The Rough (

Toronto

written and researched by

Phil Lee & Helen Lovekin

Rough GUIDES

www.roughguides.com

Contents

Toronto's architecture colour section following p.40

Canadian art colour section following p.208

Colour maps following p.240

Woodbridge

Toronto

◄◄ Hockey Hall of Fame ◄ Union Station and the CN Tower

Introduction to
Toronto

Since the 1960s, Toronto has thrown itself into a spate of serious image-building, with millions of dollars lavished on glitzy architecture, slick museums, an excellent public transport system and the redevelopment of its waterfront. As a result, Toronto – the economic and cultural focus of English-speaking Canada, and the country's largest metropolis – has become one of North America's most likeable and attractive cities.

Toronto sprawls along the northern shore of Lake Ontario, its bustling, vibrant centre surrounded by a jingle and jangle of satellite townships and industrial zones that, as "Greater Toronto", covers no less than 600 square kilometres. In the centre, huge new shopping malls and high-rise office blocks reflect the economic successes of the last two or three decades, a boom that has attracted immigrants from all over the world, transforming an overwhelmingly Anglophone city into a cosmopolitan megalopolis of over seventy significant minorities. Indeed, getting a feel for Toronto's diversity is one of the city's great pleasures. Nowhere is this better experienced than in its myriad cafés and restaurants, where standards are high and prices are low. The city also boasts a pulsating club scene, not to mention a classy programme of performing arts, from dance to theatre and beyond.

Toronto also has its share of attention-grabbing sights, mostly clustered in the city centre. The most celebrated of these is the CN Tower, the world's tallest free-standing structure, but much more enjoyable are the pick of the city's museums – for starters, there's the outstanding Art Gallery of Ontario and the delightful Gardiner Museum of Ceramic Art – and a brace of Victorian mansions. That said, these sights illustrate different facets of Toronto, but in no way do they crystallize its identity. The city remains opaque: too big and diverse to allow for a defining personality and too metamorphic to permit rigid definition. This, however, adds an air of excitement and unpredictability to the place. In fact, for many it's the surging vitality of the city that provides the most abiding memories.

What to see

oronto's central core is readily divided into three main areas: Downtown, Uptown and the waterfront. **Downtown**, bounded by Front Street to the south, Gerrard Street to the north, Spadina Avenue to the west and Jarvis Street to the east, is the most varied of the three. Here you'll find the city's most visited attractions, kicking off with the famous **CN Tower** and the

▲ Algonquin Island

Toronto today

Toronto is the **provincial capital** of Ontario, one of the ten provinces and three territories that make up Canada. The bicameral federal government meets at the nation's capital, Ottawa, on the Ontario/Québec border. Toronto achieved its present geographical dimensions in 1998 when, much to the chagrin of many locals, the six semi-independent boroughs of what had been Metropolitan Toronto were merged into one **"Megacity"**, the GTA (Greater Toronto Area). The GTA's **population** is approaching six million, making it the largest city in Canada by a long chalk – its nearest rival being Montréal, with some three and a half million inhabitants.

armadillo-like **Rogers Centre** (formerly the SkyDome) sports stadium next door. These two structures abut the **Banking District**, whose assorted skyscrapers display some of the city's most striking architecture, especially in the quartet of hulking black blocks that constitute the **Toronto Dominion Centre**. One of these blocks holds the delightful **Gallery of Inuit Art**, an exemplary collection of Inuit sculpture gathered together from the remote settlements of the Arctic north in the 1960s. Close by, **St Andrew's Presbyterian Church** is a proud reminder of the nineteenth-century city, its handsome neo-Romanesque stonework overlooking **Roy Thompson Hall**, the home of the Toronto Symphony Orchestra.

▶ Dock at The Beach

The Banking District fizzles out at Queen Street, giving way to **Nathan Phillips Square**, site of both the old and new city halls, and the sprawling **Eaton Centre**, Toronto's main shopping mall, which extends along Yonge as far as Dundas. Nearby is the much-lauded **Art Gallery of Ontario** (AGO), home to a first-rate selection of both European and Canadian works. Within easy striking distance is **Fort York**, the reconstructed British army outpost where Toronto began, and which is now stranded on the western edge of Downtown in the shadow of the Gardiner Expressway. In the opposite direction, the **St Lawrence** neighbourhood is one of the city's more distinctive, its main claim to fame being a clutch of fine old stone buildings. From here, it's another short hop east to the **Distillery District**, not actually a district at all, but rather Toronto's brightest arts and entertainment complex, which occupies a sprawling former distillery dating from the nineteenth century.

Moving north, **Uptown** runs from Gerrard as far as Dupont Street. With the exception of the **Ontario Legislative Assembly Building**, a

Out of the city

Toronto is a convenient base for exploring **southwest Ontario**, a triangular tract of land that lies sandwiched between lakes Huron and Erie. Significant parts of the region are blotched by heavy industry, but there's also mile upon mile of rolling farmland and a series of excellent attractions, the best of which are within a two- to three-hour drive of

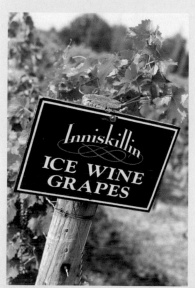

Downtown. Potential destinations include Canada's premier tourist spot, **Niagara Falls**, as well as nearby **Niagara-on-the-Lake**, a beguiling town of leafy streets and charming colonial houses, as well as site of the renowned Shaw Festival and – within the vicinity – more than twenty wineries. There's also **Goderich** and **Bayfield**, two lovely little towns tucked against the bluffs of the Lake Huron shoreline, and **Severn Sound**, home to a pair of top-notch historical reconstructions, Discovery Harbour and Sainte-Marie among the Hurons. The sound is also the front door to the **Georgian Bay Islands National Park**, whose island-studded waters are strikingly beautiful.

whopping sandstone pile on University Avenue, the principal attractions here are the museums, beginning with the wide-ranging applied art of the **Royal Ontario Museum** (ROM), where pride of place goes to the Chinese collection. Smaller and more engaging are both the **Gardiner Museum**, which holds a connoisseur's collection of ceramics, and the fascinating range of footwear displayed at the **Bata Shoe Museum**. Also of interest are a pair of intriguing old houses: **Casa Loma**, a mock-Gothic extravagance dating from 1911, and **Spadina House**, whose studied charms are the epitome of Victorian gentility.

The third part of the city centre is the Lake Ontario **waterfront**. Formerly a grimy industrial strip of wharves and warehouses, it's now flanked by deluxe condominiums and bright office blocks. This is one of the smartest parts of the city and it comes complete with open-air performance areas, bars, restaurants, shops and a couple of art galleries, including the enterprising **Power Plant Contemporary Art Gallery**. The waterfront is also where ferries leave for the **Toronto Islands**, the low-lying, crescent-shaped

Toronto's neighbourhoods

Peppered throughout Toronto are a dozen or so distinct **neighbourhoods**, enclaves which sustain a flavour all their own, even though some of them cover just a few streets. The rundown below will help you get the most from these neighbourhoods, whether you want to shop, eat or just take in the atmosphere.

The Beach (see p.90), lying south of Queen Street East between Woodbine and Victoria Park avenues, is a prosperous and particularly appealing district with chic boutiques, leafy streets and a sandy beach trimmed by a popular boardwalk. Pianist Glenn Gould was born here.

Cabbagetown (see p.77), east of Jarvis Street and roughly bounded by Gerrard Street East on its south side, Wellesley Street East to the north and the Don River to the east, is renowned for its Victorian houses. Its name comes from the district's nineteenth-century immigrants, whose tiny front gardens were filled with cabbages.

Chinatown (see p.65), or more accurately the largest of the city's four Chinatowns, is concentrated along Dundas Street West, between Bay Street and Spadina Avenue. This is one of Toronto's most distinctive neighbourhoods, packed with busy restaurants and stores selling anything from porcelain and jade to herbs and pickled seaweed.

The Gay Village (see p.176), with its plethora of bars, restaurants and bookshops, is centred on the intersection of Church and Wellesley streets.

Greektown is a burgeoning neighbourhood located along Danforth Avenue, between Pape and Woodbine. With scores of authentic restaurants, this is the place to go for Greek food.

High Park (see p.99) takes its name from the park that overlooks the Gardiner Expressway to the west of Downtown. Its main drag, Roncesvalles Avenue, is the heart of the city's large Polish community.

sandbanks that shelter the harbour and provide opportunities for city folk to go walking, swimming and sailing amidst the woods and lawns.

To get the real flavour of Toronto's core, it's best to **explore on foot**, a perfectly feasible option as distances are quite manageable. However, visiting some of the more peripheral attractions – like Casa Loma and Spadina House – can be a bit of a trek, especially in the summer when the city is often unbearably humid. Fortunately, Toronto's **public transport** system is excellent, consisting of a comprehensive, safe and inexpensive network of streetcars, buses and subways that delves into

▲ CN Tower's glass floor

Kensington Market (see p.65), just north of Dundas Street West between Spadina and Augusta avenues, is the most ethnically diverse part of town, where Portuguese, West Indian and Jewish Canadians pack the streets with tiny shops and open-air stalls. The lower half of the market, just off Dundas, concentrates on secondhand clothing, while the upper half is crowded with fresh food stalls and cafés.

Little Italy – the so-called Corso Italia – runs along College Street between Bathurst and Clinton, and is one of Toronto's livelist neighbourhoods.

Little Portugal, a crowded, vital area packed with shops and neighbourhood food joints, is focused on Dundas Street West, west of Bathurst Street as far as Dovercourt Road.

Queen Street West (see p.58), between University and Spadina, has one of the highest retail rents in the city and is home to all things trendy and expensive. The students and punks who once hung around here have moved on to what is known as **West Queen West**, between Bathurst Street and Ossington Avenue.

Rosedale is a byword for prosperity, a well-heeled neighbourhood whose leafy streets and old mansions have traditionally been home to the city's elite. Its boundaries are Yonge Street to the west, the Don Valley Parkway to the east, St Clair Avenue to the north and Bloor Street East to the south.

Yorkville (see p.76), just above Bloor Street West between Bay and Avenue Road, was "alternative" in the 1960s, with appearances by figureheads of the counterculture like Gordon Lightfoot and Joni Mitchell. Today, the alternative vibe of the place is long gone, and the district holds some of Toronto's most expensive clothing shops and art galleries, as well as several good bars and restaurants.

every nook and cranny of the city. This system also brings most of the city's **suburbs** within easy reach. The chief attraction here is **The Beach**, a delightful neighbourhood bordering Lake Ontario, just a twenty-minute streetcar ride east of Downtown – though you might also consider the excellent Ontario Science Centre, north of Downtown, the scenic Scarborough Bluffs, east of Downtown on the shores of Lake Ontario, and the nearby Toronto Zoo, one of the largest in North America.

► Paradise Restaurant, Centre Island

When to go

Toronto has a harsh **climate**. In the winter, it's often bitterly cold, with sub-zero temperatures and heavy snowfalls. January and February are usually the coldest months, though real winter conditions can begin in early November and drag on into late March. Summers, on the other hand, are hot and humid. July and August are consistently the hottest months, sometimes uncomfortably so. Spring and autumn offer the city's most enjoyable weather, with lots of warm, sunny days and balmy nights.

Toronto climate chart

	Jan	Feb	Mar	Apr	May	Jun	Jul	Aug	Sept	Oct	Nov	Dec
Average daily max temp												
max (°C)	8	8	13	19	25	28	32	32	28	23	17	12
°F	28	29	39	52	65	73	79	77	68	56	44	33
°C	-2.2	-1.7	3.9	11.1	18.3	22.8	26.1	25	20	13.3	6.7	0.6
Average daily min temp												
°F	15	15	24	35	45	54	60	58	50	39	31	20
°C	-9.4	-9.4	-4.4	1.7	7.2	12.2	15.6	14.4	10	3.9	-0.6	-6.7
Average rainfall												
in	1.9	1.8	2.3	2.6	2.6	2.6	2.8	3.2	2.8	2.5	2.6	2.4
mm	48.3	45.7	58.4	66	66	66	71	81.3	71	63.5	66	61

things not to miss

It's not possible to see everything Toronto has to offer in one trip – and we don't suggest you try. What follows is a selective taste of the city's highlights: first-class museums, great places to eat and drink and dynamic neighbourhoods to explore. Arranged in five colour-coded categories, you can browse through to find the very best things to see, do and experience. All highlights have a page reference to take you straight into the text, where you can find out more.

01 **The Royal Ontario Museum** Page **72** • Complete with its lavish new extension, the ROM is the city's largest and most diverse museum, noted for its fabulous Chinese collection.

02 **Ice hockey** Page **195** • Canadians love their ice hockey: catch the Maple Leafs at the Air Canada Centre.

03 **Toronto International Film Festival** Page **175** • North America's largest film festival is a star-studded affair held over ten days in September.

04 **Elgin and Winter Garden Theatre** Page **58** • Intriguing old double-decker theatre which has been immaculately restored.

05 **Cabbagetown** Page **77** • Take a walk through the trim Victorian terraces of this modish neighbourhood, named after its first occupants' habit of planting cabbages in the front garden.

12
■

07 Dundas Square Page **57** • Right at the heart of the city, flashy Dundas Square can sure pull in the punters for everything from "meet the celebrity" to rock gigs.

06 Kensington Market Page **65** • Check out everything from organic food to trendy clothes at Toronto's best open-air market.

09 St Lawrence Market Page **50** • The best food and drinks market in the city with an excellent line in local delicacies.

08 The CN Tower Page **40** • Like it or lump it (or a bit of both), the CN Tower is Toronto's mascot – and one of the world's best-known buildings.

11 Bata Shoe Museum Page 75 • Tickle your fancy at this fun, inventive museum, which is dedicated to footwear of every description, from Ottoman platforms to French chestnut-crushing clogs.

12 Gay Pride Page 178 • Toronto's exuberant, week-long Gay Pride attracts over 800,000 people. Join in the fun at the end of June.

10 Niagara Falls Page 104 • Get up-close to Niagara's roaring, crashing falls on a "Maid of the Mist" boat trip.

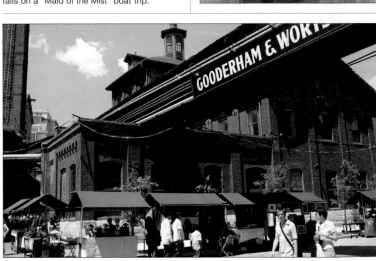

13 Distillery District Page 53 • Unbeatable assortment of art galleries, cafés, clothes shops and furniture designers – plus much else – in this revamped old distillery.

14 The
Galler
Ontario Page
prestigious gallery
a superb collection o.
Canadian art with the
of Seven to the fore, not
mention the world's larges
assemblage of Henry Moore
sculptures.

15 Toronto Islands Page **85** • The ferry trip over to the balmy Toronto Islands offers smashing views back over the city.

16 The Canadian Opera Company Page **172** • The COC is lodged in its plush new home, the Four Seasons Centre: great acoustics; catch them if you can.

17 **Ice skating at City Hall** Page **199** • Skate the winter blues away at this popular ice rink in front of City Hall.

19 **Shopping** Page **182** • The Canadians love to shop – so join in: Queen Street West is the grooviest part of town, awash with cafés, restaurants and designer clothes stores.

20 **Chinatown** Page **65** • Enjoy the sights and smells of Downtown Toronto's Chinatown, the focus of the city's sizeable Chinese community, where scores of stalls sell every Asian delicacy you can imagine and then some.

18 **Casa Loma** Page **78** • Marvel at this outlandish behemoth of a building, conceived by the incorrigibly eccentric Henry Pellatt.

Basics

Basics

Getting there

As Canada's commercial hub, Toronto is easy to reach from almost anywhere in the world. From outside of North America, flying is pretty much your only option, whereas US residents can fly, drive, take the bus or catch the train. The main airport is Toronto Pearson International, just 25km northwest of the city centre (see "Arrival" for more information).

Airfares to Toronto from the UK, Australia and New Zealand vary depending on the season, with the highest prices applying from around mid-June to early September. You'll get the best deals during the low season, mid-November through to April (excluding Christmas and New Year, when seats are at a premium and prices are hiked up). If you're flying from the US or from anywhere else in Canada, the same general strictures apply, though the market is more unpredictable, with airlines constantly moving their prices up and down.

Flights from the USA and the rest of Canada

From the USA, there are plenty of nonstop flights to Toronto on Air Canada and many US airlines. Typical budget return **fares** on major airlines are US$200–400 from New York, US$300–500 from Chicago and US$350–600 from LA. If you plan a long weekend trip, you can often find special fares, like NY–Toronto for US$150 or Chicago–Toronto for US$200. You really need to shop around to get the very best deals. Your best bet is to first try an **online agent** (see p.20), who may be able to dig up scheduled return fares for as little as half the prices quoted above. **Within Canada**, there are myriad flights to Toronto from almost all of the country's big cities and major towns; the main carrier is Air Canada. Typical budget return **fares** are Montréal to Toronto CDN$250–350, Winnipeg to Toronto CDN$300–400.

As for **flying times**, New York to Toronto takes 1hr 30min, LA to Toronto 2hr 30min, Vancouver to Toronto 2hr 10min.

From the UK and Ireland

Toronto is easily reached **from the UK** mainland by either charter or scheduled flight. The majority of flights leave from London Heathrow, with other airports offering a slim to slender range of choices; Manchester and Glasgow have the most. **From Ireland** – north or south – there are no direct nonstop flights to Toronto and the main options are either charter flights or routings via the UK mainland or a US hub airport. Keep in mind that direct, nonstop flights can often – but certainly not always – be at a premium when compared with one-stop flights.

A standard return **fare** on a scheduled flight from London Heathrow direct to Toronto with Air Canada, the principal carrier, can range from £450 to £1200 (low season/ high season). With restrictions, though, this can easily be trimmed to a very affordable £400. From Dublin or Belfast to Toronto via London with Air Canada costs more, from €750/£670, but it's often possible to save money by flying to London independently on a budget airline and then taking a separate flight from Heathrow.

The **flying time** from Heathrow to Toronto is about eight hours.

Throughout this guide, prices are given in Canadian dollars ($); where there might be any confusion between Canadian and American dollars, however, we distinguish between the two (CDN$ and US$).

From Australia, New Zealand and South Africa

There are no direct flights from **Australia or New Zealand or South Africa** to Toronto. However, Air Canada, Qantas, United and Air New Zealand have daily connecting flights from all major Australasian cities to Vancouver (via Los Angeles or Hawaii), from where they will quote you through-fares to Toronto.

From **Australia** low season Sydney–Vancouver flights start around A$2300; or A$3000 from Perth and Darwin. Expect to pay an extra A$600 to Toronto. From **New Zealand**, Air NZ/Air Canada (via LA or Hawaii) and both United and American (via LA) provide daily connections to Toronto (NZ$3300). It's also possible to fly with Qantas (via Sydney and LA) for similar fares. From **South Africa**, South Africa Airways offers services to Toronto via New York or Washington from around R16,000/R24,000 in low/high season for a return ticket. You will probably find it cheaper, though more time consuming, to fly via London on return flights that cost from R800 and then pick up a direct flight from there (see p.19).

Airlines, agents and operators

Online booking

ⓦ www.expedia.co.uk (in UK), ⓦ www.expedia .com (in US), ⓦ www.expedia.ca (in Canada)
ⓦ www.lastminute.com (in UK)
ⓦ www.opodo.co.uk (in UK)
ⓦ www.orbitz.com (in US)
ⓦ www.travelocity.co.uk (in UK), ⓦ www .travelocity.com (in US), ⓦ www.travelocity.ca (in Canada), ⓦ www.travelocity.co.nz (in New Zealand)
ⓦ www.travelonline.co.za (in South Africa)
ⓦ www.zuji.com.au (in Australia)

Airlines

Aer Lingus Republic of Ireland ☎ 0818/365 000, New Zealand ☎ 1649/3083355, South Africa ☎ 1-272/2168-32838, UK ☎ 0870/876 5000, US & Canada ☎ 1-800/IRISH-AIR; ⓦ www .aerlingus.com.
Air Canada Canada & US ☎ 1-888/247-2262, UK ☎ 0871/220 1111, Republic of Ireland ☎ 01/679 3958, Australia ☎ 1300/655 767, New Zealand ☎ 0508/747 767; ⓦ www.aircanada.com.
Air New Zealand New Zealand ☎ 0800/737000, Australia ☎ 0800/132 476, UK ☎ 0800/028 4149, Republic of Ireland ☎ 1800/551 447, US ☎ 1800-262/1234, Canada ☎ 1800-663/5494; ⓦ www .airnz.co.nz.
American Airlines US & Canada ☎ 1-800/433-7300, UK ☎ 020/7365 0777, Republic of Ireland ☎ 01/602 0550, Australia ☎ 1800/673 486, New Zealand ☎ 0800/445 442; ⓦ www.aa.com.
bmi US ☎ 1-800/788-0555, UK ☎ 0870/607 0555 or 0870/607 0222, Republic of Ireland ☎ 01/283 0700, Australia ☎ 02/8644 1881, New Zealand ☎ 09/623 4293, South Africa ☎ 11/289 8111; ⓦ www.flybmi.com.
British Airways US & Canada ☎ 1-800/AIRWAYS, UK ☎ 0844/493 0787, Republic of Ireland ☎ 1890/626 747, Australia ☎ 1300/767 177, New Zealand ☎ 09/966 9777, South Africa ☎ 114/418 600; ⓦ www.ba.com.
Canjet Airlines US & Canada ☎ 1-800-809 7777, ⓦ www.canjet.com.
Cathay Pacific US ☎ 1-800/233-2742, Canada ☎ 1-800/2686-868, UK ☎ 020/8834 8888, Australia ☎ 13 17 47, New Zealand ☎ 09/379 0861, South Africa ☎ 11/700 8900; ⓦ www .cathaypacific.com.
Continental Airlines US & Canada ☎ 1-800/523-3273, UK ☎ 0845/607 6760, Republic of Ireland ☎ 1890/925 252, Australia ☎ 1300/737 640, New Zealand ☎ 09/308 3350, International ☎ 1800/231 0856; ⓦ www.continental.com.
Delta US & Canada ☎ 1-800/221-1212, UK ☎ 0845/600 0950, Republic of Ireland ☎ 1850/882 031 or 01/407 3165, Australia ☎ 1300/302 849, New Zealand ☎ 09/9772232; ⓦ www.delta.com.
easyJet UK ☎ 0905/821 0905, ⓦ www.easyjet.com.
Emirates US & Canada ☎ 1-800/777-3999, UK ☎ 0844/800 2777, Australia ☎ 1300/303 777, New Zealand ☎ 05/0836 4728, South Africa ☎ 0861/364 728; ⓦ www.emirates.com.
Flyglobespan UK ☎ 0870/271 9000, ⓦ www.flyglobespan.com
JAL (Japan Air Lines) US & Canada ☎ 1-800/525-3663, UK ☎ 0845/774 7700, Republic of Ireland ☎ 01/408 3757, Australia ☎ 1-300/525 287 or 02/9272 1111, New Zealand ☎ 0800/525 747 or 09/379 9906, South Africa ☎ 11/214 2560; ⓦ www.jal.com or www .japanair.com.
KLM (Royal Dutch Airlines) See also Northwest/ KLM. US & Canada ☎ 1-800/225-2525, UK ☎ 0870/507 4074, Republic of Ireland ☎ 1850/747 400, Australia ☎ 1300/392 192, New Zealand ☎ 09/921 6040, South Africa ☎ 0860/247 747; ⓦ www.klm.com.

Six steps to a better kind of travel

At Rough Guides we are passionately committed to travel. We feel strongly that only through travelling do we truly come to understand the world we live in and the people we share it with – plus tourism has brought a great deal of benefit to developing economies around the world over the last few decades. But the extraordinary growth in tourism has also damaged some places irreparably, and of course climate change is exacerbated by most forms of transport, especially flying. This means that now more than ever it's important to travel thoughtfully and responsibly, with respect for the cultures you're visiting – not only to derive the most benefit from your trip but also in order to preserve the best bits of the planet for everyone to enjoy. At Rough Guides we feel there are six main areas in which you can make a difference:

• Consider what you're contributing to the local economy, and indeed how much the services you use do the same, whether it's through employing local workers and guides or sourcing locally grown produce and local services.

• Consider the environment on holiday as well as at home. Water is scarce in many developing destinations, and the biodiversity of local flora and fauna can be adversely affected by tourism. Patronise businesses that take account of this rather than those that trash the local environment for short-term gain.

• Give thought to how often you fly and what you can do to redress any harm that your trips create. Reduce the amount you travel by air; avoid short hops by air and more harmful night flights.

• Consider alternatives to flying, travelling instead by bus, train, boat and even by bike or on foot where possible. Take time to enjoy the journey itself as well as your final destination.

• Think about making all the trips you take "climate neutral" via a reputable carbon offset scheme. All Rough Guide flights are offset, and every year we donate money to a variety of charities devoted to combating the effects of climate change.

• Travel with a purpose, not just to tick off experiences. Consider spending longer in a place, and really getting to know it and its people – you'll find it much more rewarding than dashing from place to place.

Lufthansa US ☎ 1-800/3995-838, Canada ☎ 1-800/563-5954, UK ☎ 0871/945 9747, Republic of Ireland ☎ 01/844 5544, Australia ☎ 1300/655 727, New Zealand ☎ 0800-945 220, South Africa ☎ 0861/842 538; ⓦ www.lufthansa.com.
Northwest/KLM US ☎ 1-800/225-2525, UK ☎ 0870/507 4074, Australia ☎ 1-300/767-310; ⓦ www.nwa.com
Qantas Airways US & Canada ☎ 1-800/227-4500, UK ☎ 0845/774 7767, Republic of Ireland ☎ 01/407 3278, Australia ☎ 13 13 13, New Zealand ☎ 0800/808 767 or 09/357 8900, South Africa ☎ 11/441 8550; ⓦ www.qantas.com.
Ryanair UK ☎ 0871/246 0000, Republic of Ireland ☎ 0818/303 030; ⓦ www.ryanair.com.
SAS (Scandinavian Airlines) US & Canada ☎ 1-800/221-2350, UK ☎ 0871/521 2772, Republic of Ireland ☎ 01/844 5440, Australia ☎ 1300/727 707; ⓦ www.scandinavian.net.
Singapore Airlines US ☎ 1-800/742-3333, Canada ☎ 1-800/663-3046, UK ☎ 0844/800 2380, Republic of Ireland ☎ 01/671 0722, Australia ☎ 13 10 11, New Zealand ☎ 0800/808 909, South Africa ☎ 11/880 8560 or 11/880 8566; ⓦ www .singaporeair.com.
South African Airways South Africa ☎ 11/978 1111, US & Canada ☎ 1-800/722-9675, UK ☎ 0870/747 1111, Australia ☎ 1300/435 972, New Zealand ☎ 09/977 2237; ⓦ www.flysaa.com.
US Airways US & Canada ☎ 1-800/428-4322, UK ☎ 0845/600 3300, Republic of Ireland ☎ 1890/925 065; ⓦ www.usair.com.
Virgin Atlantic US ☎ 1-800/821-5438, UK ☎ 0870/574 7747, Australia ☎ 1300/727 340, South Africa ☎ 11/340 3400; ⓦ www.virgin-atlantic.com.
WestJet US & Canada ☎ 1-888/937-8538, UK, Republic of Ireland, Australia, New Zealand & South Africa ☎ 1-0800/5381 5696; ⓦ www .westjet.com.

Agents and operators

ebookers UK ☎ 0871/223 5000, Republic of Ireland ☎ 01/431 1311; ⓦ www.ebookers.com, www.ebookers.ie. Low fares on an extensive selection of scheduled flights and package deals.

North South Travel UK ☎01245/608 291, ⓦwww.northsouthtravel.co.uk. Friendly, competitive travel agency, offering discounted fares worldwide. Profits are used to support projects in the developing world, especially the promotion of sustainable tourism.
Trailfinders UK ☎0845/058 5858, Republic of Ireland ☎01/677 7888, Australia ☎1300/780 212; ⓦwww.trailfinders.com. One of the best-informed and most efficient agents for independent travellers.
STA Travel US ☎1-800/781-4040, UK ☎0871/2300 040, Australia ☎134 782, New Zealand ☎0800/474 400, South Africa ☎0861/781 781; ⓦwww.statravel.com. Worldwide specialists in independent travel; also student IDs, travel insurance, car rental, rail passes, and more. Good discounts for students and under-26s.

By Car

Getting to Toronto **by car** is easy enough but, like any other form of land travel, time is the critical factor. From New York City to Toronto you are looking at approximately 790km, which, assuming the border crossing is uneventful (see box below), translates to about ten hours' driving time. Detroit is 370km and roughly a four-hour drive away. From Montréal, it's about 540km, and driving will take you about five hours.

If you are driving a **rental car** in from the US, be sure to let the agency know that you intend to cross the border into Canada to avoid any possible misunderstandings concerning insurance. Bear in mind also that once you reach Toronto, a car may be more of a hindrance than a help, as Downtown parking and gas stations – both in short supply – are pricey.

Car rental agencies

Avis US ☎1-800/331-1212, Canada ☎1-800/879-2847, UK ☎0844/581 8181, Republic of Ireland ☎021/428 1111, Australia ☎13 63 33 or 02/9353 9000, New Zealand ☎09/526 2847 or 0800/655 111, South Africa ☎11/923 3660; ⓦwww.avis.com.
Budget US ☎1-800/527-0700, Canada ☎1-800/268-8900, UK ☎0870/156 5656,

Australia ☎1300/362 848, New Zealand ☎0800/283 438; ⓦwww.budget.com.
Dollar US ☎1-800/800-3665, Canada ☎1-800/229 0984, UK ☎0808/234 7524, Republic of Ireland ☎1800/515 800; ⓦwww.dollar.com.
Enterprise Rent-a-Car US & Canada ☎1-800/261-7331, UK ☎0870/350 3000, Republic of Ireland ☎1890/227 999; ⓦwww.enterprise.com.
Europcar US & Canada ☎1-877/940 6900, UK ☎0845/758 5375, Republic of Ireland ☎01/614 2800, Australia ☎1300/131 390; ⓦwww.europcar.com.
Hertz US & Canada ☎1-800/654-3131, UK ☎0870/040 9000, Republic of Ireland ☎01/870 5777, Australia ☎13 30 39, New Zealand, ☎0800/654 321, South Africa ☎21/935 4800; ⓦwww.hertz.com.
National US ☎1-800/227-7368, UK ☎0870/400 4588, Australia ☎0870/600 6666, New Zealand ☎03/366 5574; ⓦwww.nationalcar.com.
SIXT US & Canada ☎1-888/749-8227, UK ☎0870/156 7567, Republic of Ireland ☎06/120 6088, Australia ☎1300/660 660, South Africa ☎0860/031 666; ⓦwww.sixt.com.
Thrifty US & Canada ☎1-800/847-4389, UK ☎01494/751 540, Republic of Ireland ☎1800/515 800, Australia ☎1300/367 227, New Zealand ☎0800/737 070; ⓦwww.thrifty.com.

By Bus

Toronto is a major hub for **bus** travel and all long-distance services pull into the main coach terminal, right in the centre of town on Bay Street (see p.24). There are several carriers, but the largest is Greyhound, which provides fast and frequent buses to Toronto from lots of places both in the US and Canada. Journey times are significant – buses from New York take eleven hours, six from Detroit, fifteen from Chicago and eight from Montréal – but prices are very reasonable: the return fare from Chicago costs around US$200, about the same from New York.

By rail

Arriving from the USA, two **rail** companies (Amtrak in the US and VIA Rail in Canada)

Crossing the US/Canada border

Crossing the US/Canada border is often quick and easy – providing you have the correct documentation (see "Entry requirements", p.29). At other times, it can be a real pain as the customs officials get down to the serious business of searching cars and potential visitors with vim and gusto: needless to say, this can take hours.

combine to offer a regular daily service from New York to Toronto via Buffalo and Niagara Falls. The whole journey takes thirteen hours (which includes a wait of about an hour and a half at the border) and costs around US$100 one-way, though discounts and special deals are legion especially if you book well ahead. Within Canada, VIA Rail has frequent trains to Toronto from Montréal, Ottawa and points east as well as a once-daily service from Winnipeg and points west as far as Vancouver. A standard single fare from Montréal costs about CDN$230, CDN$600 from Vancouver, but once again discount deals are commonplace particularly if you book well in advance.

All these trains pull into Toronto's Union Station in the heart of the city.

Bus and rail contacts

Amtrak US ☎ 1-800/USA-RAIL, 🌐 www.amtrak.com.
Greyhound US ☎ 1-800/231-2222, 🌐 www.greyhound.com; Canada ☎ 1-800/661-8747, 🌐 www.greyhound.ca.
Trailways buses US ☎ 1-800/776-7548, 🌐 www.trailwaysny.com.
VIA Rail ☎ 1-888/VIA-RAIL, 🌐 www.viarail.ca.

Arrival

Located 25km northwest of the city centre, Toronto Pearson International Airport is linked to almost every important metropolis in the world, as well as every major Canadian town and city. The vast majority of visitors to Toronto arrive by plane.

Toronto's **bus** and **train stations** are conveniently located Downtown and they link Toronto to a wide range of Canadian and American cities. Those arriving **by car** will find the city encircled by motorways, a straightforward drive except during rush hour when traffic congestion can be a real pain.

By air

Arriving **by air**, you'll almost certainly land at **Toronto Pearson International**, about forty minutes by car from Downtown. The airport has two main terminals, one devoted to international flights, the other to domestic and US flights. Both terminals have a full range of facilities, including money-exchange offices, ATMs and free hotel hotlines. A free airport shuttle – The Link Train – connects the terminals.

From the airport on the Airport Express bus

The **Airport Express bus** (daily, every 20–30min, 5am–1am; ☎ 905/564-3232, 🌐 www.torontoairportexpress.com) picks up passengers outside both terminals and proceeds Downtown, taking between forty and sixty minutes to get there – though heavy traffic can make the journey considerably longer. The bus drops passengers at the coach station and seven of Toronto's major hotels: the *Westin Harbour Castle*, *Fairmont Royal York*, *InterContinental*, *Sheraton Centre*, *Bond Place*, *Holiday Inn on King* and the *Delta Chelsea Inn*. **Tickets** for the airport bus can be purchased either at the kiosks next to the bus stop outside each of the terminal buildings or from the driver. A one-way fare costs $20, $33 return.

From the airport by TTC bus

Much less expensive, if rather more time-consuming, are the several bus services linking the airport with the city's subway network. The two fastest are operated by

All prices quoted are in **Canadian dollars**, unless otherwise stated.

the **TTC** (Toronto Transit Commission): the **Airport Rocket** (#192; Mon–Sat 5.30am–1.30am & Sun 8am–1am every 15–40min; $2.75 one-way) takes about twenty minutes to reach Kipling subway station, at the west end of the subway network. From there, it takes another twenty minutes or so by subway (which operates Mon–Sat 6am–1am, Sun 9am–1am) to get Downtown. The second option, **TTC bus #58A**, links the airport with Lawrence West subway station, to the north of Downtown (daily 5am–1am every 15–40min; 45min; $2.75 one-way). Buses leave from designated stops outside Terminal 1; payment can be made to the driver.

From the airport by limo and taxi

An **airport limo service** (a shared taxi system) operates at both terminals and the journey Downtown costs about $46 per person. Unlike taxis, the price is fixed – an important consideration if you arrive (or leave) during rush hour; the disadvantage is that they (mostly) only leave when they're full. Individual **taxis** charge about the same – say $50 from the airport to the city centre – but fares are metered.

Toronto City Centre Airport

The city's second and much smaller airport, the **Toronto City Centre Airport**, is on Hanlan's Point in Toronto harbour, close to Downtown at the foot of Bathurst Street. One airline rules the roost here, Porter Airlines (☎416/619-8622 or 1-888/619-8622, ⓦwww.flyporter.com), which offers flights to a number of US and Canadian destinations, including Chicago (Midway), Halifax in Nova Scotia, Montréal, Ottawa, Québec City and New York (Newark). From the airport, there's a free minibus service to the *Royal York Hotel*, on the corner of Front Street West and York Street.

By bus and by train

Toronto's **coach terminal** (ⓦwww.toronto coachterminal.com) is located at 610 Bay St, metres from Dundas Street West and a five-minute walk from the subway stop at the corner of Yonge and Dundas. If you're arriving late at night, note that the bus station's immediate environs are unsavoury – though it only takes a couple of minutes to reach more reassuring parts of Downtown. Nonetheless, if you're travelling alone and late at night, it's probably best to take a taxi to your ultimate destination.

All incoming **trains** arrive at **Union Station**, at the junction of Bay Street and Front Street West. The complex, which is the hub of the city's public transportation system, includes a subway station and holds the main terminal for the **GO trains and buses** that service the city's suburbs. Details of GO services are available at their station ticket offices, by phone on toll-free ☎1-888/438-6646 (within Toronto ☎416/869-3200) and on their website, ⓦwww.gotransit.com.

By car

From Niagara Falls and points west along Lake Ontario, most traffic arrives via the QEW (Queen Elizabeth Way), which funnels into the Gardiner Expressway, an elevated motorway (notorious for delays) that cuts across the southern side of Downtown, just south of Front Street. From the east, most drivers opt for the equally busy Hwy-401, which sweeps along Lake Ontario before veering off to slice through the city's suburbs north of Downtown. Driving in from the north, take Hwy-400, which intersects with Hwy-401 northwest of the centre, or Hwy-404, which meets Hwy-401 northeast of the centre. Note that on all routes you can expect delays during rush hours (roughly 7.30–9.30am and 4.30–6.30pm).

To relieve congestion on Hwy-401, an alternative motorway, Hwy-407ETR (ⓦwww407etr .com), has been built further north on the city's outskirts. It was North America's first all-electronic toll highway: instead of tollbooths, each vehicle is identified by an electronic tag (a transponder), and the invoice is posted later. Toll charges are fixed but vary – at peak times vehicles are charged 19.25¢ per kilometre – and there's also a small supplementary charge per trip for any vehicle without a transponder; these vehicles are identified by licence plate photos. If you rent a car, be aware that rental companies slap on an extra administration charge (of around $15) if you take their vehicles on this road.

For more on car hire, see p.22.

City transport and guided tours

Fast, frequent and efficient, Toronto's public transportation system is operated by the Toronto Transit Commission (TTC), whose integrated network of subways, buses and streetcars (or trams) serves virtually every corner of the city. The TTC operates a 24-hour information line on ☏416/393-4636 with operator assistance available daily from 8am to 6pm; they also have a website, ⓦwww.ttc.ca.

With the exception of Downtown, where all the major sights are within easy walking distance of one another, your best option is to use **public transport** to hop between attractions – especially in the cold of winter or the sultry summertime. Much to its credit, the TTC has gone to great lengths to assure the **safety** of its passengers: all subway stations have well-lit DWAs (Designated Waiting Areas), intercom connections with TTC staff, and closed-circuit TV for monitoring. In addition, TTC buses operate a **Request Stop Program**, which allows women travelling alone late at night (9pm–5am) to get off buses wherever they want and not just at regular TTC stops. A similarly positive approach has been adopted for **passengers with disabilities**, who can use a dedicated service, Wheel-Trans (see p.36).

As for **fares**, on every part of the TTC system a single journey costs $2.75 (local students and seniors over 65 years $1.85; children ages 2–12 $0.70; children under two free). Paper tickets are available at all subway stations and from bus and streetcar drivers. Metallic tokens can also be used, but these are only issued at subway stations and they are impossibly small and difficult to keep track of. More economically, a **batch of five tickets** or tokens can be bought for $11.25, or $22.50 for ten, at any subway station and at many convenience stores and

newsstands. Each ticket or token entitles passengers to one complete journey of any length on the TTC system. If this involves more than one type of transport, it is necessary to get a paper transfer at your point of entry. Streetcar and bus drivers issue them, as do the automatic machines located at every subway station. A **day pass** costs $9 and provides one adult with unlimited TTC travel all day. On Saturdays and Sundays, the same pass can also be used as a family ticket, covering up to six people with a maximum of two adults.

The subway

Toronto's **subway**, the core of the city's public transportation network, is a simple, three-line system (see our map at the back of the book). There are two main lines: one cuts east to west along Bloor Street and Danforth Avenue, while the other forms a loop with Union Station at its head; north of Union, one part of this subway line runs along University Avenue, the other along Yonge Street. Transferring between the two subway lines is possible at three stations only: Spadina, St George and Bloor-Yonge. The subway **operates** Mon–Sat 6am–1.00am, Sun 9am–1.00am.

Buses and streetcars

The subway provides the backbone of the TTC system, but its services are faithfully

Orientation and street numbers

Yonge Street is Toronto's principal north–south artery. Main drags perpendicular to Yonge use this intersection to change from west to east – Queen Street West, for example, becomes Queen Street East when it crosses Yonge. Note, therefore, that 1000 Queen Street West, for example, is a long way from 1000 Queen Street East.

supplemented by **buses** and **streetcars**. The system couldn't be simpler, as a bus and/or streetcar station adjoins every major subway stop. Hours of operation vary with the route, but are comparable with subway times; there is also a limited network of **night buses** running along key routes hourly or so between 1am and 6am.

Commuter lines

In addition to subways, streetcars and buses, the TTC runs several **commuter lines**. The most useful is the **Scarborough Rapid Transit**, a streetcar service that picks up passengers at the eastern terminus of the Bloor-Danforth subway line and makes a five-stop trek to the heart of Scarborough, a Toronto suburb (see p.91). Transfers from the rest of the TTC network are valid on the Scarborough Rapid Transit. Finally, **GO trains** (☎416/869 3200, ⓦwww.gotransit .com) arrive and depart from Union Station, and link the city's various suburbs and satellite towns. There are no free transfers from the TTC system to GO train lines, though these are primarily used by commuters and are little used by tourists based in the city.

Taxis

Taxis cruise the city in numbers and can be hailed from any street corner. Give the driver your destination and ask the approximate price before you start. Fares are generally reasonable and are based on a fixed tariff per kilometre plus a small pick-up charge. As an example, a ride from Union Station to the far side of Cabbagetown should cost around $12. Taxis can also be reserved in advance; of the multitude of companies to choose from, two of the most reliable are Co-op Cabs (☎416/504-2667) and Diamond Taxicab (☎416/366-6868). Toronto taxi drivers anticipate a **tip** of ten to fifteen percent on the total fare.

Guided tours

Guided tours are big business in Toronto and the range of what's on offer is exemplary – from heritage walks and boat cruises through to the more predictable coach tours. One of the best options is the **free Heritage Toronto Walks** (☎416/392-1973, ⓦwww .heritage toronto.org) organized by the city's Heritage Board. Running from late April to September, about twenty different walks are offered once or twice each season, exploring everything from the old "Mansions of Jarvis Street" and "Nature on the Toronto Waterfront" to "The Yorkville Music Scene of the 1960s" and the Cabbagetown neighbourhood (see p.77). No reservations are required; you just turn up at the appointed time and place; walks take between one and a half and two and a half hours.

Amongst the commercial guided tour operators, Gray Line (☎1-800/594-3310 or 416/594-3310, ⓦwww.grayline.ca) operates ten-hour coach trips to Niagara Falls (all year, 1 or 2 daily; $130) and twelve-hour excursions to Georgian Bay (see p.124), including an island cruise (June–Oct; one daily; $80). Perhaps of more appeal, Gray Line also runs **hop-on, hop-off city tours** in double-decker buses. These vehicles shuttle around the city centre between 9am and 4pm, appearing at regular intervals (30min–1hr) at about twenty major attractions; a full-fare ticket costs $34. One good place to join the tour is the stop on the corner of York and Front streets, near the CN Tower. On all Gray Line trips, there are concessionary fares for seniors (age 60+) and children (ages 5–11). For more information on guided city tours, see p.199.

If you want to take a **boat trip**, the Mariposa Cruise Line (☎416/203-0178; ⓦwww.mariposacruises.com) offers a good range of lake and harbour tours from mid–May to September; boats depart from the jetty beside the Queen's Quay Terminal building, at the foot of York Street. Alternatively, the Great Lakes Schooner Company (☎416/203-2322; ⓦwww .greatlakesschooner.com) features genuine sailing trips on a three-master, the Kajama (June–Aug; 1–3 daily; $20). There are lots of other nautical options – and the annual Visitor Guide, available at the Ontario Tourism Travel Information Centre (see p.36), outlines most of them.

The media

Toronto does well for newspapers and magazines, some of which are free, as well as for radio stations. By contrast, the TV channels on offer, both terrestrial and cable, are largely uninspiring until after 11pm, at which point any number of truly strange and exotic programmes are launched at the unwary. Many shows that are deemed too risqué for general North American audiences find their previews on Toronto TV channels during the wee hours.

Newspapers and magazines

Toronto has two first-rate daily **newspapers**, the *Globe and Mail* and the *Toronto Star*. Both provide insight into every facet of the city, but the *Globe and Mail* is better for international coverage, the *Star* for local stuff. The *Globe* is also Canada's main nationwide newspaper, its only rival being the comparable, if more right-wing, *National Post*. As for **magazines**, the most popular is *Toronto Life* (Ⓦwww.torontolife.com), which has an entertaining range of feature articles and also does an excellent line of listings publications: "Where to Get Good Stuff Cheap" is a particular favourite and tends to sell out quickly.

Amongst several literary publications, one deserving of special note is the twice-yearly *Brick* (Ⓦwww.brickmag.com), which serves up an eclectic mix of book reviews, poetry, essays, memoirs and interviews. For serious aficionados of local 'zines and comics, The Beguiling, 601 Markham St (☎416/533-9168, Ⓦwww.beguiling.com), is a must-visit, as it stocks the gamut of the indie publications.

TV and radio

Canadian **TV** is dominated by US sludge and slurry, though the publicly subsidized Canadian Broadcasting Corporation (CBC) does fight a rearguard action for quality programmes, from drama through to documentary. The main local TV station is the chatty and rather inconsequential City TV. Cable television is commonplace, both in private homes and in the vast majority of hotel and motel rooms.

As regards **radio**, CBC Radio One (99.1 FM) is Toronto's frequency for the Canadian Broadcasting Corporation, an excellent source for public affairs, news and arts programming. For just news, try CFTR (680 AM) or CFRB (1010 AM). For easy rock, tune in to CHUM (104.5 FM) or MIX (99.9 FM). Harder rock is found on Q 107 (107.1 FM), and alternative sounds are on CFNY (102.1 FM). CISS (92.5 FM) does country, and CFMX (96.3 FM) or CBC Two (94.1 FM) are good for classical. There are also two excellent student stations that feature alternative and world artists, as well as news and events: CKLN (88.1 FM) from Ryerson Polytechnic, and CIUT (89.5 FM) from the University of Toronto.

Travel essentials

Addresses

Yonge Street is Toronto's principal north–south artery. Main drags perpendicular to Yonge use this intersection to change from west to east – Queen Street West, for example, becomes Queen Street East when it crosses Yonge. Note, therefore, that 1000 Queen Street West, for example, is a long way from 1000 Queen Street East. Where a number is prefixed to the street number, this indicates an apartment or suite number in a block at the same street address. As with US usage, the "first floor" is what would be the ground floor in Britain; the "second floor" is one floor above ground level, and so on.

Costs

By continental European standards, Toronto is very reasonably priced, with most basic items – from maps through to food and clothing – **costing** significantly less than back home. US residents, Australians and New Zealanders, on the other hand, will find prices about the same – maybe a little higher, but not by much. Historically, Toronto has been a reasonably priced destination for British travellers too, though at time of writing the slide in the value of sterling makes the city quite a bit more expensive than home. Generally speaking, dining and drinking in Toronto are inexpensive, as is public transport, whereas accommodation, which is almost certainly going to be your major outlay, can be expensive, though there are plenty of bargains.

On average, if you're prepared to buy your own picnic lunch, stay in bargain-basement hostels or university residences, and stick to the least expensive bars and restaurants, you could get by on around CDN$60 a day. Staying in a modest chain hotel, eating out in medium-range restaurants most nights and drinking regularly in bars, you'll get through at least CDN$150 a day, with the main variable being the cost of your room. On CDN$230 a day and upwards, you'll be limited only by your energy reserves – though if you're planning to stay in the best hotels and make every night a big night out, this still won't be enough. As always, if you're travelling alone you'll spend much more on accommodation than you would in a group of two or more: most hotels do have single rooms, but they're fixed at about seventy percent of the price of a double. See also "Taxes", p.35.

Crime and personal safety

There's little reason why you should ever come into contact with either the Toronto Police Service or the Ontario Provincial Police, who safeguard the rest of the province: Toronto is one of the safest cities in North America and, generally speaking, you can explore the city without fear of harassment or assault. Few citizens carry arms, muggings are uncommon, and street crime less commonplace than in many other major North American cities – though the usual cautions about poorly lit urban streets and so forth stand. Nonetheless, certain parts of Toronto are decidedly shady with pockets of seedy roughness dotted here and there seemingly at random. Consequently, and especially until you are familiar with the city's layout, it's always best to err on the side of caution. One such area is to the east of Yonge on Sherbourne Street to the south of Queen Street East. Using public transport, even late at night, isn't usually a problem – but if in doubt take a taxi. Note also that the police are diligent in enforcing traffic laws.

If you are a victim of crime, you'll need to go to the **police** to report it, not least because your insurance company will require a police report. Remember to make a note of the crime report number – or, better still, ask for a copy of the statement itself. Don't expect a great deal of concern if your loss is relatively small, and don't be surprised if the process of completing forms and formalities takes ages. If you are detained by the police, the arresting officer(s) must identify him/herself. At the police station, detainees have the right to free but reasonable use of a telephone and legal counsel. For certain sorts of suspected offence – primarily terrorist-, gun- and drug-related – the police may strip-search detainees.

Currency

See Money and exchange.

Electricity

Electricity in Canada is supplied at an alternating current of 110 volts and at a frequency of 60Hz, the same as in the US. Visitors from the UK will need transformers for appliances like shavers and hair dryers, and a plug converter for Canada's two-pin sockets.

Emergencies

For police, fire and ambulance **emergencies**, call ☏911.

Entry requirements

Citizens of the EU, Norway, Iceland and many Commonwealth countries, including Australia and New Zealand, only need a **valid passport** to enter Canada. The rules regarding US citizens entering Canada changed in 2009 with US citizens now required to carry a passport or, in some cases but never on planes, a Passport Card. Note that a US driver's licence alone is not sufficient proof of citizenship.

All visitors to Canada have to complete a **Welcome to Canada form**, effectively a customs declaration form, which you'll be given on the plane or at the US–Canadian border. On the form, you have to indicate the purpose of your visit from three options – study, business or personal. At point of entry, the immigration officer decides the length of stay permitted – usually not more than three months. The officers rarely refuse entry, but they may delve deep, asking you for details of your schedule and likely destinations and enquiring as to how much money you have and what job you do; they may also ask to see a return or onward ticket. If they ask where you're staying and you give the name and address of friends, don't be surprised if they check. Note also that although passing

overland between the US and Canada is usually straightforward, there can sometimes be long delays, especially if your vehicle is at the receiving end of a spot search. Officers at the more obscure border entry points can be real sticklers.

For **visits of more than six months**, study trips and stints of (temporary) employment, contact the nearest Canadian embassy, consulate or high commission for authorization prior to departure. Once inside Canada, if you need an extension of your stay or want to change the basis on which you were admitted, you must apply to the nearest Canada Immigration Centre (◉www.cic.gc.ca) at least thirty days before the expiry of the authorized visit.

Canadian high commissions, embassies and consulates abroad

For the official list of all Canada's high commissions, consulates and embassies, consult ◉www.voyage.gc.ca.

Australia High Commission, Commonwealth Ave, Canberra ACT, ☏02/6270 4000, ◉www.australia.gc.ca. Consulates in Melbourne, Perth and Sydney.

Ireland Embassy, 7 Wilton Terrace, Dublin 2 ☏01/234 4000, ◉www.ireland.gc.ca.

New Zealand High Commission, 125 The Terrace, Wellington 6143 ☏04/473 9577, ◉www.newzealand.gc.ca.

UK High Commission, Canada House, Trafalgar Square ☏020/7258 6600, ◉www.unitedkingdom.gc.ca. Honorary consulates in Belfast, Cardiff and Edinburgh.

USA Embassy, 501 Pennsylvania Ave NW, Washington DC 20001 ☏202/682-1740, ◉www.washington.gc.ca/. Consulates in Atlanta, Boston, Buffalo, Chicago, Dallas, Denver, Detroit, Honolulu, Los Angeles, Miami, Minneapolis, New York, San Francisco, and Seattle.

Foreign consulates in Toronto

Australia Suite 1100, South Tower, 175 Bloor St E, ☏416/323-1155.

Ireland Suite 1210, 20 Toronto St ☏416/366-9300.

New Zealand Suite 2308, 2nd Floor, 965 Bay St ☏416/947-9696.

United Kingdom Suite 2800, 777 Bay St ☏416/593-1267.

United States 360 University Ave ☏416/595-1700.

Health

You'd be daft to visit Canada without a travel insurance policy covering potential medical expenses. Canada has an excellent **health service**, but non-residents are not entitled to free health care, and **medical costs** can be astronomical. If you have an accident, medical services will get to you quickly and charge you later. **Doctors** and **dentists** can be found listed in the Yellow Pages, though for **medical emergencies** (as well as fire and police) call ☎911. If you are carrying medicine prescribed by your doctor, also bring a copy of the **prescription** – first, to avoid problems at customs and immigration and, second, for renewing medication with Canadian doctors as required.

As you would expect, Toronto has scores of **pharmacies**. In particular, Shopper's Drug Mart has several central locations, including 181 Bay St at Front (☎416/777-1300); the Royal Bank Plaza, 200 Bay St (☎416/865-0001); and 66 Wellington St West (☎416/365-0927). For a holistic apothecary, try The Big Carrot, at 348 Danforth Ave (☎416/466-2129, ⓦwww.thebigcarrot.ca), a large whole-foods co-op with a wide selection of herbal remedies and health products; it is located three blocks east of Broadview Avenue.

Specific health problems

Canada requires no specific vaccinations, but problems can arise if you venture out into the backcountry – Algonquin Provincial Park (see p.122) being a case in point. Here, although **tap water** is generally safe to drink, it's prudent to ask first. You should also always boil backcountry water for at least ten minutes to protect against the **Giardia parasite** (or "beaver fever"). The parasite thrives in warm water, so be careful about swimming in hot springs – if possible, keep nose, eyes and mouth above water. Symptoms are intestinal cramps, flatulence, fatigue, weight loss and vomiting, all of which can appear up to a week after infection. If left untreated, more unpleasant complications can arise, so see

a doctor immediately if you think you've contracted it.

Blackfly and **mosquitoes** are notorious for the problems they cause hikers and campers, and are especially bad in areas near standing water and throughout most of northern and much of central Ontario. Horseflies are another pest. Late April to June is the blackfly season, and the mosquito season is from June until about October. If you're planning an expedition into the wilderness, you'd be well-advised to take three times the recommended daily dosage of **vitamin B complex** for two weeks before you go, and to take the recommended dosage while you're in Canada; this cuts down bites by up to seventy-five percent.

Once you're there, **repellent creams** and sprays may help: the best are those containing DEET. The ointment version of Deep-Woods Off is the best brand, with 95 percent DEET. If you're camping or picnicking you'll find that burning coils or candles containing allethrin or citronella can help. If you're walking in an area that's rifo with pests, it's well worth taking a **gauze mask** to protect your head and neck; wearing white clothes and no perfumed products also makes you less attractive to the insects. Once bitten, an **antihistamine cream** like phenergan is the best antidote. On no account go anywhere near an area marked as a blackfly mating ground – people have died from bites sustained when the creatures are in heat. Also dangerous is **West Nile virus**, a mosquito-born affliction with life-threatening properties; up until now, the virus has only appeared in a handful of places in southern Ontario, but it may spread – so pay attention to local advice.

If you develop a large rash and flu-like symptoms, you may have been bitten by a tick carrying lyme borreliosis (or "**lyme tick disease**"). This is easily curable, but if left untreated can lead to nasty complications, so again see a doctor as soon as possible. It's spreading in Canada, especially in the more southerly and wooded parts of the country, so you should check on its prevalence with the local tourist authority. It also may be advisable to buy a strong tick

In a **medical emergency**, call ☎911.

repellent and to wear long socks, trousers and sleeved shirts when walking.

In backcountry areas, look out for **poison ivy**, which grows in most places, but particularly in a belt across southern Ontario and Quebec, where poison-ivy ointment is widely available. If you're likely to be walking in affected areas, ask at tourist offices for tips on where it is and how to recognize it. The ivy causes itchy open blisters and lumpy sores up to ten days after contact. If you do come into contact with poison ivy, wash your body and clothes as soon as possible, smother yourself in calamine lotion and try not to scratch. In serious cases, hospital emergency rooms can give antihistamine or adrenalin jabs.

Insurance

Prior to travelling, you should take out an **insurance policy** to cover against theft, loss and illness or injury. Before paying for a new policy, however, it's worth checking whether you already have some degree of coverage: credit card companies, home-insurance policies and private medical plans sometimes cover you and your belongings when you're abroad.

After exhausting the possibilities above, you'll probably want to contact a specialist travel insurance company, or consider the travel insurance deal we offer (see box below). A typical travel insurance policy provides cover for the loss of baggage, tickets and – up to a certain limit – cash or cheques, as well as cancellation or curtailment of your journey. Most of them exclude so-called dangerous sports unless an extra premium is paid. Many policies can be chopped and changed to exclude coverage you don't need: for

example, sickness and accident benefits can often be excluded or included at will. If you do take medical insurance, ascertain whether benefits will be paid as treatment proceeds or only after return home, and whether there is a 24-hour medical emergency number. When securing baggage cover, make sure that the **per-article limit** will cover your most valuable possession. If you need to make a claim, keep receipts for medicines and medical treatment. In the event you have anything stolen, you must obtain a **crime report statement** or number from the police.

Internet and email

Most of Toronto's hotels and many of its B&Bs provide **internet/email access** for their guests either free or at minimal charge. There's also free internet/email access at the city's public libraries, one of the more convenient of which is the Toronto Reference Library, 789 Yonge St at Cumberland (Mon–Thurs 9.30am–8.30pm, Fri 9.30am–5pm & Sat 9am–5pm, plus mid-Sept to late June Sun 1.30–5pm; ☎416/395-5577, ⓦwww .torontopubliclibrary.ca; see p.77). The city has a gaggle of internet cafés too, though of course they all levy charges.

The site ⓦwww.kropla.com gives useful details of how to plug your laptop in when abroad, phone codes around the world, and information about electrical systems in different countries.

Selected internet cafés

Cyber Orbits 1 Gloucester St ☎416/920-5912. Open 24hr.
Internet Café 370 Yonge St ☎416/408-0570. Open daily 6am–1am.

Rough Guides travel insurance

Rough Guides has teamed up with Columbus Direct to offer you travel insurance that can be tailored to suit your needs. Products include a low-cost backpacker option for long stays; a short break option for city getaways; a typical holiday package option; and others. There are also annual multi-trip policies for those who travel regularly. Different sports and activities (trekking, skiing, etc) can be usually be covered if required.

See our website (ⓦwww.roughguides.com/website/shop) for eligibility and purchasing options. Alternatively, UK residents should call ☎0870/033 9988; Australians should call ☎1300/669 999 and New Zealanders should call ☎0800/55 9911. All other nationalities should call ☎+44 870/890 2843.

Selected websites

ⓦ**www.canada.gc.ca** The Canadian government tells all – or all that it wants its citizens to know?

ⓦ**www.canadianhockey.ca** Proof positive that Canadians are passionate about their national sport, ice hockey.

ⓦ**www.gaytoronto.com** A useful starting point if you're looking to find out what's happening on the male scene, but it has precious little information for women. There's a useful bulletin board service, which has an accommodation section.

ⓦ**www.theglobeandmail.com** Canada's premier national newspaper, the *Globe and Mail*, online.

ⓦ**www.martiniboys.com** Perhaps the best online guide to Toronto's hottest and coolest bars and clubs, as well as intelligent, well-written restaurant reviews.

ⓦ**www.nlc-bnc.ca** National Library of Canada website offering information on all things Canadian, ordered by subject.

ⓦ**www.thestar.com** The *Toronto Star* is arguably the city's best newspaper and its website is strong on news, sports and weather. There's also a regularly updated "what's on" section covering local music, film and TV schedules.

ⓦ**www.statcan.gc.ca** Statistics Canada is a national agency that analyses a whole raft of information to see where the country is going and how it is getting there.

ⓦ**www.pc.gc.ca** Parks Canada operates this excellent website with detailed information on all of Canada's national parks and national historic sites.

Net Space 275 Queen St W ☎416/597-2005. Open daily 8am–1am.
Net Space 2 2305 Yonge St ☎416/486-9071. Open daily 8am–1am.

Libraries

The main Downtown library is the **Toronto Reference Library**, 789 Yonge St, at Cumberland (Mon–Thurs 9.30am–8.30pm, Fri 9.30am–5pm & Sat 9am–5pm, plus mid-Sept to late June Sun 1.30–5pm; ☎416/395-5577, ⓦwww.torontopubliclibrary.ca; see p.77).

Mail

Canada Post (ⓦwww.canadapost.ca) operates service counters in scores of locations, mostly as a discrete part of a larger retail outlet, principally pharmacies and stationery stores. Usual opening hours are Monday to Friday 9am to 6pm and Sat 9am to noon. Specific **post offices** are thinner on the ground, but there are a number dotted across the city centre. One of the handiest is inside the Atrium on Bay mall, 20 Dundas St West at Yonge St (Mon–Fri 9am–6pm & Sat 9am–5pm). If you're posting letters to a Canadian address, always include the **postcode** or your mail may never get there. Apart from Canada Post service counters and offices, stamps can be purchased from the lobbies of larger hotels, airports, train stations and many retail outlets and newsstands. Canada Post's services are reliable, both inbound and outbound.

Maps

The **maps** in this guide should be perfectly adequate for most purposes, but if you want something a tad more comprehensive, the best bet is the rip-proof, waterproof **Rough Guide Toronto Map** (1:16,000 to 1:27,000), which has an accurate index and pinpoints recommended restaurants, bars, sights and shops.

If you plan to venture out into the wilds of Ontario, the best resource available is MapArt's (ⓦwww.mapart.com) excellent Ontario Road Atlas (mostly 1:250,000), a 108-page book that retails at around $20; for shorter trips, Rand McNally's (ⓦwww.randmcnally.com) Ontario map is both clear and accurate.

Metric measurements

Officially at least, Canada uses the **metric system** with distances in kilometres, temperatures in degrees Celsius, and foodstuffs, petrol and drink sold in grams, kilograms or litres. Such is the economic clout of the

USA, however, that many items are sold and/or gauged in imperial measurements, from gallons through to miles.

Money and exchange

Canadian **currency** is the Canadian **dollar** ($), made up of 100 cents (¢). Coins come as 1¢ (penny), 5¢ (nickel), 10¢ (dime), 25¢ (quarter), $1 and $2. The $1 **coin** is known as a "loonie", after the bird on one face; no one's come up with a suitable name for the newer $2 coin – "twoonie" has been tried but hasn't really caught on. There are **notes** of $5, $10, $20, $50 and $100. US dollars are widely accepted, but generally – banks, etc apart – on a one-for-one basis – not a good deal as the US dollar is (usually) worth more than its Canadian counterpart. Exchange rates at the time of writing are £1=C$1.77, US$1=C$1.18, €1=C$1.61, A$1=C$0.85, NZ$1=C$0.70. For the most up-to-date rates, check ⓦwww.oanda.com.

Banks are legion and, although opening hours vary, all are **open** Mon–Fri 10am–3pm at the very least. Two central locations for the Toronto Dominion (TD) bank, one of the city's largest, are 77 Bloor St at Bay St and 65 Wellesley St East. Toronto has plenty of **ATMs**, with a particular concentration in the city centre, and almost all of them accept a host of debit cards. If in doubt, check with your bank to find out whether the card you wish to use will be accepted – and if you need a new (international) PIN. You'll rarely be charged a transaction fee, as the banks make their profits from applying different exchange rates. Credit cards can be used in ATMs too, but in this case transactions are treated as loans, with interest accruing daily from the date of withdrawal. All major credit cards, including American Express, Visa and MasterCard, are widely accepted in Toronto.

Opening hours and public holidays

Shopping is a major Toronto pastime and opening hours are therefore very generous, with most shops open seven days a week, usually from 9.30am/10am until anywhere from 8pm to 10pm Monday to Thursday; on Friday quite a few places close a little earlier, at 6pm or 7pm; weekend hours are usually Saturday 9.30am/10am to 6pm or 7pm, and Sunday noon to 6pm. In addition, convenience stores, like 7-Eleven, are routinely open much longer, often round the clock. Office hours are more restricted, characteristically Monday to Friday 9/9.30am to 4.30/5pm. Most major museums are open daily from around 10am to 5pm or 5.30pm, with one late night a week, usually Wednesday or Thursday until 8pm or 9pm. As for restaurants, these are usually open daily from 11am to 11pm, with or without an afternoon break, from around 2.30/3pm to 5/6pm. Bars are open daily from 11am to 2am. Most offices are closed on public holidays, but – with the probable exception of Christmas and the New Year – not bars, restaurants, shops, museums and hotels. Public transport keeps moving on public holidays, too, operating a skeleton service.

Metric conversions

All figures are approximate:
1 centimetre = 0.39 inches; 1 inch = 2.5cm; 1 foot = 30cm.
1 metre (100cm) = 1.1 yards or 39 inches; 1 yard = 0.9m.
1 kilometre (1000m) = 0.6 miles; 1 mile = 1.6km; 8km = 5mi.
1 hectare (10,000sq m) = 2.5 acres; 1 acre = 0.4ha.
1 litre = 2.1 US pints; 1 US pint = 0.5 litres; 1 US quart = 0.9 litres.
1 litre = 0.3 US gallons; 1 US gallon = 3.8 litres.
1 litre = 1.8 UK pints; 1 UK pint = 0.6 litres.
1 litre = 0.2 UK gallons; 1 UK gallon = 4.5 litres.
1 kilogram or kilo (1000g) = 2.2lb; 1lb = 45g/0.45kg; 1oz = 28g.

Temperatures

°C	-10	-5	0	5	10	15	20	25	30	35
°F	14	23	32	41	50	59	68	77	86	95

Public holidays

New Year's Day Jan 1
Good Friday varies; March/April
Easter Sunday varies; March/April
Victoria Day third Monday in May
Canada Day July 1
Labour Day first Monday in Sept
Thanksgiving second Monday in Oct
Christmas Day Dec 25
Boxing Day Dec 26
Also widely observed, but not official public holidays are:
Easter Monday varies; March/April
Simcoe Day first Monday in Aug
Remembrance Day Nov 11

Phones

Public telephones are commonplace in Toronto, though the rise of the mobile phone/cell phone means that their numbers will not increase and may well diminish. All are equipped for the hearing-impaired, and for making domestic or international calls; most accept **pre-paid calling cards** and **credit cards** in addition to coins. **Local calls** cost 25¢ from a public phone, but are free on private phones (though not usually hotel phones). All phone books contain maps of the Downtown core and display Toronto Transit Commission (TTC) routes; the Yellow Pages, a compendium of all business phone numbers, grouped by service, are especially informative.

When dialling any Canadian number, either local or long-distance, you must include the **area code** – usually ☏416 or ☏647 in Toronto. **Long-distance calls** – to numbers beyond the area code from which you're dialling – must be prefixed with "1". On public telephones, this "1" secures an operator intercept; the operator will tell you how much money you need to get connected. Thereafter, you'll be asked to shovel money in at regular intervals – so unless you're making a reverse-charge/collect call you'll need a stack of quarters (25¢ pieces) handy.

To confuse matters, some connections within a single telephone code area are charged at the long-distance rate, and thus need the "1" prefix; a recorded message will tell you this is necessary as soon as you dial the number. To save the hassle of carrying all this change, you could consider buying a **telephone card** either back home or here in Toronto. In Toronto, there are a number of telephone charge cards to choose from, with one of the more widely available being Bell's Prepaid Calling Card, which is sold in several denominations. For further details of this and other Bell phone cards, contact their customer service department on ☏1-800/668 6878, ⊛www.bell.ca.

Note also that many businesses, especially hotels, have toll-free numbers (prefixed by ☏1-800 or 1-888). Some of these can only be dialled from phones in the same province, others from anywhere within Canada, and a few from anywhere in North America; as a rough guideline, the larger the organization, the wider its toll-free net. Finally, remember that although most hotel rooms have phones, there is almost always an exorbitant surcharge for their use.

International calls

To phone abroad from Canada, dial the appropriate international access code as below, then the number you require, omitting the initial zero where there is one.
Australia ☏0061
New Zealand ☏0064
Republic of Ireland ☏00353
South Africa ☏0027
UK ☏0044
USA ☏001

To phone Canada from abroad, dial the local international access code (00 in many countries), followed by the code for Canada (1), then the area code, followed by the number.

Mobile/cell phones

Canada's **mobile phone** (cell phone) network works on GSM 1900, which means that mobiles/cells bought in Europe, Australia and New Zealand need to be triband to gain cellular access. As you would expect, the mobile network covers all of Toronto, but out in rural Ontario **coverage** can be patchy. If you intend to use your mobile/cell phone in Toronto, note that call charges can be excruciating – particularly galling is the supplementary charge that you often have to pay on incoming calls – so check with your

Useful phone numbers

Directory enquiries from private phones Local, regional and long-distance within North America ☎411; international, call the operator ☎0.
Directory enquiries from public phones Local/regional ☎411; long-distance within North America ☎1+ area code + 555-1212; international, call the operator ☎0.
Emergencies Police, fire and ambulance ☎911.
Operator Domestic and international ☎0.

supplier before you depart. Text messages, on the other hand, are usually charged at ordinary rates. You might also consider buying either a SIM card or a pay-as-you-go phone when you get to Canada from any one of the many local suppliers.

Post

See "Mail".

Smoking

Smoking has long been prohibited in all public buildings, including train stations, as well as on flights and bus services. In the last few years, these restrictions have been widened and smoking is now banned inside restaurants, bars and cafés.

Taxes

Virtually all prices in Canada for everything from bubble-gum to hotel rooms are quoted **without tax**, which means that the price you see quoted is not the price you'll end up paying. Across the province of Ontario, which includes Toronto, there's a **Provincial Sales Tax (PST)** of eight percent on most goods and services, though this is replaced by a **Room Tax** of five percent on accommodation. These taxes are supplemented by the **Goods and Services Tax (GST)**, a five percent levy applied nationwide on just about everything you can think of. Visitors can claim a PST rebate on certain outgoings (but nothing from the GST). The rules are complicated, but broadly **PST rebates** mainly apply to shopping receipts where you have spent $625 or more (before tax). Claim forms are available at many hotels, shops and airports. Return them, with all original receipts, to the address given on the form. Those returning overland to the US can claim their rebate at selected border duty-free shops. For more

information, call ☎905/432-3431 or consult ⓦwww.rev.gov.on.ca/English/taxes/.

Taxis

There are lots of **taxi firms** to choose from – try Co-op Cabs (☎416/504-2667) or Diamond Taxicab (☎416/366-6868).

Time zones

Toronto is on **Eastern Standard Time (EST)**, the same time zone as New York City, which is five hours behind Greenwich Mean Time. Toronto is also three hours ahead of Pacific Standard Time (PST), fifteen hours behind Australian Eastern Daylight Time (EDT) and seventeen hours behind New Zealand – except for periods during the changeovers made in the respective countries to and from daylight saving.

Tipping

Almost everywhere you eat or drink, the service will be fast and friendly – thanks to the institution of **tipping**. Waiters and bartenders depend on tips for the bulk of their earnings and, unless the service is dreadful, you should top up your bill by fifteen percent or more. A refusal to tip is considered rude and mean in equal measure. If you're paying by credit card, there's a space on the payment slip where you can add the appropriate gratuity.

Toilets – public

Public **toilets** – or 'restrooms' – are rare: try hotel lobbies, any shopping centre, subway stations (particularly Union Station), or the Toronto Reference Library (see p.77).

Tourist information

The excellent **Ontario Tourism Travel Information Centre**, at street level inside the

Toll-free information numbers and websites

Ontario Tourism ☎ 1-800/ONTARIO (668-2746), ⓦ www.ontariotravel.net.
Tourism Toronto ☎ 1-800/499-2514, ⓦ www.seetorontonow.com.

Atrium on Bay mall, 20 Dundas St West at Yonge (Mon–Fri 10am–9pm, Sat 10am–6pm & Sun noon–5pm; ☎ 1-800/ONTARIO, or within Toronto 1-416/314-5899), stocks a comprehensive range of information on all the major attractions in Toronto and throughout Ontario. Most of the stuff is free, including reasonably good-quality city maps, the Ride Guide to the city's transport system, and entertainment details in the monthly magazine *Where*. Ontario Tourism will also book hotel accommodation on your behalf both in Toronto and across all of Ontario. They also sell the City Pass (see p.39) and operate an all-encompassing **website**, ⓦ www.ontariotravel.net, which is particularly strong on practical information.

Surprisingly, **Tourism Toronto**, the city's official visitor and convention bureau, does not have an information office, but it does run a telephone information line, whose operators can handle most city queries and will make hotel reservations on your behalf (Mon–Fri 8.30am–6pm; ☎ 1-800/499-2514 or 416/203-2500). You can also scour bags of information and book accommodation on their website, ⓦ www.seetorontonow.com.

Travellers with disabilities

Toronto is one of the best places in the world to visit if you have **mobility** problems or other physical **disabilities**. All public buildings are required to be wheelchair-accessible and provide suitable toilet facilities, almost all street corners have dropped kerbs, and public telephones are specially equipped for hearing-aid users. In addition, the city's public transport system, operated by the TTC (see p.25; ⓦ www.ttc.ca), is disability-friendly, its bespoke **Wheel-Trans** operation providing

a door-to-door transit service seven days a week (Mon–Fri 6am–1am, Sat & Sun 7am–12.30am). Further Wheel-Trans information, including registration details, are available on the TTC website and ☎ 416/393-4222. For other TTC route, fare and schedule information, call either ☎ 416/393-4636 or 416/393-4555.

Travelling with children

Most of the time, Toronto does a good job in keeping **children** in good spirits. Many attractions are specifically designed to cater for families; children's menus are commonplace; an extra bed or two will be rolled out in most hotel and motel rooms with a minimum of fuss; swimming pools and assorted sports facilities are ubiquitous; and children get concessionary rates just about everywhere, from buses to museums. For more information, see Chapter 15, Kids' Toronto, pp.203-206.

Underground Toronto

For better or worse, Toronto has the world's largest **underground shopping complex** (ⓦ www.toronto.ca/path), over one thousand shops and stores spread out along a seemingly endless network of subterranean pedestrian walkways and mall basements. The network links over forty office towers and several major hotels and, best of all, keeps city folk well away from the extremes of their climate. The network stretches north from Union Station to the Eaton Centre and the coach terminal, and west–east from the CBC Broadcasting Centre to the King Street subway; **access points** – of which there are many – sport a multi-coloured sign inscribed "**PATH**".

The City

The City

Downtown Toronto

T he skyscrapers etched across **Downtown Toronto**'s skyline witness the clout of a city that has discarded the dowdy provincialism of its early years to become the economic and cultural focus of English-speaking Canada. There's no false modesty here, kicking off with Toronto's mascot, the **CN Tower**, and continuing with the **Rogers centre**, formerly the **SkyDome**, the flashy stadium built for the Blue Jays and Argonauts sports teams. Close by, the plush and extravagant *Royal York Hotel* marks the start of the **Banking District**, a brisk and bustling part of the city whose herd of tower blocks proceeds north to Queen Street. Here, modern behemoths like the **Toronto Dominion Centre** and the gold-coated **Royal Bank Plaza** are beacons of modern-day prosperity, but there are older high rises too, like the **Dominion Bank** and the **Canada Permanent Trust building**, whose sumptuous designs (c.1920) trumpet the aspirations of previous generations. Toronto's business elite also funded one of Downtown's most enjoyable art galleries, the outstanding **Toronto Dominion Gallery of Inuit Art**.

At Queen Street, the Banking District gives way to the central **shopping area**, which revolves around the sprawling **Eaton Centre**. Immediately to the west is **City Hall**, another striking example of modern design, and the **Art Gallery of Ontario**, which houses the province's finest collection of paintings, as well as an entire gallery of sculptures by Henry Moore. Finally, on the western periphery of Downtown is **Fort York**, an accurate and intriguing reconstruction of the British stockade established here in 1793.

Downtown is best explored on **foot**, though the tower blocks can be a bit claustrophobic and local complaints that the city centre lacks a human dimension are legion. To be fair, this sentiment has been taken into account, and although it's a bit late in the day, efforts have been made to make the Downtown core more people-friendly, with plazas, pavement cafés and street sculptures.

Toronto City Pass

If you are a diligent sightseer, you may be able to save money with the **Toronto City Pass**. Valid for nine days, the pass entitles visitors to free entrance to six of the city's most popular attractions – the CN Tower (see p.40), the Hockey Hall of Fame (see p.49), the Royal Ontario Museum (see p.72), Casa Loma (see p.78), the Ontario Science Centre (see p.96) and Toronto Zoo (see p.91). It costs $64 ($43 for 4 to 12-year-olds) and can be purchased at any of the six sights.

The CN Tower

Much to the dismay of many Torontonians, the **CN Tower**, 301 Front St West (daily 9am–10pm, sometimes later; observation deck & glass floor $22, Sky Pod $5 extra; ☏416/868-6937, ⓦwww.cntower.ca; Union subway), has become the city's symbol. It's touted on much of the city's promotional literature, features on thousands of postcards and holiday snaps and has become the obligatory start to most tourist itineraries. From almost anywhere in the city, it's impossible to

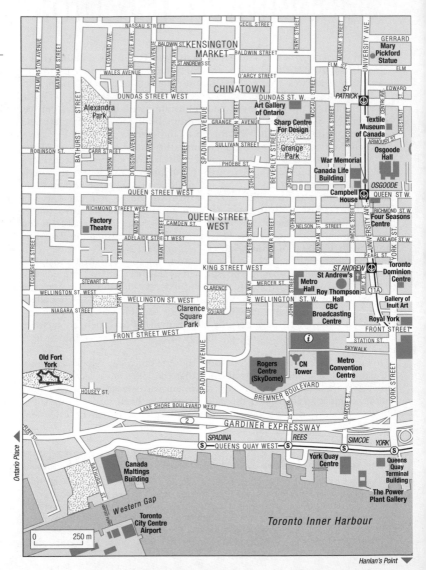

Toronto's architecture

In its early days, Toronto was every inch a utilitarian city – one with few frills and no pretence, where almost everything was subordinate to the needs of industry and commerce. As the city spread across the flatlands bordering Lake Ontario, little thought was given to public space, though big-deal politicians and business people broke the flow by erecting monuments to their own prestige. The string of doughty structures they created still dot the city, and in recent years they have been leavened and lightened by a battery of more playful buildings by some of the big names in world architecture.

Ontario Legislative Assembly Building ▲

Old City Hall ▼

Union Station ▼

Victorian high points

Toronto began with **Fort York**, which was built by the British in standard frontier style, its top-heavy blockhouses and cottage-like officers' quarters an excellent illustration of function defining form. As Toronto expanded the frontier aesthetic disappeared and the city's movers and shakers built themselves big, clumpy stone buildings in the Romanesque Revival style – though one contemporary wag preferred to term the style 'penitentiary'. It's to this period that Toronto owes the **Ontario Legislative Assembly Building**, **Old City Hall** and **Casa Loma**, a trio of monstrous masterpieces whose finely carved details – from gargoyles to coats of arms – can't help but entertain. The last two were designed by the rumbustious Edward James Lennox, the leading Toronto architect of his day, who dotted the city with his creations – and fell out with the city council big time.

There are buildings with a much lighter touch from this period too, most memorably the intricate facade of the **Elgin and Winter Garden Theatre**, a double-decker Vaudeville theatre that remains in use today; and the smooth Beaux Arts design of **Union Station**, with its long line of columns and grand, evocative friezes. All these buildings have the flavour of North America, but many of the old college buildings of the University of Toronto are deliberately reminiscent of England's Oxford and Cambridge, the neo-Gothic **Hart House** being a case in point. A further architectural nod to class-ridden England can be seen in **Spadina House**, Toronto's most elegant Victorian home – complete with a conservatory trap door that enabled the gardeners to come and go unseen by their employers.

Reaching for the sky

In the 1960s, the business elite got stuck into building the skyscrapers that still dominate the Banking District. Pride of place here goes to the sleek, unadorned towers of the **Toronto Dominion Centre**, whose set of reflective black blocks were designed by Ludwig Mies van der Rohe. In the 1970s, the much-lauded architect I.M. Pei added a real whopper of a building on behalf of the **Canadian Imperial Bank of Commerce**, Boris Zerafa weighed in with the gold-layered towers of the **Royal Bank Plaza**, and the railway conglomerate CN somehow ended up with the **CN Tower**, now, for better or more likely for worse, the city's emblem. In 1992, the **BCE Place** – now Brookfield Place – office block was given a light and airy gloss by Santiago Calatrava's glassy Allen Lambert Galleria, a six-storey pedestrian thoroughfare that looks a little like the rib cage of a giant dinosaur. This was all serious stuff, but in the mid-1990s there was, at last, a whiff of architectural whimsy: in 1995 Canada's own Raymond Moriyama chose to make the exterior of the new **Bata Shoe Museum** look like a shoe box, its roof set at an angle to suggest a lid resting on an open box. The design proved

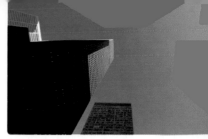

▲ Toronto Dominion Centre

▼ Allen Lambert Galleria

▼ Bata Shoe Museum

Architectural top five

▶▶ **The Ontario Legislative Assembly Building** see p.66.

▶▶ **The Art Gallery of Ontario's Frank Gehry extension** see p.60.

▶▶ **The Toronto Dominion Centre** see p.45.

▶▶ **The Sharp Centre for Design** see p.65.

▶▶ **The Michael Lee-Chin Crystal at the ROM** see p.72.

Sharp Centre for Design ▲

Art Gallery of Ontario ▼

instantly popular with most city folk, but in 2004 they were asked to rise to the challenge of a much more idiosyncratic structure, the **Sharp Centre for Design**, an addition to the dour brickwork of the Ontario College of Art. Conceived by the English architect Will Alsop, the Sharp consists of a giant black-and-white-panelled rectangular "table-top", perched high up at roof level and supported by huge multi-coloured steel legs; some have hated it, more have loved it, and whatever else it does, it certainly brings a smile. Influences can be hard to pin down, but Alsop's work may well have helped lure other well-known architects to Toronto. Frank Gehry designed the new extension to the **Art Gallery of Ontario** (the AGO), which consists of two parts – a striking glass and wood north facade on Dundas Street and a four-storey titanium and glass wing on the AGO's south side. There's also been a revamping of the **Royal Ontario Museum** (ROM), in which the stunning **Michael Lee-Chin Crystal**, named after its benefactor but designed by the renowned architect Daniel Libeskind, comprises six large crystal-shaped aluminium-and-glass cubes. This is prestige architecture at its most conspicuous and it has put a real spring in the step of the city. So, too, has the revamping of the waterfront: the large, dog-eared warehouses and wharves of yesteryear have been cleared away to be replaced by brisk and efficient condominium blocks, whose occupants enjoy wide views of Lake Ontario, and a set of leisure facilities – from cycling tracks to art galleries and open-air auditoria – that have become something of a focus for a city that has always been short of public space.

miss its slender form poking high above the skyline, reminding some of French novelist Guy de Maupassant's quip about another famous tower: "I like to lunch at the Eiffel Tower because that's the only place in Paris I can't see it."

Unlikely as it may seem, the celebrity status of the CN Tower was entirely unforeseen, its origins plain and utilitarian. In the 1960s, the Canadian Broadcasting Company (CBC) teamed up with the railway conglomerate Canadian National (CN) to propose the construction of a bigger and better transmission antenna. CBC eventually withdrew from the project, but CN, who owned the land and saw a chance for profit, forged ahead. Much to the company's surprise,

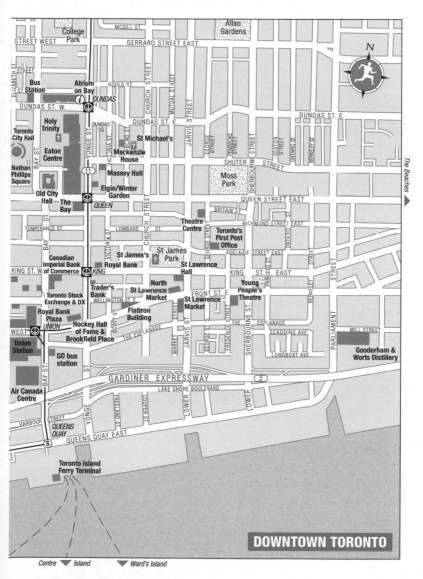

DOWNTOWN TORONTO

they found that the undertaking stirred intense public interest – so much so that long before the tower was completed, in April 1975, it was clear that its potential as a tourist sight would be huge: today, broadcasting only accounts for about twenty percent of the tower's income, with the rest provided by the two million visitors who throng here annually. Come early (especially on school holidays) to avoid the crowds.

The **tallest freestanding structure in the world**, the sleek and elegant tower tapers to a minaret-thin point 553m (1815ft) above the city centre; details of its construction are provided in a series of **photographs** and **touch-screen diplays** on the mezzanine level just beyond the main access ramp and security check-in. This background information is extremely interesting, revealing all sorts of odd facts and figures, though it is hardly reassuring to know that the tower is hit by lightning between sixty and eighty times a year.

From the foot of the tower, **glass-fronted elevators** whisk you up the outside of the structure to the indoor and outdoor **Look Out level** galleries at 346m. These circular galleries provide views over the whole of the city, which appears flattened and without much perspective - though markers help by pointing out the most conspicuous sights. This is also where you'll find the *360 Restaurant* (which slowly revolves around the tower, taking 72 minutes to make one revolution), and the reinforced **glass floor** – a vertigo thrill that goes some way to justifying the tower's pricey admittance fee. You are, however, still 100m from the top of the tower, with a separate set of lifts carrying visitors up to the **Sky Pod**, a confined little gallery that, frankly, doesn't justify the extra expense. On the way down, the lifts deposit passengers at the ground-floor souvenir shop, which adjoins an arcade full of (eminently missable) simulated film rides of bungee jumping and so on; there is an extra charge for these.

Rogers Centre and the Metro Convention Centre

Next door to the CN Tower, at 1 Blue Jays Way, stands the **Rogers Centre**, formerly the **SkyDome** (frequent guided tours depending on event schedules; call ☏416/341-2770 for latest timetable; $13.25; Ⓦwww.rogerscentre.com), which is home to two major Toronto sports teams – the Argonauts, of Canadian football fame, and the Blue Jays baseball team (for more on both teams, see Chapter 14, Sports and outdoor activities). Opened in 1989, the SkyDome seats about 60,000 and is used for special events and concerts, as well as sports. It was the first stadium in the world to have a fully retractable roof, an impressive feat of engineering with four gigantic roof panels mounted on rail tracks that together take just twenty minutes to cover the stadium's eight acres of turf and terrace. With every justification, the SkyDome was much heralded by the city, but however ingenious the design, the building itself is really rather ugly, and, despite the best efforts of artist **Michael Snow** – who added a pair of giant cartoon sculptures to the exterior: *The Audience Part 1* and *Part 2* – it looks like a giant armadillo when the roof is closed. Hour-long **guided tours**, worth it only if you are sticking around for an event, begin with a fifteen-minute film about the stadium's construction. The ensuing walking tour takes in a team dressing room, the Blue Jays Hall of Fame, and a stroll on the playing field.

▲ Michael Snow's The Audience at the Rogers Centre

On the other side of the CN Tower, the **Metro Convention Centre** straddles the rail lines into Union Station (see below), with the dreary North Building on one side, and the smart, chic South Building, with its acres of glass and steel, on the other. The former faces onto Front Street West, and the latter onto Bremner Boulevard. The South Building has the main entrance, where the foyer displays *The Turtle Pond* – a delightful mosaic of frogs, frogspawn and turtles. Here also, just outside the building, is an engaging sculpture of two whopping woodpeckers pecking away at a steel tree.

Union Station and the Air Canada Centre

A sheltered walkway called the **Skywalk** leads from the Metro Convention Centre to **Union Station** (Front St W and Bay St), a distinguished Beaux Arts structure designed in 1907 and finally completed in 1927. The station's exterior is imposing, with its long serenade of Neoclassical columns, but the interior is the real highlight, the vast **main hall** boasting a coffered and tiled ceiling of graceful design. Like other North American railway stations of the period, Union Station has the flavour of a medieval cathedral, with muffled sounds echoing through its stone cloisters, and daylight filtering through its high arched windows. The station's grandiose quality was quite deliberate. In the days when the steam train was the most popular form of transport, architects were keen to glorify the train station, and, in this case, to convey the idea of Canada's vastness – a frieze bearing the names of all the Canadian cities reachable by rail at the time of construction runs around the hall.

A short walk south from Union Station, the **Air Canada Centre**, 40 Bay St (☎416/815-5500, ⓦwww.theaircanadacentre.com), is home to hockey's Maple

Leafs and basketball's Raptors; see Chapter 14, Sports and outdoor activities, for more on these two teams. Hour-long **tours** of the Air Canada Centre ($12) are available, and include a visit to a dressing room and the Esso Maple Leafs Memories and Dreams Suite, which looks at the team's history.

The Royal York Hotel

Directly opposite the west end of the railway station, the **Royal York Hotel**, 100 Front St W, was the largest and tallest building in the British Empire when it opened in 1929. The architects were Montréal's Ross and Macdonald and they opted for the Beaux Arts style to match Union Station, but in lieu of the formal symmetries of its neighbour, they gave the *Royal York* a cascading, irregular facade with stylistic flourishes reminiscent of a French château. Originally, the hotel had its own concert hall, mini-hospital and twelve-thousand-book library, and each of its one thousand rooms had a radio, private shower and bath. The hotel soon became a byword for luxury, where every well-heeled visitor to the city stayed, and although other, newer hotels have usurped its pre-eminent position in the last decade or two, a recent refurbishment has restored it as a favourite with visiting bigwigs. For full contact details, as well as what it costs to stay here, see p.128.

The Banking District and Fort York

Opposite the east end of Union Station, the **Banking District**, which extends north as far as Queen, kicks off with the **Royal Bank Plaza**, 200 Bay St, where the two massive towers were designed by local architect Boris Zerafa during the construction boom of the mid-1970s. Each tower is coated with a thin layer of gold, and despite Zerafa's assertion that the gold simply added texture to his creation, it's hard not to believe that the Royal Bank wanted to show off a bit too.

Selling air

In one of the city's stranger ordinances, Toronto's buildings were once decreed to have a "**notional maximum altitude**". Owners of historic properties were not allowed to extend their buildings upwards, but they were permitted to **sell the empty space** between their roofs and the notional maximum to builders of new structures. Consequently, developers literally bought empty space and added it on to the maximum height they were already allowed for their buildings, thus creating the skyscrapers that the ordinance seemed to forbid.

The arrangement enhanced neither the old nor the new buildings, and was followed up by an even stranger agreement. By the late 1980s, preservationists had convinced the city that no more of the city's old buildings should be demolished. Developers, however, still wanted to build new Downtown buildings, and several deals emerged where a new complex would incorporate or literally engulf the old – the most extreme example being **Brookfield Place** at the corner of Yonge and Front streets (see p.50).

In between the *Royal York Hotel* and the Royal Bank, a gated **stone stairway** climbs up from Front Street West to a tiny plaza overseen by a phalanx of skyscrapers. It's a delightful spot, in a heart-of-the-city sort of way, and **Catherine Widgery**'s *City People* (1989), a folksy set of life-size aluminium figures attached to the stairway's walls, adds a touch of decorative élan. The walkway continues down to Wellington Street West, just a few metres from the southern tower – now the Waterhouse Tower – of the **Toronto Dominion Centre**, whose four reflective black blocks straddle Wellington Street between Bay and York. Arguably the most appealing of the city's modern skyscrapers, the four towers are without decoration, achieving an austere beauty that can't help but impress. Begun in 1964, they were designed by **Ludwig Mies van der Rohe** (1886–1969), one of the twentieth century's most influential architects. Rohe was influenced by a wide range of architectural styles, including Prussian Classicism and Russian Constructivism; he also served as the director of Bauhaus. In his last decades, he refined his architectural vision, seeking to establish contemplative, neutral spaces guided by his maxim-cum-motto "Less is more"; the Toronto Dominion Centre is a case in point.

The Toronto Dominion Gallery of Inuit Art

The **Toronto Dominion Gallery of Inuit Art**, in the south – or Waterhouse – tower of the Toronto Dominion Centre (Mon–Fri 8am–6pm, Sat & Sun 10am–4pm; free), boasts an outstanding collection of Inuit sculpture. Spread over two levels, the collection's hundred-or-so pieces are owned by the Dominion Bank, who commissioned a panel of experts to celebrate Canada's Centennial in 1965 by collecting the best of post-war Inuit art. All the favourite themes of Inuit sculpture are here, primarily **animal and human studies** supplemented by a smattering of **metamorphic figures**, in which an Inuit adopts the form of an animal, either in full or in part. Other sculptures depict **deities**, particularly Nuliayuk the sea goddess (also known as Sedna). Inuit religious belief was short on theology, but its encyclopedic animism populated the Arctic with spirits and gods, the subject of all manner of Inuit folk tales. Christianity destroyed this traditional faith, but the legends survived and continue to feature prominently in Inuit art. Most of the sculptures are in **soapstone**, a greyish-blue stone that is easy to carve, though there are bone, ivory and caribou-antler pieces too. The only problem is the almost total lack of labelling, though a free **introductory booklet**, available from the rack at the start of the gallery, does provide some assistance.

Four sculptures are exhibited in the **foyer**, beside the revolving doors, and although they are sometimes rotated it's here you can expect to see **Johnny Inukpuk**'s raw, elemental *Mother Feeding Child* (1962), an exquisite piece in which a woman holds her child in an all-encompassing embrace. Hailing from Port Harrison, on the eastern shores of Hudson Bay, Inukpuk was one of the first Inuit sculptors to establish a reputation in the south, and his work has been collected since the late 1950s. Another of his soapstone sculptures is usually displayed in the foyer as well – the *Tattooed Woman*, a fine, almost fierce portrayal of a woman in traditional attire, whose eyes stare out into the distance.

Upstairs, distributed among a dozen glass cabinets, is a superb selection of soapstone sculptures. In the first cabinet are two striking representations of Sedna, one by **Saggiak**, the other by **Kenojuak Ashevak**, both carved in Cape Dorset in 1965. Half-woman, half-seal, **Sedna**, the goddess of the sea and sometimes of life itself, is one of the key figures of Inuit mythology. Her story is a sad one. She was deceived by a young man, who posed as a hunter, but was in fact a powerful shaman. Sedna married him and he promptly spirited her away from her family. Sedna's father gave chase and rescued his daughter, but on the return journey they were assailed by a violent storm conjured by the shaman. Terrified, the father threw his daughter overboard, and when she repeatedly attempted to get back into the boat, he chopped off her fingers and then her hands. These bits and pieces became whales, seals, walruses and fish, but Sedna herself sank to the depths of the ocean, where she remains.

Other striking works to look for include the magnificent *Bear*, by Cape Dorset's **Pauta Saila**, located four cabinets along from the Sedna sculptures. The bear is crudely carved, but the jaws are all that's needed to convey the animal's ferocity, and the blurring of the trunk and the legs gives the appearance of great strength. There's also a wise-looking, but somehow anguished, half-crow, half-human figure another couple of cabinets down, also dating from the 1960s, though not attributed to any particular sculptor.

To St Andrew's Presbyterian Church

Crossing over Wellington Street, and walking between the other three towers of the Toronto Dominion Centre, you soon pass **Joe Fafard**'s herd of grazing cows – seven extraordinarily realistic **bronze statues** that have proved immensely popular with the city's office workers. From here, it's a short detour west along King Street to **St Andrew's Presbyterian Church**, 75 Simcoe St (daily 9am–4pm; free; St Andrew subway). Marooned among the city's skyscrapers, this handsome sandstone structure is a reminder of an older Toronto, and its Romanesque Revival towers and gables have a distinctly Norman appearance. Built in 1876 for a predominantly Scottish congregation, the church has a delightful interior, its cherrywood pews and balcony sloping down towards the chancel with dappled light streaming in through the stained-glass windows. St Andrew's has an admirable history of social action. Since the earliest days of the city's settlement, St Andrew's, along with many other Toronto churches, has played a leading role in the fight against poverty and homelessness.

Roy Thompson Hall, Metro Hall and the CBC Broadcasting Centre

Across Simcoe Street from St Andrew's, **Roy Thompson Hall**, the home of the Toronto Symphony Orchestra (see p.172), was completed in 1982 to a design by Canada's own Arthur Erickson. The hall looks like an upturned soup bowl by day, but at night its appearance is transformed, its glass-panelled walls radiating a skein of filtered light high into the sky. Next door, **Metro Hall**'s trio of glass-and-steel office blocks is set around an attractive plaza of water fountains and lawns. Built in the early 1990s, the complex represents a break from the brash architectural harshness of previous decades and a move toward more fluid, people-friendly designs.

To the south, Metro Hall faces the **CBC Broadcasting Centre**, 250 Front St West, a ten-storey edifice whose painted gridiron beams make the building aesthetically bearable, but not much more. Since its foundation in 1936, **CBC** (the Canadian Broadcasting Corporation) has built up an international reputation for the impartiality of its radio and television news and, although it carries commercials unlike the UK's BBC, it remains in public ownership and is directly responsible to Parliament. CBC used to offer guided tours of the Broadcasting Centre, but these have been discontinued, at least for the moment. You can, however, still visit the **CBC museum** (Mon–Fri 9am–5pm; free;

ⓦwww.cbc.ca/museum), where, amongst a series of modest exhibits, vintage CBC TV shows are shown in a mini-theatre. In addition, three sets of push-buttons – one set each for public affairs, news and kids' programmes – access about forty brief programme clips, from perceptive comments on the US war in Vietnam to the heart-rending moment in 1980 when Terry Fox, who had lost a leg from cancer, had to abandon his attempt to run across Canada. Less impressive is the 1969 report on Toronto's Yorkville (see p.76), a particularly potty piece of social scaremongering in which the reporter claims – amongst much else – that the assorted drug-addled hippies would "make love to anyone".

From the CBC Broadcasting Centre, it's a brief stroll east to the former Toronto Stock Exchange (see p.48) or a twenty-minute hoof west to Fort York (see p.47).

Fort York

Modern-day Toronto traces its origins to **Fort York** (late May to Aug daily 10am–5pm; Sept to late May Mon–Fri 10am–4pm, Sat & Sun 10am–5pm; $8; ⓣ416/392-6907, ⓦwww.fortyork.ca), a **colonial stockade** built in 1793 on the shores of Lake Ontario to bolster British control of the Great Lakes. Since then, landfill has pushed the lakeshore southwards and marooned the fort, which was attractively reconstructed in the 1930s, in the shadow of the (elevated) Gardiner Expressway just to the west of Bathurst Street. There are **two entrances** to the fort – a (well-signed) main entrance off Lakeshore Boulevard West along Fleet Street and then Garrison Road; and a pedestrians' back entrance via a path off Bathurst Street. To get to the latter, head west along Front Street from the CBC Broadcasting Centre, turn left onto Bathurst, walk over the bridge and the path is on the right; to shorten the walk, take the King Street tram west to King and Bathurst. To reach the front entrance, take either the Bathurst streetcar along Bathurst Street (#511) or streetcar #509 from Union Station, and get off on **Fleet Street** at the foot of Garrison Road; from here the fort is a ten-minute walk.

Fort York was initially a half-hearted, poorly fortified affair, partly because of a lack of funds, but mainly because it was too remote to command much attention – never mind that the township of York was the capital of Upper Canada. However, in 1811, a deterioration in Anglo-American relations, that was soon to lead to war, put it on full alert. There was a sudden flurry of activity as the fort's ramparts and gun emplacements were strengthened, but it was still too weak to rebuff the American army that marched on York in 1813. Hurriedly, the British decided to evacuate and blow up the gunpowder magazine to stop its contents falling into enemy hands. Unfortunately, they completely underestimated the force of the explosion, and killed or wounded ten of their own men in addition to 260 of the advancing enemy, the fatalities including the splendidly named American general Zebulon Montgomery Pike. After the war, Fort York, which the Americans occupied only briefly before abandoning it, was rebuilt and its garrison made a considerable contribution to the development of Toronto, as York was renamed in 1834. The British army moved out in 1870 and their Canadian replacements stayed for another sixty years; the fort was opened as a **museum** in 1934. Throughout the summer, **costumed guides** give the low-down on colonial life and free **plans** of the fort are issued at reception.

The fort

The fort's carefully restored earth and stone **ramparts** are low-lying and thick and constructed in a zigzag pattern, both to mitigate against enemy artillery and

The Fenian raids

During the American Civil War, the British continued to trade with the Confederacy, much to the chagrin of the Union army. After the war, tensions between the two countries abated, though many northerners still hankered for retribution – no group more so than the **Fenian Brotherhood,** formed by Irish exiles in New York in 1859. Many of these Irishmen had a deep and abiding hatred for the British, whose cruel administration of their homeland had caused the Catholic population endless suffering. To the Brotherhood, Britain's continued control of Canada was unbearable, and they hoped to capitalize on the residue of ill-feeling left from the Civil War to push the US into military action against its northern neighbour. Their tactics were simple: they organized a series of **cross-border raids,** several of which were aimed against Fort York, hoping that if they provoked a military retaliation from the British, the US government would feel obliged to come to their aid and invade Canada. The most serious Fenian raid crossed the border in 1866 with a thousand men. The British drove the Fenians out without too much difficulty, and although there were significant casualties, Congress didn't take the military bait.

to provide complementary lines of fire. They enclose a haphazard sequence of log, stone and brick buildings, notably a couple of well-preserved **blockhouses,** complete with heavy timbers and snipers' loopholes. In one of them – **Building No.5** on the plan – an introductory video outlines the history of the fort and an exhibit explores the various military crises that afflicted Canada from the 1780s to the 1880s, especially the War of 1812. Here also is a small but particularly good display on late eighteenth- and early nineteenth-century **artillery**. The prize pieces are a 1793 British rampart gun, a cross between a rifle and an artillery piece, and a hot-shot furnace for heating cannon balls. A certain **Lieutenant Colonel Shrapnel,** who saw military service in Canada, wasn't at all impressed by cannon balls and invented his own much more lethal shell, which fragmented on impact. To prove his invention, Shrapnel arranged a test firing at the arsenal in Woolwich, back in London, and a card copy of the results is displayed here; needless to say, the top brass were suitably persuaded.

Moving on, **Building No.6** started out as a magazine but ended up as a storehouse. Its ground floor now holds a modest display on the role of black soldiers and settlers in the early history of Ontario. The Upper Canada legislature actually banned the importation of slaves in 1793, forty years before slavery was abolished right across the British Empire. Up above, an archeological section displays the various bits and pieces unearthed at the fort – buckles, brooches, plates, clay pipes, tunic buttons and so forth. The most interesting piece is a "**Sacred to Love**" stick pin, an example of the mourning jewellery that was popular amongst Victorians. Across the fort, **Building No.4,** the Blue Barracks, is a 1930s reconstruction of the junior officers' quarters, whilst **Building No.3** is the former Officers' Quarters and Mess. The latter boasts several period rooms and two original money vaults, hidden away in the cellar. Opposite, the stone and brick powder magazine – **Building No.8** – has two-metre-thick walls and spark-proof copper and brass fixtures.

The Toronto Stock Exchange

Doubling back from the CBC Centre (see p.46) along Wellington Street West, it's a brief walk to the old **Toronto Stock Exchange,** 234 Bay St, whose crisp architectural lines have been badly compromised by its incorporation within a tower block that imitates – but doesn't match – the sober blocks of the adjacent

Toronto Dominion Centre (see p.45). Nevertheless, the original facade has survived in good nick, its stone lintel decorated with muscular Art Deco carvings of men at work. Curiously enough, and seemingly unnoticed by the captains of capital, an unknown stonemason couldn't resist adding a subversive subtext when he carved the main frieze: look closely and you'll see that the top-hatted figure – the capitalist – is dipping his hand into a worker's pocket. Inside, the routinely modern ground floor is used to accommodate the **temporary exhibitions** of the **Design Exchange** (Mon–Fri 10am–5pm, Sat & Sun noon–5pm; $5 admission charged for most exhibitions; Ⓦ www.designexchange.org), or "**DX**", whose purpose is to foster innovative design. Displays may cover everything from local furniture design to prototype plans for making the city more environmentally friendly. Very different is the **trading floor** up above, which has been preserved in all its Art Deco pomp, its geometric panelling decorated with a series of delightful ribbon murals celebrating industry.

The CIBC buildings

Across the street from the Exchange, the formidable (and formidably named) **Canadian Imperial Bank of Commerce**, 199 Bay St, is a stainless-steel behemoth erected in the 1970s to a design by renowned architect **Ieoh Ming Pei** (born 1917). Hailing from China, where his father was a prominent banker, Pei moved to the United States in the 1930s, and it was there that he eventually established a worldwide reputation for sleek modern designs, seen in buildings such as the John Hancock Tower in Boston and the glass pyramids at the Louvre museum in Paris. Pei's CIBC tower is typical of his work, its sheer, overweening size emphasized by its severe angles and sleek trajectory. The tower stands in sharp contrast to the former **CIBC building**, next door to the north at 25 King St West. This older structure, erected just after the stock market crash of 1929, has a restrained stone exterior, where the cathedral-like doors, draped with carved reliefs, merely hint at the magnificent chandeliers, gilt-coffered ceilings and precise marble tracery within.

The Royal and Trader's banks

Heading east from the former CIBC building, you'll soon reach the former **Royal Bank**, 2 King St East, which was designed by Ross and Macdonald, also the creators of Union Station and the *Royal York Hotel*. Clumsily modernized on the ground floor, the austere symmetries of the building as a whole still impress, as do the classical columns and decorative motifs that were gracefully worked into the lower floors of the main facade.

A quick step to the south, **Trader's Bank**, 67 Yonge St at King (no public access), was **Toronto's first skyscraper**, a fifteen-storey structure completed in 1906. The owners were apprehensive that the size of the building might prompt accusations of vanity, so they insisted on overhanging eaves and stumpy classical columns in an effort to make it look shorter. They need not have bothered: as soon as it was finished visitors thronged the bank and the top floor was turned into an observation deck. Newer skyscrapers now dwarf Trader's, of course, and the once unhindered view is long gone.

The Hockey Hall of Fame

From Trader's Bank, it's a short haul south to the **Hockey Hall of Fame**, 30 Yonge St at Front St West (late June to Aug Mon–Sat 9.30am–6pm, Sun

10am–6pm; Sept to late June Mon–Fri 10am–5pm, Sat 9.30am–6pm, Sun 10.30am–5pm; $13, children aged 4–13 & seniors $9; ⊤416/360-7765, Ⓦwww .hhof.com), a highly commercialized, ultra-modern tribute to Canada's national sport – though you wouldn't think so from the outside. The only part of the Hall visible from the street is the old **Bank of Montréal building**, a Neoclassical edifice dating back to 1885. The bank is actually one of Toronto's finer structures – its intricately carved stonework is adorned by a dainty sequence of pediments and pilasters – but its incorporation into the Hall of Fame is awkward. The bank's entrance has been blocked off and the interior bowdlerized to house a collection of hockey trophies.

The **entrance** to the Hockey Hall of Fame is below ground in the adjacent **Brookfield Place**, a large retail complex on the west side of Yonge Street between Front and Wellington streets (and still known by most Torontonians by its old name of BCE Place). Inside the museum are a series of **exhibition areas**, featuring a replica of the Montréal Canadiens' locker room, copious biographical details of the sport's great names and descriptions of the various National Hockey League (NHL) teams. Much of this is geared toward the enthusiast, but there's plenty to keep the less-obsessed entertained as well, notably the mini **ice-rink**, where visitors can blast away at hockey pucks, and two small theatres showing **films** of hockey's most celebrated games. The film of the 1972 "World Summit Series" between the USSR and Canada records what must rank as one of the most gripping sporting events ever, a tense confrontation infused with Cold War resonance. Finally, the **trophy room**, located inside the old bank building, contains the very first **Stanley Cup**, donated by Lord Stanley, the Governor General of Canada, in 1893. An English aristocrat, Stanley was convinced that sports raised the mettle of the men of the British Empire. Concerned that Canadian ice hockey lacked a trophy of any stature, he inaugurated the Stanley Cup, which has become the defining emblem of the sport. For more on ice hockey, see Sports and outdoor activities, pp.194–202.

The St Lawrence District

One of the city's oldest neighbourhoods, the **St Lawrence District**, lying just to the east of Yonge St, between The Esplanade, Adelaide Street East and Frederick Street, enjoyed its first period of rapid growth after the War of 1812. In Victorian times, St Lawrence became one of the most fashionable parts of the city, and although it hit the skids thereafter, it was revamped and (partly) gentrified in the late 1990s.

The best approach is along Front Street East, heading east from Yonge. From this direction, you'll soon spot the distinctive trompe l'oeil **mural** on the back of the **Flatiron building**, a sturdy office block of 1892, which fills in the narrow triangle of land between Wellington and Front streets. From here, it's a short hop to **St Lawrence Market** (Tues–Thurs 8am–6pm, Fri 8am–7pm & Sat 5am–5pm; Ⓦwww.stlawrencemarket.com), at Front and Jarvis, a capacious 1844 red-brick building that holds the city's best food and drink market. Spread out across the main and lower levels are stalls selling everything from fish and freshly baked bread to international foodstuffs, all sorts of organic edibles and **Ontario specialities** – cheese, jellies, jams and fern fiddleheads to name but four. The market is at its busiest on Saturday.

Up above, and reachable by the elevator beside the main entrance, is the old city council chamber – the front part of today's market served as the town hall from 1845 to 1899 – and this is where you'll find the **Market Gallery** (Tues–Fri 10am–4pm & Sat 9am–4pm; free). This displays regularly rotated **exhibitions**, often of sketches and photographs drawn from the city's archives. Visiting the market on Saturdays also means that you can drop by the **North St Lawrence**

▲ The Flatiron building

Market, an authentic farmers' market (Sat 5am–5pm) housed in the long brick, muralled building opposite, on the north side of Front Street. The same premises are also used for a Sunday antique market (dawn to 5pm).

St Lawrence Hall

Behind North St Lawrence Market, just along Jarvis Street, stands **St Lawrence Hall**, one of the city's most attractive Victorian buildings, an expansive edifice whose columns, pilasters and pediments are surmounted by a dinky little cupola. Dating from 1850, the hall was built as the city's main meeting-place, with oodles of space for balls, public lectures and concerts. Some performances were eminently genteel, others decidedly mawkish – it was here that the "Swedish songbird" **Jenny Lind** (1820–87) made one of her Canadian appearances – and yet others more urgent, like the anti-slavery rallies of the 1850s. The bad taste award goes to the American showman and circus proprietor **P.T. Barnum** (1810–91), one-time mayor of his hometown of Bridgeport, Connecticut, and author of the bizarre *The Humbugs of the World*. It was Barnum who saw the potential of his fellow Bridgeportonian, the diminutive Charles Sherwood Stratton, aka **Tom Thumb** (1838–83), exhibiting him as a curiosity here in St Lawrence Hall as well as anywhere else where people were willing to pay. Stratton was just 60cm (2ft) tall when he first went on tour.

St James Cathedral

On the other side of King Street, a couple of hundred metres west from St Lawrence Hall, rises the graceful bulk of **St James Anglican Cathedral** (Mon–Fri 7.30am–5.30pm, Sat 9am–5pm & Sun 8am–5.30pm; free; ⓦwww .stjamescathedral.on.ca), whose yellowish stone is fetchingly offset by copper-green roofs and a slender spire. An excellent example of the neo-Gothic style once popular in every corner of the British Empire, the cathedral boasts scores of pointed-arch windows and acres of sturdy buttressing. Inside, the nave is supported by elegant high-arched pillars and flanked by an ambitious set of **stained-glass windows** that attempts to trace the path by which Christianity reached Canada from Palestine via England. It's all a little confusing, but broadly speaking, the less inventive windows depict Biblical scenes, whereas those that focus on English history are the more ingenious. These stained-glass windows were inserted at the end of the nineteenth century, but those of **St George's Chapel**, in the southeast corner of the church, were added in 1935 to celebrate the Silver Jubilee of King George V. They exhibit an enthusiastic loyalty to the British Empire that is echoed in many of the cathedral's funerary plaques: take, for example, that of a certain **Captain John Henry Gamble**, who was born in Toronto in 1844 but died on active service in the Khyber Pass in 1879; his stone is in the west transept. Spare a thought also for poor old **William Butcher**, a native of Suffolk, in England, who fell to his death when he was working on the cathedral spire, aged just 27; his stone is in the main entrance way.

Toronto's First Post Office

Located about five-minutes' walk northeast of St James Cathedral, in a tatty part of town, **Toronto's First Post Office**, 260 Adelaide St East (Mon–Fri 9am–4pm, Sat & Sun 10am–4pm; free), occupies an old brick building that dates back to 1833. Returned to something approaching its original appearance, and staffed by costumed volunteers, the **museum** gives the flavour of the times and features displays on postal history. It also doubles up as a working post office, where visitors can write a letter with a quill pen, seal it with wax and tie it up with a ribbon.

From the post office, it takes about twenty minutes to walk west to Nathan Phillips Square (see below) or, heading southeast, around fifteen minutes to reach the Distillery District.

The Distillery District

The **Distillery District** (ⓦ www.thedistillerydistrict.com) is home to Toronto's newest arts and entertainment complex, sited in the former **Gooderham and Worts distillery**, an extremely appealing industrial "village" on Mill Street, near the foot of Parliament Street. In use as a distillery until 1990, this rambling network of over forty brick buildings once constituted the largest distillery in the British Empire. It was founded in 1832, when ships could sail into its own jetty, though landfill subsequently marooned it in the lee of the railway lines and the tail end of the Gardiner Expressway. Since its demise, the distillery has been sympathetically redeveloped by a small group of entrepreneurs, who chose to integrate many of the original features into the revamp – including its quirky walkways and bottle runways – and, with refreshing integrity, to exclude all multinational chains. One of the architectural highlights is the **Pure Spirits building**, which features French doors and a fancy wrought-iron balcony.

Amongst much else, the complex holds art galleries and artists' studios, furniture designers, a chocolatier, bakeries, shops, a microbrewery, a visitor centre (offering guided tours) and a couple of performance venues. As for **opening times**, most of the galleries and shops start daily at 9am or 10am and close down at 6pm, whereas the cafés and bars hang on till late.

To get to the Distillery District by **public transport**, take the King Street streetcar (#504) east to Parliament and make the five-minute walk from there.

Nathan Phillips Square and City Hall

Back in the city centre, on Queen Street, **Nathan Phillips Square** is one of Toronto's most distinctive landmarks, the whole caboodle designed by the Finnish architect **Viljo Revell** (1910–64), a determined functionalist who was lucky to survive World War II when, as a member of the crew, his warship was sunk by mines in 1941. The square is framed by an elevated walkway and focuses on a reflecting pool, which becomes a skating rink in winter, and it's overlooked by Revell's **City Hall**, whose twin curved glass and concrete towers stand behind and to either side of a mushroom-topped entrance. In front of this is *The Archer*, a **Henry Moore** sculpture resembling nothing so much as a giant propeller. Surprising as it seems today, when such architectural designs are relatively commonplace, Revell won all sorts of awards for this project, which was considered the last word in 1960s dynamism – though today its weather-stained blocks look rather dejected. In its creation, however, the square became a catalyst for change. Named after its sponsor, Nathan Phillips, Toronto's first Jewish mayor, the space suddenly provided the kind of public gathering place the city so sorely lacked, kick-starting the process by which the private Toronto of the 1950s became the extrovert metropolis of today.

Standing in the southwest corner of Nathan Phillips Square, a statue of **Winston Churchill** (1874–1965) recalls Toronto's British connection. Inscribed upon the statue are four famous quotations, one of which is drawn from the barnstorming speech Churchill delivered to the Canadian House of Commons on December 30, 1941 in the dark days of World War II: "[The losing French] generals advised France's divided cabinet 'In three weeks, England will have her neck wrung like a chicken'. Some chicken! Some neck!"

Had Revell's grand scheme been fully implemented, the city would have bulldozed the **Old City Hall**, a flamboyant pseudo-Romanesque building that dominates the east side of the square. Completed in 1899, it was designed by **Edward J. Lennox**, who developed a fractious relationship with his paymasters on the city council. They had a point: the original cost of the building had been estimated at $1.77 million, but Lennox spent an extra $750,000 and took all of eight years to finish the project. Nevertheless, Lennox had the last laugh, carving gargoyle-like representations of the city's fathers on the capitals of the columns

Glenn Gould

In the 1970s, anyone passing the Eaton's department store around 9pm on any day of the year might have seen the door unlocked for a distracted-looking figure swaddled in overcoat, scarves, gloves and hat. This character, making his way to a recording studio set up for his exclusive use inside the store, was perhaps the most famous citizen of Toronto and the most charismatic pianist in the world – **Glenn Gould**.

Not the least remarkable thing about Gould was that very few people outside the CBS recording crew would ever hear him play live. In 1964, aged just 32, he retired from the concert platform, partly out of a distaste for the accidental qualities of any live performance, partly out of hatred for the cult of the virtuoso. Yet no pianist ever provided more material for the mythologizers. He possessed a memory so prodigious that none of his acquaintances was ever able to find a piece of music he could not

▲ Glenn Gould

instantly play perfectly, but he loathed much of the standard piano repertoire, dismissing romantic composers such as Chopin, Liszt and Rachmaninoff as little more than showmen. Dauntingly cerebral in his tastes and playing style, he was nonetheless an ardent fan of Barbra Streisand – an esteem that was fully reciprocated – and once wrote an essay titled "In Search of Petula Clark". He lived at night and kept in touch by phoning his friends in the small hours of the morning, talking for so long that his monthly phone bill ran into thousands of dollars. Detesting all blood sports (a category in which he placed concert performances), he would terrorize anglers on Ontario's Lake Simcoe by buzzing them in his motorboat. He travelled everywhere with bags full of medicines and would at the top of the front steps and placing his name on each side of the building – something the city council had expressly forbidden him to do. Lennox was also responsible for the construction of Casa Loma (see p.78).

The Eaton Centre

Across the street from the Old City Hall, **The Bay department store**, at Queen and Yonge, is the present incarnation of the **Hudson's Bay Company**, which played a crucial role in the development of colonial Canada (see box, p.56). A second-floor walkway spans Queen Street to connect The Bay with the whopping **Eaton Centre** (Mon–Fri 10am–9pm, Sat 9.30am–7pm, Sun noon–6pm; Ⓦ www .torontoeatoncentre.com; Queen or Dundas subways), a three-storey assortment of shops and restaurants spread out underneath a glass-and-steel arched roof. By shopping-mall standards, the design is appealing, and the flock of fibreglass **Canada**

never allow anyone to shake his hand, yet soaked his arms in almost scalding water before playing to get his circulation going. At the keyboard he sang loudly to himself, swaying back and forth on a creaky little chair made for him by his father – all other pianists sat too high, he insisted. And even in a heatwave he was always dressed as if a blizzard were imminent. To many of his colleagues, Gould's eccentricities were maddening, but what mattered was that nobody could play like Glenn Gould. As one exasperated conductor put it, "the nut's a genius".

Gould's first recording, Bach's *Goldberg Variations*, was released in 1956 and became the best-selling classical record of that year. Soon after, he became the first Western musician to play in the Soviet Union, where his reputation spread so quickly that for his final recital more than a thousand people were allowed to stand in the aisles of the Leningrad hall. On his debut in Berlin, a leading German critic described him as "a young man in a strange sort of trance", whose "technical ability borders on the fabulous". The technique always dazzled, but Gould's fiercely wayward intelligence made his interpretations controversial, as can be gauged from the fact that **Leonard Bernstein**, conducting Gould on one occasion, felt obliged to inform the audience that what they were about to hear was the pianist's responsibility, not his. Most notoriously of all, Gould had a very low opinion of Mozart's abilities, going so far as to record the Mozart sonatas in order to demonstrate that Wolfgang Amadeus died too late rather than too soon. Gould himself **died suddenly** in 1982 at the age of 50 – the age at which he had said he would give up playing the piano entirely.

Gould's **legacy of recordings** is not confined to music. He made a trilogy of radio documentaries on the theme of solitude: *The Quiet in the Land*, about Canada's Mennonites; *The Latecomers*, about the inhabitants of Newfoundland; and *The Idea of North*, for which he taped interviews with people who, like himself, spent much of their time amid Canada's harshest landscapes. Just as Gould's Beethoven, Bach and Mozart sounded like nobody else's, these were documentaries like no others, each a complex weave of voices spliced and overlaid in compositions that are overtly musical in construction. However, Gould's eighty-odd piano recordings are the basis of his enduring popularity, and nearly all of them have been reissued on CD and DVD, spanning Western keyboard music from Orlando Gibbons to Arnold Schoenberg. One of the most poignant is his second version of the *Goldberg*, the last record to be issued before his death.

geese suspended from the ceiling – *Flight Stop* – adds a touch of flair; they are the work of **Michael Snow**, who also spruced up the Rogers Centre (see p.194). The geese were actually the subject of a bitter wrangle between Snow and the Eaton Centre. In December 1981, the Eaton Centre placed red bows round the neck of the geese, an act that so enraged Snow that he ended up taking them to court, arguing that the bows distorted and mutilated his work. He won and the geese have been bow-less ever since.

The Hudson's Bay Company

The story of the **Hudson's Bay Company** – of which The Bay department stores are just an arm – begins in 1661, when two Frenchmen, Médard Chouart des Groseilliers and Pierre-Esprit Radisson, reached the southern end of **Hudson Bay** overland and realized this was the same vast and icy inland sea described by earlier seafaring explorers. They returned to Québec laden with **furs**, but as soon as they got back the French governor arrested them for trapping without a licence. Understandably peeved, they turned to England, where Charles II's cousin, Prince Rupert, persuaded the king to finance an expedition to Hudson Bay to test the Frenchmen's claims regarding the abundance of furs. Charles equipped two ships, the *Eaglet* and the *Nonsuch*, and, after a mammoth voyage, the *Nonsuch* returned with a fantastic cargo of furs, which led to the incorporation of the Hudson's Bay Company by Charles II on May 2, 1670. The Company was granted wide powers, including exclusive trading rights to the entire Hudson Bay watershed – to be called **Rupert's Land**.

The **HBC** was a joint-stock company, the shareholders annually electing a governor and committee to hire men, order trade goods and arrange fur auctions and shipping. By 1760, **trading posts** had been built at the mouths of all the major rivers flowing into Hudson Bay; these were commanded by **factors**, who took their policy orders from London. The orders were often unrealistic and presumed that native trappers would bring furs to the posts – whereas the rival Montréal-based **North West Company** operated with mainly Francophone employees, who spent months in the wilderness hunting with the natives. Unsurprisingly, the NWC was prone to undercut the HBC's trade and there was intense competition between the two across the north of the continent, occasionally resulting in violence. In 1821 a compromise was reached and the two companies **merged**. They kept the name Hudson's Bay Company and the British parliament granted the new, larger company a commercial monopoly from Hudson Bay to the Pacific. Parliament also refined the administrative structure of the expanded HBC. A North American chief factor was appointed and his councils dealt increasingly with local trading concerns, though the London governor and committee continued to have the last word.

The extensive **monopoly** rights ceded to the new company were fiercely resented by local traders, and, in a landmark case of 1849, a west Canadian jury found a trader by the name of Sayer guilty of breaking the monopoly, but then refused to punish him. Thereafter, in practice if not by law, the Company's stranglehold on the fur trade was dead and buried. Furthermore, the HBC's quasi-governmental powers seemed increasingly anachronistic and when a company official, James Douglas, became governor of British Columbia in 1858, the British government forced him to resign from the HBC. This marked the beginning of the end of the Company's colonial role.

In 1870, the HBC sold Rupert's Land to Canada. In return it received a cash payment, but, more importantly, retained the title to the lands on which the trading posts had been built. Given that the trading posts often occupied land at the heart of the new cities in the west, this was a remarkably bad deal for Canada – and a great one for the HBC. Subsequently, the HBC became a major real-estate developer and **retail chain**, a position it maintains today as part of a multinational corporation owned by the USA's NRDC Equity Partners.

Maps of the shopping mall are displayed on every floor, but the general rule is the higher the floor, the more expensive the shop. The centre takes its name from **Timothy Eaton** (1834–1907), an immigrant from Ulster who opened his first store here in 1869. His cash-only, fixed-price, money-back-guarantee merchandising revolutionized the Canadian market and made him a fortune. Soon a Canadian institution, Eaton kept a grip on the pioneer settlements in the west through his mail-order catalogue, known as the "homesteader's bible" – or the "**wish book**" among native peoples – whilst Eaton department stores sprang up in all of Canada's big cities. In recent years, however, the company has struggled to maintain its profitability and the branch in the Eaton Centre has been taken over by Sears.

About two-thirds of the way along the Eaton Centre from Queen Street – just before Sears – a side exit leads straight from Level 3 to the **Church of the Holy Trinity**, a quirky nineteenth-century structure whose yellow brickwork is surmounted by a flourish of matching turrets and chimneys. Much to its credit, the church campaigns hard on issues of poverty, and beside its entrance stands the **Toronto Homeless Memorial**, which lists those who have died as a result of their homelessness. The church also figures in Canadian movie history. It was here, with the church set against the skyscrapers that crowd in on it, that Canadian director **David Cronenberg** filmed the last scene of *Dead Ringers*. The dubious moral content of the film – the unscrupulous exploits of twin rogue gynaecologists, both played by Jeremy Irons – prompted Cronenberg to defend his subject matter coyly: "I don't have a moral plan. I'm a Canadian."

Dundas Square

The Eaton Centre ends (or begins) at the corner of **Dundas and Yonge streets**, once the city's main intersection. By the 1990s, the junction looked tatty and neglected, but thereafter the city council began a thoroughgoing revamp, the key part of which was the construction of a public piazza, **Dundas Square**, with water jets and a giant video screen showing ads and promotional videos. It's a popular meeting spot, and further developments are planned.

Mackenzie House and St Michael's Cathedral

It's hardly an essential visit, but the **Mackenzie House** (Jan–April Sat & Sun noon–5pm, May–Aug Tues–Sun noon–5pm, Sept–Dec Tues–Fri noon–4pm, Sat & Sun noon–5pm; $6; Dundas subway), a brief walk east of Dundas Square at 82 Bond St, is of some interest as the home of **William Lyon Mackenzie** (1795–1861). Born in Scotland, Mackenzie moved to Toronto where he scraped together a living publishing *The Colonial Advocate*, a radical anti-Tory newspaper. Frustrated with the politics of the colony's early leaders, Mackenzie was one of the instigators of the Rebellion of 1837 (see p.218), after which he was exiled to the US for twelve years before being pardoned. Mackenzie lived in this house between 1859 and 1861, and it has been restored to an approximation of its appearance at the time, complete with a print shop (c.1845) whose workings are demonstrated by costumed guides.

From the Mackenzie House, it's a few paces south to **St Michael's Cathedral** (Mon–Sat 6am–6pm, Sun 6am–10pm; free; ⓦ www.stmichaelscathedral.com), an imposing neo-Gothic edifice whose sturdy brickwork dates back to the middle of the nineteenth century. Broadly patterned on York Minster in the UK, this Catholic cathedral boasts a soaring, crocketted spire, a handsome set of pointed windows along the nave, attenuated buttresses and perky dormer windows – but somehow the whole caboodle still manages to look a tad sullen. Inside, the capacious three-aisled nave is flanked by mini-shrines and permeated with the whiff of burning candles. The **stained-glass windows** are the church's pride and joy and they divide into two types: machine-embossed windows made in the US and Canada and hand-blown, more subtly coloured windows imported from France. The three (French) windows at the east end of the church, above the high altar, are particularly fine, the central one depicting the Crucifixion set against a deep blue background.

The Elgin and Winter Garden Theatre Centre

Across from the Eaton Centre, just north of Queen Street at 189 Yonge, the **Elgin and Winter Garden Theatre Centre** (guided tours only, Thurs at 5pm & Sat at 11am; 90min; $10; ☏416/325-5015; Queen subway) is one of the city's most unusual attractions. The first part of the **guided tour** covers the **Elgin**, an old vaudeville theatre whose ornate furnishings and fittings, including a set of splendid gilt mirrors, have been restored after years of neglect. The Elgin was turned into a cinema in the 1930s and, remarkably enough, its accompaniment, the top-floor **Winter Garden**, also a vaudeville theatre, was sealed off. Such double-decker theatres were first introduced in New York in the late nineteenth century, and soon became popular along the whole of the east coast, but only a handful have survived. When this one was unsealed, its original decor was found to be intact, the ceiling hung with thousands of paint-preserved beech leaves, illuminated by coloured lanterns. In the event, much of the decor still had to be replaced, but the restoration work was painstakingly thorough and the end result is delightful. Vaudeville was an informal business, with customers coming and going as they saw fit and performances following each other nonstop. Consequently, every vaudeville theatre had a ready supply of **backcloths**, and several were discovered when the Winter Garden was unsealed; they are now a feature of the tour.

Osgoode Hall, Campbell House and Queen Street West

Immediately to the west of Nathan Phillips Square, along Queen Street, stands **Osgoode Hall** (no public access), an attractive Neoclassical pile built in the nineteenth century for the Law Society of Upper Canada. Looking like a cross between a Greek temple and an English country house, it's protected by a fancy wrought-iron **fence** originally designed to keep cows and horses off its immaculate lawn. Across Queen Street, at the corner of University, the glittering new **Four Seasons Centre for the Performing Arts** is home to both the Canadian Opera Company (see p.172) and the National Ballet of Canada (see p.172). Close by, in the middle of University Avenue, stands a **War Memorial** honouring those Canadians who fought for the British imperial interest in the South African (or Boer) War at the start of the twentieth century. The memorial features two Canadian soldiers of heroic disposition, and the column is engraved with the names of the battles where Canadian regiments fought.

The elegant Georgian mansion on the west side of University Avenue is **Campbell House** (Tues–Fri 9.30am–4.30pm, Sat noon–4.30pm; plus late May to early Oct Sun noon–4.30pm; ☎416/597-0227; $4.50; Ⓦwww .campbellhousemuseum.ca; Osgoode subway), originally built on Adelaide Street for Sir William Campbell, Chief Justice and Speaker of the Legislative Assembly – and transported here in 1972. There are regular **guided tours** of the period interior, which is distinguished by its immaculately carved woodwork and sweeping circular stairway, and these provide a well-researched overview of early nineteenth-century Toronto. At the time, Campbell was a leading figure among the ruling elite, and a surprisingly progressive one too, eschewing the death penalty whenever possible, and even awarding the radical William Mackenzie (see p.57) damages when his printing press was wrecked by a mob of Tories in 1826.

Beyond the Campbell House, **Queen Street West** between University and Spadina is one of the grooviest parts of the city, its assorted cafés and bars attracting the sharpest of dressers. Meanwhile, the alternative crew of students and punks who once hung around here have moved further west, out to what is known as **Queen West West**, between Spadina and Bathurst. In the daytime, this whole section of Queen Street is a great place to be – but at night it's even better.

The Canada Life building and the Textile Museum of Canada

Built at the end of the 1920s, the monumental **Canada Life building** rises up behind Campbell House, its imposing Beaux Arts lines capped by a chunky Art Deco tower that is in its turn topped off by a **weather beacon**: the cube on top turns white for snow, red for rain and green for sun, whilst lights running down from the cube mean it's getting colder, up for hotter. The Canada Life building is, however, but one of a long sequence of bristling tower blocks, which march up **University Avenue** as it slices across the city, running north from Front Street to the Ontario Legislative Assembly Building (see p.66). Strolling north up University from Queen Street West, it only takes a couple of minutes to reach **Armoury Street**, the site of the old city armoury and the spot where the province's soldiers mustered before embarking overseas for the battlefields of both world wars.

Just off Armoury Street, the **Textile Museum of Canada**, housed in part of an office block at 55 Centre Ave (daily 11am–5pm, Wed till 8pm; $12; ☎416/599-5321, Ⓦwww.textilemuseum.ca), offers a rolling programme of

temporary exhibitions. International in outlook, the museum has featured everything from contemporary domestic textile pieces through to traditional work – for example Oriental rugs and hooked mats from Newfoundland and Labrador. The displays are often very good and are frequently supplemented by practical **demonstrations** of different textile techniques.

Back on the east side of University Avenue, head north from Dundas Street West and, just beyond Elm Street, look for the bust of **Mary Pickford** (1893–1979). Pickford was born in Toronto, but left on a theatrical tour at the tender age of eight. She dropped her original name – Gladys Mary Smith – when she began working as a motion-picture extra in Hollywood in 1909. Renowned as "America's sweetheart", she earned the cinematic sobriquet with her cute face and fluffy mop of hair, which enabled her to play little-girl roles well into her thirties.

From the Pickford statue, it's a short walk north to the Ontario Legislative Assembly building (see p.66) and a similarly brief excursion southwest to the Art Gallery of Ontario (see below).

The Art Gallery of Ontario (AGO)

Located just west of University Avenue along Dundas Street West, the **AGO**, the **Art Gallery of Ontario** (Tues, Sat & Sun 10am–5.30pm; Wed, Thurs & Fri 10am–8.30pm; $18, seniors $15, students & children aged 6–12 years $10; free Wed 6–8.30pm; St Patrick subway; ☎416/979-6648, ⓦwww.ago.net), is celebrated both for its wide-ranging collection of **foreign and domestic art** and its excellent temporary exhibitions. It's also just emerged from a thorough-going revamp in which the architect **Frank Gehry**, who is perhaps most famous for the Guggenheim Museum in Bilbao, has transformed the AGO's appearance with a startling **glass and wood north facade** on Dundas and a new, four-storey **titanium and glass wing** overlooking Grange Park to the south. The remodelling has added acres of extra gallery space and the AGO's permanent collection – plus the temporary exhibitions – are now exhibited on **four main floors**: the Concourse Level is distinguished by the clumsily named "Inuit Visible Storage display" of Inuit art; Level 1 is largely devoted to European art and photography; Level 2 holds a wonderful collection of Canadian paintings as well as a battery of Henry Moore sculptures; Level 3 has hospitality suites; Level 4 has a regularly rotated selection of contemporary art, as does Level 5. Museum **maps** are issued free at reception; there is a café, a restaurant, a large gift and bookshop, and the AGO runs a first-rate programme of **free guided tours**.

Concourse Level: Inuit art

Soapstone sculptures form the bulk of the AGO's collection of **Inuit art**. Highlights include **Pauta Saila**'s (1916–92) light-hearted *Dancing Bear* and **Joe Talirunili**'s (1906–76) *Migration*, in which a traditional Inuit boat – an *umiak* – is crowded with Inuit seemingly bent on escaping danger. Talirunili carved a large number of migration boat scenes throughout his long career, the inspiration derived from a dramatic incident in his childhood when the break-up of the pack ice caught his family unawares, forcing them to hurriedly evacuate their encampment. Look out also for the work of **John Tiktak** (1916–81), generally regarded as one of the most talented Inuit sculptors of his generation. The death of Tiktak's mother in 1962 had a profound effect on him, and his *Mother and Child* forcefully expresses this close connection, with the figure of the child carved into the larger figure of the mother. Tiktak's *Owl Man* is another fine piece, an excellent example of the metamorphic – half-human, half-animal – figures popular amongst the Inuit, as is **Thomas Sivuraq**'s (born 1941) *Shaman Transformation*.

Level 1: the European collection

The AGO possesses an eclectic sample of **European fine and applied art**, including ivory and alabaster pieces, exquisite cameos and fine porcelain, as well as **European sculptures** by the likes of Barbara Hepworth. Early **paintings** include some rather pedestrian Italian altarpieces, Pieter Brueghel the Younger's incident-packed *Peasant Wedding*, and a strong showing of **Dutch painters** of the Golden Age – Rembrandt, Van Dyck, Frans Hals and Goyen to name but four. Look out also for Carel Fabritius's exquisite *Portrait of a Lady with a Handkerchief*, one of only a few of the artist's works to have survived the powder-magazine explosion that killed him in Delft in 1654 – though the authorship of the painting has been disputed. **French painters** are much in evidence, too, with distinguished works including *St Anne with the Christ Child* by Georges de la Tour and *Venus Presenting Arms to Aeneas* by Poussin. Amongst the **Impressionists**, there's Degas's archetypal *Woman in the Bath*, Renoir's screaming-pink *Concert*, and Monet's wonderful *Vétheuil in Summer*, with its hundreds of tiny jabs of colour.

Level 1: The Grange

At the back of the AGO, entered from Level 1, is **The Grange**, an early nineteenth-century brick mansion with Neoclassical trimmings built by the Boultons, one of the city's most powerful families. The last of the line, William Henry – "a privileged, petted man ... without principle", according to a local journalist – died in 1874, and his property passed to his widow, Harriette, who promptly married an English expatriate professor named Goldwin Smith. The latter enjoyed Toronto immensely, holding court and boasting of his English connections, and when he died in 1910 (after Harriette) he bequeathed the house to the fledgling Art Museum of Toronto, the predecessor of the AGO. The Grange has recently been restored to its mid-nineteenth-century appearance and **guides** will show you around, enthusiastically explaining the ins and outs of life in nineteenth-century Toronto. Several of Harriette's **paintings** have survived, and while the **antique furnishings** and fittings are appealing, it's the beautiful wooden staircase that really catches the eye.

Level 2: the Canadian collection

Level 2 has perhaps the finest collection of **Canadian paintings** in the world, the bulk of which was gifted to the AGO by **Kenneth Thomson** (1923–2006), a Canadian businessman and art collector who was, at the time of his death, the ninth-richest person in the world. The Thomson family made its initial fortune from newspapers, owning a string of prestigious dailies, including Canada's *Globe & Mail* and London's *The Times* and *Sunday Times*, before moving into financial data services. Kenneth Thomson himself was a remarkably modest man, with a keen sense of humour, whose courteous, gentle manner – never mind his generous sponsoring of the AGO – made him one of the city's most popular figures.

Canadian eighteenth-century painting

The AGO owns a small but intriguing assortment of paintings by **eighteenth-century Canadians** and the majority are exhibited here on Level 2. One especially noteworthy canvas is a curiously unflattering *Portrait of Joseph Brant* by **William Berczy** (1748–1813). A Mohawk chief, **Joseph Brant** (1742–1807) was consistently loyal to the British, his followers fighting alongside them during the American War of Independence. Brant's reward was a large chunk of Ontario land and a string of official portraits – and this was one of them. Brant is shown in a mix of European and native gear; he carries an axe and has a Mohawk hairdo, but wears a dress coat with a sash – an apt reflection of his twin loyalties. Brant spoke English fluently, even translating parts of the Bible into Mohawk, and was a Freemason and Anglican to boot, feted by high society during a visit to England in 1776. At the same time, under his Mohawk name, Thayendanega (Two Bets), Brant was a powerful figure in the Iroquois Confederacy, leading one of its four main clans in both war and peace.

Canadian nineteenth-century painting

Early to mid-nineteenth-century Canadian paintings on Level 2 at the AGO include the cheery *Passenger Pigeon Hunt* by **Antoine Plamondon** (1802–95). Trained in Paris, Plamondon worked in the Neoclassical tradition, but here he allows some freedom of movement amongst the young hunters, with the St Lawrence River as the backdrop. From eastern Canada comes **John O'Brien** (1832–91), who is well represented by *The Ocean Bride leaving Halifax Harbour*. Self-taught, O'Brien specialized in maritime scenes, turning out dozens of brightly coloured pictures of sailing ships and coastal settings. Look out also for the canvases of one of the era's most fascinating figures, Irish-born **Paul Kane** (1810–71; see box below), notably his *Landscape in the Foothills with*

Paul Kane

Born in Ireland, **Paul Kane** emigrated to Toronto in the early 1820s. In 1840, he returned to Europe, where, curiously enough, he was so impressed by a touring exhibition of paintings of the American Indian that he promptly decided to move back to Canada. In 1846, he wrangled a spot on a westward-bound **fur-trading expedition**, beginning an epic journey: he travelled from Thunder Bay to Edmonton by canoe, crossed the Rockies by horse, and finally returned to Toronto two years later. During his trip, Kane made some seven hundred sketches, which he then painted onto canvas, paper and cardboard. Like many early Canadian artists, Kane's paintings often displayed a conflict in subject and style – that is, the subject was North American but the style European; indeed, it wasn't until the Group of Seven (see *Canadian art* colour section) that a true Canadian aesthetic emerged.

In 1859, Kane published *Wanderings of an Artist among the Indian Tribes of North America*, the story of his long travels. It includes this account of **Christmas dinner** at Fort Edmonton: "At the head, before Mr Harriett, was a large dish of boiled buffalo hump; at the foot smoked a boiled buffalo calf...one of the most esteemed dishes among the epicures of the interior. My pleasing duty was to help a dish of mouffle, or dried moose nose, [while] the worthy priest helped the buffalo tongue and Mr Randall cut up the beaver's tails. The centre of the table was graced with piles of potatoes, turnips and bread conveniently placed so that each could help himself without interrupting the labours of his companions. Such was our jolly Christmas dinner at Edmonton."

Cornelius Krieghoff

Born in Amsterdam, **Cornelius Krieghoff** trained as an artist in Düsseldorf before emigrating to New York, where, at the age of just 21, he joined the US army, serving in the Second Seminole War in Florida. Discharged in 1840, Krieghoff immediately re-enlisted, claimed three months' advance pay and deserted, hot-footing it to Montréal with the French-Canadian woman he had met and married in New York. In Montréal, he picked up his brushes again, but without any commercial success – quite simply no one wanted to buy his paintings. That might have been the end of the matter, but Krieghoff moved to **Québec City** in 1852 and here he found a ready market for his paintings among the well-heeled officers of the British garrison, who liked his folksy renditions of Québec rural life. This was the start of Krieghoff's most productive period. Over the next eight years he churned out dozens of souvenir pictures – finely detailed, anecdotal scenes that are his best work. In the early 1860s, however – and for reasons that remain obscure – he temporarily packed in painting, returning to Europe for five years before another stint in Québec City, though this time, with the officer corps gone, he failed to sell his work. In 1871, he went to live with his daughter in **Chicago** and died there the following year, a defeated man.

Buffalo Resting and *At Buffalo Pound*, where bison are pictured in what looks more like a placid German valley than a North American prairie. There's also his *Indian encampment on Lake Huron*, a softly hued oil on canvas painting dating to 1845. Equally interesting is the work – and life – of the prolific **Cornelius Krieghoff** (1815–72; see box above). The AGO owns a healthy sample of Krieghoff's paintings, including characteristic winter scenes like his *Settler's Log House* and *The Portage Aux Titres*, whose autumnal colours surround a tiny figure struggling with a canoe.

Folksy and/or romanticized country scenes and landscapes ruled the Canadian artistic roost from the 1850s through to the early twentieth century. By and large this was pretty routine stuff, but **Homer Watson**'s (1855–1936) glossy Ontario landscapes, with their vigorous paintwork and dynamic compositions, made him a popular and much acclaimed artist – Queen Victoria even purchased one of his paintings, and Oscar Wilde dubbed him "the Canadian Constable". The AGO possesses several Watson paintings, most memorably *The Old Mill* and *The Passing Storm*, two especially handsome and well-composed canvases, but his *Death of Elaine* – inspired by a Tennyson poem – is a bizarrely unsuccessful venture into ancient legend, the eponymous maiden looking something like a stick insect.

From the same period come a couple of important paintings by the Newfoundlander **Maurice Cullen** (1866–1934), beginning with the precise angles and dappled brushwork of *Moret in Winter*, which is generally regarded as the beginning of Canadian Impressionism. Cullen was trained in Paris, where he was greatly influenced by the work of Monet, producing this French river-scape just before he returned to Canada, where he applied a similar approach to the landscapes of the St Lawrence River, as in his *The Last Loads*.

Canada's Group of Seven

One of the most distinctive artists of the **Group of Seven**, displayed here on Level 2, was **Lawren Harris** (1885–1970), whose 1922 *Above Lake Superior* is a pivotal work, its clarity of conception, with bare birch stumps framing a dark mountain beneath Art Deco clouds, quite exceptional. Equally stirring is his surreal *Lake Superior* (1923), one of several paintings inspired by the wild, cold landscapes of the lake's north shore. Harris was also partial to urban street scenes and the AGO has several – including two of Toronto – each painted in a careful pointillist style very different from his wilderness works.

The *West Wind* by **Tom Thomson** (1877–1917) is another seminal work, an iconic rendering of the northern wilderness that is perhaps the most famous of all Canadian paintings. Thomson was the first to approach the wilderness with the determination of an explorer and a sense that it could encapsulate a specifically Canadian identity. A substantial sample of his less familiar (but no less powerful) works are part of the AGO collection, including the moody *A Northern Lake*, the Cubist-influenced *Autumn Foliage 1915*, the sticky dabs of colour of *Maple Springs*, and his *Autumn's Garland*, an oil on panel finished the year before he died. There is also a whole battery of preparatory sketches of lakes and canyons, waterfalls and forests, each small panel displaying the vibrant, blotchy colours that characterize Thomson's work.

J.E.H. MacDonald (1873–1932) was fond of dynamic, sweeping effects, and his panoramic *Falls, Montreal River* sets turbulent rapids beside hot-coloured hillsides. MacDonald also produced the startling sweep of *October Shower Gleam* and the superbly observed *Rowan Berries*. His friend **F.H. Varley** (1881–1969) dabbled in portraiture and chose soft images and subtle colours for his landscapes, as exemplified by the sticky-looking brushstrokes he used for *Moonlight after Rain*. The talents of **A.J. Casson** (1898–1992) are perhaps best recalled by the jumble of snow-covered roofs of his *House Tops in the Ward*, and his bright and rather formal *Old Store at Salem*, which offers a break from the scenic preoccupations of the rest of the Seven. There are also the vital canvases of **A.Y. Jackson** (1882–1974), most notably the bold colours and forms of his *Yellowknife Country* and the carpet-like surface of *Algoma Rocks, Autumn*, painted in 1923. Yet another member of the Group of Seven, **Arthur Lismer** (1885–1969), spent every summer at his cottage in Georgian Bay, north of Toronto, where he concentrated on painting shoreline and island vistas; the AGO has several prime examples. A contemporary of the Group – but not a member – the gifted **Emily Carr** (1871–1945) focused on the Canadian west coast in general, and its dense forests and native villages in particular, as in her dark and haunting *Thunderbird* of 1930 and the deep green foliage of both *Indian Church* and *Western Forest*, dating to 1929.

For more on the Group of Seven, see *Canadian Art* colour section.

The Henry Moore Sculpture Centre

Also on Level 2 is the world's largest collection of sculptures by **Henry Moore** (1898–1986), with the emphasis firmly on his plaster casts, alongside a few of his bronzes. Given a whole gallery, the sheer size and volume of Moore's output is impressive, but actually it was something of an accident that his work ended up here at all. In the 1960s, Moore had reason to believe that London's Tate Gallery was going to build a special wing for his work. When the Tate declined, Moore negotiated with the AGO instead, after being persuaded to do so by the gallery's British representative, Anthony Blunt – the art expert who was famously uncovered as a Soviet spy in 1979.

Levels 4 and 5: contemporary art

Spread over two levels, the AGO's collection of **contemporary art** showcases work by European, British and American artists from 1960 onwards. Around two hundred pieces are exhibited in total and they cover a wide range of media, from painting, sculpture and photography through to film and installation. The displays are changed fairly regularly, but prime pieces you can expect to see include Andy Warhol's *Elvis I* and *II*, Mark Rothko's strident *No. 1 White and Red* and Claes Oldenburg's quirky if somewhat frayed *Giant Hamburger*.

The Sharp Centre for Design

Immediately to the south of the AGO, along McCaul Street, the Ontario College of Art and Design occupied a plain brick building until the extraordinary **Sharp Centre for Design** was added to it in 2004. Created by the English architect **Will Alsop** – his first building in North America – the centre comprises a giant black-and-white-panelled rectangular "table-top", perched high up at roof level and supported by mammoth multi-coloured steel legs; it holds art studios, theatres and so forth and has variously been described as "adventurous" and "ludicrous". Regardless, it certainly is big.

Chinatown and Kensington Market

Back on Dundas, the Art Gallery of Ontario is fringed by **Chinatown**, a bustling, immensely appealing neighbourhood cluttered with **shops**, **restaurants** (for recommendations, see Chapter 8) and **street stalls** selling any and every type of Asian delicacy. The boundaries of Chinatown are somewhat blurred, but its focus, ever since the 1960s, when the original Chinatown was demolished to make way for the new City Hall, has been Dundas Street West between Beverley Street and Spadina Avenue. The first Chinese to migrate to Canada arrived in the mid-nineteenth century to work in British Columbia's gold fields. Subsequently, a portion of this population migrated east, and a sizeable Chinese community sprang up in Toronto in the early twentieth century. Several more waves of migration – the last influx following the handing over of Hong Kong to mainland China by the British in 1997 – have greatly increased the number of Toronto's Chinese, bringing the population to approximately 280,000 (about eleven percent of the city's total).

Next door to Chinatown, just north of Dundas Street West, between Spadina and Augusta avenues, lies Toronto's most ethnically diverse neighbourhood, pocket-sized **Kensington Market**. It was here, at the turn of the twentieth century, that Eastern European immigrants squeezed into a patchwork of modest little brick and timber houses that survive to this day. On Kensington Avenue they established an **open-air street market**, the main feature of the neighbourhood ever since, a lively, entertaining bazaar whose stall owners stem from many different backgrounds. The lower half of the market, just off Dundas Street, concentrates on **secondhand clothing**, while the upper half is crowded with **fresh food stalls and cafés**. Even if you don't want to actually buy anything, Kensington Market is one of the city's funkiest neighbourhoods and a great place to hang out.

Uptown Toronto

Spreading north from Gerrard Street, **Uptown Toronto** is something of an architectural hodgepodge, with perhaps the handiest starting point being **University Avenue**, whose bristling, monochromatic office blocks stomp up towards the imposing Victorian stonework of the **Ontario Legislative Assembly Building**, one of the city's most distinctive structures. The Assembly Building marks the start of a small **museum district**, made up of the delightful **Gardiner Museum of Ceramic Art** and the large but somewhat incoherent **Royal Ontario Museum**, which possesses one of the country's most extensive collections of applied art. The Assembly Building is also close to the prettiest part of the sprawling **University of Toronto** campus, on and around King's College Circle.

Moving north, office blocks and shops choke Bloor Street West, though it's here you'll find the fanciful **Bata Shoe Museum**, as well as the ritzy little neighbourhood of **Yorkville**. From here, it's a short subway ride or a thirty-minute walk to the city's two finest historic homes: the neo-baronial **Casa Loma** and the debonair **Spadina House** next door, both covered by the **Toronto City Pass** (see p.39).

Uptown's principal east–west corridor, **Bloor Street**, intersects with **Yonge Street**, the main north–south drag, which cuts a lively, if somewhat seedy, route north from Gerrard Street, lined along the way with **bars, cafés and shops**. At Wellesley Street, Yonge makes its way through the edge of the **Gay Village**, but the only sights hereabouts are further east in **Cabbagetown**, a pleasant old neighbourhood of leafy streets and terrace houses.

The Ontario Legislative Assembly Building

Peering down University Avenue, from just north of College Street, the pink sandstone mass of the **Ontario Legislative Assembly Building** dates to the 1890s (frequent 30min guided tours: late May to early Sept daily 9am–4pm, mid-Sept to late May Mon–Fri 10am–4pm; free; ☎416/325-7500, ⓦwww .ontla.on.ca; Queen's Park subway). Elegant it certainly isn't, but although the building is heavy and solid, its ponderous symmetries do have a certain appeal, with block upon block of roughly dressed stone assembled in the full flourish of the Romanesque Revival style. Seen from close up, the design is even more engaging, its intricacies a pleasant surprise: above the chunky columns of the main entrance is a sinuous filigree of carved stone, adorned by mythological creatures and gargoyle-like faces. The main facade also sports a Neoclassical frieze in which the **Great Seal of Ontario** is flanked by allegorical figures representing art, music, agriculture and so forth.

Inside, the foyer leads to the wide and thickly carpeted **Grand Staircase**, whose massive timbers are supported by gilded iron pillars. Beyond is the capacious **Legislative Chamber**, where the formality of the mahogany and sycamore panels is offset by a series of whimsical little **carvings** – look for the owl overlooking the doings of the government and the hawk overseeing the opposition benches. Under the Speaker's gallery, righteous **inscriptions** have been carved into the pillars, which is a bit of a hoot considering the behaviour of the building's architect, Richard Waite. Waite was chairman of the committee responsible for selecting an architect, and, as chairman, he selected himself.

A fire burned down the building's **west wing** in 1909, and to avoid a repeat performance, Parliament had its replacement built in marble the following year. No expense was spared in the reconstruction, so there was an awful fuss when one of the MPPs (Members of the Provincial Parliament) noticed what appeared to be blemishes in the stone on several of the pillars. The blotches turned out to be **dinosaur fossils**, and nowadays they are pointed out on the **guided tour**. The provincial assembly typically sits from late September to late June, with breaks at Christmas and Easter, and although guided tours avoid the chamber when the body is in session, the **visitors' gallery** is open to the public during its deliberations Monday through Thursdays; call for further details and times.

Queen's Park

Back outside, in front of the main entrance, are a pair of Russian **cannons** that were captured during the Crimean War. Queen Victoria gave them to the city in 1859 in honour of those Canadian regiments who had fought alongside the British during the siege of Sevastopol. The cannons are flanked by a series of **statues** of politicians and imperial bigwigs that spread across the manicured lawns of **Queen's Park**. Two of the more interesting are just a few metres to the east of the assembly's main entrance, beginning with **Queen Victoria**, who sits on her throne with a rather paltry crown on her head. Strangely, Victoria looks very male and, as if to compensate, her bust appears much too large for her slender frame. The adjacent statue of **John Graves Simcoe** (see p.217) is a much happier affair, with the one-time lieutenant-governor of Upper Canada cutting a dashing figure with a tricorn hat in one hand and a cane, held at a jaunty angle, in the other.

On the west side of the building stands a **bust** of anti-Tory radical William Lyon Mackenzie (see p.57 & p.218) and immediately behind it is an overblown **memorial** to "The struggle for responsible government" – that is, the campaign for representative government as opposed to rule by British appointees. Mackenzie was one of the first figures of any note to champion this cause. Behind the memorial is a **plaque** honouring the **Mac-Paps**. Named after the joint leaders of the Rebellion of 1837 – Mackenzie and Louis Joseph Papineau – the Mac-Paps were a 1500-strong Canadian battalion of the International Brigades, who fought for the Republicans against Franco and the Fascists in the Spanish Civil War of the 1930s. The plaque is attached to a hunk of rock from the Spanish town of Gandesa, scene of some of the war's bloodiest fighting.

There's more **statuary** behind the Legislative Building on the other section of Queen's Park. Here, right in the middle of the greenery, lording over the pigeons and the squirrels, is a heavyweight equestrian statue of King Edward VII

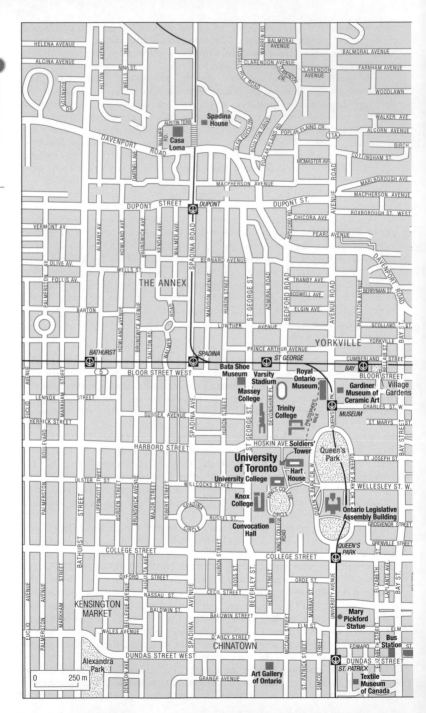

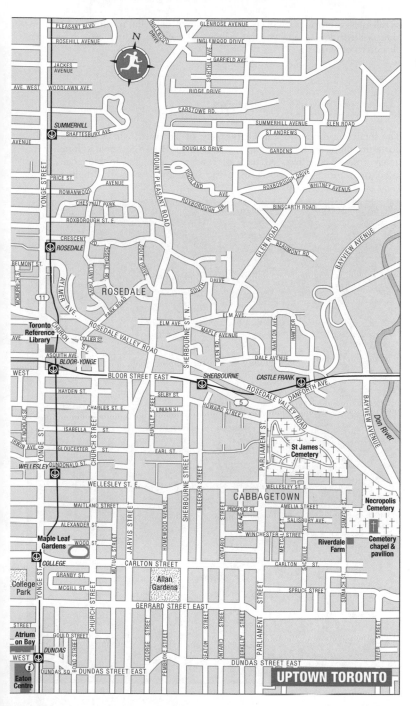

UPTOWN TORONTO

in full-dress uniform. Originally plonked down in Delhi, this imperial leftover looks a bit forlorn – and you can't help but feel the Indians must have been pleased to off-load it.

University of Toronto

The sprawling campus of the **University of Toronto**, which extends south-north from College to Bloor and east-west from Bay to Spadina, is dotted with stately college buildings and halls of residence. The best-looking (and most interesting) are to be found close to the Legislative Assembly Building at the

▲ University of Toronto

John Strachan

Toronto's first Anglican bishop was the redoubtable **John Strachan** (1778–1867), a one-time schoolmaster who made a name for himself in the War of 1812. The Americans may have occupied Toronto easily enough, but Strachan led a spirited civil resistance, bombarding the occupiers with a deluge of requests and demands about everything from inadequate supplies to any lack of respect the Americans showed to private property. Perhaps surprisingly, the Americans treated Strachan's complaints very seriously, though they did get mightily irritated. After the war, Strachan turned his formidable energies to education. All of bourgeois Toronto believed in the value of university education, but the problem was agreeing on who should provide it, as Canada's various religious denominations all wanted a piece of the educational action.

In 1827, Strachan obtained a royal charter for the foundation of Toronto's first college of higher education, but his plans for an Anglican-controlled institution were resisted so forcibly that **King's College**, as Strachan's college was called, didn't open its doors until 1843. Even then, Strachan's triumph was short-lived: Anglican control lasted just six years before the provincial government secularized the institution and renamed it the **University of Toronto**.

Over the ensuing decades the university was browbeaten by theological colleges that considered a secular university to be immoral, but by the turn of the twentieth century the University of Toronto had made a name for itself, ultimately becoming one of North America's most prestigious educational institutions. It was here that **insulin** was discovered in 1921, and here that **Marshall McLuhan**, who taught at the university, wrote his seminal *The Medium is the Message*.

west end of Wellesley Street, beginning on **Hart House Circle**. Here, the ivy-covered walls, neo-Gothic architecture and cloistered quadrangles of **Hart House** are reminiscent of Oxford and Cambridge – just as they were designed to be. Primarily a students' social and cultural facility, Hart House dates from the early twentieth century, its communal rooms culminating in the cavernous **Great Hall**, with its high timber ceiling and acres of wood panelling.

Hart House is named after **Hart Massey** (1823–96), a member of the Massey family that made a vast fortune from the manufacture of farm machinery. One of the last of the clan to be directly associated with the company was **Vincent Massey** (1887–1967), an extraordinarily influential man, sometimes ribbed as Canada's representative in heaven. Vincent was the one-time Chairman of the National Gallery, Chancellor of the University of Toronto, and the first native-born Governor-General of Canada from 1952 to 1959. Hart House was built at Vincent's instigation, and he also helped equip it with a sizeable collection of **modern Canadian paintings**, in which the Group of Seven (see *Canadian Art* colour section) makes a strong showing. The collection is too large to display at any one time, so the exhibits are regularly rotated, and they can be viewed in some of the public rooms of Hart House and sometimes in its **Justina M. Barnicke Gallery** (Mon–Wed 11am–5pm, Thurs & Fri 11am–7pm, Sat & Sun 1–5pm; free; ☎416/978-8398, ⓦwww.jmbgallery.ca). The gallery, which has just two small rooms, runs a lively programme of temporary exhibitions and has a sound reputation for showcasing the work of less well-known, modern Canadian painters from the 1920s onwards.

The Soldiers' Tower

Hart House is attached to the **Soldiers' Tower**, a neo-Gothic memorial erected in 1924 to honour those students who had died in World War I. It adjoins an arcaded **gallery**, which is inscribed with a list of the war dead as well as Canadian **John McCrae**'s *In Flanders Fields*, arguably the war's best-known poem: "... We are the Dead. Short days ago/We lived, felt dawn, saw sunset glow,/Loved and were loved, and now we lie,/In Flanders fields ... ." Optimistically, the builders of the memorial didn't leave any space to commemorate the dead of any future war – so the names of the university students killed in World War II had to be inscribed on the walls under the arches at the foot of the tower.

King's College Circle

Hart House Circle leads into the much larger **King's College Circle**, where an assortment of university buildings flanks a large field. On the north side of the field stands **University College**, a rambling Romanesque-style structure, whose turrets and heavy-hooped windows frame an imposing if somewhat surly central tower. Further around the circle, the rough sandstone masonry of **Knox College**, dating from 1874, repeats the studied Gothicism of its neighbours, whereas the adjacent **Convocation Hall** makes a break for a lighter tone, its elegant rotunda having been erected in the 1920s.

Philosopher's Walk

Backtracking to Hart House Circle, walk through the arch of the Soldiers' Tower, turn right along Hoskin Avenue and – just before you reach the traffic island – watch for the footpath on the left. This is **Philosopher's Walk**, an easy, leafy stroll, which leads north, slipping around the back of (but still giving access to) the Royal Ontario Museum on its way to Bloor Street West.

The Royal Ontario Museum

Usually known as the **ROM**, the **Royal Ontario Museum**, at 100 Queen's Park (Mon–Thurs 10am–5.30pm, Fri 10am–9.30pm, Sat & Sun 10am–5.30pm; $22, seniors $19, children aged 4–14 $15, free after 4.30pm on Wed; ☎416/586-8000, ⓦwww.rom.on.ca; Museum subway), is Canada's largest and most diverse museum and, among much else, it possesses a vast collection of fine and applied art drawn from every corner of the globe. What's more, the permanent collection is supplemented by an ambitious programme of temporary exhibitions and there are three hands-on galleries for children, the CIBC **Discovery Gallery**, the Digital Gallery and the Gallery of Biodiversity.

Facing onto Queen's Park, the ROM's **original building** is a substantial and serious-minded stone structure whose precise neo-Gothic symmetries are embellished with Art Deco flourishes. However, this structure is now overshadowed by a large and flashy extension – known as the **Michael Lee-Chin Crystal** – whose six crystal-shaped, aluminium-and-glass cubes were completed in 2007. Lee-Chin, a wealthy businessman, footed the bill, but the design was the brainchild of **Daniel Libeskind**, a Polish-born American architect, who has won a veritable raft of commissions since he turned from academic theory to architectural practice in 1998.

At the time of writing, the interior layout of the ROM is still in flux, but broadly speaking the permanent collection is divided into two categories – **World Culture** and **Natural History**. The Natural History galleries are on Level 2, whereas the World Culture galleries are on two floors – Level 1 (mainly

China, Korea, Japan and early Canada) and Level 3 (principally the Pacific, Egypt, Classical Greece, Europe). Many of the galleries are named after individual sponsors, which can be a little confusing, so be sure to pick up a free **museum plan** at the entrance. The ROM has two particularly impressive sections, its internationally acclaimed **Chinese collection** and the assorted fossils of the **Age of Dinosaurs gallery**.

Level 1: the old entrance hall

The domed and vaulted **old entrance hall** of the original ROM building is an extravagant affair, whose ceiling is decorated with a brilliant mosaic of imported Venetian glass. Bolted into the adjacent stairwells are four colossal and stunningly beautiful Native Canadian **crest poles** (commonly but erroneously referred to as totem poles). Dating from the 1880s, and the work of craftsmen from the Haida and Nisga'a peoples of the west coast, these poles – the tallest is 24.5 metres high – are decorated with stylized carvings representing the supernatural animals and birds that were associated with particular clans.

Level 1: the Sigmund Samuel Gallery of Canada

Concentrated in the Sigmund Samuel Gallery, the ROM's **early Canadian collection** is especially strong on furniture, silverware, ceramics and glass. There's also an intriguing collection of late eighteenth- and early nineteenth-century **trade silver** with examples of the assorted knick-knacks – brooches, earrings, crucifixes, medals and the like – which European traders swapped with natives for furs. Here also is the iconic *Death of Wolfe* by **Benjamin West**. The British general James Wolfe inflicted a crushing defeat on the French outside Québec City in 1759, but was killed during the battle. West's painting transformed this grubby colonial conflict into a romantic extravagance, with the dying general in a Christ-like pose, a pale figure held tenderly by his subordinates. West presented the first version of his painting to the Royal Academy of Arts in 1771 and it proved so popular that he spent much of the next decade painting copies.

Level 1: the Chinese collection

Level 1 has no fewer than four galleries devoted to its world-class **Chinese collection**, which spans six millennia, from 4500 BC to 1900 AD. Perhaps the most stunning of the four is the **Bishop White Gallery of Chinese Temple Art**, which displays three large and extraordinarily beautiful Daoist and Buddhist wall paintings dating from around 1300 AD. Two of them are a matching pair of Yuan Dynasty **murals** depicting the lords of the Northern and Southern Dipper, each of whom leads an astrological procession of star spirits.

Other key exhibits in the Chinese galleries include a remarkable collection of toy-sized **tomb figurines**, comprising a couple of hundred ceramic pieces representing funerary processions of soldiers, musicians, carts and attendants. Dating from the early sixth to the late seventh century, they re-create the habits of early China – how people dressed, how horses were groomed and shod, changes in armoury and so forth. There is also a fabulous collection of **snuff bottles**, some carved from glass and rock crystal, others from more exotic materials like amber, ivory, bamboo and even tangerine skin. Europeans introduced tobacco to China in the late sixteenth century, and although smoking did not become popular in China until recent times, snuff went down a storm and anyone who was anybody at court was snorting the stuff by the middle of the seventeenth century. The most popular component of the Chinese collection, however, is its **Ming Tomb**. The aristocracy of the Ming Dynasty (1368–1644 AD) evolved an elaborate style of monumental funerary sculpture and architecture, and the ROM holds the only example outside of China, though it is actually a composite tomb drawn from several sources rather than an intact, original whole. Central to the Ming burial conception was a Spirit Way, an avenue with large-scale carved figures of guards, attendants and animals placed on either side. At the end of the alley was the tumulus, or burial mound – in this case the tomb house of a seventeenth-century Chinese general by the name of Zu Dashou.

Level 2: The Age of Dinosaurs

Amongst the assorted Natural History galleries on Level 2, the highlight is the **Age of Dinosaurs** section, which holds the ROM's splendid collection of **fossil-skeletons**, the pick being those retrieved from the Alberta Badlands, near Calgary in western Canada. These Badlands are the richest source of dinosaur fossils in the world, having yielded over three hundred complete skeletons and 35 dinosaur species – ten percent of all those known today. Many of the Alberta dinosaur fossils have been dispatched to museums across the world, but the ROM still has a first-rate sample; the rampant herd of **Allosaurus** – a Jurassic-period carnivore of large proportions and ferocious appearance – commands the most attention.

Level 3: the European Collection

The ROM's **European Collection** includes a string of period rooms, mostly English, from the sixteenth to the eighteenth century, as well as eclectic collections of Arms and Armour, Art Nouveau and Art Deco, metalwork, glass and ceramics. Amongst the latter is a superb collection of Delftware and Italian majolica. There are also significant collections from Classical Greece, Imperial Rome, and Etruria.

Level 3: the Egyptian collection

The ROM plays a strong suite when it comes to **Ancient Egypt**, owning several finely preserved mummies, including the richly decorated sarcophagus of a certain Djedmaatesankh, a court musician who died around 850 BC. Even more unusual is the assortment of mummified animals, including a crocodile, a hawk and a weird-looking cat. There is also the intriguing **Punt Wall**, a 1905 plaster cast of the original in Queen Hatshepsut's temple in Deir el-Bahri, Egypt. The events depicted on the wall occurred in the year 1482 BC, and represent a military expedition to Punt, which lay south of Egypt near present-day Somalia.

The Gardiner Museum of Ceramic Art

The **Gardiner Museum of Ceramic Art** (Mon–Thurs 10am–6pm, Fri 10am–9pm, Sat & Sun 10am–5pm; $12; ☏416/586-8080, ⓦwww.gardinermuseum .on.ca; Museum subway), just across the street from the ROM at 111 Queen's Park, holds a superb collection of ceramics. Spread over three small floors, the museum's exhibits are beautifully presented, and its key pieces are well labelled and explained. An audioguide is also available.

On the main floor, the **pre-Columbian** section is particularly fine, composed of over three hundred pieces from regions stretching from Mexico to Peru. One of the most comprehensive collections of its kind in North America, it provides an intriguing insight into the lifestyles and beliefs of the Maya, Inca and Aztec peoples. The sculptures are all the more remarkable for the fact that the potter's wheel was unknown in pre-Columbian America, and thus everything was necessarily hand-modelled. Some of the pieces feature everyday activities, but it's the **religious sculptures** that mostly catch the eye, from wonderfully intricate Mexican incense burners to the fantastical zoomorphic gods of the Zapotecs.

Also on the main floor is an exquisite sample of fifteenth- and sixteenth-century tin-glazed **Italian majolica**, mostly dishes, plates and jars depicting classical and Biblical themes designed by Renaissance artists. The early pieces are comparatively plain, limited to green and purple, but the later examples are brightly coloured, reflecting technological change: in the second half of the fifteenth century, Italian potters learnt how to glaze blue and yellow, and then ochre. Perhaps the most splendid pieces are those from the city – and pottery centre – of **Urbino**, including two wonderful plates, one portraying the fall of Jericho, the other the exploits of Hannibal.

Up above, the second floor has both Japanese and Chinese porcelain plus an especially pleasing sample of eighteenth-century **European porcelain**, most notably hard-paste wares (fired at very high temperatures) from Meissen, Germany. On this floor also is a charming menagerie of Italian *commedia dell'arte* figurines, doll-sized representations of theatrical characters popular across Europe from the middle of the sixteenth to the late eighteenth century. The predecessor of pantomime, the *commedia dell'arte* featured stock characters in improvised settings, but with a consistent theme of seduction, age and beauty; the centrepiece was always an elderly, rich merchant and his attractive young wife.

Bata Shoe Museum

Within easy walking distance of the Gardiner, the **Bata Shoe Museum**, 327 Bloor St West at St George St (Mon–Sat 10am–5pm, Thurs till 8pm, Sun noon–5pm; $12; ☎416/979-7799, ⓦwww.batashoemuseum.ca; St George subway), was designed by **Raymond Moriyama**, the much-lauded Canadian architect whose other creations include the Ontario Science Centre (see p.96), the Scarborough Civic Centre and the Toronto Reference Library (see p.77). Moriyama is not without his architectural critics, but his accomplished designs demonstrate a soft and subtle charm in their preference for unusual angles and wavy, rounded lines. For the Bata Museum, which opened in 1995, Moriyama chose to make the exterior look like a shoe box, the roof set at a jaunty angle to suggest a lid resting on an open box. It is not, perhaps, one of his most successful creations, but it seems to have satisfied the woman who was funding it all – **Sonja Bata** of the Bata shoe manufacturing family – who had the museum built to display the extraordinary assortment of footwear she had spent a lifetime collecting.

A leaflet issued at **reception** steers visitors around the museum, starting with an introductory section on **Level B1** entitled "**All About Shoes**", which presents an overview on the evolution of footwear, kicking off with a plaster cast of the oldest human footprint ever discovered (roughly 3,700,000 years old). Among the more interesting exhibits in this section are pointed shoes from **medieval Europe**, where different social classes were allowed different lengths of toe, and tiny **Chinese silk shoes** used by women whose feet had been bound. Banned by the Chinese Communists when they came to power in 1949, foot binding was common practice for over a thousand years, and the "ideal" length of a woman's foot was a hobbling three inches. A small adjoining section is devoted to **specialist footwear**, most memorably French chestnut-crushing clogs from the nineteenth century; inlaid Ottoman platforms designed to keep aristocratic feet well away from the mud; and a pair of Dutch smugglers' clogs with the heel and sole reversed to leave a footprint intended to hoodwink any following customs officials.

Moving on, **Level G** features a large glass cabinet showcasing all sorts of **celebrity footwear**. The exhibits are rotated regularly, but look out for Buddy Holly's loafers, Eminen's sneakers, Marilyn Monroe's stilettos, Princess Diana's red court shoes, Shaquille O'Neal's colossal Reebok trainers and Elton John's ridiculous platforms. **Level 2** and **Level 3** are used for **temporary exhibitions** that draw extensively on the museum's permanent collection – there's not nearly enough room to show everything at the same time.

Yorkville

From both the Bata Museum and the Gardiner, it's the briefest of walks to the chic and well-heeled **Yorkville neighbourhood**, whose epicentre is Cumberland Street and Yorkville Avenue between Bay Street and Avenue Road. Jam-packed with chichi **cafés, restaurants and shops**, Yorkville makes for a pleasant stroll (especially if you've got some spare cash), one of its most agreeable features being

▲ Yorkville

the **old timber-terrace houses** that are still much in evidence. These same houses have actually seen much grimmer days: in the late 1950s, Yorkville was run down and impoverished, but then the hippies arrived and soon turned the area into a countercultural enclave – a diminutive version of Haight-Ashbury, with Joni Mitchell and Gordon Lightfoot in attendance. Things are much less inventive today – big cars and big jewellery – but the **Village Gardens**, at the corner of Cumberland and Bellair streets, is a particularly appealing and cleverly designed little park. The centrepiece is a hunk of granite brought from northern Ontario, and around it are arranged a variety of neat little gardens, displaying every native Ontario habitat from forest to wetlands.

The Toronto Reference Library

Located at the east end of Cumberland Street, east of Yorkville at 789 Yonge St, the **Toronto Reference Library** (Mon–Thurs 9.30am–8.30pm, Fri 9.30am–5.30pm, Sat 9am–5pm, plus mid-Sept to late June Sun 1.30–5pm; ☎416/393-7131, Ⓦwww.torontopubliclibrary.ca) occupies a striking modern building designed by Canada's own **Raymond Moriyama** (see p.75). The exterior is actually a good deal less becoming than the interior, whose five floors are arranged around a large and airy floor-to-ceiling atrium with a pool and waterfall. As you would expect, the library possesses an enormous stock of books, CDs and audiobooks, as well as around a hundred public-access PCs, which are divided into two groups – those which can be booked ahead of time and those which are used instantly for a maximum of fifteen minutes; Internet access on all the computers is free.

Amongst the library's many sections, the fourth-floor **Periodicals Centre** has Canadian source materials dating back to the eighteenth century, as does the adjoining **Genealogy and Local History Collection**. Regular **exhibitions** illustrate various aspects of the special collections, but it's the fifth-floor **Arthur Conan Doyle Room** (Tues, Thurs & Sat 2–4pm; free) that steals the show, boasting the world's largest collection of books, manuscripts, letters and so forth written by Conan Doyle, including of course the illustrious Sherlock Holmes series.

Cabbagetown

The precise boundaries of **Cabbagetown**, southeast of the Toronto Reference Library, continue to be a matter of dispute between local historians and real estate agents – the former try to narrow the area and the latter try to expand it – but, roughly speaking, this Victorian neighbourhood is bounded by Gerrard Street to the south, Parliament Street to the west, Wellesley Street to the north, and the Don River valley to the east.

Cabbagetown got its name from the nineteenth-century Irish immigrants who settled here and grew cabbages in their yards instead of (the more traditional) flowers. Contemporary residents have embraced the vegetable and even have their own flag with a large, leafy cabbage prominently displayed at the centre. The neighbourhood once had a reputation for substandard homes and dire living conditions, prompting novelist Hugh Garner to anoint it "the largest Anglo-Saxon slum in North America". Today, however, with most of the houses neatly renovated, Cabbagetown has become a haven for the city's hip and moderately well-to-do.

Specific sights in Cabbagetown are thin on the ground, but **Metcalfe Street**, running one block east of Parliament Street, does possess a particularly appealing ensemble of **Victorian houses**, as does adjoining **Winchester Street**. Common architectural features include high-pitched gables, stained-glass windows, stone lintels and inviting timber verandas. At the east end of Winchester Street, the entrance to one of the city's oldest cemeteries is marked by a handsome Gothic Revival **chapel** and matching **pavilion**, whose coloured tiles and soft yellow brickwork date to the middle of the nineteenth century. Inside the **cemetery**, the gravestones are almost universally modest and unassuming, but their straightforward accounts of the lives of the dead give witness to the extraordinary British diaspora that populated much of Victorian Canada. Cabbagetown is also home to the **oldest neighbourhood festival** in Toronto; for details, see p.210.

Casa Loma

To the northwest of the Yorkville neighbourhood, it's a five-minute walk from Dupont subway station up the slope of Spadina Road to the corner of Davenport Road, where a flight of steps leads to Toronto's most bizarre attraction – **Casa Loma**, at 1 Austin Terrace (daily 9.30am–5pm; last admission 4pm; $18, parking $2.75 per hour; ☎416/923-1171, ⓦwww.casaloma.org). A folly to outdo almost every other folly, Casa Loma is an enormous towered and turreted mansion built to the instructions of Sir Henry Pellatt and his architect Edward J. Lennox between 1911 and 1914. A free map of the house is available at the reception, as are **audioguides**.

Sir Henry Pellatt

Sir Henry Pellatt (1859–1939) made a fortune by pioneering the use of hydro-electricity, harnessing the power of Niagara Falls (see pp.104–109) to light Ontario's expanding cities. Determined to become a man of social standing, Pellatt threw his money around with gusto. He levered his wife into a key position as a leader of the Girl Guides and managed to become a major general of the Queen's Own Rifles, bolstering his appointment by taking 640 soldiers to a military training camp in Aldershot, in England, at his own expense. Pellatt's enthusiasm for the British interest went down well, and he even secured a knighthood, though he was never fully accepted by the old elite – for one thing, he was fond of dressing up in a costume that combined a British colonel's uniform with the attire of a Mohawk chief.

In 1911, Pellatt started work on Casa Loma, gathering furnishings from all over the world and even importing Scottish stonemasons to build a wall around his six-acre property, the end result being an eccentric mixture of medieval fantasy and early twentieth-century technology. Pellatt spent more than $3 million fulfilling his dream, but his penchant for reckless business dealings finally caught up with him, forcing him to move out and declare himself bankrupt in 1923. He died penniless sixteen years later, his dramatic fall from grace earning him the nickname "Pellatt the Plunger".

The house

A clearly numbered route goes up one side of the house and down the other. It begins on the ground floor in the **Great Hall**, a pseudo-Gothic extravaganza with an eighteen-metre-high cross-beamed ceiling, a Wurlitzer organ and enough floor space to accommodate several hundred guests. Hung with flags, heavy-duty chandeliers and suits of armour, it's a remarkably cheerless place, but, in a touch worthy of Errol Flynn, the hall is overlooked by a balcony at the end of Pellatt's second-floor bedroom; presumably, Sir Henry could, like some medieval baron, welcome his guests from on high.

Pushing on, the **library** and then the walnut-panelled **dining room** lead to the **conservatory**, an elegant and spacious room with a marble floor and side-panels set beneath a handsome Tiffany domed glass ceiling. Well-lit, this is perhaps the mansion's most appealing room, its flowerbeds kept warm even in winter by the original network of steam pipes. The nearby **study** was Sir Henry's favourite room, a serious affair engulfed by mahogany panelling and equipped with two secret passageways, one leading to the wine cellar, the other to his wife's rooms – a quintessential dichotomy. Also of note is the ground-floor **Oak Room**, which comes complete with an elaborate stucco ceiling and acres of finely carved oak panelling.

On the second floor, **Sir Henry's Suite** has oodles of walnut and mahogany panelling, which stands in odd contrast to its 1910s white-marble, high-tech bathroom, featuring an elaborate multi-nozzle shower. **Lady Pellatt's Suite** wasn't left behind in the ablutions department either – her bathroom had a bidet, a real novelty in George V's Canada – though she had a lighter decorative touch, eschewing wood panelling for walls painted in her favourite colour, Wedgwood Blue, with pastel furniture to match. This suite also contains a small display on Lady Pellatt's involvement with the Girl Guides, a uniformed organization encouraging good imperial habits: self-reliance, honesty, self-discipline and so forth. In the photos, Lady Pellatt looks serious and concerned, the girls suitably keen and dutiful.

At the other end of the main second-floor corridor are the **Round Room**, with its curved doors and walls, and the smartly decorated **Windsor Room**, named after – and built for – the Royal Family, in the rather forlorn hope that they would come and stay here. Of course they never did; Pellatt was much too parvenu for their tastes. Up above, the third floor holds a mildly diverting display on Pellatt's one-time regiment, the **Queen's Own Rifles**, tracing its involvement in various campaigns from the suppression of the Métis rebellion in western Canada in 1885 through to World War I and beyond. The most interesting features are the old photographs and the potted biographies of some of the regiment's bravest, medal-winning soldiers. From the third floor, wooden staircases clamber up to two of the house's **towers**, where you'll have pleasing views over the house and gardens.

Back on the ground floor, stairs lead down to the Lower Level, which was where Pellatt's money ran out and his plans ground to a halt. Work never started on the bowling alley and shooting range he had designed, and the **swimming pool** only got as far as the rough concrete basin that survives today – never mind that Pellatt conceived a marble pool overlooked by golden swans. Pellatt did, however, manage to complete the 250-metre-long **tunnel** that runs from the house and pool to the **carriage room** and **stables**, where his thoroughbred horses were allegedly better-treated than his servants, chomping away at their oats and hay in splendid iron and mahogany stalls. The stables are a dead end, so you'll have to double back along the tunnel to reach the house and the exit.

The gardens

Before you leave, spare time for the **terraced gardens** (May–Oct daily 9.30am–4pm; no extra charge), which tumble down the ridge at the back of the house. They are parcelled up into several different sections and easily explored along a network of footpaths, beginning on the terrace behind the Great Hall. Highlights include the Rhododendron Dell, the lily pond and waterfall of the Water Garden and the Cedar Grove, a meadow garden flanked by cool, green cedars.

Spadina House

Quite what the occupants of **Spadina House** (guided tours only: April–Aug Tues–Sun noon–5pm plus holiday Mon noon–5pm; Sept–Dec Tues–Fri noon–4pm, Sat & Sun noon–5pm; Jan–March Sat & Sun noon–5pm; $8; ℡416/392-6910, ⊛www.toronto.ca; Dupont subway) must have thought when Casa Loma went up next door can only be imagined, but there must have been an awful lot of curtain-twitching. The two houses are a study in contrasts – Casa Loma a grandiose pile and Spadina an elegant Victorian property of genteel appearance dating from 1866.

Spadina was built by **James Austin**, an Irish immigrant from County Armagh, who was a printer's apprentice before becoming a successful businessman and a co-founder of the Toronto Dominion Bank. After his death, Spadina House passed to Albert Austin, who enlarged and modernized his father's home, adding billiard and laundry rooms, a garage and a refrigerator room to replace the old ice house. Albert's property eventually passed to his three daughters, who lived in the house until the last of the sisters, Anna Kathleen, moved out in 1983, the year before she died. Anna bequeathed Spadina House to the City of Toronto, which now manages and maintains the place. The Austins' uninterrupted occupation of the house means that its furnishings are nearly all genuine family artefacts, and they provide an intriguing insight into the family's changing tastes and interests.

Narrated by enthusiastic volunteers, the **guided tour** is a delight. Particular highlights include the conservatory trap door that allowed the gardeners to come and go unseen by their employers, an assortment of period chairs and sofas designed to accommodate the largest of bustles, the original gas chande-liers and a couple of canvases by **Cornelius Krieghoff** (see p.63). Pride of place, however, goes to the **Billiard Room**, which comes complete with an inventive Art Nouveau decorative frieze dating from 1898, and the **library**, equipped with a sturdy oak bureau and a swivel armchair in the manner of the designs of England's William Morris. On the first floor, look out for the unusual arcaded arches and wooden grills above the bedroom doors. These were installed in the 1890s as part of a scheme to improve the circulation of air as recommended by Florence Nightingale (1820–1910), who became famous in every corner of the British Empire as the nurse who took over the military hospital at Scutari during the Crimean War of the 1850s.

After touring the house, be sure to wander the **garden** (same times; no extra cost), with its neat lawns and colourful borders.

The waterfront and the Toronto Islands

There is much to enjoy on the shore of Lake Ontario, despite its industrial blotches and the heavy concrete brow of the Gardiner Expressway. Footpaths and cycling trails nudge along a fair slice of **the waterfront**, and the Harbourfront Centre offers a year-round schedule of activities – music festivals, theatre, dance and the like. Here also is the adventurous Power Plant Contemporary Art Gallery, as well as Ontario Place, a leisure complex spread over three man-made islands that provides all sorts of kids' entertainment throughout the summer.

Even better are the **Toronto Islands**, whose breezy tranquillity attracts droves of city-dwellers during Toronto's humid summers. It only takes fifteen minutes to reach them by municipal ferry, but the contrast between the city and the islands could hardly be more marked, not least because the islands are almost entirely **vehicle-free**; many locals use wheelbarrows or golf buggies to move their tackle, while others walk or cycle.

The waterfront and around

Toronto's grimy docks – a swathe of warehouses and factories that was unattractive and smelly in equal measure – once blighted the shoreline nearest the city centre. Today it's another story: the port and its facilities have been concentrated further east, beyond the foot of Parliament Street, while the **waterfront** west of Yonge Street has been redeveloped in grand style, sprouting luxury condominium blocks, jogging and cycling trails, offices, shops and marinas. The focus of all this activity is the **Harbourfront Centre**, whose various facilities include an open-air performance area and the **Power Plant Contemporary Art Gallery**. To reach the Harbourfront Centre by **public transport**, take streetcar #509 or #510 from Union Station and get off at Queens Quay Terminal, the second stop.

The Harbourfront Centre

The centrepiece of Toronto's downtown waterfront is the ten-acre **Harbourfront Centre**, an expanse of lakefront land stretching from the foot of York Street in

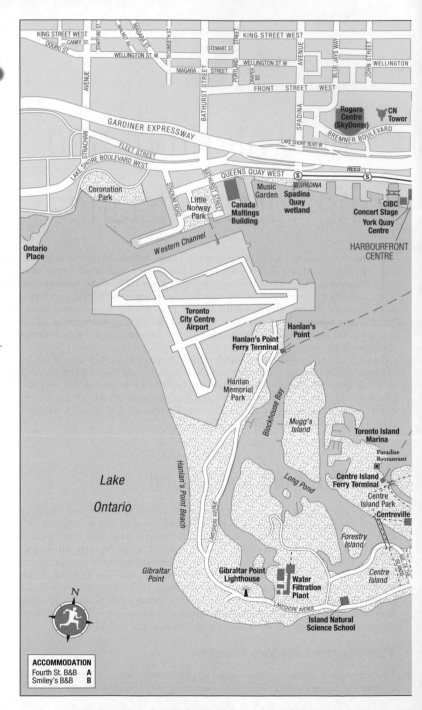

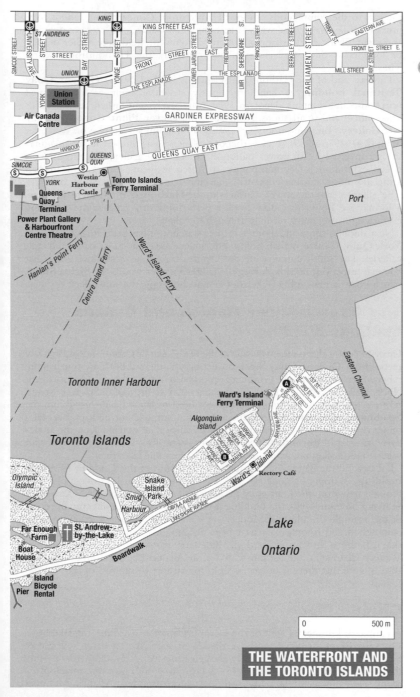

THE WATERFRONT AND
THE TORONTO ISLANDS

the east to the conspicuous outdoor Harbourfront Concert Stage, about five-minutes' walk away to the west. This is one of Toronto's most creative quarters, and many of the city's artistic and cultural events are held here, either outside or indoors at one of several venues, principally the Harbourfront Centre Theatre.

The east end of the Harbourfront Centre is marked by the **Queens Quay Terminal building**, a handsome, glassy structure built as a combined warehouse and shipping depot in 1927. Attractively refurbished, it now holds cafés, offices and smart shops. Next door, the **Power Plant Contemporary Art Gallery** (Tues–Sun noon–6pm, Wed noon–8pm; $4, but free on Wed after 5pm; ☎416/973-4949, ⓦ www.thepowerplant.org) is housed in an imaginatively converted 1920s power station. Every year, the gallery presents about a dozen exhibitions of contemporary art, often featuring emerging Canadian artists. It's mostly cutting-edge stuff; indecipherable to some, exciting to others. The gallery shares the power station with the **Harbourfront Centre Theatre**, a former ice house that now hosts a performing arts programme featuring everything from poetry readings through to ballet.

Next door to the west, another former warehouse has been turned into the **York Quay Centre**, which holds performance areas, meeting spaces and craft galleries. The south entrance of the Centre lets out to a shallow pond that converts into a skating rink during the winter. Further west is the **Sirius Stage**, which boasts a graceful fan-like roof designed to suggest a ship's deck.

The Toronto Music Garden and Canada Maltings building

Cross the footbridge on the west side of the Harbourfront Centre and you're a few metres from **Queens Quay West**, once a busy boulevard but now much more subdued, separated from the Gardiner Expressway by a raft of brand-new apartment blocks. Walking west along the road, it's about 600m to the foot of Spadina Avenue, where a tiny slice of old industrial land has been reclaimed and turned into the **Spadina Quay wetland** – not much to write home about perhaps, but still a minor concession to the lakeshore's original habitat. The wetland abuts the attractively landscaped **Toronto Music Garden**, essentially a series of rockeries with vague musical allusions, which meanders west along the lakeshore.

Just beyond the Music Garden lurk the giant silos of the **Canada Maltings building**, an imposing concrete hulk erected in 1928 for the storage of barley brought here from the Prairies by the ships that once thronged the St Lawrence Seaway. Closed in 1987, the building is derelict today, but architecturally – as a prime example of industrial Modernism – it's much too fine a structure to be demolished, and Torontonians have been debating its future for years. On its far side is Bathurst Street, and the dinky little ferry that shuttles across the narrow Western Channel to the Toronto City Centre Airport (see p.24) on the Toronto Islands; note that there is no access from the airport to the rest of the Toronto Islands.

Ontario Place

A couple of kilometres west of the Harbourfront Centre along the lakeshore, **Ontario Place**, at 955 Lakeshore Blvd West (late May & early Sept Sat & Sun 10am–6pm; June–Aug mostly, though times can vary, daily 10am–8pm; day pass covering most rides $45; ☎416/314-9900, ⓦ www.ontarioplace .com), rises out of the lake like some sort of postmodern Atlantis. Architect

Eberhard Zeidler was given a mandate to create "leisure space in an urban context", and he came up with these three artificial islands, or "pods", covering 95 acres with landscaped parks, lagoons and canals. The attractions here are almost entirely themed around water, and rides like the Rush River Raft Ride, the Purple Pipeline and the Pink Twister provide exciting ways to get dizzy and wet. Visitors looking for less frenetic activities can rent **pedal boats** (available at all of the park's various lagoons) or two-seater aquatic bicycles, which are used to thrash through the canals that separate the pods.

Both an amusement park and an entertainment complex, Ontario Place was the template for facilities like Disney's EPCOT Center in Florida, and it teems with young families and teenagers during the day. The atmosphere at night tends to be a bit more mature, particularly at the **Molson Amphitheatre**, which puts on a series of summer concerts dominated by headliner rock groups.

Also at Ontario Place is the **Cinesphere**, whose distinctive geodesic dome, containing a 750-seat theatre with a curved, six-storey screen, was the world's first IMAX theatre when it opened in 1971; IMAX technology was developed by the Toronto-based IMAX Corporation in 1967. Distinguishing IMAX from normal cinema, the frames of an IMAX film are physically larger than in any other processing format. The film runs through a behemoth projector at 24 frames per second and the screens average 20m (65ft) in height. The cumulative sensation is one of being immersed in the film, and it has certainly proved a popular formula – there are now IMAX theatres all over the world. To see an IMAX film here, it's a good idea to book ahead, either online or by phone; tickets cost $8–17 each. To get to Ontario Place by **public transport**, take the Harbourfront streetcar (#509) from Union Station to Exhibition Place, then walk south through the Exhibition grounds, over the Lakeshore bridge and into Ontario Place; the walk takes about ten minutes.

The Toronto Islands

Originally a sandbar peninsula, the **Toronto Islands**, which arch around the city's harbour, were cut adrift from the mainland by a violent storm in 1858. First used as a summer retreat by the Mississauga Indians, the islands went through various incarnations during the twentieth century: they once hosted a baseball stadium, where slugger Babe Ruth hit his first professional home run, saw fun fairs featuring horses diving from the pier, and even served as a training base for the Norwegian Air Force during World War II. Today, this archipelago, roughly 6km long and totalling around 800 acres, seems worlds away from the bustle of Downtown, a perfect spot to relax and unwind – and a place where visitors' **motor cars are banned**.

The city side of the archipelago is broken into a dozen tiny islets dotted with cottages, leisure facilities, verdant gardens and clumps of woodland. By comparison, the other side of the archipelago is a tad wilder and more windswept, consisting of one long sliver of land, which is somewhat arbitrarily divided into three "islands": from the east, these are **Ward's Island**, a quiet residential area with parkland and wilderness; **Centre Island**, the busiest and most developed of the three; and **Hanlan's Point**, which leads round to Toronto's pint-sized

Mrs Simcoe and the Toronto Islands

Mrs Elizabeth Simcoe (1766–1850), the energetic wife of the lieutenant-governor of Upper Canada, John Graves Simcoe, arrived in York, today's Toronto, in 1793 and returned to England three years later. An avid diarist, Mrs Simcoe recorded the day-to-day happenings of colonial life in her diary, a lively, attractively illustrated text dotted with shrewd observations and descriptions of Canada's flora. Mrs Simcoe took a shine to the Toronto Islands – or the peninsula, as it was then – and rode there frequently. Her first jaunt is recorded as follows: "We met with some good natural meadows and several ponds. The trees are mostly of the poplar kind, covered with wild vines, ... [and] on the ground were everlasting peas creeping in abundance, of a purple colour. I am told they are good to eat when boiled ... The diversity of scenes I met with this morning made the ride extremely pleasant. I was very near riding into what appeared a quicksand ... [which was] ... the only unpleasant incident that occurred this day." If this extract whets your appetite, *The Diary of Mrs John Graves Simcoe*, although currently out of print, is still available at the World's Biggest Bookstore (see p.184).

City Centre Airport (see p.24). Hanlan's Point also holds the city's best **sandy beach** – though, as Lake Ontario is generally regarded as being too polluted for swimming, most visitors stick to sunbathing.

Practicalities

Passenger **ferries** bound for the Toronto Islands depart from the mainland **ferry terminal**, which is located metres from the conspicuous *Westin Harbour Castle Hotel*, between the foot of Yonge and Bay streets. To get to the ferry terminal from Union Station, take the #509 or #510 streetcar and get off at the first stop – Queen's Quay (Ferry Docks). The islands have three **ferry docks** – one each on Ward's Island, Centre Island and Hanlan's Point. The ferries to Ward's Island and Hanlan's Point run year-round, while the ferry shuttling visitors over to Centre Island only operates from spring to fall. During peak season (May to early Sept), ferries to all three islands depart at regular intervals, either every half-hour, every forty-five minutes, or every hour; at other times of the year, it's usually hourly. Ferries begin running between 6.30am and 9am and finish between 9pm and 11.30pm, depending on the service and the season. For schedule details, telephone ☎416/392-8193. Regardless of the time of year, a return **fare** for adults is $6.50, or $4 for seniors (over 65) and students. Cyclists are allowed to take their **bikes** with them unless the ferry is jam-packed, and **rollerblades** are permitted, but must be removed while on board.

From May to September, **bike rental** is available on Centre Island from **Island Bicycle Rental** (☎416/203-0009), a five- to ten-minute walk from the Centre Island ferry dock at the foot of the pier. They open daily at around 10.30am and stock ordinary bicycles, tandems and even quadracycles, but the only advance reservations they accept are for groups of ten or more. Ordinary bikes cost $7 per hour plus a fully refundable deposit of $10; photo ID is required. **Canoe and paddle boat rental** is available on Centre Island too, from the **Boat House**, a five- to ten-minute walk from the Centre Island ferry dock. Hiring a boat allows you to paddle round the islands' network of mini-lagoons and reach a couple of tiny wooded islets that are otherwise impossible to reach. Aside from walking, cycling and rowing, the other means of conveyance is a free and fairly frequent **trackless train** that runs across the islands throughout the summertime; you can board the train at any point along its circuitous route. As regards eating and drinking, it's all fast-food stuff except for the **Rectory Café** (May–Sept daily 10am–9pm, rest of year Wed–Sun 11am–5pm), on Ward's Island, where they serve tasty snacks and light meals. Finally, note that **cars** are not allowed on the Toronto Islands without a special permit and these are only available to island residents.

Several hours are needed to explore the islands by bike, a full day if you are on foot, or you can overnight at one of the islands' two B&Bs (see p.133).

Ward's Island

Named after the Ward family, who settled on the then-peninsula in 1830, **Ward's Island** holds the cosiest of little hamlets, whose narrow lanes are flanked by antique wooden cottages that seem to blend seamlessly into the surrounding greenery. The island is home to approximately seven hundred full-time residents, but remains one of the least-developed of the chain – the landscape is still dominated by primeval-looking scrub, reed and birches mixed with wild apple trees and grape vines. The cottages edge up towards a curving, sandy beach and a pleasant **boardwalk**, which scoots along the Lake Ontario side of the island, with a network of paths exploring the rest of the terrain. A trio of narrow footbridges connects Ward's with its tiny neighbours – **Algonquin Island**, with yet more dinky little cottages, wild **Snake Island** and private **Snug Harbour**, the first of three inter-connected islets that are owned by the Canadian yacht club. The **Rectory Café**, easily the best place to eat on the islands and with an attractive patio, is metres from the Algonquin footbridge.

Centre Island

Most of the summer season's action takes place on **Centre Island**, with ferries arriving at its dock carrying boatloads of day-trippers. The first things you'll see as the ferry sails in is the landscaped gardens abutting the dock and the *Paradise Restaurant*, a favourite watering hole for the thirsty sailors of the adjacent Toronto Island Marina. From the dock, it's a five-minute walk east to **Centreville** (June–Aug daily, plus May & Sept weekends, 10.30am–5pm, 6pm, 7pm or 8pm; ☎416/203-0405, ⓦwww.centreisland.ca), a children's amusement park with charmingly old-fashioned rides. There are around thirty rides altogether, including paddle boats shaped as swans, a carousel, a Ferris wheel and a rollercoaster. Each ride costs a specified number of tickets, from two to board the carousel up to a maximum of six to experience the rollercoaster. Individual tickets are $1, or you can splash out on an all-day pass costing $30 for adults (and anyone over four feet tall), or $21 for kids under four feet. At the east end of Centreville is **Far Enough Farm**, a small farm and petting zoo popular with very young children.

Just to the south of Centreville, a footbridge spans the narrow waterway that bisects Centre Island to reach the **Avenue of the Islands**, a wide walkway surrounded by trim gardens. At its southern end, this walkway extends into a forked **pier** that pokes out beyond the stone breakwater into the lake. Island Bicycle Rental (see p.86) is located at the foot of the pier and boat rental is available from the Boat House, near to – and clearly signposted from – the Avenue of the Islands; from the Boat House you can paddle off through the islands and get to places, like wooded and uninhabited **Forestry Island**, which are otherwise inaccessible.

One other minor attraction, just east of the Avenue of the Islands, across the water from Far Enough Farm, is the Anglican **St Andrew-by-the-Lake**, a long and slender clapboard church dating from 1884.

③ Hanlan's Point

Hanlan's Point is named after another old island family, who first settled here at Gibraltar Point, on the island's southwestern tip, in 1862. The most famous member of the family was **Edward "Ned" Hanlan**, who earned Canada's first

▲ Gibraltar Point lighthouse

Olympic gold medal as a champion rower, a skill he honed rowing back and forth to the mainland. The Hanlans built a hotel-resort on the island and others followed, though none has survived and neither has an old amusement park, which was demolished in the 1930s to make way for what is now the Toronto City Centre Airport (see p.24); there's a **statue** of Ned in his pomp by the Hanlan's Point ferry dock.

Ferries arrive on the northeast side of the island just outside the airport precincts. From the dock, a combined **footpath and bicycle trail** runs south, passing behind – and just east of – **Hanlan's Point Beach**, a long stretch of tawny sand which is generally regarded as one of the city's best beaches. Frankly, this is not much of a boast, but it is enough to attract a fair few sunbathers, though swimmers – given the polluted nature of the lake – are few and far between. Part of the beach is for the clad; in the other part – in the ungainly words of the park's department signs – "clothing [is] optional". Altogether, the beach is perhaps more valued as an environmentalist's haven, and generations of budding biologists have been nurtured at the nearby Toronto Islands Natural Science School, which teaches city children about the flora and fauna of both the islands and Lake Ontario.

The school is on the south side of the island, beyond the **Gibraltar Point Lighthouse**, a sturdy limestone structure with a dark-pink, iron top. Erected at the beginning of the nineteenth century, the original lighthouse was sixteen metres high, and equipped with a lamp that burned sperm oil. This setup was updated in the 1830s, when the lighthouse was heightened by about four metres and its lamp replaced by one fuelled by coal oil; an electric lamp was installed in 1916. In its early days, when Toronto harbour was crowded with sailing ships, the Gibraltar was a vitally important beacon. It also achieved notoriety when its first keeper, a certain **Radan Muller**, disappeared in 1815. The *York Gazette* was quick to pronounce Muller of "inoffensive and benevolent character", and was pleased to report that the police had detained two suspects in his disappearance. In the event, the suspects – two soldiers from Fort York (see p.47) – were never charged, but popular legend continued to assert their guilt. The story went that they dropped in on Radan for a drinking session, and a quarrel ensued in which the lighthouse keeper was accidentally killed. More murkily, it's possible that Radan was a whisky smuggler, and the fight started over the profits of some contraband booze. Whatever the truth, the remains of Radan's body were finally discovered by a later keeper in 1893, buried in a shallow grave just to the west of the lighthouse – quite enough to fuel endless **ghost stories**.

The suburbs

Toronto's **suburbs** today are the very opposite of the manicured lawns, car culture and demographic consistency that characterized them in the Fifties and Sixties. In a city that anticipates 2.6 million more inhabitants by 2030, where there are 150 languages spoken and where fifty percent of the citizens are foreign-born, it is the suburbs, especially **Scarborough**, **Etobicoke**, **East York**, and **North York** where hundreds of thousands of new Canadians settle, bringing with them customs, cuisines and architecture to spice up strip malls, residential areas and public spaces. A recent example of this is the **BAPS Shri Swaminarayan Mandir** – the stunning Hindu temple in Etobicoke, which became an immediate hit with all Torontonians, regardless of faith, as a treasured architectural addition when it went up in 2007 (see p.98).

Toronto's 1960s suburban expansion was fuelled by a period of unprecedented affluence, which saw governments willing to build and maintain huge cultural projects – often on large out-of-town sites where land was cheap. The **Toronto Zoo**, the **Ontario Science Centre** and **Black Creek Pioneer Village** – in Scarborough, East York and North York respectively – are three such examples, all of them drawing tourists and residents alike from the Downtown core. These large-scale man-made attractions are not the only reason to venture out to the suburbs, however: spots like **High Park**, the **Scarborough Bluffs** and **The Beach**, along with the parkland, ravines and rivers that web through the urban and suburban sprawl, offer swaths of nature on the city's doorstep. For more on making the most of Toronto's green spaces and wilderness areas, see chapter 14, "Sports and outdoor activities".

As for getting out to the suburbs, Toronto's extensive **public transport** system takes passengers to the city's perimeters for the single (adult) fare of $2.75. On weekends, suburban bus and train schedules operate less frequently; contact the Toronto Transit Commission (TTC) for route information at ☎416/393-4636 or ⓦwww.ttc.ca.

The Beach

The Beach, until recently known in the plural, is located east of Downtown Toronto. In the 1890s and 1900s it was what the Toronto Islands are today: a summer play area on the shores of Lake Ontario. Today The Beach is more residential but overall has retained the look and feel of a turn-of-the-century seaside resort. It has a three-kilometre boardwalk, ample Queen Anne-style houses with generous front porches, and a charming bandshell in Kew Park, which serves as the main stage for the neighbourhood's many festivals. The Beach's successful preservation is remarkable considering Toronto's Downtown core is only twenty minutes away by streetcar.

There are two main sections to The Beach community: **Kew Beach** and **Balmy Beach**, separated from one another by a tiny inlet at the foot of Silver-birch Avenue. The former is the site of **Kew Beach Park**, situated just below Queen Street – a picture-perfect spot with rolling, grassy hills and a sandy beachfront that is delightful even on a packed Sunday afternoon. Slightly west of Kew Beach is **Cherry Beach**, a car-free favourite among hikers, cyclists and bird-watchers, thanks to the nearby bird sanctuaries on the Toronto Islands. Cherry Beach begins at **Ashbridges Bay Park**, which is at the corner of Lakeshore Boulevard East and Coxwell Avenue. Signs inside the park point out the **Martin Goodman Trail**, a hiking route that spans the entire Toronto waterfront to link into the Bruce Trail, a long-distance trail that runs from the Niagara Escarpment to Tobermory at the tip of the Bruce Peninsula in Georgian Bay (for more on this trail, see. p.199).

To get to The Beach from Downtown on **public transport**, take the #501 Queen streetcar east to the stretch between Woodbine and Neville Park stops – about a twenty-minute ride.

Scarborough

Northeast of Downtown, **Scarborough** is perhaps the most dynamic and diverse of Toronto's "inner" suburbs. In terms of major attractions it offers the **Toronto Zoo**, the **Scarborough Bluffs** and adjacent **marina**, plus a number of parks and gardens including the idiosyncratic **Guildwood Park**. It has natural grandeur and offers unimpeded views of Lake Ontario – even if the urban sprawl along the arterial roadways gives no hint of the natural beauty that often lies just beyond the major thoroughfares. Many of these thoroughfares have been enlivened in the last few years by Scarborough's explosive population growth, with new arrivals all making their mark. Entrepreneurs from Hong Kong and mainland China, for example, have transformed boring strip malls into islands of Far East culture, with restaurants, herbalists, and storefront feng shui practitioners. In contrast, some of Toronto's wealthiest enclaves are tucked away discreetly along the many ravines and rivers, notably **Highland Creek** and **Rouge River**, along the lakefront.

Toronto Zoo

When the **Toronto Zoo** (for opening hours and admission prices, see "Zoo practicalities", p.94) reopened in 1974 after the cramped Riverdale Zoo (now Riverdale Farm, see p.204) was closed, it re-emerged as something entirely new: it was the first zoo without cages. Designed by architect Raymond Moriyama (who also designed The Bata Shoe Museum and the Toronto Reference Library), the new Toronto Zoo housed its occupants in biospheric pavilions and outdoor enclosures. Although these habitats are the norm for any credible zoological attraction today, they were a huge innovation at the time, and marked the first step in the gradual disappearance of the sad, caged menagerie-type of zoo.

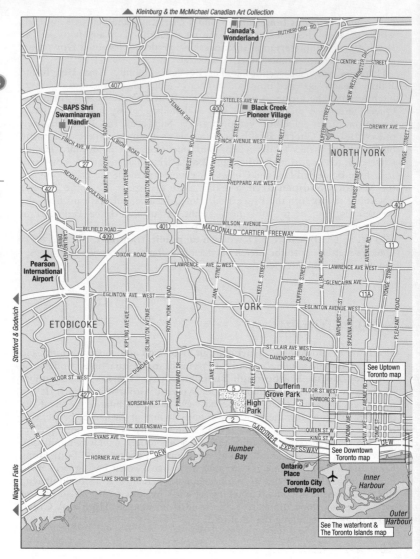

With over five thousand animals representing 460 species, the Toronto Zoo occupies a 287-hectare (710-acre) site on the edge of the Rouge Valley, making it one of the world's largest zoos. The natural setting overlaps indigenous species' habitat with the zoo denizens' enclosures, and raccoons, chipmunks, beavers and foxes from the surrounding woodland are frequently spotted. Hardy species such as moose, Siberian tigers, snow leopards, elk, camels and wolves live outdoors in large, landscaped paddocks. Other animals live in simulations of their own environments, represented by six **zones**: **Indo-Malaya**, **Africa Savannah and Rainforest**, **the Americas**, **Australasian**, **Canadian Domain**, and **Eurasia**. Six pavilions or biospheres – African Rainforest, Indo-Malayan,

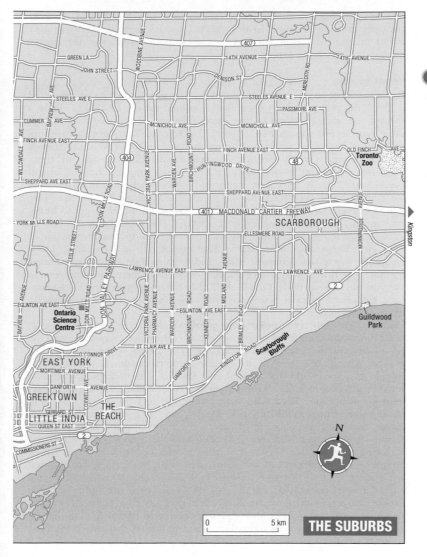

Americas, Malayan Woods, Australasian – are filled with flora indigenous to the resident fauna. The **Zoomobile monorail** ($7) zips around the vast site past grizzly bears, musk, oxen and tapirs, and is a boon to young visitors or those with mobility issues. Otherwise there are 10km of **trails** connecting pavilions and enclosures.

The zoo partakes in a Species Survival Plan for creatures from frogs to elephants and ultimately seeks to successfully reintroduce animals into their natural environment. The publicity machine goes into media overdrive when zoo babies are born, with highly publicized naming contests. In all cases, however, the Toronto Zoo takes its role as an environmental educator seriously. Its conservation programmes, including breeding habitat recovery and species reintroduction, have protected species such as the Vancouver Island marmot, the trumpeter swan, black-footed ferrets and the highly unglamorous Mexican axolotl.

What to see

By far the most popular pavilion is the two-acre **gorilla habitat**. Completed in 2000, this is the world's largest indoor habitat for the Lowland Gorilla, a species now so endangered in their natural habitat of central Africa that all their sizeable populations live in zoos. The Toronto Zoo's gorilla breeding program is in concert with an international attempt to prevent the species from becoming entirely extinct. As well as including an ark for these magnificent primates' physical survival, the habitat supports their social and psychological needs. They have communal spaces and room to roam, trees for climbing and nests for privacy. There's also a unique "interactive" **log**, where visitors can sit on one end and gorillas on the other to get to know one another – albeit through a safety barrier. For those lucky enough to experience such an encounter, the moment of inter-species recognition is both electrifying and unforgettable. The habitat also includes an outdoor enclosure where the dominant males and females hold sway. The younger members of this Lowland Gorilla clan were born here, an achievement the Toronto Zoo is justly proud of. (Other breeding programme successes have included Sumatran tiger cubs and, in a Canadian first, two Komodo dragon hatchlings.)

Another big draw is the **polar bear pool**, which features a step-down glass wall to view the white bears when they cavort underwater. Having admired the polar bears, you should also check out the **grizzly bears**, who never seem like they are having quite as much fun as their northern cousins. On the opposite side of the zoo world, the Australasian Pavilion has undergone extensive revision and now includes a **Great Barrier Reef** exhibit featuring a 23-feet-long (7m-long) tank filled with over a thousand reef fish species. If you're visiting with **younger children** make life easy and take them to the **Discovery Zone**, an educative playground close to the front entrance and Education Centre. From April to October it encompasses the Splash Island Waterpark, including the Waterside Theatre featuring an ever-changing roster of family programming. Youngsters can also enjoy pony rides, camel rides, face painting and simulator rides – Gorilla Rainforest Ride, Swimming with Dolphins Ride and a Canyon Coaster Rides (all tickets $5–$6) – and close encounters with less exotic creatures such as prairie dogs, skunks, or warthog piglets. There are several seasonal and year-round restaurants dominated by fast food outlets. In addition to the expected gift shops there is a plant nursery that reflects the zoo's activities in habitat restoration.

Zoo practicalities

Toronto Zoo (☏416/392-5900, ⓦwww.torontozoo.com) is **open** every day except Christmas (Jan to mid-March 9.30am–4.30pm; mid-March to late May 9.30am–6pm; late May to early Sept 9am–7pm; early Sept to mid-Oct 9am–6pm; mid-Oct to Dec 9.30am–4.30pm; last admission an hour before closing). **Admission** is $20, with discounts for seniors ($14) and children aged 4–12 ($12). Children aged 3 and under go free. The zoo can be reached by **public transport** in about fifty minutes from Downtown: catch the Sheppard East (#85B) bus from the Sheppard subway station year-round, or the Scarborough (#86A) bus from Kennedy Road during the summer season. Both buses go right up to the Zoo's main entrance. Arriving **by car**, take Hwy-401 to Scarborough (exit 389) and drive north on Meadowvale Road, following the signs for the zoo.

Scarborough Bluffs

Toronto's easternmost edge got its European name when Elizabeth Simcoe, wife of Upper Canada's first lieutenant-governor, sailed past and remarked how they reminded her of the **Scarborough** cliffs in England. The **Bluffs** are part of a prehistoric shoreline known as the Iroquois Shoreline and they mark an extent of the preglacial Lake Iroquois, the sixth Great Lake. Both for their great natural beauty and geological significance, the Scarborough Bluffs are preserved within three parks, the most significant of which is **Bluffer's Park**, a 473-acre waterfront space featuring supervised beaches (July and Aug), picnic areas sheltered in groves, snack bars, sports facilities – with everything from cricket and lacrosse to bocce and soccer – a public **marina** for recreational sailors and a private yacht club.

Smaller but nevertheless impressive is **Cathedral Bluffs Park**, where spires of eroded sandstone cliffs rise more than 90m above Lake Ontario, and **Scarborough Heights Park**. All three Bluff parks are part of a continuous strip of lakeshore parkland. To reach Bluffer's Park by **public transport** take the Kingston Road (#12) bus to the Brimley Road stop, from where it's a pleasant five-minute walk to the waterfront. **By car** simply follow Brimley Road south from Kingston Road straight downhill towards Lake Ontario. Scarborough Heights is on Fishleigh Drive, just south of Kingston Road. The waterfront is a short walk south that pleasantly turns from cityscape to country meadow. For more **information** about these or any of Toronto's parks call ☎416/392-8186 or visit ⓦ www.toronto.ca/parks.

▲ Bluffer's Park

Guildwood Park

Another scenic stop along the bluffs is **Guildwood Park** (daily dawn to dusk; ☎416/392-8188; free), spread over the grounds of a large estate acquired in 1932 by Spencer and Rosa Clark, who turned it into a **colony for artists and craftspeople**. Today, the Ontario Crafts Council's Guild Shop on Cumberland Avenue in Yorkville (see p.189) continues as part of that legacy. The Clarks also formed a collection of over seventy **architectural ornaments** from the historic Toronto buildings that were torn down to make way for the skyscrapers that dominate the skyline today. Huge keystones and fanciful patios, gateways, arches and doorways minus their buildings dot the Guildwood Park grounds. (Unfortunately, the Clarks' pseudo-Georgian house did not have a benefactor, and after years of fighting off demolition it burned down in Dec 2008.) Guildwood Park's uninterrupted view of Lake Ontario amid the eclectic, even surrealistic collection of architectural fragments and sculptures makes it a popular spot for film shoots and photographers of all kinds, especially for weddings. The formal gardens are laid out country-estate style, while the wetlands and woods that surround Guildwood have a good cross-section of local flora and some fauna, including increasingly rare woodpeckers.

To get to Guildwood Park by **public transport**, take the Morningside (#116) bus from Kennedy subway station. If you're **driving**, turn south onto Guildwood Parkway from Kingston Road.

East York and North York

Unlike the other cities of Metropolitan Toronto forced to amalgamate into the "Megacity" in 1998 (see p.220), **North York** was lucky enough to have a mayor who went on to become the Toronto megacity mayor – which meant that this suburb emerged from that unfortunate civic exercise in relatively good shape, gaining a new subway line, relocated corporate head offices, jimmied metropolitan boundaries and a real estate boom. Smaller, quieter **East York** is wedged between old Toronto, Scarborough and North York; both suburbs are directly north of Downtown. These two suburbs are filled with attractive, affluent neighbourhoods such as Lawrence Park and Bayview Village, that have their own little clusters of pretty stores, good restaurants and gourmet food shops, as well as one of Toronto's most troubled neighbourhoods, along the axis of Jane Street and Finch Avenue, in North York.

East York gets on itineraries for the excellent **Ontario Science Centre**, while North York's main draw is **Black Creek Pioneer Village**.

The Ontario Science Centre

Since its creation in 1969, the chief purpose of the **Ontario Science Centre**, 770 Don Mills Rd, at Eglinton Avenue East (daily 10am–5pm, and until 6pm Dec 26–Jan 3; $18, seniors and 13–17s $13.50, children 4–12 $11; ☎416/696-1000, ⓦwww.ontariosciencecentre.ca) has been to expose children and young people to the creative workings of science and technology. Today it is the most visited cultural attraction in Canada. It has over six hundred mostly interactive exhibits on the environment, biology, communications and technology in ten exhibition halls built on a wooded ravine site. Three main halls are connected by glassed-in walkways, escalators and bridges that follow the undulating contours of the landscape. Successive facelifts have included additions such an OMNIMAX Theatre and the Weston Family Innovation Centre, which explores the creative side of cutting-edge scientific innovation. Exhibits also tackle subjects at the forefront of scientific inquiry and social concerns. The **Question of Truth** hall, for example, considers supposed scientific "facts" used to validate errors in reasoning from the Ptolemaic universe to racism. Similarly, an exhibit on the **Genome Project** has an ancillary exhibit exploring notions of race. Less weighty exhibits use science to see the world differently utilizing varieties of unconventional musical "instruments" (play music on a water fountain or on pieces of junk; make metal dance; try a word harp, for example), and there are blockbuster exhibits to encourage repeat visits. One of the most popular is **The Human Body**, where visitors can discern the inner workings of human biology through life-sized three-dimensional displays and various quizzes and games. There's also information on complex medical advances like bioengineering, DNA fingerprinting and immunology, all presented in an easily accessible format. Other halls focus on subjects like communications, space and sport. The **Weston Family Innovation Centre** focuses on the latest innovations, debates and challenges in science today.

Like the exhibitions, the **OMNIMAX Theatre** is a big draw at the OSC. The 320-seat theatre features a 24-metre-high wraparound screen with digital sound that creates an enveloping cinematic experience. Admission to the OMNIMAX shows is extra ($12–20). You can get to the Ontario Science Centre in twenty to thirty minutes by **public transport** from Downtown: take the Yonge subway line north to Eglinton station and transfer to the Eglinton East (#34) bus, getting off at Don Mills Road – you will see the Centre beyond its parking lots. Alternatively, take the Bloor–Danforth line east to Pape and then the Don Mills (#25) bus to St Dennis Drive. If you're **driving**, take the Don Valley Parkway and follow the signs from the Don Mills Road North exit. In all cases the signage is excellent and the huge complex is very hard to miss.

Black Creek Pioneer Village

Change may be rampant everywhere else but it's always 1860 in North York's **Black Creek Pioneer Village** (May & June Mon–Fri 9.30am–4pm, Sat & Sun 11am–5pm; July to early Sept Mon–Fri 10am–5pm, Sat & Sun 11am–5pm; early Sept to Dec Mon–Fri 9.30am–4pm, Sat & Sun 11am–4.30pm; $13, children 5–15 $9; ☎416/736-1740, Ⓦwww.blackcreek.ca). Around 25km northwest of Downtown at 1000 Murray Ross Parkway, near the intersection of Steeles Avenue and Jane Street, this 35-building living history "museum" is staffed by interpreters dressed in period costume performing the daily tasks and activities of an **Ontario village** in the 1860s, including open-hearth cooking, blacksmithing, milling, printing, various farming chores, and tending the heritage gardens. From May to December visitors are bystanders to enactments of the various dramas of pioneer life. Of particular interest are the "**Herstory**" **tours** that explore various myths and realities of Ontario women's lives in nineteenth-century rural communities. Special candlelight **Christmas events** and dinners are hot tickets in December (and in a nod to the surrounding community, Hindu Federation Day is also celebrated in Aug).

It takes about 45 minutes to get here on **public transport**: take the Yonge subway line to Finch station then board the Steeles bus (#60 B, D or E) and get off at Murray Ross Parkway (about a 3min walk from the front entrance). **By car**, travel north on Hwy-400 and exit on Steeles Avenue East, then turn west on Murray Ross Parkway, one block east of Jane Street.

BAPs Shri Swaminarayan Mandir

Around 30km northwest of Downtown, at 61 Claireville Drive on the very northern edge of Etobicoke, the spectacular **BAPS Shri Swaminarayan Mandir** (daily 9am–8pm; ☎416/798-2277) rises from the corner of Hwy-427 and Finch Avenue like an intricately carved limestone and marble island, a testament as much to change in Toronto as to faith. In the short space of eighteen months and at a reputed cost of forty million dollars, some 1800 specially trained, faith-based craftsmen from 26 sites made the Hindu temple in India and then shipped it in over three hundred containers to Canada to be assembled in Toronto and opened in 2007 by Prime Minister Harper with great fanfare. The most arresting part of the complex is the stone **Mandir**, a huge building with a lace-like interior carved from white marble and limestone and intended for deep meditation. While visitors are welcome, the buildings are places of worship and visitors are asked to wear clothing that covers their shoulders and knees. Special tours can be arranged by calling ahead. It takes about an hour (or more if the traffic's bad) to reach the temple on **public transport** from Downtown: take the Yonge subway line to Finch Station and catch the #36 Finch Bus west.

Canada's Wonderland

Immediately recognizable by its fake mountain, **Canada's Wonderland** (May–Sept variable opening hours; day-pass covering all rides $31.49 excluding taxes; ☎905/832-7000, ⓦwww.canadas-wonderland.com) offers over two hundred attractions, 65 different **rides** and thirteen bone-rattling **rollercoasters**, scattered over a vast site about 30km north of Downtown in the suburban township of Vaughan. Visiting the park is an all-day proposition: in addition to the rollercoasters, there's a twenty-acre water park called **Splash Works** with sixteen water slides and Canada's largest outdoor wave pool, go-karts, mini-golf and roaming cartoon characters, such as Fred Flintstone and Sponge Bob Square Pants. Live action Hollywood stunt shows with elaborate pyrotechnic effects bring out everyone's inner 10-year old. As well as hosting big-name rock concerts, there are also cultural festivals held here, featuring food, music and family activities from various ethnic communities (the Russian and Eastern European Festival Matryoshka is one such example). On-site facilities include three large theatres, fast-food and licensed restaurants, kitsch-laden shops, and wheelchairs, strollers and lockers.

Canada's Wonderland is located on Hwy-400; if you're **driving** from Downtown, exit at Rutherford Road and follow the signs. To get here by **public transport**, catch the Wonderland Express GO bus from Yorkdale or York Mills subway stations. Buses leave every hour and take forty minutes; an adult one-way fare is $4.90 or $9.80 return.

McMichael Canadian Art Collection

Situated in the village of Kleinburg, about 45km northwest of downtown Toronto, the **McMichael Canadian Art Collection** (daily 10am–4pm; $15, children 5 and under free; ☎905/893-1121, ⓦwww.mcmichael.com) is entirely dedicated to collecting and exhibiting **Canadian art**. Housed in a series of handsome timber and stone buildings in the beautiful wooded Humber River valley, the collection originally belonged to Robert and Signe McMichael, devoted followers of the Group of Seven (see *Canadian Art* colour section). The McMichaels opened their home and art gallery to the public in the early 1960s, and in 1965 they turned their property over to the Province of Ontario.

On the **Lower Level**, a series of small galleries focuses on various aspects of the **Group of Seven**'s work. Gallery Two, for example, begins with the artistic friends and contemporaries who influenced the Group's early style, while Gallery Three zeroes in on the Group's spiritual founder, Tom Thomson, who died in a canoeing accident three years before the Group showed as a collective. The galleries boast fine paintings here by J.E.H. MacDonald, Lawren Harris, Edwin Holgate, F.H. Varley and L.L. Fitzgerald, as well as works by their great contemporary Emily Carr. Other artists who later became associated with the Group of Seven, notably A.J. Casson, are also strongly represented. For those unfamiliar with the Group's work, Lawren Harris's huge, luminous canvasses of Lake Superior Islands, icebergs , mountains and increasingly abstract depictions of the far north are a revelation; and the gallery devoted to the Group's portraiture encourages a deeper appreciation of their work.

The **Upper Level** is devoted primarily to modern **First Nations art** and **Inuit sculpture and prints**, notably the great **Norval Morriseau**, founder of the Woodland School of "X-ray" painting. Rotating temporary exhibitions appear on this level as well. The gallery's recent efforts towards acquiring **contemporary Canadian art** – as opposed to simply collecting and preserving works by the Group of Seven and their contemporaries – generated much controversy until a string of special exhibitions, successful with both the art critics and the box office, quelled further dispute and reintroduced the collection to a younger audience.

After viewing the paintings, allow time to stroll the woodland footpaths surrounding the McMichael Gallery. Free maps are available at reception, pointing the way to installations of sculpture, Tom Thomson's old studio shack, moved here from Rosedale in 1962, and the graves of six Group members.

The easiest way to get here is **by car** (about 50min): from Downtown, take Hwy-401 to Hwy-400 north to Major Mackenzie Drive; turn left (west) on Major Mackenzie Drive to Islington Avenue, then turn right (north) on Islington Avenue to the village of Kleinburg. **Public transport** requires a few transfers: from the Islington subway (on the Bloor–Danforth line), take bus #37 north to Steeles and Islington, then transfer to the York Region bus #13, continuing up Islington to the McMichael Collection entrance. Alternatively, a taxi ride from Islington subway station is about $30.

High Park and Roncesvalles districts

West of downtown Toronto, the High Park and Roncesvalles districts are in a state of flux: over the past few years comparatively inexpensive real estate has attracted young urban families exchanging their lofts for lawns. The shops, cafés and restaurants are quickly changing to keep up with the newcomers' tastes but traces of the Eastern European neighbourhoods remain.

The **High Park district**, flanking the large and verdant High Park, about 5km west of Yonge Street, was once the enclave of Toronto's **Polish community**, which has a long tradition in the city. Poles began settling in Toronto in the middle of the nineteenth century, with subsequent waves of immigration spurred by famine, revolution and war, especially World War II. In the 1950s, along with other Eastern Europeans, they gravitated here to the High Park area, and many Polish families remain today, notwithstanding the recent demographic shifts. By contrast, the strip known as the **Roncesvalles neighbourhood** – running along Roncesvalles Avenue – has changed more dramatically, its little Ukrainian and Eastern European bakeries, perfumed by rye bread and caraway seeds, rapidly being replaced with hip hotdog eateries and alternative clubs and bars.

High Park and Roncesvalles districts are for the most part architecturally undistinguished, consisting of a low tangle of early twentieth-century brick buildings. On the south side of the Gardiner Expressway, however, by the shore of Lake Ontario, is the former site of the **Sunnyside Amusement Park** with its gorgeous Art Deco Bathing Pavilion, and beside it the **Palais Royale dance hall** – Toronto's "it" spots from 1922 to 1955. Sunnyside featured amusements such as all-girl baseball teams and big band swing, including Duke Ellington, Count Bassie, and Guy Lombardo and his Royal Canadians. The **bathing pavilion** survived demolition and remains open during the summer, although the 1925 pool was fully renovated in the 1980s (1755 Lakeshore Blvd W ☎416-531-2233). There is also a little café, a boardwalk along the Lake Ontario beachfront and the western perimeter of the Martin Goodman Trail (see p.91).

High Park

High Park itself is a 161-hectare (399-acre) rectangle of greenery that attracts over a million visitors annually. The park was originally the estate of John George Howard whose descendants bequeathed the property to the city. Their Regency-style home, **Colborne Lodge** (March 10–Oct 10am–4pm; Nov–Feb Sat & Sun noon–4pm; free), is now a museum, restored to its mid-nineteenth-century appearance. John Howard was a keen water colourist and selections of his work are displayed at the lodge. John and his wife Jemima were buried a short stroll north of the lodge beneath the large stone cairn.

The northern half of the park is perfect picnic territory, with tended **lawns** and a scattering of sports facilities. While two-thirds of High Park remains in its natural oak savannah, the park's southwest corner boasts the charming **Hillside Gardens**, a manicured stretch that borders the wooded slopes above **Grenadier Pond**, supposedly named after the drowned British grenadiers who crashed through the ice while parading here in winter (one lurid local legend has a young skater spotting a grinning grenadier frozen under the ice). The pond's ecosystem is currently in a state of recovery after being unbalanced by surrounding neighbourhoods' drain runoffs, and the bass and pike population as well as the indigenous plants are gradually returning. The reclamation of the landscape can be scrutinized from a nearby teahouse and **café**. Midway through the park is the **amphitheatre and stage** for the Canadian Stage Company's popular summer Shakespeare production, Dream in High Park, as well as an annual outdoor poetry slam called The Scream in High Park Literary Festival (ⓦwww.thescream.ca).

Getting here is straightforward: the north side of the park is a short walk from the High Park subway station; the south and east sections are reached on bus #80, which leaves Keele subway station.

Dufferin Grove Park

In 1995 a group of residents of the neighbourhood near the west-end **Dufferin Grove Park** (875 Dufferin St; Dufferin subway) attempted unsuccessfully to lobby the city for a much-needed community centre. Unwilling to admit defeat, these resourceful community activists built a communal **wood-fired oven** inside the park instead. Today there are two large brick, wood-burning ovens about the size of low-slung garden sheds in Dufferin Grove Park. Bread is baked Thursdays between 8am and 2pm by a volunteer organization calling itself Friends of Dufferin Grove Park, also known as "park bakers". The bread is sold at the park's year-round **Farmers' Market**, held Thursdays 3–7pm, and the funds support numerous community projects and activities. Other fundraising, outdoor culinary activities in the park include pizza bakes and communal Friday Night Suppers. The Dufferin Grove bread ovens appear to be an original community project that the Friends of Dufferin Grove Park want to share: their "Cooking With Fire in Public Space" should be read by all community activists; see Ⓦ www.dufferinpark.ca/oven/bakeoven.html, or call ☎ 416/392-0913 for more information. The park also features more conventional facilities such as a winter skating rink, a summer soccer pitch, baseball diamond, a wading pool, and badminton nets.

5

Day-trips

One of the most celebrated sights in North America, **Niagara Falls** is without a doubt the most popular day-trip destination from Toronto. A vast arc of water crashing over a 52-metre cliff, the falls are just 130km south of the city, along and around the heavily industrialized Lake Ontario shoreline. They adjoin the uninspiring **town of Niagara Falls**, which bills itself as the "Honeymoon Capital of the World" – and its hotels and motels have the heart-shaped double beds to prove it. Much more enticing, especially as a place to overnight, is the charming little town of **Niagara-on-the-Lake**, whose colonial villas abut Lake Ontario 26km downstream from the falls.

Less familiar, to foreigners at least, is the **Lake Huron shoreline**, 210km west of Toronto across a thick band of fertile farmland, whose southern reaches are dotted with pretty little country towns, most memorably **Goderich** and **Bayfield**. The first possesses a charming small-town air and one key sight, the fascinating **Huron Historic Gaol**; the second is graced by leafy streets and elegant clapboard villas, a far cry from the fast-food joints and neon billboards of many a Canadian town. In between Toronto and the Lake Huron shoreline is **Stratford**, a pleasant, middling little village, which puts on North America's largest classical theatre festival every year from May to November.

A couple of hours north of Toronto by car is **Severn Sound**, the southeastern inlet of **Georgian Bay**, whose bare, glacier-shaved rocks, myriad lakes and spindly pines were immortalized by the Group of Seven painters (see p.63). This is one of the most beautiful parts of southern Ontario, and, although the region is dotted with country cottages, its pristine landscapes have been conserved in the **Georgian Bay Islands National Park**, accessible by water taxi from the tiny resort of **Honey Harbour**. Also on Severn Sound are two outstanding historical reconstructions: the seventeenth-century Jesuit complex of **Sainte-Marie among the Hurons** and the British naval base at **Discovery Harbour**, founded outside Penetanguishene in 1817.

Buses and trains link Toronto with Niagara Falls, but otherwise you'll be struggling to reach any of the other destinations mentioned above by **public transportation**; car rental is, however, reasonably priced – see p.22 for more information.

DAY-TRIPS

Kingston ▶

◀ Goderich & Bayfield

◀ Stratford

Algonquin Park

Georgian Bay

Georgian Bay Islands

Severn Sound

Honey Harbour

Penetanguishene

Ste Marie among the Hurons

Midland

Nottawasaga Bay

Lake Simcoe

Richmond Hill • Markham

Kleinburg •

Toronto

See Toronto maps

Lake Ontario   CANADA
                USA

Niagara-on-the-Lake

Niagara Falls

Welland •

Buffalo

CANADA
USA

Lake Erie

N

0   25 km

Niagara Falls

In 1860, thousands watched as **Charles Blondin** walked a tightrope across **Niagara Falls**. Midway, he paused to cook an omelette on a portable grill, and then had a marksman shoot a hole through his hat from the *Maid of the Mist* boat, fifty metres below. As attested by Blondin's antics, and by the millions of waterlogged tourists who jam the tour boats and observation points, Niagara Falls is a dramatic attraction – but the stupendous first impression doesn't last long. To prevent each year's crop of visitors from getting bored, the Niagarans have created an infinite number of vantage points. You can take in the 52-metre cascade from boats, viewing towers, helicopters, cable cars and even tunnels in the rock face behind the falls. Of these options, the tunnels and boats best capture the extraordinary force of the waterfall, a perpetual white-crested thundering pile-up that had composer Gustav Mahler bawling "At last, fortis-simo!" over the din.

Arrival

From Toronto, there are fast and frequent **Coach Canada buses** (℡1-800/461-7661, ⓦwww.coachcanada.com) to the town of Niagara Falls and there's also a less frequent VIA **train** service (℡1-888/842-7245, ⓦwww.viarail.ca). By train or bus, the journey time from Toronto is about two hours. The train is the more scenic way to travel, but delays on the return leg – on which the evening train originates in New York – can be a real pain. If you're travelling by **car**, a day is more than enough time to see the falls and squeeze in a visit to Niagara-on-the-Lake, just 26km downstream.

Trains to Niagara Falls pull in at the **VIA train station** on Bridge Street, in the commercial heart of the town, 3km north of the falls themselves. The **bus station** is across the street at Bridge Street and Erie Avenue. **Car drivers** should be aware that **parking** anywhere near the falls can be a major hassle in the summer. Try to arrive before 9.30am when there's usually space in the car park beside Table Rock House, metres from the waterfall; any later and you can expect a long line. Another hassle can be crossing the **international border** over to the US; it only takes a few minutes to walk across Rainbow Bridge from Canada into the US, but the return journey can take literally hours, depending on border control.

Information – and the Great Gorge Adventure Pass

For **visitor information**, steer clear of the gaggle of privately run tourist centres that spring up here and there, now and again, and head instead for the main **Niagara Parks information centre** (℡905/371-0254 or 1-877/642-7275, ⓦwww.niagaraparks.com), at the Table Rock complex beside the falls. Here, and elsewhere, but only from mid-April to late October, you can purchase the **Niagara Falls Great Gorge Adventure Pass**, the most productive of several discount deals on offer, a combined ticket covering four of the main attractions (Journey Behind the Falls, Maid of the Mist, White Water Walk and the Butterfly Conservatory) plus all-day transportation on the People Mover system; the pass can also be purchased at each of the four attractions and currently costs $35 for adults and $22 for children aged 6–12.

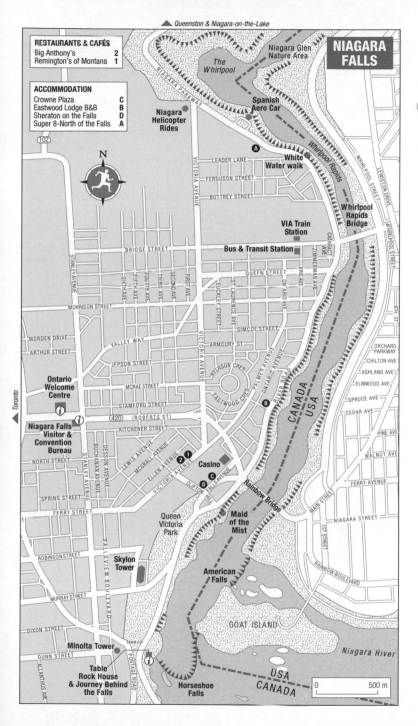

▲ Queenston & Niagara-on-the-Lake

NIAGARA FALLS

RESTAURANTS & CAFÉS
Big Anthony's   2
Remington's of Montana 1

ACCOMMODATION
Crowne Plaza   C
Eastwood Lodge B&B   B
Sheraton on the Falls   D
Super 8-North of the Falls A

Niagara Glen
Nature Area

The
Whirlpool

Spanish
Aero Car

(102)

Niagara
Helicopter
Rides

NIAGARA PARKWAY

Whirlpool Rapids

LEWISTON DRIVE

WHIRLPOOL STREET

N

LEADER LANE

White
Water walk

FERGUSON STREET

BUTTREY STREET

VIA Train
Station

Whirlpool
Rapids
Bridge

Bus & Transit Station

VICTORIA AVENUE

CATARACT AVE

ZIMMERMAN AVE

ERIE AVE

QUEEN STREET

BRIDGE STREET

STANLEY AVENUE

SIXTH AVE

FIFTH AVE

FOURTH AVE

THIRD AVE

SECOND AVE

FIRST AVE

ST LAURENCE AVE

BUCKLEY STREET

ONTARIO AVE

8TH ST

MORRISON STREET

VALLEY WAY

SIMCOE STREET

ORCHARD
PARKWAY

MORDEN DRIVE

JEPSON STREET

ARMOURY ST

CHILTON AVE

ARTHUR STREET

MCRAE STREET

RYERSON CRES

PALMER AVENUE

ASHLAND AVE

ELMWOOD AVE

Ontario
Welcome
Centre
ⓘ

STAMFORD STREET

EASTWOOD CRES

RIVER ROAD

CANADA

USA

SPRUCE AVE

CEDAR AVE

(420) (ROBERTS ST)

Ⓑ

Niagara Falls
Visitor &
Convention
Bureau
ⓘ

KITCHENER STREET

PINE AVE

NORTH STREET

LEWIS AVENUE

MCGRALL AVENUE

ELLEN AVENUE

BUCHANAN AVENUE

DESSON AVENUE

STANLEY AVENUE

WALNUT AVE

SPRING STREET

VICTORIA HILL

CLIFTON HILL

2 ❶
Casino
Ⓒ
Ⓓ

FALLS AVENUE

FERRY AVENUE

FERRY STREET

ROBINSON STREET

FALLSVIEW BOULEVARD

Queen
Victoria
Park

Rainbow Bridge

MAIN STREET

1ST STREET

NIAGARA STREET

MURRAY STREET

Maid of the
Mist

RAINBOW BOULEVARD

Skylon
Tower

American
Falls

DIXON STREET

Minolta Tower

GOAT ISLAND

Niagara River

DUNN STREET

Table
Rock House
& Journey Behind
the Falls

PORTAGE ROAD

ALLANTHUS AVE

Horseshoe
Falls

USA
CANADA

0   500 m

▲ Toronto

There's also the municipal **Niagara Falls Tourism Office**, just off Stanley Avenue beside the Skylon Tower at 5400 Robinson St (Mon–Fri 8am–6pm, Sat & Sun 10am–6pm; ℡905/356-6061, ⓦwww.niagarafallstourism.com), which has a full range of information on the town and the falls and will – if required – help you find a place to stay.

Getting around

Next door to the bus station is **Niagara Transit** (℡905/356-1179, ⓦwww .niagarafalls.ca), which operates a limited range of town and suburban services. The most useful is the **Falls Shuttle** (mid-May to early Oct daily every 30min–1hr; single ticket $2.25), which runs across town, stopping – amongst many other places – at the foot of Clifton Hill, a few minutes walk from the falls. The Shuttle links with the very handy Niagara Parks' **People Mover System** (late May to mid-Oct daily 9/10am–6pm, 8/9pm; ⓦwww .niagaraparks.com), whose buses travel 30km along the riverbank between Queenston Heights Park, downriver (north) from the falls – a little more than halfway towards Niagara-on-the-Lake – and the Rapids' View car park just to the south, pausing at all the major attractions in between. People Movers appear at twenty-minute intervals and an all-day pass costs $7.50, $4.50 for children ages 6–12.

There's also public transport from Niagara Falls to Niagara-on-the-Lake with **5-0 Transportation** (℡905/358-3232 or 1-800/268-7429, ⓦwww.5-0taxi .com), whose minibuses run two or three times daily in each direction; a single adult fare costs $10, $18 return. There is, however, no public transport up-river beyond the Rapids' View car park.

Accommodation

Niagara Falls is billed as the "Honeymoon Capital of the World", which means that many of its **motels and hotels** have an odd mix of plain and basic rooms and gaudy suites with heart-shaped bathtubs, waterbeds and the like. Quite what the connection is between water and nuptial bliss is hard to fathom – but there it is. In summer, hotel and motel rooms fill up fast and prices rocket, so either ring ahead or seek help from Niagara Falls Tourism (see p.104). Out of season it's a buyer's market, which means that haggling can often bring the price way down. The least expensive choices are out along **Lundy's Lane**, an extremely dispiriting motel strip that extends west of the falls for several kilometres. You're much better off spending a little more to stay either in the **Clifton Hill area**, which has – once you've adjusted to it – a certain kitsch charm, or on leafy **River Road**, running downriver from the foot of Clifton Hill. If you want a room with a decent **view of the falls**, you'll be paying premium rates. The premier hotels on **Falls Avenue**, beside Clifton Hill, and **Fallsview Boulevard**, on top of the ridge directly above the falls, offer the best views but you should always check the room before you shell out: descriptions can be fairly elastic and some rooms claiming to be in sight of the falls require minor gymnastics for a glimpse.

Crowne Plaza Hotel **5685 Falls Ave** ℡905/374-4444 or 1-800/263-7135, ⓦwww .niagarafallshotels.com/brock/. Just metres from the foot of Clifton Hill, this is one of Niagara's older and most attractive hotels, a tidy tower block with Art Deco flourishes whose upper storeys (and more expensive rooms) have splendid views over the American Falls. Marilyn Monroe stayed here in Room #801 while filming *Niagara* – and you can stay here too for no extra charge. Formerly the *Hotel General Brock*. Doubles from $150.

Eastwood Lodge B&B 5359 River Rd
℡905/354-8686, ⒲www.bbcanada.com/685
.html. Six commodious, a/c en-suite
bedrooms in a rambling old villa with wide
balconies and attractive garden. Doubles
from $139.

Sheraton on the Falls 5875 Falls Ave
℡905/374-4445 or 1-888/229-9961,
⒲www.niagarafallshotels.com/sheraton/. A
walloping skyrise, whose upper floors have
wondrous views of the American Falls. Large
and well-appointed rooms with supremely
comfortable beds. Doubles from $150.

Super 8 – North of the Falls 4009 River Rd
℡905/356-0131 or 1-800/565-0035, ⒲www
.niagarawatersedgeinn.com. Comfortable if
unexceptional motel in attractive location,
flanked by parkland near the Aero Car (see
p.108). Doubles from $70 to as much as
$500 at peak times.

The falls

Though you can hear the growl of the **falls** from miles away, nothing quite prepares you for your first glimpse – the fearsome white arc shrouded in clouds of dense spray, with riverboats struggling far below. There are actually two cataracts, as the USA's tiny **Goat Island** (which must be one of the wettest places on earth) divides the accelerating water into two channels: on the American side, the river slips over the precipice of the **American Falls**, 320m wide but still only half the width of **Horseshoe Falls**, on the Canadian side. The spectacle is even more extraordinary in winter, when snow-covered trees edge a jagged armoury of freezing mist and heaped ice blocks.

This may look like a scene of untrammelled nature, but it isn't. Since the early twentieth century, **hydroelectric schemes** have greatly reduced the water flow, and all sorts of tinkering has spread what's left of the Niagara River more evenly across the falls' crest line. As a result, the process of **erosion** – which has moved the falls some 11km upstream in twelve thousand years – has slowed from one metre a year to just 30cm. This obviously has advantages for the tourist industry, but the environmental consequences of harnessing the river in such a way are still unclear.

Beside Horseshoe Falls, **Table Rock House** has a small, free **observation platform** and elevators that travel to the base of the cliff, where **tunnels** (Jan–June Mon–Fri 9am–5.30pm, Sat & Sun 9am–7.30pm; June–Sept Mon–Fri 9am–8.30pm, Sat & Sun 9am–9.30pm; Sept & Oct daily 9am–8pm; Nov & Dec daily 9am–7pm; $12), grandly named the "**Journey Behind the Falls**", lead to points directly behind the waterfall – and here you really do get a sense of its power. For a more panoramic view, a small **Incline Railway** ($2) takes visitors up the hill behind Table Rock House to the **Minolta Tower**, 6732 Fallsview Boulevard (daily: June–Sept 9am–11pm, Oct–May 9am–10pm; $8; ⒲www .niagaratower.com), which has its own elevated observation decks.

Back at Table Rock House, a wide and often crowded path leads north along the cliffs above the gorge, with the manicured lawns of **Queen Victoria Park** to the left and views of the American Falls to the right. At the end of the park is **Clifton Hill**, the main drag linking the riverside with the town of Niagara Falls. From the jetty below Clifton Hill, **Maid of the Mist boats** edge out into the river and push up towards the falls, an exhilarating and extremely damp trip that no one should miss (daily: May to late June 9.45am–4.45/5.45pm; late June to early Aug 9am–7.45pm; early to late Aug 9am–7.15pm; Sept to late Oct 9.45am–4.45/5.45pm; boats leave every 15min in high season, otherwise every 30min; $14.50, $8.90 for children ages 6–12, including waterproofs; ℡905/358–5781, ⒲www.maidofthemist.com).

Clifton Hill itself is a tawdry collection of fast-food joints and bizarre attractions, from the innocuous "House of Frankenstein" to the eminently missable "Ripley's Believe It or Not!" where, amongst other wonders, you can spot a cat with two heads. Just off Clifton Hill, near the Rainbow Bridge on Falls Avenue, is one of the town's two 24-hour **casinos**, a bristlingly modern structure where – to use the old cliché – college kids can watch their parents fritter away their inheritance; the other is up on Fallsview Boulevard. If you're keen to avoid all this commercialization, then stick to the **riverside** where the Niagara Parks Commission keeps everything in order. There are a string of attractions further downstream, beginning with the White Water Walk, 3km away (see below).

Eating

There are literally dozens of cheap chain **restaurants** and fast-food joints along and around Clifton Hill, but for something rather more distinctive you'll have to venture a little further afield – to **Victoria Avenue** at the top of Clifton Hill, though even here pickings are thin.

Big Anthony's 5677 Victoria Ave ☎ 905/354-9844. Tasty, reasonably priced Italian food at this small, well-known restaurant named after a one–time professional wrestler, pictures of whom decorate the walls. Pizzas from $12. Close to Clifton Hill.

Remington's of Montana 5657 Victoria Ave ☎ 905/356-4410. Bright, attractively decorated restaurant, serving well–prepared steaks and seafood. Steaks from $15 and up.

Downstream from the falls

The **Niagara River Recreation Trail** is a combined bicycle and walking track that travels the entire length of the Niagara River from Lake Erie down to Lake Ontario; for most of its 58km it runs parallel to the main road, the scenic **Niagara Parkway**. Downstream from the falls, trail and parkway cut across the foot of Clifton Hill (see p.107) before continuing north for a further 3km to reach the **White Water Walk** (daily: April to mid-May 9am–4.30pm; mid-May to mid-June 9am–6pm; mid-June to early Sept 9am–7pm; early Sept to late Nov 9am–5pm; $8.50). This comprises an elevator and then a tunnel, which leads to a boardwalk overlooking the Whirlpool Rapids, where the river seethes and fizzes as it makes an abrupt turn to the east.

From here, it's a further 1km along the parkway to the brightly painted **Whirlpool Aero Car** (daily: early March to late June 9am–4.45pm; late June to early Sept 9am–7.45pm; early Sept to mid-Nov 9am–4.45pm; $11), a cable-car ride across the gorge that's as near as you'll come to emulating Blondin's tightrope antics.

Niagara Glen to the Butterfly Conservatory

Pushing on, it's another short hop to the **Niagara Glen Nature Reserve** (daily dawn–dusk; free), where paths lead down from the clifftop to the bottom of the gorge. It's a hot and sticky trek in the height of the summer, and strenuous at any time of the year, but rewarding for all that – here at least (and at last) you get a sense of what the region was like before all the tourist hulla-baloo. Nearby, about 800m further downstream along the parkway, lies the Niagara Parks Commission's pride and joy, the immensely popular **Niagara Parks Botanical Gardens** (daily dawn–dusk; free), whose various themed gardens – rose, parterre and so forth – flank the huge, climate-controlled **Butterfly Conservatory** (daily: early March to mid-June 9am–6pm; mid-June to early Sept 9am–9pm; early Sept to early Oct 9am–6pm; early Oct to early March 9am–5pm; $11), which houses over two thousand exotic butterflies in a tropical rainforest setting.

Queenston Heights Park and Queenston

About 3km further on, **Queenston Heights Park** marks the original location of the falls, before the force of the water – as it adjusts to the hundred-metre differential between lakes Erie and Ontario – eroded the riverbed to its present point, 11km upstream. Soaring above the park is a grandiloquent monument to **Sir Isaac Brock**, the British-born general who was killed here in the War of 1812, leading a head-on charge against the invading Americans.

From beside the park, the Niagara Parkway begins a curving descent down to the little village of **QUEENSTON**, whose importance as a transit centre disappeared in 1829 when the falls were bypassed by the Welland Canal, which runs west of the river between lakes Erie and Ontario. In the village, on Queenston Street, the **Laura Secord Homestead** (guided tours: early May to June Mon–Fri 9.30am–3.30pm, Sat & Sun 11am–5pm; July to early Sept daily 11am–5pm; $4.50) is a reconstruction of the substantial timber-frame house of Massachusetts-born Laura Ingersoll Secord (1775–1868). It was from here, during the War of 1812, that Secord proved her dedication to the imperial interest by walking 30km through the woods to warn a British platoon of a surprise attack planned by the Americans. As a result, the British and their native allies laid an ambush and captured over five hundred Americans at the Battle of Beaver Dams. The house itself is of elegant proportions and equipped with period furnishings and fittings; the tour provides an intriguing introduction to Secord's life and times.

From Queenston, it's about 12km to Niagara-on-the-Lake.

Niagara-on-the-Lake

Boasting elegant clapboard houses and verdant, mature gardens, all spread along tree-lined streets, **NIAGARA-ON-THE-LAKE**, 26km downstream from the falls, is one of Ontario's most charming little towns, much of it dating from the early nineteenth century. The town was originally known as Newark and became the first capital of Upper Canada in 1792, but four years later it lost this distinction to York (Toronto) because it was deemed too close to the American frontier, and therefore vulnerable to attack. The US army did,

The Shaw Festival

Showcasing the work of the second-largest repertory theatre company in Canada after Stratford's (see p.115), Niagara-on-the-Lake's **Shaw Festival** is the only festival in the world devoted solely to the works of George Bernard Shaw and his contemporaries. Indeed, it is mandated to produce only plays written in the playwright's lifetime (1856–1950), which the company refer to as "plays about the beginning of the modern world". Performances are held in four theatres. The largest is the Festival Theatre, a modern structure seating 850 people at 10 Queen's Parade and incorporating the Studio Theatre; the other two theatres are the Court House, a nineteenth-century stone building at 26 Queen Street, and the Royal George, with its fancy Edwardian interior at 85 Queen Street. **Ticket prices** for the best seats at prime weekend performances hit $110, but most seats go for around $50. The box office for all four theatres is on ☎1-800/511-7429, or book online at ⓦ www.shawfest.com. The festival runs from April to late November.

in fact, cross the river in 1813, destroying the town, but it was quickly rebuilt and renamed. Even better, it has managed to avoid all but the most sympathetic of modifications ever since, except just away from the centre down on Melville Street, where a rash of new development and a marina add nothing to the appeal of the place. Niagara-on-the-Lake attracts a few too many day-trippers for its own good, but the crowds are rarely oppressive, except on weekends in July and August. The town is also popular as the location of one of Canada's most acclaimed theatre festivals, the **Shaw Festival**, which celebrates the works of George Bernard Shaw with performances from April to late October, and is surrounded by **wineries**, many of which welcome visitors (see box, p.113).

Arrival and information

A reliable **minibus service** linking Niagara Falls and Niagara-on-the-Lake is provided two or three times daily by **5-0 Transportation** (☎905/358-3232 or 1-800/667-0256, ⓦwww.5-0taxi.com), who charge $10 for the one-way fare, $18 return. The Niagara-on-the-Lake **tourist office** is on the main drag at 26 Queen St, in the lower level of the Court House (daily:

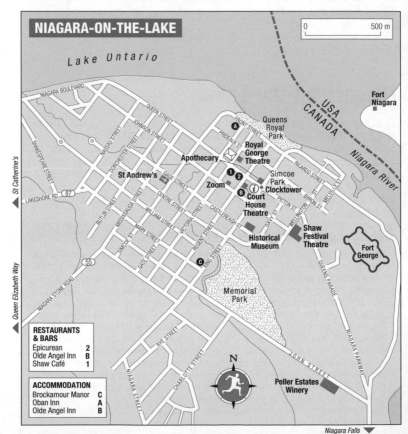

NIAGARA-ON-THE-LAKE

0 — 500 m

Lake Ontario

Niagara Boulevard

Queen Street

Johnson Street

Mary Street

Nassau Street

Dorchester Street

Simcoe Street

Gate Street

Mississauga Street

Centre Street

Victoria Street

Regent Street

King Street

Gage Street

Front Street

Prideaux St

Ricardo Street

Davy St

Castlereagh St

Picton St

Byron St

Melville St

Wellington

Shakespeare Street

St Catherine's ◀

Lakeshore Rd

87

Butler Street

William Street

55

Niagara Stone Road

Queen Elizabeth Way ◀

Rye Street

Niagara Street

Charlotte Street

John Street

Queens Parade

Niagara Parkway

USA
CANADA

Niagara River

Fort Niagara ■

Queens Royal Park

Royal George Theatre

Apothecary

St Andrew's

Zoom

ⓐ

① ②

ⓘ Clocktower

Simcoe Park

ⓑ **Court House Theatre**

Historical Museum

Shaw Festival Theatre

Fort George

ⓒ

Memorial Park

N

Peller Estates Winery

RESTAURANTS & BARS
Epicurean   **2**
Olde Angel Inn   **B**
Shaw Café   **1**

ACCOMMODATION
Brockamour Manor   **C**
Oban Inn   **A**
Olde Angel Inn   **B**

Niagara Falls ▼

▲ Niagara-on-the-Lake

May–Oct 10am–7.30pm; Nov–April 10am–5pm; ☎905/468-1950, ⓦwww
.niagaraonthelake.com). They issue town maps and operate a free **room
reservation service**, which can be a great help in the summer when the
town's hotels and B&Bs – of which there are dozens – get very busy.

It only takes a few minutes to stroll from one end of town to the other, but
to venture further afield – especially to the falls – you might consider renting a
bicycle from Zoom, out at 2017 Niagara Stone Rd, which doubles as Hwy-55
(☎905/468-2366 or 1-866/811-6993, ⓦwww.zoomleisure.com).

Accommodation

Brockamour Manor 433 King St, at Mary ☎ 905/468-5527, ⊛ www.brockamour.com. This elegant B&B has six en-suite guest rooms ranging from the commodious Sir Brock's Bedchamber to the two smaller rooms in the old servants' quarters. With its high gables and wide veranda, the house itself is a splendid affair dating from 1812, surrounded by an attractive wooded garden. Doubles from $225.

Oban Inn 160 Front St ☎ 905/468-2165 or 1-866/359-6226, ⊛ www.obaninn.ca. A delightful and luxurious hotel across from the lake and within easy walking distance of the town centre. The original Oban burnt to the ground in 1992, but its replacement was built in full-flush colonial style, with an elegant wooden veranda. The gardens are beautiful and the breakfasts are first-rate. Doubles from $260.

Olde Angel Inn 224 Regent St, just off Queen St ☎ 905/468-3411, ⊛ www.angel-inn.com. Dating from the 1820s, this is the oldest inn in town. Offers a handful of simple but perfectly adequate rooms in the main building and a couple of annexe-cottages too. Doubles $100.

The Town

It's the general flavour of Niagara-on-the-Lake that appeals, rather than any specific sight, but **Queen Street**, the main drag, does hold a pretty **clock tower** and the **Apothecary** (mid-May to Sept daily noon–6pm; free), which is worth a peep for its beautifully carved walnut and butternut cabinets, crystal gasoliers and porcelain jars. Nearby, the town's finest building is the church of **St Andrews**, at Simcoe and Gage streets, a splendid illustration of the Greek Revival style dating to the 1830s. The church has a beautifully proportioned portico and the interior retains the original high pulpit and box pews. From here, it's a brief stroll to the **Niagara Historical Museum** at 43 Castlereagh St and Davy (daily: May–Oct 10am–5pm; Nov–April 1–5pm; $5; ⊛ www.niagarahistorical.museum), whose accumulated tackle trawls the early history of the town and includes mementoes of the Laura Secord family (see p.109). Also of interest is the fenced **burial plot in Simcoe Park**, at King and Byron streets, which holds the earthly remains of 25 Polish soldiers who died here during the great influenza epidemic of 1918–1919.

Polish soldiers in Niagara-on-the-Lake

In the later stages of World War I, over twenty thousand **Poles** mustered in the US to form a Polish brigade. It was a delicate situation, as the Allies needed the soldiers but the Poles were committed to the creation of an independent Poland at a time when their country was ruled by Russia, an ally of the US. In the event, policy differences with the US government prompted the Poles to move over the border to Niagara-on-the-Lake, where they established a base camp. Paid and equipped by France, the Poles were trained by Canadian officers and then shipped off in batches to fight on the Western front, thereby deferring their attempts to create an independent Poland. At the end of the war, with the Tsar gone and the Bolsheviks in control of Russia, the Polish brigade – or **"Blue Army"** as it was called from the colour of their uniform – crossed Germany to return to their homeland, where they played a key role in the foundation of an independent Poland. The graves of the 25 soldiers here in Niagara recall these historical complexities, and a wooden shrine has been erected in their honour.

Ontario wines

Until the 1980s **Canadian wine** was something of a joke. The industry's most popular product was a sticky, fizzy concoction called "Baby Duck", and other varieties were commonly called "block-and-tackle" wines, after a widely reported witticism of a member of the Ontario legislature: "If you drink a bottle and walk a block, you can tackle anyone." This state of affairs was, however, transformed by the **Vintners Quality Alliance** (VQA; ❦www.vqaontario.com), who have, since 1989, come to exercise tight control over wine production in Ontario, which produces around eighty percent of Canadian wine. The VQA's appellation system distinguishes between – and supervises the quality control of – two broad types of wine. Those wines carrying the **Provincial Designation** on their labels must be made from one hundred percent Ontario-grown vines from an approved list of European varieties of grape and selected hybrids; those bearing the **Geographic Designation** (ie, Niagara Peninsula, Pelee Island or Lake Erie North Shore), by comparison, can only use *Vitis vinifera*, the classic European grape varieties, such as Riesling, Chardonnay and Cabernet Sauvignon. As you might expect from a developing wine area, the results are rather inconsistent, but the **Rieslings** have a refreshingly crisp, almost tart flavour with a mellow, warming aftertaste – and are perhaps the best of the present range, white or red. More than twenty **wineries** are clustered in the vicinity of **Niagara-on-the-Lake**, and most are very willing to show visitors around. Local tourist offices carry a full list with opening times, but one of the most interesting is **Inniskillin**, Line 3 (Service Road 66), just off the Niagara Parkway, about 5km south of Niagara-on-the-Lake (daily: May–Oct 10am–6pm; Nov–April 10am–5pm; ☎905/468-2187, ❦www.inniskillin.com). Here you can follow a free self-guided tour or take a guided tour ($5), sip away at the tasting bar and buy at the wine boutique. Inniskillin has produced a clutch of award-winning vintages and played a leading role in the improvement of the industry. They are also one of the few Canadian wineries to produce **ice wine**, an outstanding sweet dessert wine made from grapes that are left on the vine till December or January, when they are hand-picked at night while frozen; there is also a slightly tarter sparkling ice wine. The picking and the crushing of the frozen grapes is a time-consuming business and this is reflected in the price – from about $60 per 375ml bottle of either sparkling or regular. Even handier for Niagara-on-the-Lake is the **Peller Estates winery**, which follows the same visitor format as Inniskillin, but is within walking distance of the town centre at 290 John St East (call for times on ☎905/468-4678; ❦www.peller.com).

Fort George

There's more military stuff not too far away at the one-time British outpost of **Fort George** (May–Oct daily 10am–5pm; April & Nov Sat & Sun only 10am–5pm; $11.70, ❦www.pc.gc.ca), located 700m southeast of the town centre via Picton Street. In the early nineteenth century, so many of the fort's soldiers were hightailing it off to the States that the British had to garrison it with the Royal Canadian Rifle Regiment, a troop of primarily married men approaching retirement who were unlikely to forfeit their pensions by deserting. If they did try and were caught, they were branded on the chest with the letter "D" (for "Deserter"), and were either lashed or transported to a penal colony – except in wartime, when they were shot.

Built in the 1790s as one of a line of stockades that was slung across the Great Lakes to protect Canada from the US, the original Fort George was destroyed during the War of 1812, but the site was thoroughly excavated and the fort

▲ Peller Estates winery

reconstructed in splendid style in the 1930s. Today, the palisaded **compound**, with its protective bastions, holds about a dozen buildings, among them the officers' quarters and two log blockhouses, which doubled as soldiers' barracks. The difference between the quarters and the barracks is striking. The former are comparatively spacious and were once – as recorded on shipping lists – furnished with fancy knick-knacks, while the latter housed the men and some of their wives (six wives out of every hundred were allowed to join the garrison) in the meanest of conditions. A tunnel links the main part of the fort with one of the exterior bastions, or ravelins, which is itself the site of a third, even stronger blockhouse. The only original building is the **powder magazine** of 1796, its interior equipped with wood and copper fittings to reduce the chances of an accidental explosion; as an added precaution, the soldiers working here went barefoot. There are also ninety-minute lantern-light **ghost tours** of the fort – good fun with or without an apparition (May–June Sun 8.30pm; July & Aug Sun, Mon, Wed, Thurs & Fri 8.30pm; Sept Sun 7.30pm; $10; ☎905/468-6621). Tours begin at the car park in front of the fort; **tickets** can be purchased either in advance at the fort's gift shop, or from the guide at the beginning of the tour.

Eating and drinking

By sheer weight of numbers, the day-trippers set the gastronomic tone hereabouts, but one or two good **cafés and restaurants** have survived the flood to offer tasty meals and snacks.

Epicurean 84 Queen St. Inexpensive but very competent café, featuring Mediterranean dishes. Vegetarian options offered most days; sandwiches $6–9. Daily 9am–9pm.

Olde Angel Inn 224 Regent St. With its low-beamed ceilings and flagstone floors, this is the town's most atmospheric pub, serving a first-rate range of draught imported and domestic beers.

Also offers filling and very affordable bar food – Guinness steak-and-kidney pies and so forth from $9 – and has a smart à la carte restaurant at the back. Just off Queen St.

Shaw Café and Wine Bar 92 Queen St, at Victoria. This café-restaurant caters to theatre-goers rather than day-trippers. The decor is a tad overdone, but the pastas and salads (from $10) are appetizing and well prepared. Closes 8pm.

Stratford, Goderich and Bayfield

Heading west from Toronto, you eventually escape the city's sprawling suburbs and satellite townships to emerge in **rural Ontario**, a sprawling chunk of flat and fertile farmland that extends as far as the shores of Lake Huron. The first place which calls for a stop is **Stratford**, an attractive little town about 160km from Toronto that is famous for its theatre festival – and has a goodly crop of B&Bs as a consequence. From here it's another short haul (about 60km) to the **Lake Huron shoreline**. Popular with holidaying Canadians, the lakeshore is trimmed by sandy beaches and a steep bluff, which is interrupted by the occasional river valley. Lake Huron is much less polluted than Lake Ontario, the sunsets are beautiful, and in **Goderich** and neighbouring **Bayfield** it possesses two of the most appealing places in the whole of the province.

Stratford makes for an easy day-trip from Toronto, but Lake Huron is a tad too far for comfort and it's better to stay the night – Bayfield has the choicer accommodation. There are good **bus and train** services from Toronto to Stratford, but there is no **public transport** to either Goderich or Bayfield.

Stratford

STRATFORD is a likeable town of 30,000 people, whose downtown is brightened by the meandering **River Avon** and a grandiose **city hall**, a brown-brick confection of cupolas, towers and limestone trimmings. More importantly, the town is home to the **Stratford Festival**, which started in 1953 and is now one of the most prestigious theatrical occasions in North America, attracting no fewer than half a million visitors each and every year.

The Stratford Festival

Each season, North America's largest classical repertory company puts on the **Stratford Festival** (☎1-800/567-1600, ⊕www.stratfordfestival.ca), featuring two of Shakespeare's tragedies and one of his comedies; this programme is augmented by other classical staples – Molière, Sheridan, Johnson and so forth – as well as by the best of modern and musical theatre. The festival also hosts a lecture series, various tours (of backstage and a costume warehouse, for example), music concerts, an author reading series and meet-and-greet sessions with the actors. The festival runs from mid-April to early November and there are performances in four downtown locations – the Festival, Tom Patterson, Avon and Studio theatres. Regular **tickets** cost anywhere between $40 and $100 depending on the performance and seat category, though there are all sorts of discount deals for students, seniors, same-day performances and previews; many plays are, however, sold out months in advance. Call or consult the website for the latest news.

Arrival and information

From Stratford **VIA train station**, on Shakespeare Street, it's a fifteen-minute stroll north via Downie Street to the town's **main crossroads**, where Downie, Ontario and Erie streets meet, just metres from the south bank of the River Avon. Greyhound **buses** use a flag stop on St Patrick Street and from here it's about five-minutes' walk north to these same crossroads. There are two tourist offices. The main one is **Tourism Stratford** at 47 Downie St (Jan–March Mon–Fri 8.30am–4.30pm; April & Nov–Dec Mon–Fri 8.30am–4.30pm & Sat 10am–4pm; May–Oct Mon 9am–5pm, Tues–Sat 9am–8pm & Sun 9am–5pm; ☎519/271-5140 or 1-800/561-7926, ⓦwww.visitstratfordontario.ca). The second is the seasonal **Visitor Information Centre** located by the river on York Street, immediately northwest of the town's main intersection.

Accommodation

Stratford has over 250 guesthouses and B&Bs plus around a dozen hotels and motels, but **accommodation** can still be hard to find during the Festival's busiest weekends, usually in July and August. The walls of the tourist offices are plastered with pictures and descriptions of many of these establishments, and standards (and prices) are high. Both offices will help you find somewhere to stay.

Avonview Manor B&B 63 Avon St ☎519/273-4603, ⓦwww.bbcanada.com/avonview. Occupying an expansive Edwardian villa overlooking the north bank of the River Avon, this enjoyable B&B has four tastefully decorated and immaculately maintained bedrooms. Doubles from $105.
Deacon House B&B Inn 101 Brunswick St ☎519/273-2052, ⓦwww.bbcanada.com/1152 .html. Six lovely guest rooms – all en suite

– in a good-looking, centrally located Edwardian villa with a wide veranda. From $110.
Duggan Place B&B Inn 151 Nile St ☎519/273-7502 or 1-888-394-1111, ⓦwww .dugganplace.com. Well-kept Victorian villa with four en-suite rooms; two have private balconies overlooking a splendid garden. A 5min walk from the town centre. From $140.

Eating

The town has a hatful of excellent **cafés** and **restaurants**, with one of the best being *Fellini's Italian Café & Grill*, 107 Ontario St (Mon–Fri 11.30am–8pm), which offers a delicious range of fresh pizzas and pastas from $9 and up. Alternatives include the tasty snacks and light meals of *Tango Café & Grill*, 104 Ontario St (Sun 8am–4pm, Mon–Thurs 7am–5pm, Fri & Sat 8am–8pm), and pastries and gourmet coffees at *Balzac's Coffee Ltd*, 149 Ontario St.

Goderich

Perched on the edge of Lake Huron, **GODERICH** is a delightful country town of eight thousand inhabitants that dates back to 1825. Its main distinction is its geometrically planned centre, comprising a set of wide, tree-lined avenues that radiate out from a handsome **central circus** – which is itself dominated by a white stone courthouse. From the circus, the four main streets follow the points of the compass, with North Street leading to the compendious **Huron County Museum** (Jan–April Mon–Fri 10am–4.30pm & Sat 1–4.30pm; May–Dec Mon–Sat 10am–4.30pm & Sun 1–4.30pm; $5, $7.50 with jail, see p.117; ⓦwww.huroncounty.ca/museum/), which concentrates on the exploits of the district's pioneers. Highlights include a fantastic array of farm implements, from simple hand tools to gigantic, clumsy machines like a steam-driven thresher.

There's also a beautifully restored Canadian Pacific steam engine, as well as exhibition areas featuring furniture and military memorabilia.

From the museum, it's a ten-minute walk to the high stone walls of the **Huron County Gaol**, at 181 Victoria St (mid-May to early Sept daily 10am–4.30pm; $5; ⓦ www.huroncounty.ca/museum/): to get there, walk up to the far end of North Street, then turn right along Gloucester Terrace and it's at the end of the street on the right. This joint courthouse and jail was constructed between 1839 and 1842, but the design was very unpopular with local judges, who felt threatened by the proximity of those they were sentencing. The other problem was the smell: several judges refused to conduct proceedings because of the terrible odour coming from the privies in the exercise yard below and, in 1856, the administration gave in and built a new courthouse in the middle of the central circus. On a visit, don't miss the original **jailer's apartment** and a string of well-preserved **prison cells**, which reflect various changes in design between 1841 and 1972, when the prison was finally closed. The worst is the leg-iron cell for "troublesome" prisoners, where unfortunates were chained to the wall with neither bed nor blanket.

Back in the centre, **West Street** leads the 1km through a cutting in the bluffs to the harbour and salt workings on the **Lake Huron shoreline**. From here, a footpath trails north round the harbourside silos to the **Menesetung Bridge**, a former railway crossing that is now a pedestrian walkway spanning the Maitland River. On the far side of the river, you can pick up the **Maitland Trail**, which wanders down the north bank of the river as far as the marina. In the opposite direction, the shoreline has been tidied up to create a picnic area, but, although the sunsets are spectacular, the beach itself is a tad scrawny.

Practicalities

Goderich **tourist office** (mid-May to Aug daily 9am–7pm; Sept to mid-May Mon–Fri 9am–4.30pm; ☎519/524-6600 or 1-800/280-7637, ⓦwww.goderich.ca) is at Nelson and Hamilton streets, beside Hwy-21, a couple of minutes' walk northeast of the central circus. They have details of the town's **bed-and-breakfasts**, which average about $75 for a double. Amongst them, one of the more appealing options is the centrally located *Colborne Bed & Breakfast*, at 72 Colborne St (☎519/524-7400 or 1-800/390-4612, ⓦwww.colornebandb.com; doubles from $80), which has four straightforward guest rooms in an early twentieth-century home. All four are en suite and have air conditioning.

Goderich's best **restaurant** is *Thyme on 21*, in a restored Victorian house right in the centre at 80 Hamilton St (Tues–Fri & Sun 11.30am–2pm & Wed–Sat 5–10pm; ☎519/524-4171). They serve an imaginative menu featuring local ingredients with main courses averaging $20 at night, less at lunch times; reservations are advised.

Bayfield

Pocket-sized **BAYFIELD**, just 20km south of Goderich, is an extraordinarily pretty and prosperous small town with handsome timber villas nestling beneath a canopy of ancient trees. The townsfolk have kept modern development at arm's length – there's barely a neon sign in sight, never mind a concrete apartment block – and almost every house has been beautifully maintained. Historical plaques give the low-down on the older buildings that line Bayfield's short **Main Street**, and pint-sized **Pioneer Park**, on the bluff overlooking the lake, is a fine spot to take in the sunset. Bayfield is mainly a place to relax and unwind, but you can also venture down to the **harbour** on the north side of the village, where, in season, you can pick wild mushrooms and fiddleheads along the banks of the Bayfield River.

Practicalities

Bayfield **tourist office** (May–Sept daily 10am–6pm; ☎519/565-5549, ⓦwww .villageofbayfield.com), in the village hall beside the green at the end of Main Street, will help you find **accommodation** – though their assistance is only necessary in July and August, when vacancies can get thin on the ground.

Amongst Bayfield's **B&Bs**, one great choice is *Clair on the Square*, 12 The Square (☎519/565-2135, ⓦwww.claironthesquare.ca), which occupies a charming Victorian villa right in the centre of the village. It offers comfortable, attractive double rooms ($150), all en suite and decorated in a crisp, modern-meets-traditional style. The village also boasts the best **hotel** for miles around in the *Little Inn of Bayfield*, at 26 Main St (☎519/565-2611 or 1-800/565-1832, ⓦwww.littleinn.com). Housed in a modernized nineteenth-century timber-and-brick building with a lovely wraparound veranda, most of the delightfully furnished rooms (from $190), with their pastel shades and bright and airy demeanour, have whirlpool baths, and many have balconies too.

The *Little Inn of Bayfield* also has a superb **restaurant** (☎519/565-2611), whose speciality is fresh fish from Lake Huron – perch, pickerel and steelhead; mains average $30.

Severn Sound

The sheltered southern shore of **Severn Sound**, some 150km north of Toronto along Hwy-400, is one of the most beguiling parts of Ontario, its creeks and bays dotted with tiny ports, its deep-blue waters studded by thousands of rocky little islets. There's enough here for several day-trips, beginning with two of the province's finest historical reconstructions – **Discovery Harbour**, a British naval base, and **Sainte-Marie among the Hurons**, a Jesuit mission. Be sure, also, to spare some time for the wonderful scenery of the **Georgian Bay Islands National Park**, whose glacier-smoothed, Precambrian rocks and wispy pines were so marvellously celebrated by the Group of Seven painters (see *Canadian Art* colour section) and by the likes of the Canadian author Alice Munro, one of whose characters revels, "What drew her in – enchanted her actually – was the very indifference, the repetition, the carelessness and contempt for harmony, she found on the scrambled surface of the Precambrian shield."

Greyhound (☎1-800/661-TRIP, ⓦwww.greyhound.ca) runs several **buses** daily from Toronto to the regional towns of **Penetanguishene** and **Midland**. Beyond that, however, local bus services are very patchy, and your best bet is to **rent a car** in Toronto (for car rental details, see p.22).

Penetanguishene

Homely **PENETANGUISHENE** ("place of the rolling white sands" in Ojibwa) is the westernmost town on Severn Sound, and the site of one of Ontario's first European settlements – a Jesuit mission founded in 1639 and

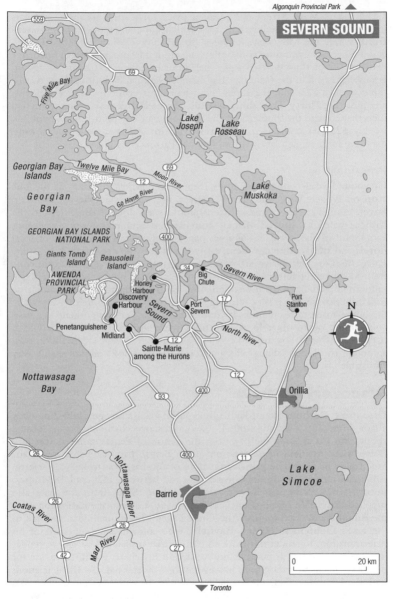

then abandoned a decade later following the burning of Sainte-Marie (see p.121). Europeans returned some 150 years later to establish a trading station, where local Ojibwa exchanged pelts for food and metal tools, but the settlement remained insignificant until the British built a naval dockyard here following the War of 1812. This attracted both French- and English-speaking shopkeepers and suppliers, and even today Penetanguishene is one of the few places in southern Ontario to maintain a bilingual tradition.

The town's **Main Street** is a pleasant place for a stroll, its shops and bars installed behind sturdy redbrick facades, which slope down towards the **waterfront**, where the MS *Georgian Queen* (☎705/549-7795 or 1-800/363-7447, ⓦwww.georgianbaycruises.com) offers an enjoyable programme of **summer cruises**. The pick are the two-and-a-half-hour excursion to Cedar Springs, on Beausoleil Island in the Georgian Bay Islands National Park (June–Sept two or three weekly; $22), and the three-and-a-half-hour cruise to Minicognashene, amongst the **Thirty Thousand Islands**, the collective name for the myriad islets that confetti the southern reaches of Georgian Bay (mid-June to Sept 2–4 weekly; $25). It's advisable to make **reservations** at least a day ahead of time; for more on Georgian Bay Islands National Park, see p.122.

Practicalities

Greyhound's daily bus service from Toronto and Midland pauses at the **bus stop** on Robert Street East, at Peel Street, immediately to the east of Main Street. From here, it's a five- to ten-minute walk down Main Street to the harbour, where the **tourist office** (Mon–Fri 9am–5pm plus summer weekends 9am–5pm; ☎705/549-2232, ⓦwww.penetanguishene.ca) has details of local **hotels** and **B&Bs**. Amongst them, easily the pick is the delightful 🏕 *No.1 Jury Drive B&B*, 1 Jury Drive (☎705/549-6851, ⓦwww.jurydrbb.huronia.com; from $120), whose four comfortable en-suite guest rooms occupy an attractive modern house built in traditional style near Discovery Harbour (see below); the leafy suburban setting is very relaxing and the breakfasts are superb – especially the home-made carrot muffins. If you decide to use Penetanguishene as a base, you can zip off to other local attractions with **Union Taxi**, 2 Robert St E (☎705/549-7666). For **food**, the *Blue Sky Family Restaurant*, 32 Main St, is an agreeable small-town diner offering good-quality snacks and meals at very affordable prices.

Discovery Harbour

Discovery Harbour (late May to June Mon–Fri 10am–5pm; July–Aug daily 10am–5pm; $6; ☎705/549-8064, ⓦwww.discoveryharbour.on.ca), located about 5km north along the bay from the centre of Penetanguishene on Jury Drive, is an ambitious reconstruction of the British naval base that was established here in 1817. The primary purpose of the base was to keep an eye on American movements on the Great Lakes, and between 1820 and 1834 up to twenty Royal Navy vessels were stationed here. Ships from the base also supplied the British outposts further to the west and, to make navigation safer, the Admiralty decided to chart the Great Lakes. This monumental task fell to the base's **Lieutenant Henry Bayfield**, who informed his superiors of his determination "to render this work so correct that it shall not be easy to render it more so". He was as good as his word, and his charts remained in use for decades. The naval station was, however, more short-lived. By 1834, relations with the US were sufficiently cordial for the navy to withdraw, and the base was turned over to the army, who maintained a small garrison here until 1856.

Staffed by enthusiastic **costumed guides**, the sprawling site spreads along a hillside above a tranquil inlet, its green slopes scattered with accurate reconstructions of everything from a sailors' barracks to several period houses, the prettiest of which is the **Keating House**, named after the base's longest-serving adjutant, Frank Keating. Only one of the original buildings survives, the dour limestone **Officers' Quarters**, which dates from the 1840s, but the complex's pride and joy is the working harbour-cum-dockyard. Here, a brace of fully rigged **sailing ships**, the HMS *Bee* and HMS *Tecumseth*, have been rebuilt to their original nineteenth-century specifications.

Sainte-Marie among the Hurons

One of Ontario's most arresting historical attractions, the reconstructed Jesuit mission of **Sainte-Marie among the Hurons** (early May & late Oct Mon–Fri 10am–5pm; late May to mid-Oct daily 10am–5pm; $9.25–11.25; ☎705/526-7838, ⓦwww.saintemarieamongthehurons.on.ca) marks the site of a crucial episode in Canadian history. In 1608, the French explorer **Samuel de Champlain** returned to Canada convinced that the only way to make the fur trade profitable was by developing partnerships with native hunters. Three years later, he formed an alliance with the **Huron** of southwest Ontario, cementing the agreement with a formal exchange of presents. However, his decision to champion one tribe against another – and particularly his gift of firearms to his new allies – disrupted the balance of power among the native societies of the St Lawrence and Great Lakes areas. Armed with Champlain's rifles, the Huron attacked their ancient enemies, the **Iroquois**, with gusto, inflicting heavy casualties; the Iroquois licked their wounds, determined to get even whenever they could. Meanwhile, in 1639, the **Jesuits** had established their centre of operations here at Sainte-Marie. They converted a substantial minority of the native people to Christianity, thereby undermining the social cohesion of the Huron – but much more importantly they had unwittingly infected and enfeebled the Huron with three European sicknesses: measles, smallpox and influenza.

In 1648 the **Dutch**, copying Champlain, began to sell the Iroquois firearms, and in March of the following year the Iroquois launched a full-scale invasion of Huron territory, or **Huronia**, slaughtering their enemies as they moved in on Sainte-Marie. Fearing for their lives, the Jesuits of Sainte-Marie burned their settlement and fled. Eight thousand Hurons went with them; most starved to death on the islands of Georgian Bay, but a few made it to Québec. During the campaign, two Jesuit priests, fathers **Brébeuf and Lalemant**, were captured at the outpost of Saint-Louis (near present-day Victoria Harbour), where they were bound to the stake and tortured – as per standard Iroquois practice. Despite the suffering brought upon the Hurons, it was the image of Catholic bravery and Iroquois cruelty that long lingered in the minds of French Canadians.

The mission is about 12km east of Penetanguishene off Hwy-12; there are **no buses**, but Penetanguishene's Union Taxi (☎705/549-7666) will take you there for about $18.

The Mission

A visit to Sainte-Marie starts in the **reception centre** with a film show that provides some background information before the screen lifts dramatically away to reveal the painstakingly restored **mission site**. There are 25 wooden buildings here, divided into two sections: the Jesuit area with its watchtowers, chapel, forge, living quarters, well-stocked garden and farm buildings, complete with pigs, cows and hens; and the native area, including a hospital and a pair of bark-covered long houses – one for Christian converts, the other for heathens. Fairly spick-and-span today, it takes some imagination to see the long houses as they appeared to Father Lalemant, who saw "... a miniature picture of hell ... on every side naked bodies, black and half-roasted, mingled pell-mell with the dogs ... you will not reach the end of the cabin before you are completely befouled with soot, filth and dirt". **Costumed guides** act out the parts of Hurons and Europeans with great vim, answering questions and demonstrating crafts and skills, though they show a certain reluctance to eat the staple food of the region, sagamite, a porridge of cornmeal seasoned with rotten fish. The grave in the simple wooden **church of St Joseph** between the Christian and native areas is the place where the (remaining) flesh of Brébeuf and Lalemant was interred after the Jesuits had removed the bones for future use as reliquaries.

A path leads from the site to the excellent **museum**, which traces the story of the early exploration of Canada with maps and displays on such subjects as fishing and the fur trade, seen in the context of contemporary European history. This leads into a section on the history of the missionaries in New France, with particular reference to Sainte-Marie. Information on the archeology of the site follows: the mission's whereabouts were always known even though Victorian settlers helped themselves to every chunk of stone – from what was known locally as "the old Catholic fort" – because the Jesuits had deposited the necessary documentation in Rome. Excavations began on the site in the 1940s and work is still in progress.

The Martyrs' Shrine

The eight Jesuits who were killed in Huronia between 1642 and 1649 are commemorated by the **Martyrs' Shrine** (mid-May to mid-Oct daily 9am–9pm; $3; ⓦwww.martyrs-shrine.com), a twin-spired, 1920s church which overlooks Sainte-Marie from the other side of Hwy-12. Blessed by Pope John Paul II in 1984 – when he bafflingly remarked that it was "a symbol of unity of faith in a diversity of cultures" – the church, along with the assorted shrines and altars in its grounds, is massively popular with pilgrims. Inside, the transepts hold a number of saintly reliquaries, most notably the skull of Brébeuf, and a stack of crutches discarded by healed pilgrims.

Georgian Bay Islands National Park

Georgian Bay Islands National Park consists of a scattering of about sixty islands spread between Severn Sound and Twelve Mile Bay, approximately 50km to the north. The park's two distinct landscapes – the glacier-scraped rock of the Canadian Shield and the hardwood forests and thicker soils of the south – meet

---

Algonquin Provincial Park

A giant slab of untamed wilderness, **Algonquin Provincial Park** (ⓦwww .algonquinpark.on.ca) boasts dense hardwood and pine forests, canyons, rapids, scores of lakes and, amongst a rich wildlife, loons, beavers, moose, timber wolves and black bears. The nearest entrance is a slowish 260km north of Toronto, too far for a day-trip, but worth considering for a longer excursion. To get there, make your way to Huntsville on Hwy-11 and then continue 45km along Hwy-60 to the park's west gate, where there is a visitor centre. Canoeing and hiking are the big deals here, and several Toronto companies offer all-inclusive wilderness packages, including meals, permits, guides, equipment and transport to and from Toronto. The pick of the bunch is **Call of the Wild**, 23 Edward St, Markham, Ontario (ⓣ905/471-9453 or 1-800/776-9453, ⓦwww.callofthewild.ca), which runs a varied programme that includes three-day ($400) and five-day ($650) canoeing trips deep into the park.

▲ Georgian Bay Islands National Park

at the northern end of the largest and most scenic island, **Beausoleil**. This beautiful island is a forty-minute boat ride west of **Honey Harbour**, the park's nearest port, which contains little more than a jetty, a couple of shops and a few self-contained hotel resorts.

Beausoleil has eleven short **hiking trails**, including two that start at the Cedar Spring landing stage on the southeastern shore: Treasure Trail (3.8km), which heads north behind the marshes along the edge of the island, and the Christian Trail (1.5km), which cuts through beech and maple stands to balsam and hemlock groves overlooking the rocky beaches of the western shoreline. At the northern end of Beausoleil, the Cambrian (2km) and Fairy trails (2.5km) are delightful routes through harsher glacier-scraped scenery, while, just to the west, the Dossyonshing Trail (2.5km) tracks through a mixed area of wetland, forest and bare granite that covers the transitional zone between the two main landscapes.

Practicalities

Honey Harbour is around 170km north of Toronto – take Hwy-400 and watch for the turn-off onto Route 5 (Exit 156), just beyond **Port Severn**. The **national park visitor reception** in Honey Harbour (late May to early Sept Mon–Fri 9am–4.30pm, Sat 8am–4pm & Sun noon–4pm; ☎705/526-9804) provides a full range of information on walking trails and flora and fauna.

There's no public transport to Honey Harbour, so having your own car is essential. Several Honey Harbour operators run **water taxis to Beausoleil**, with a one-way trip costing $40–50 in summer, a few dollars less in spring and fall. Among them, Honey Harbour Boat Club (☎705/756-2411), about 700m beyond the park office, is probably your best bet. There are no set times, but in summer boats leave for Beausoleil quite frequently. Fares to several of the park's other islands are negotiable. In all cases, advance **reservations** are required, and you should be sure to agree on a pick-up time before you set out. With less time to spare, the national park's **Georgian Bay Islands Day Tripper boat** leaves from Honey Harbour three times daily (Thurs to Mon) in July and August bound for Beausoleil, where passengers get four hours' hiking time. The round-trip fare is $16, plus $5.80 park admission; for further details and reservations, call ☎705/526-8907. Prospective hikers and campers bound for Georgian Bay Islands National Park need to come properly equipped – this is very much a wilderness environment. And whatever you do, don't forget the insect repellent.

If you decide to stay overnight, Beausoleil has eleven small **campsites**. The charge is $15 a night and all operate on a self-registration, first-come, first-served basis, with the exception of Cedar Spring, where the **visitor centre** (☎705/726-8907) near the main boat dock takes reservations for an additional $10. The campsites can get packed to the gills, so check availability before departure.

Listings

Listings

Accommodation

Toronto offers a wide variety of **accommodation**. In the last few years, a number of quirky new boutique **hotels** have shaken up the city's hotel scene, playing a positive role in neighbourhood rejuvenation at the same time. (This is particularly the case with the **Drake Hotel** and its same-block neighbour, the **Gladstone**; see p.131.) At the other end of the scale are the international luxury hotels with designer interiors and glamorous penthouse suites. Balancing things out is a good selection of unadventurous but comfortable mid-priced hotels, offering standard amenities such as in-room mini bars, coffee-makers, data ports, and often with a restaurant, pool and fitness centre on site.

Although most **bed–and–breakfasts** are necessarily not as central as the city's hotels, they tend to be slightly cheaper and take you off the beaten path into Toronto's vibrant neighbourhoods where you can feel like a local. For longer stays there are also **vacation suite hotels** and **short-let apartments** that provide greater privacy than the average B&B and are more economical than a hotel.

Budget-conscious travellers might want to consider Toronto's hostels, but the best deal in town remains the **summer residences** at local universities.

During peak season (late June to Aug), and especially around popular summer events like Gay Pride, Caribanna and the Toronto International Film Festival (see p.175 for dates) it is best to **book** your accommodation in advance.

Unless otherwise indicated, you'll find all of the accommodation listed in this chapter marked on the relevant colour **map** at the back of this book.

Hotel deals online

When hotels began offering special rates to online booking services, **published rack rates** became more a suggestion than a guide to the cost of a room. A little pre-trip research on the internet will uncover excellent hotel **deals** and seasonal packages, and many places offer the best available rate found prior to or within 24 hours of booking. Hotels will also post special offers or value-added **packages** (combined with spas, theatre tickets, meals, for example) on their own websites. The following sites are useful for finding accommodation offers;

Ⓦ www.expedia.ca   Ⓦ www.ontariotravel.net
Ⓦ www.quikbook.com   Ⓦ www.redToronto.com
Ⓦ www.tourismtoronto.com

Hotels

Any Downtown **hotel** will be sufficiently close to all the main attractions and easily accessible by public transport. **Rates** vary considerably; in general, though, a clean, centrally located hotel room starts at $130–170; note that the prices quoted below reflect rates for double occupancy during high season, in Canadian dollars, before tax (see p.35).

Differing weekend and weekday prices may apply, and rates will often be cheaper outside the summer months, assuming a large convention is not driving room rates up during your visit.

Downtown

Bond Place 65 Dundas St E, at Victoria St ☎416/362-6061 or 1-800/268-9390, ✆www .bondplace.ca. Subway: Dundas. Steps away from the Eaton Centre and bustling Dundas Square, *Bond Place* comes with the usual conveniences, and its rates are reasonable, starting at $129–159.

The Cosmopolitan 8 Colborne St, at Yonge St ☎416/350-2000, ✆www.cosmotoronto.com. Subway: King. All 97 suites feature hardwood floors and special air purifiers, and guests receive a complimentary continental breakfast and a gemstone on their pillows at night instead of a chocolate. Rates range from $349 to $1500.

Delta Chelsea Inn 33 Gerrard St W, at Yonge St ☎416/595-1975 or 1-877/814-7706, ✆www .deltachelsea.com. Subway: Dundas. With 1500 guest rooms, six restaurants, ballrooms and conference facilities, and an indoor waterslide (The Corkscrew), this huge hotel's expertise is family stays. Day care, a family pool and play centres are available for young children. Average rates are around $159–309, but check for online deals.

🎿 **Fairmont Royal York** 100 Front St W ☎416/368-2511 or 1-800/257-7544, ✆www.fairmont.com/royalyork. Subway: Union. The *Fairmont Royal York* has gone green, with a rooftop herb garden and apiary. Down in the lobby, mosaic floors, coffered ceilings and massive chandeliers create a property fit for a queen – indeed, the hotel maintains a suite for HRM when she visits. Dependable quality, unflappable staff and a central location keep this historic hotel a favourite. Average rates for low and high season are around $209–339.

Grand Hotel & Suites Toronto 225 Jarvis St, at Dundas St E ☎416/863-9000 or 877/324-7263, ✆www.grandhoteltoronto.com. This 177-suite property has soaring cathedral ceiling suites on the third floor, heated whirlpools on the

rooftop, and enough marble in the lobby to fit out a Moscow subway station. Rates from $179.

Hilton Toronto 145 Richmond St W, at University Ave ☎416/869-3456 or 800/267-2281, ✆www.hilton.com. Subway: Osgoode; streetcar: Queen (#501). A dramatic lobby area featuring wood, stone, steel and water makes an immediate impression. Guest rooms are on par with other contemporary interiors. On the edge of the Queen Street West area, and neighbour to the new Four Seasons Opera House, the *Hilton Toronto* includes all the chain's dependable features. Average rates start at $299.

Holiday Inn on King 370 King St W, at Peter St ☎416/599-4000 or 800/263-6364, ✆www.hiok .com. Streetcar: King (#504). All four hundred rooms and suites were recently refreshed in that ubiquitous chocolate wood, clean-line look. Offers the amenities and services you'd expect, and is close to theatres, clubs and restaurants, and the Rogers Centre (formerly the SkyDome). Average rates are $211–339.

Hotel Le Germain 30 Mercer St, at John St ☎416/345-9500 or 1-866/7345-9501, ✆www .germaintoronto.com. Streetcar: King (#504). There are 118 rooms and four suites with fireplaces and a balcony, plus a two-storey apartment suite for those on a generous budget. The latest tweaks include a rooftop putting green and "vineyard". A dramatic lobby, attention to service and an attentive staff complement the glam surroundings. Rates from $285 to $355.

🎿 **Hotel Victoria** 56 Yonge St, at King St W ☎416/363-1666 or 1-800/363-8228, ✆www.toronto.com/hotelvictoria.Subway: King. This adorable, affordable Downtown hotel is a real gem. There are 56 well-appointed, comfortable rooms to choose from and the service is comprehensive. Rates range from $130 to $159.

InterContinental Toronto Centre 225 Front St W, at Simcoe St ☎416/597-1400 or 800/422-7969, @www.torontocentre.intercontinental.com. **Subway: Union.** Adjacent to the Metro Toronto Convention Centre, this snazzy place is an obvious choice for business travellers. The well-equipped rooms include mini bars, dataports and coffee-makers, and there's a decent on-site spa. Rates range from $253 to $783.

Le Méridien King Edward 37 King St E ☎416/863-3131 or 1-800/543-4300, @www .lemeridien-kingedward.com. **Subway: King; Streetcar: King (#504).** Built to last by by E.J. Lennox (see p.54) in 1903, the "King Eddy" maintains its opulent Beaux Arts character with grand staircases and a galleried lobby presided over by King Edward VIII's larger-than-life portrait above the fireplace. A much-needed refurbishment is restoring its waning lustre. Average rates are around $249–419.

Marriott Toronto Downtown Eaton Centre 525 Bay St, at Yonge St ☎416/597-9200 or 1-800/597-5911, @www.marriotteatoncentre .com. **Subway: Dundas.** If staying right next door to a large, famous shopping mall (the Eaton Centre) is your idea of heaven, search no further. Amenities include an indoor pool, down-filled duvets, flat-screen TVs, and a well-trained staff. Average rates range from $349 to $449.

Metropolitan 108 Chestnut St, at Dundas St ☎416/977-5000 or 1-800/668-6600, @www .metropolitan.com. **Subway: St Patrick.** This attractive hotel, filled with flowers and Deco-style furniture, is close to the Art Gallery of Ontario and Downtown shopping. Rooms are done out in blond woods and restful neutrals, and equipped with high-speed internet access and multiple phones. There's also an excellent restaurant on site, *Lai Wah Hein* (see p.144). Rates are around $265–440.

Novotel Toronto Centre 45 The Esplanade ☎416/367-8900 or 800/668-6835, @www .novoteltorontocentre.com. **Subway: Union.** The *Novotel* boasts 262 comfortable guest rooms, an indoor pool, fitness centre and a Downtown location. Average rates range from $129 to $450.

Pantages Suites and Hotel Spa 200 Victoria St, at Dundas St ☎416/362-1777 or 1-866/852-1777, @www.pantageshotel.com. **Subway: Dundas.** Right in the midst of the Cannon Theatre, the Elgin and Winter Garden Theatre Centre and Massey Hall, the *Pantages*' great location is matched by dramatic guest rooms: luxurious Egyptian cotton sheets, air purifiers and little water fountains are standard amenities. Rooms start around $259; suites from $299.

Renaissance Toronto Hotel Downtown 1 Blue Jays Way, at Spadina Ave ☎416/341-7100 or 800/237-1512, @www.marriott.com. **Subway: Union; Streetcar: King (#504).** The *Renaissance Toronto*'s claim to fame is its location: a bank of rooms, the main lounge and the restaurant look right onto the Rogers Centre's baseball diamond and are in huge demand during Blue Jays games or Argo play-offs. Rates start around $179 for a city-view room, going up to $2000 for the Rogers Convention Suite.

Sheraton Centre Toronto 123 Queen St W, at University Ave ☎416/361-1000 or 800/325-3535, @www.sheraton.com. **Subway: Queen.** All 1377 stylish rooms and suites feature ultra body-conforming mattresses that some travellers claim to be hooked on. Other *luxe* features include a lobby waterfall, indoor/ outdoor pool, and interior terraced gardens. Standard rates from around $239.

SoHo Metropolitan 318 Wellington St W, at Blue Jays Way ☎416/977-5000 or 1-800/668-6600, @www.metropolitan.com. **Streetcar: King (#504).** This chic boutique hotel has 72 guest rooms and eighteen suites featuring glass-walled, marble-clad bathrooms, maple furnishings and full-length windows that open. The *Soho Met* also boasts an exceptional restaurant (*Sen5es*, see p.146), and bar/lounge. Rates start at $245.

Strathcona Hotel 60 York St, at Wellington St ☎416/363-3321 or 1-800/268-8304, @www .thestrathconahotel.com. **Subway: Union.** This attractive, affordable hotel comes with all the standard amenities, a great location across from the *Fairmont Royal York*, and its own individual style. A real find. July rates start at $145.

Travelodge Toronto Downtown West 621 King St W, at Bathurst St ☎416/504-77441 or 1-800/578-7878, @www.travelodgetorontodowntown.com. **Streetcar: King (#504).** Alas, the cheesy Sixties facade was shorn off and replaced with standard corporate blah, but this place offers good value on an increasingly pricey strip. Add-ons include complimentary continental breakfast, free high-speed internet connection and cheap parking. Standard rates are around $129–139.

The waterfront

Radisson Hotel Admiral 249 Queens Quay W
☎416/203-3333 or 1-800/333-3333, ⓦwww
.radissonadmiral.com. Subway: York Quay.
Located on the waterfront, this 157-room
family hotel features an indoor pool, on-site
restaurant, and standard amenities. Its pier-
side location is tempting for lake-lovers and
the view is splendid. Average rates are
$188–309.

Westin Harbour Castle 1 Harbour Square
☎416/869-1600 or 800/228-3000, ⓦwww
.westin.com/harbourcastle. York Quay stop on
the LRT from Union. This 977-room hotel sits
right on Lake Ontario's edge. The Toronto
Island ferry terminal is next door and St
Lawrence Market and the Distillery District
are an easy walk away. Rooms offer
dramatic views, data ports, flat-screen TVs,
and Heavenly Dog beds for canine guests.
Further creature comforts include a gym,
restaurants and bars, and an indoor pool.
Standard rates start at $319.

Uptown

**Best Western Primrose 111 Carlton St, at Jarvis
St** ☎416/977-8000 or 1-800/268-8082, ⓦwww
.torontoprimrosehotel.com. Subway: College;
streetcar: Carlton/College (#506). The *Primrose*
has all the basic amenities you'd expect
from a large chain hotel (coffee-makers, free
local calls, data lines and so on), plus a
pool, gym, restaurant and bar. Average
rates are around $169–179.

**Comfort Hotel Downtown Toronto 15 Charles St
E, at Yonge St** ☎416/924-1222, ⓦwww.toronto
.com/comfortdowntown. Subway: Bloor-Yonge
(Hayden exit). With an excellent location, just
close enough to Yonge, the *Comfort Hotel*
offers the brand's standard amenities, and
wireless high-speed internet access, and
recently revamped rooms. Rates at
$124–174.

**Courtyard By Marriott Downtown Toronto 475
Yonge St, at Alexander St** ☎416/924-0611 or
800/847-5075, ⓦwww.marriott.com/yyzcy.
Subway: Carlton. On the edge of Toronto's
Gay Village, this Marriott offers a smoke-free
policy, wired and wireless internet access,
and an indoor pool with whirlpool. Doubles
range from $149 to $399.

**Days Hotel & Conference Centre 30 Carlton St,
at Yonge St** ☎416/977-6655 or 800/367-9601,
ⓦwww.dayshoteltoronto.ca. Subway: College.
Head here for perfectly comfortable

chain-style rooms plus a pool, exercise
room and a seriously convenient location,
half a block from Yonge St. Shopping,
eateries and a multiplex cinema are steps
away. Best available rates $109–139.

Four Seasons 21 Avenue Rd, at Cumberland St
☎416/964-0411 or 1-800/332-3442, ⓦwww
.fourseasons.com. Subway: Bay (Cumberland
exit). This luxurious hotel, in the glitzy heart
of Yorkville, hosts some of the city's most
illustrious guests, especially during the
Toronto Film Festival. The very glam
Avenue Bar is always perfect for special
occasions. Average rates range from $395
to $415.

Hazelton Hotel 118 Yorkville Ave, at Avenue Rd
☎416/963-6300, ⓦwww.thehazeltonhotel
.com. Subway: Bay (Cumberland exit). Large
rooms with high ceilings, private balconies,
leather wall panelling and the latest toys in
home entertainment are what you'll find at
the *Hazelton*, as well as a health club, spa,
pool and, of course, a private screening
room. Rates start around $450.

**Howard Johnson Yorkville 89 Avenue Rd,
north of Yorkville Ave,** ☎416/964-1220,
ⓦwww.hojo.com. Subway: Bay. This budget-
friendly, 69-room classic is a block from
the upscale Yorkville and Annex neighbourhoods and is far cheaper than the
immediate competition. Guests enjoy
complimentary breakfasts, colour TV and
inexpensive parking. Children under 12
stay free. Comfortable, surprise-free rooms
and an attentive staff make this a real find.
Rates at $169–189.

**Madison Manor Boutique Hotel 20 Madison Ave,
at Bloor St W,** ☎416/922-5579, ⓦwww
.madisonavenuepub.com. Subway: St George.
With 23 rooms and six suites on four floors
(staircase only), this charming Victorian
mansion sits in the heart of the Annex
neighbourhood. The architectural elements
have been respected and all rooms come
with en-suite bathrooms, satellite TV,
voicemail service and complimentary
breakfast. The *Madison Pub & Restaurant* is
right next door for a lively Sat night. Rates
at $99–$189.

Park Hyatt Toronto 4 Avenue Rd, at Bloor St W
☎416/977-4823 or 800/333-3333, ⓦwww
.parkhyatttoronto.com. Subway: Museum or Bay.
This luxury hotel offers large, well-appointed
rooms, all with high-end amenities and
internet gadgets, at a premium price. Other
features include the *Rooftop* cocktail bar

with spectacular skyline views, a spa, and a *Morton's Steakhouse* (see p.153). Rates start around $330.

Ramada Plaza Toronto 300 Jarvis St at Carlton St ☎ 416/977-4823 or 1-800/567-2233, ⓦ www.ramadaplazatoronto.com. Streetcar: Carlton/College (#506). Aimed primarily at business travellers, this reliable, central chain hotel offers recently refurbished rooms and suites as well as an exercise room and pool. Standard rates are around $129–199.

Sutton Place 955 Bay St, at Wellesley St ☎ 416/924-9221 or 866/378-8866, ⓦ www .suttonplace.com. Subway: Wellesley. Classy *Sutton Place* offers luxury service for very reasonable prices, as well as a stellar location, close to Yorkville, Yonge St, the Gay Village, and the University of Toronto's leafy, gothic campus. With rates from as low as $155, this is one of the best finds in town.

Wellesley Manor Boutique Hotel 29 Wellesley St E, at Yonge St ☎ 416/927-8156, ⓦ www .wellesleymanor.ca. Subway: Wellesley. This recently redecorated Victorian manor offers eleven en-suite rooms, with satellite TV, 27-inch LCD TVs, high-speed internet connection, and a central location steps from Yonge Street's hub-bub, and five minutes from Bloor West's shopping. Rates start at $119.

West End

🏃 **Drake Hotel 1150 Queen St W, at Beaconsfield St ☎ 416/531-5042 or 1-866/372-5386, ⓦ www.thedrakehotel.ca.**

▼ The Drake Hotel

Streetcar: Queen (#501). The *Drake* instantly became the city's "it" spot when it reopened in 2004. The lounge/dining room just got a glitzy refurbishment but the café and patios retain their edgy atmosphere and the "Crash Pad" rooms rock with their glass-walled bathrooms, Ugly Dolls on the pillows, and customized furniture. Doubles are around $189–239.

🏃 **Gladstone Hotel 1214 Queen St W, at Gladstone Ave ☎ 416/531-4635, ⓦ www .gladstonehotel.com. Streetcar: Queen (#501).** Continuously open since 1889, the *Gladstone* follows the dictum "new ideas in old buildings". All the rooms have been designed by different local artists, right down to the wallpaper, and communal areas serve as art galleries. The splendid hand-operated cage elevator is still working, operated by Hank Young, the "Gladstone Cowboy". Rates range from $185 to $475.

The airport

Delta Toronto West Airport 5444 Dixie Rd, at Highway 401 ☎ 905/624-1144 or 800/737-3211, ⓦ www.deltatorontoairportwest.com. Most airport strip hotels don't cater to families but this one has plenty to offer: accompanied children under 17 stay free, there are children's menus, an indoor pool, a leafy garden – and even pets are welcome. An exercise room, business centre, and 24hr room service ensure business travellers are well looked after too. Free shuttle service to the airport. High season rack rates $189–289.

Holiday Inn Select Toronto International Airport 970 Dixon Rd, at Airport Road ☎ 416/675-7611 or 800/524-8436, ⓦ www.hiselect.com /yyz-inintlapt. This 445-room chain offers standard features, a polyglot staff and the largest outdoor pool on the airport strip. Other amenities include an exercise room, whirlpool and a full business centre. Average rates are around $189–289.

Sheraton Gateway Hotel in Toronto International Airport Terminal 3, Toronto International Airport ☎ 905/238-0159 or 800-668-9887, ⓦ www .sheraton.com/torontoairport. Attached to Terminal 3, the *Sheraton Gateway's* rooms literally overlook the runways and offer corporate amenities such as free bottled water, ergonomic chairs, a full conference and business centre, and free shuttle service to Terminal 1. Note that as the hotel is inside the airport, guests will need their passports. Check the site for details. Rates start at $265.

Stage West All Suite Hotel & Theatre Restaurant 5400 Dixie Rd ☎905/238-0159 or 800/668-9887, ⍟www.stagewest.com. An airport strip hotel with a difference: not only are all the rooms suites, with separate sitting and bedroom areas, fridges and microwaves, but there's also a six-hundred-seater theatre restaruant offering light, professionally performed shows. A heated, saltwater pool and water slide round out the facilities. Queen suites start around $129–159.

Suburbs

Old Mill Inn & Spa 21 Old Mill Rd ☎416/236-2641 or 866/653-6455, ⍟www.oldmilltoronto.com. Subway: Old Mill. Site of Toronto's first lumber mill and a tea garden since 1914, this historic property on the Humber River is a country retreat in the city. Mock-Tudor beams, oak furniture, dancing on the terrace and afternoon tea are all wonderfully old-school. The 46 rooms and thirteen suites each have fireplaces, jet tubs and flat-screen TVs, and the hotel's latest addition is a full-service spa. Room rates are around $205–375.

Short-let apartments and suite hotels

Once the preserve of academics and lobbyists, **short-let apartments** and **suite hotels** are growing in number and popularity. Like B&Bs, they give self-reliant guests a chance to feel part of the city but with greater privacy. The combination of self-service, a kitchenette and inexpensive or free parking can represent considerable savings, particularly for families or groups of friends.

Annex Rentals ☎416/839-9943, ⍟www .annexrentals.com. Beautiful one- and two-bedroom rental properties in historic houses in and around the Annex neighbourhood, let by the week, the month or longer. Design features include mosaic tile bathrooms, cathedral windows with leaded glass, custom-designed kitchens, and furnishings with unique flourishes that go big on the wow factor. Weekly rentals begin at $1000, with monthly rates from $2400.

Cambridge Suites Hotel 15 Richmond St E, Downtown ☎416/368-1990 or 1-800/463-1990, ⍟www.cambridgesuiteshotel.com. Subway: Queen. Offering high-end comfort and privacy, this place offers hotel services (including a restaurant and fitness centre) in apartment-like, two-room suites. Well located, close to theatres, shops and restaurants. Average rates are around $219–259 per night.

Coach House in the Annex 117 Walmer Rd, Uptown ☎416/899-0306, ⍟www.thecoach house.ca. Subway: Spadina. There are two fully self-contained suites here: the separate, split-level Coach House and the Apartment Suite in the main house, both set in a pretty garden. Amenities include fresh flowers, bathrobes, high-speed internet connection, and TVs and VCRs. Daily rates start at $145; enquire about weekly or monthly rates.

Posh Digs 414 Markham St, at Ulster St, Uptown ☎416/964-6390, ⍟www.poshdigs.ca. Streetcar: Carlton/College (#506). The three self-contained suites with either balconies or a garden are in a Victorian property, a block from the College Street strip. Parking, TV and VCR, internet, private phone (with free local calls), bathrobes and complimentary food basket are all part of the package. Rates start at $125–200 per night; weekly and monthly rates negotiable.

The Suites at 1 King West 1 King St W, at Yonge St, Downtown ☎416/924-9221 or 866/470-5464, ⍟www.onekingwest.com. Subway: King. Once the Dominion Bank of Canada, a 51-storey tower was grafted on top and became *The Suites at 1 King West*. The rooms have light walls, white linens, dark wood accents and black marble kitchenette countertops. Nicely done and very central. Suites are around $179–350.

Town Inn Suites 620 Church St, at Charles St E, Uptown ☎416/964-3311 or 800/387-2755, ⍟www.towninn.com. Subway: Bloor-Yonge (Hayden St exit). Long an insider favourite, the *Town Inn* offers comfortable, centrally located suites for the cost of a budget hotel room. Facilities include an indoor pool and an outdoor tennis court. Junior queen suites start at $179.

Bed-and-breakfasts

Toronto's deluxe **bed-and-breakfasts** can be as expensive as a good downtown hotel room, and in terms of quality and services many are more like inns. What B&Bs offer, however, that most hotels cannot is an intimate setting and a feel for what it's like to live in one of Toronto's neighbourhoods. Travellers with special needs, concerns or feedback should contact the Federation of Ontario Bed and Breakfast Accommodation (℡519/568-8878, ⓦwww.fobba.com), or Toronto City Bed and Breakfasts (ⓦwww.torontocitybandb.com).

Ainsley House Bed & Breakfast 19 Elm St (east of Mt Pleasant), Uptown ℡416/972-0533 or 888/423-3337, ⓦwww.ainsleyhouse.com. **Subway: Sherbourne.** An easy walk from Yonge and Bloor, this Rosedale mansion offers six rooms, two with shared bath and four en-suite. Free parking available; deposits required. Two-night minimum stays, starting at $49–69 per night.

Bonnevue Manor B&B 33 Beaty Ave, near Jameson Ave, High Park (see "Toronto's Suburbs" map at the end of the book) ℡416/5336-1455, ⓦwww.bonnevuemanor.com. **Streetcar: Queen (#501) or King St (#504).** This turreted Victorian mansion with its original wraparound veranda is close to High Park and the Roncesvalles neighbourhood. Its nine rooms and suites, all with private baths, and some with their own fireplaces, start at $99, with a two-night minimum stay.

Baldwin Village Inn Bed and Breakfast 9 Baldwin St, at McCaul St, Downtown ℡416/591-5359, ⓦwww.baldwininn.com **Streetcar: Carlton/College (#506) or Dundas (#505).** On the edge of Kensington Market and Chinatown, this charming property is surrounded by a mish-mash of cultures, religions, artists' studios, and restaurants. Alas, no private baths. Two-night minimum stay, at $105–115 per night.

Fourth Street B&B 22 Fourth St, Ward Island (see map, pp.82–83) ℡416/203-0771, ⒠fourthstbb@hotmail.com. **Ferry: Ward Island.** The epitome of a traditional Toronto Island house, *Fourth Street B&B* offers one guest room (with shared bath), use of the kitchen, full breakfasts and the free use of bicycles for guests. Available year-round. Two-night minimum stay, starting at $100 per night; weekly and monthly rates negotiable.

The Mulberry Tree 122 Isabella St, at Jarvis St, Uptown ℡416/960-5249, ⓦwww.bbtoronto.com. **Subway: Wellesley.**

▼ The Mulberry Tree

A delightful and reliable B&B in a tastefully decorated heritage home, *The Mulberry Tree* is cosy, friendly, comfortable and close to Downtown. Rates around $130–135.

Smiley's B&B 4 Dacotah Ave, Algonquin Island (see map, pp.82–83) ℡416/203-8599, ⓦwww.erelda.ca. Located on Algonquin Island, *Smiley's* offers the small but lovely "Belvedere" room, perched at the top of the house, year-round, or the self-contained Studio Suite, with its own entrance, sitting area, bathroom and kitchen, available for nightly rental from May–Oct, and weekly or monthly rental otherwise. The Belvedere starts at $80 a night; the Studio at $180. Cash deposit required upon reservation.

University residences and hostels

From the third week in May to the end of August, Downtown **student residences** owned by the University of Toronto and Ryerson University are available to budget-wise tourists on a daily, weekly or monthly basis. Clean, affordable and relatively private, these rooms and suites are frequently the best bargain in town. Most residences require a deposit depending on the length of your stay. Students with valid IDs may get a discount of around ten percent, so enquire at reception.

Toronto's range of **hostels** continues to grow and improve, with several of the more recently opened ones being agreeable options. Most have private or family rooms as well as dormitories.

Canadiana Backpackers Inn 42 Widmer St, at Adelaide St, Downtown ☏416/598-9090 or 877/215-1225, ⓦwww.canadianalodging.com. **Streetcar: Queen (#501).** This Canuck-themed hostel is on a tiny side street close to nightclubs, the CN Tower, and Queen St W. Accommodation ranges from single and double private rooms to quad rooms (including Girls Only) and six- to eight-bed dorms. Special features include free pancake and maple syrup breakfasts, coffee and tea, internet access, daily events and a movie screening room. Dorm bed $27; single private $75. Ask about student discounts.

Global Village Backpackers 460 King St W, at Spadina Ave, Downtown ☏416/703-8540 or 1-888/844-7875, ⓦwww.globalbackpackers .com. **Streetcar: King (#504).** This former honkey-tonk hotel has four private/family rooms; everything else is dormitory-style (including Girls Only) with men's and women's shared bathrooms. Close to the Queen St W action as well as the King W strip. Special features include free wi-fi, a games room and an on-site pub and rooftop access. Dorm bed $27; quads (four to a room) $29 per person; private room (one double bed) $72 per room. Check website for discounts.

Hostelling International (HI) – Toronto 76 Church St, at Adelaide St, Downtown ☏416/971-4440 or 877/848-8737, ⓦwww .hostellingtoronto.com. **Streetcar: Dundas (#505).** The neighbourhood has successfully resisted gentrification but this hostel is a clean, well-run example of the HI collective. Dorms/family rooms, quads and private rooms (single and double) available with internet access, coin-operated laundry, an on-site café and the usual shared kitchen

and TV lounge. Rates go from $32 per person up to $90 double or single; discounts available if you present your ISIC card or HI membership.

Neill-Wycik 96 Gerrard St E, at Victoria St, Downtown ☏416/977-2320 or 800/268-4358, ⓦwww.neill-wycik.com. **Subway: Dundas; streetcar: Dundas (#505).** Fifteen of the 22 floors are arranged into units containing four private bedrooms, two bathrooms and a kitchen area with a fridge and stove – perfect if you're traveling with familiy or friends. Close to Dundas Square and the Eaton Centre, as well as the Gay Village, the hostel offers daily housekeeping, continental breakfast and in-room phones. Doubles in July start at $64.

University of Toronto, St Michael's College 81 St Mary's St, at Bay St, Uptown ☏416/926-7296, ⓦwww.utoronto.ca/stmikes. **Subway: Bay (Bay St exit).** This is the college where media prophet Marshall McLuhan taught for much of his career. From mid-May to mid-Aug singles and doubles are available at weekly rates, including maid service. Singles for non-students start at $170 per week (one-week minimum stay).

University of Toronto, Victoria College 140 Charles St W, Uptown ☏416/585-4524, ⓦwww .vicu.utoronto.ca. **Subway: Museum.** Close to Yorkville and Bloor West shopping, the Royal Ontario Museum, nightclubs, lounges and restaurants, and surrounded by intriguing architecture, the no-frills accommodation offers singles with shared bathrooms and and a handful of suites with private bathrooms from May to mid-Aug. Linens, towels, housekeeping services and breakfast are provided. Singles start at $59.50 per night; weekly and monthly rates available.

7

Cafés and light meals

Toronto's thriving **cafés** are the seam in the city's social fabric. Locals head there for a morning latte, a quick meal, an evening drink, or just to meet up with friends for some social activity. The scene gets especially busy during the summertime when cafés move tables and chairs onto terraces and sidewalks, providing excellent vantage points for people-watching or just hanging about.

These places can also provide the best testing-ground for young, talented chefs looking to make a name for themselves, often with inventive combinations of the huge variety of ethnic dishes gone mainstream. Most recently they've been catering to Toronto's ever-growing number of **locivors** – who aim to eat locally produced food, wherever possible – by showcasing local and regional cheeses, breads, fresh produce, meats and lake fish.

We've grouped spots into two broad categories: places that are best for beverages and socializing (though you'll find even these usually serve snacks), and places (typically low-key, informal restaurants) that make a good place for **light meals**.

Cafés

Downtown

Balzac's 55 Mill St, at Parliament St ☎416/207-1709, ⊛www.balzacscoffee .com. Streetcar: King (#504); bus: Parliament St (#65A from Castle Frank station). In the midst of the nineteenth century Distillery

▼ Balzac's

District, *Balzac's* has the look and feel of an Old Montréal loft, and serves mostly espresso-type coffees, plus some sweets to go with them.

Casa Acoreana Café 235 August Ave, at Baldwin St ☎416/593-9717. Streetcar: Carlton/College (#506). Basically a shed attached to the neighbouring spice store, where patrons can enjoy their brew while perched on a variety of jittery seating. Excellent espressos and hot chocolate – pure Kensington Market.

I Deal Coffee 84 Naussau St, at Bellevue St ☎416/364-7700. Streetcar: Carlton/College (#506). Also at 162 Ossington Ave, at Queen St W ☎416/534-7700. Streetcar: Queen (#501). The proprietor is devoted to his coffee craft with a specialist's passion evident in every delicious sip.

Moon Bean Coffee 30 St Andrews St, off Spadina Ave ☎416/595-0327. Streetcar: Spadina (#510). One of the early coffee roasteries, *Moon Bean* has hung in long

135

enough to become a Kensington Market institution. In addition to coffees, juices and teas, patrons can snack on a solid selection of daily soups, sandwiches and pastries. **Tequila Bookworm 512 Queen St W, at Portland St** ☎647/436-4648, ⓦ www .tequilabookwormblogspot.com. **Streetcar: Queen (#501).** A recent move means more space (second-storey patio), more books and more live performances. The menu features wraps, Belgian waffles, espresso coffees, beers and some smart cocktails.

Uptown

Café Doria 1094 Yonge St, at Roxborough St W ☎416/944-0101. **Subway: Rosedale.** A charming little coffee bar serving up forti-fying espressos for patrons worn out from shopping at the many beautiful antique stores nearby. Sandwiches and small pizzas are good and the pasties are excellent. **The Coffee Mill 99 Yorkville Ave, at Hazelton Ave** ☎416/967-383, ⓦ www.coffeemillrestaurant .com. **Subway: Bay.** Nothing changes at this Hungarian establishment, dating back to Yorkville's boho days when the likes of Joni Mitchell and Neil Young were getting their start in the neighbourhood's coffee houses. It serves espresso-type coffees, including the hard-core Turkish variety, and is famed for its rib-sticking goulash. **Jet Fuel Coffee Shop 519 Parliament St, at Aberdeen Ave** ☎416/968-9982, ⓦ www .jetfuelcycling.blogspot.com. **Streetcar: Carlton/ College (#506).** An unofficial club house of bicycle couriers. It only serves beverages that can be made with an espresso machine (tea included), and imports a few baked goods for dunking. **Linuxcaffe 326 Harbourd St, at Grace St** ☎416/534-2116, ⓦ www.linuxcaffe.ca. **Subway: Christie.** *Linuxcaffe* offers three basics: dark roasted coffees; top-notch panini, burritos and soup made from resolutely local produce; and, finally, linux software. You have to pay for the food and coffee. **Manic Coffee 426 College St, at Bathurst St** ☎416/966-3888, ⓦ www.maniccoffee.com. **Streetcar: Carlton/College (#506).** There are serious roasteries and then there's *Manic*. Fresh Fifties-style pies and pastries from *Wanda's Pie in the Sky* make fine accompaniments. **MBCo 100 Bloor St W, at Bellair St** ☎416/961- 6226, ⓦ www.mbco.ca. **Subway: Bay (Bellair exit).** This swanky sliver of a sandwich

bar/café faces the Yorkville Park, not Bloor St. Serves a large selection of beautifully prepared and presented wraps, sandwiches and pastries along with espresso-type drinks, beers, or wines.

MoRoCo Chocolate Boutique, Salon & Cocoa Bar 99 Yorkville Ave, at Hazelton Ave ☎416/961-2202, ⓦ www.morocochocolate .com. **Subway: Bay.** If Vivienne Westwood designed a playhouse out of Wedgewood and filled it with top-grade chocolate, coffee and hors'd'oeuvre-like menu items you would have, approximately, *MoRoCo*. Unlike most Yorkville eateries that take conspicuous consumption seriously, this witty Rococo-inspired café just wants to have fun. **Pusateri's Café 57 Yorkville Ave, at Bay St** ☎416/785-9100, ⓦ www.pusateris.com. **Subway: Bay (Bay exit).** Few cafés offer star-gazing as well as valet parking, but this one, attached to the downtown branch of Toronto's best purveyors of fine food, is the ultimate Yorkville daytime glam spot. If watching visiting movie stars do their grocery shopping isn't your idea of an inter-esting time, perhaps the fact that *Pusateri's* only uses lilly coffee will entice you here. **Tim Horton's 1170 Bay St, at Bloor St** ☎416/975-4464, ⓦ www.timhortons.com. **Subway: Bay (Bay exit).** Tim Horton played hockey for the Toronto Maple Leafs so naturally his eponymous coffee chain was an immediate hit, famed for such innova-tions as selling the bits punched out of doughnuts to form the holes as "Tim Bits". Sandwiches, soups and stews are served along with doughnuts, crullers, muffins and buns. This branch is open 24/7.

East End

Athens Pastries 509 Danforth Ave, at Fenwick Ave ☎416/463-5144. **Subway: Chester.** This café-bakery sells sweet and savoury Greek pastries with coffee, and nothing else. Huge trays of fresh baklava, spanakopita and a delectable custard and filo confection empty out in rapid succession as sit-down or take-away customers file in for their filo pastry fix. **Dark Horse Espresso Bar 682 Queen St E, at Hamilton St** ☎647/436-3460, ⓦ www .darkhorseespresso.com. **Streetcar: Queen (#501).** No menus here: *Dark Horse* gets right down to the coffee. Daily muffins and pastries take the edge off the caffeine blast. **Tango Palace Coffee Co. 1156 Queen St E, near Leslie St** ☎416/465-8085. **Streetcar: Queen**

(#501). *Tango* serves up huge cups and bowls of *café au lait*, cappuccinos and just plain coffee with a bewildering variety of sweets, all to the strains of jitterbug and doo-wop tunes. Some savoury snacks are also available.

West End

Alternative Grounds 333 Roncesvalles Ave, at Howard Park Ave ☎4126/534-5543, ⦿www .alternativegrounds.com. **Streetcar: Dundas (#505).** Toronto's first exclusively Free Trade coffee roastery is as much about lifestyle and outlook as it is about a cup of Joe. Learn about the growers' collectives where your coffee, tea or chocolate came from, recycle with maximum green, or even get a hot beverage to stay or go.
Beaver Café 1192 Queen St W, at Gladstone Ave ☎416/537-2768, ⦿www.thebeavertoronto.com. **Streetcar: Queen (#501).** Stop smirking! The beaver is Canada's national rodent and the *Beaver Café* wears its patriotic heart on its sleeve with a kitsch Canadiana decor. The menu, on the other hand, has pronounced Mediterranean leanings – panini sandwiches stuffed with a wide choice of fillings are a signature item.
Café Bernate 1024 Queen St W, near Power St ☎416/535-2835. **Streetcar: Queen (#501).** This

24-hour food

If you find yourself awake and hungry between 3am and 6am, or if you're just heading home after a long night, these establishments will be open to serve you.

7 Charles Street West	p.140
Fran's	p.142
Golden Griddle	p.142
Mars Restaurant (Fri–Sat)	p.142
Mel's Montréal Delicatessen	p.142
Tim Horton's	p.136

charming neighbourhood café seems almost ladylike, rising with ease and calm above the general hub-bub of galleries, shops and clubs. The menu offers a wide variety of sandwiches, daily soups and sweets with the usual varieties of coffees and teas.
Lakeview Lunch 1132 Dundas St W, at Shaw St ☎416/530-0871. **Streetcar: Dundas (#505).** The sign outside proudly proclaims "Established in 1949" and this deco diner hasn't changed much since. An absolute must for those who proclaim an interest in authentic greasy spoons. Starting at $5.

Light meals

Somewhere in between Toronto's more casual cafés and its full-blown restaurants are smaller, informal and generally inexpensive dining spots that make a perfect place for **light meals**. These are often the best places to sample the diverse cuisines that the city has to offer, at very affordable prices.

Asian fusion

Foxley 207 Ossington Ave, at Dundas St W, West End ☎416/534-8520. **Streetcar: Queen (#501).** Chef Tom Thai's latest establishment gives the Pan-Asian treatment to local produce (think beef cheeks in green curry). There's an emphasis on fish, and the duck prosciutto is raved about. Pickings are slim for vegetarians but everyone can indulge in dessert, especially the black rice pudding. Mains start around $12.
Kubo Radio Asian Pub 894 Queen St E, near Logan Ave, East End ☎416/406-5826, ⦿www .kubo.com. **Streetcar: Queen (#501).**This long, skinny space is filled to the rafters with jars of pickles, bottles of wine and packages of

Asian comestibles and serves up a medley of noodles, salads, spicily seasoned seafood and lake fish, vegetarian dishes and plenty of innovative sake martinis. Weekly theme nights and fun staff keep the party vibe going weekday or weekend.
Lee 603 King St W, at Portland St, Downtown ☎416/504-7867, ⦿www .susur.com/lee. **Streetcar: King (#504).** Maestro chef Susur Lee's eponymous tapas/dim sum restaurant is his lighter, more affordable venue compared to his next-door *Madeline's* (see p.145). Small, treat-size dishes for sharing offer up explosions of tastes, textures and daring pairings. The signature Singapore Slaw, featuring nineteen separate ingredients, is a must-try, as is the duck

confit. Summer grazing on the red velvet patio benches is as special as it gets. Dishes start at $9. Reservations are advisable.

Red Tea Box 696 Queen St W, at Euclid Ave, West End ☎416/203-8882. Streetcar: Queen (#501). The ultimate in feminine Asian fusion: small tables covered in decorative cloths and an assortment of antimacassared chairs make up the front tearoom; there's also a larger room out back beside a garden patio. Bento boxes of dainty fusion dishes are the house speciality, along with an array of teas served in china teapots and a choice of dramatically decorated cakes.

Shanghai Cowgirl 538 Queen St W, at Ryerson Ave, Downtown ☎416/203-6623, ⓦwww .shanghaicowgirl.com. Streetcar: Queen (#501). Worlds collide at this chrome-plated diner turned fusion palace. Gourmet burgers and spicy Asian noodles (both start at $7.95) share space on the menu, and the retro lunch counter buzz turns clubland when weekend DJs arrive.

Silk Road Café 341 Danforth Ave, at Hampton Ave, East End ☎416/63-8660, ⓦwww .silkroadcafe.com. Subway: Chester. Greektown is not where you'd expect to find a Pan-Asian menu, but Tom Wong's establishment is a neighbourhood favourite. A house speciality is the spicy Turfan noodles with beef ($8.95). There's a good selection of vegetarian dishes and appetizers as well.

Spring Rolls 40 Dundas St W, at Yonge St, Downton ☎416/585-2929, ⓦwww.springrolls .ca. Subway: Dundas. Also at other locations. A broad range of Asian cuisines and influences make up *Spring Rolls'* menu, which features stir-fries, soups, noodles, satay, salads and plenty of vegetarian options (mains from $8.99). The Dundas St location is highly recommended, not least for the people-watching.

British

Chippy's 893 Queen St W, at Gore St, Downtown ☎416/866-7474, ⓦwww.chippys.ca. Streetcar: Queen (#501). *Chippy's* serves decidedly upscale fish and chips: haddock, cod, halibut and even salmon are paired with hand-cut chips and dressed with a luscious variety of savoury sauces. Meals start at $6.99.

Epic Fairmont Royal York, 100 Front St W, at York St, Downtown ☎416/368-2511, ⓦwww .fairmont.com/RoyalYork. Subway: Union. Between 2.30pm and 4pm *Epic* serves Toronto's most enticing high tea, featuring dainty, delectable finger sandwiches, little fruit tarts and assorted pastries, scones, Grand Marnier crumpets with honey and, of course, a wide variety of speciality teas to choose from. Royal Tea $25.

🏃 **House on Parliament** 456 Parliament St, at Carlton St, Downtown ☎416/925-4074. Streetcar: Carlton/College (#506). This excellent Cabbagetown pub serves good, affordable food that provides for a variety of dietary choices – their veggie burger is arguably the best in town – and features British stalwarts like steak and kidney pie. There's a rib-sticking weekend brunch and roast beef dinners with all the fixings on Sun. Dishes start at at $7.75.

Caribbean

Ackee Tree 170 Spadina Ave, at Queen St W, Downtown ☎416/866-98730, ⓦwww.ackeetree .com. Streetcar: Queen (#501). All the Jamaican classics are here: curried goat, peas (as in kidney or pinto beans) and rice with oxtail, a good vegetarian selection, and plenty of jerk – plus free internet access when you buy from the menu. Mains start around $9.

Ali's West Indian Roti Shop 1446 Queen St W, Suburbs ☎416/532-7701. Streetcar: Queen (#501). *Ali's* Trinidadian-style *dhalpoori roti* comes stuffed with your choice of meat, seafood or vegetarian options. Plated stews are also available. Island-style soursop juice and ginger beer ice cream are on hand to cool spice-excited palates. *Roti*s start around $5.50.

Irie Food Joint 745 Queen St W, at Palmerston Ave, West End ☎416/366-4743, ⓦwww .iriefoodjoint.com. Streetcar: Queen (#501). *IFJ*'s menu acknowledges the many different traditions that braid the West Indian culinary knot, featuring classics like caliloo soup, jerk chicken, and braised oxtail with rice and peas. Less expected is the roast pork in hosin sauce, or Island-inspired pastas. Surprisingly affordable in such a trendy, attractive dining space. Mains start around $11.

The Real Jerk 709 Queen St E, at Broadview Ave, East End ☎416/463-6055, ⓦwww.therealjerk .com. Streetcar: Queen (#501). *The Real Jerk* is a Toronto tradition, and continues to dish up generous platters of hot, spicy chicken and beef. Even vegetables get jerked. On offer as well are platters of seafood, rotis, the original Rasta Pasta and a selection of vegetarian dishes, all served up with the requisite sides of rice and peas and coleslaw. Mains start at $8.75.

Ritz Caribbean Foods 450 Yonge St, at College St, Uptown ☎416/934-1480. Subway: College. All the West Indian standards – roti, callaloo, jerk and ackee and saltfish – are served up until the wee hours. Eat at tables or take away. Items start at $5.

Chinese

Bright Pearl Seafood 346-348 Spadina Ave (upstairs), at St Andrews St, Downtown ☎416/979-3988, ⓦwww.brightpearlseafood.com. Streetcar: Spadina (#510) or Carlton/College (#506). You have to love a restaurant that proudly posts an award for "best maintained washrooms" on its website. The famous yellow stucco exterior, replete with huge lion statues, paws aloft, and the one-hundred-item all-day dim sum make this slice of culinary theatre popular with locals and tourists alike. Servers zip around the vast, pink banquet hall with carts explaining the dim sum contents of the little bamboo baskets, dishes and trays; you can also order from the menu. Mains start at $10.90, dim sum at $3.

Champion House 480 Dundas St W, at Spadina Ave, Downtown ☎416/977-8282. Streetcar: Dundas (#505). Best known for its Peking Duck – a lengthy experience involving some pleasant theatricality in the service. Vegetarians are also catered for, with tofu and gluten standing in for meat. Mains start at $8.95.

Lee Garden 331 Spadina Ave, at Baldwin St, Uptown ☎416/593-9524. Streetcar: Carlton/College (#506). This unpretentious storefront is where super-chefs like Susur Lee take the family when they go out for Chinese. Local atmosphere abounds and the waiters are like squad commanders as they marshal patient customers in this Cantonese favourite to their tables. Although seafood is high on the list, Lee Garden is famous for its grandfather smoked chicken. Mains start around $11.

Liu Liu Hot Pot 149 Baldwin St, at Spadina Ave, Downtown ☎426/593-8858. Streetcar: Carlton/College (#506) or Spadina (#510). Look for the sign "Famous for Sichuan Hot Pot". As with European fondue, diners sit around a special pot, placed over a burner and filled with bubbling, spicy stock into which they dip a selection of meats, vegetables or fish until cooked. If you're the solitary type you can order soups to go. Group hot pots are around $25.

Mother's Dumplings 79 Huron St, at Dundas St W, Downtown ☎416/217-2008, ⓦwww.mothersdumplings.com. Streetcar: Dundas (#505). Steamed, boiled and pan-fried dumplings, just like owner-chef's mum taught her to make, come in a seemingly unending variety by the dozen. There are also pancakes, steamed buns and noodle dishes. Dumplings start at $4.99 per dozen. Cash only.

Swatow 309 Spadina Ave, at Dundas St, Downtown ☎416/977-0601. Streetcar: Dundas (#505). All the money saved on decor and atmospheric lighting goes into the food, which is old-style Cantonese and Fuk-kin: congee, soups, numerous noodle and rice dishes, chicken and fresh-from-the-tank seafood are dished up at a frenetic pace to happy diners at communal tables. Mains start around $8.

Yung-Sing Pastries 22 Baldwin St, at McCaul St, Uptown ☎416/979-2832. Streetcar: Carlton/College (#506).The paragon of Toronto cheap-eats. For under $5 you can fill up on the ever-popular Chinese buns (the BBQ pork is their number one seller) and delectable custard tarts.

French

Bonjour Brioche 812 Queen St E, at DeGrassi St, East End ☎416/406-1250. Streetcar: Queen (#501). This patisserie-café draws hordes from all over the city with its jewel-like fruit tarts, buttery croissants, puffy brioche and delectable pissaladière, a variation on pizza from Provence. The sit-down menu is a blackboard full of soups, sandwiches, omelettes and quiches. There's usually a line for Sunday brunch, and almost everything is eaten by 2pm, so come early. Items start at $8. Cash only.

Indian

Kama 214 King St W (downstairs), at Simcoe St, Downtown ☎416/599-5262. Streetcar: King (#504). Located across from Roy Thompson Hall, Kama offers a light, modern interpretation of Indian classics. Nothing on the menu is too hot, too buttery, or too exotic. Mains start at $9.95.

Rangoli 1392 Yonge St, at Rosehill Ave, Uptown ☎416/967-4111, ⓦwww.rangolirestaurant.ca. Subway: St. Claire. Perfectly coiffed WASP ladies rub shoulders with burkha-clad women at this oasis of fragrant tandoori. Patient staff explain the menu to all: tandoori fish, tikka and chicken *khurchan* sing with heat and fresh herbs. Vegetarians are well served and there's a full selection of *naan*, *parantha* and *roti* to slup up every last drop. Mains start at $9.95 and the luncheon buffet is a bargain.

Udupi Palace 1460 Gerrard St E, at Craven Rd, East End ☎416/405-8138, ⓦwww.udupipalace .com. **Streetcar: Carlton/College (#506).** Southern Indian, all-vegetarian snacks like *dosa* and *uthapam* – a feathery pancake served with various savoury toppings – share the menu with Schezwan-influenced soup, reflecting Toronto's current craze for Hakka, a blend of Indian and Chinese cuisines. Items start at $3.99.

Italian

7 Charles Street West 7 Charles St W, at Yonge St, Uptown ☎416/928-9041, ⓦwww.7westcafe .com. **Subway: Bloor-Yonge.** This Victorian house has been reborn as a three-floor, 24/7 café. The first floor is a traditional bistro-type dining area, the second an espresso café-bar, and the third is like a friend's attic, complete with a tiny back patio. The simple food, available on the first two floors, is relatively inexpensive and has an Italian twist. The desserts are lovely and there's a bargain-basement brunch on Sun. Items start around $6.

Café Diplomatico 594 College St, at Gore St, Uptown ☎416/534-4637, ⓦwww.diplomatico .ca. **Streetcar: Carlton/College (#506).** Known locally as "the Diplo", this no-nonsense remnant of an earlier time has managed to hold its own among newer, chichi neighbours. Good-sized, no-nonsense pizzas with a range of market-fresh toppings, and a wide selection of sandwiches are served inside or on the packed patio.

John's Italian Café 27 Baldwin St, at McCaul St, Downtown ☎416/5596-8848. **Streetcar: Carlton/College (#506).** An unpretentious, somewhat rustic, café specializing in pizzas (the pesto and goat's cheese deserves its lofty reputation) and pastas, with Italian *dolce* for desserts. The fantastic patio stays open as long as weather permits. Pizzas start around $15.

Kit-Kat Italian Bar & Grill 297 King St W, at John St, Downtown ☎416/977-4461, ⓦwww.kitkattoronto.com. **Streetcar: King (#504).** It's hard not to love *Kit-Kat*. The patio

and front are squeezed for space, but the back booths (out with the kitchen and a growing tree) give you room to spread out and dig into large platters of uncomplicated Italian basics, like *osso bucco*, pasta primavera or a really tasty polenta baked with gorgonzola. Lots of dishes are meant for sharing and the excellent staff guide patrons through the choices of the day with élan. Pastas start around $14.95.

Seven Numbers 307 Danforth Ave, at Bowden St, East End ☎416/469-5183, ⓦwww .sevennumbers.com. **Subway: Chester.** If fate denied you the opportunity to be born into an Italian family that took joy in nurturing you with simple food cooked well, Rosa Marinuzzi and son Tony can help: *Seven Numbers* dishes up antipasti, salads, pastas, seafood, mains and *dolce* that your mother would have made if she could cook like Rosa. Reservations recommended.

Terroni 57A Adelaide St E, at Church St, Downtown ☎416/203-3093. **Streetcar: (#501). Also at 720 Queen St W, Downtown** ☎416/504-0320. **Streetcar: Queen (#504).** ⓦwww.terroni.ca. When the beloved Victoria St branch moved around the corner to the ornate, historic Adelaide Street Courthouse, there was a collective intake of breath. Then a star was born: all the best elements of the menu's original roster of salad, pizza, pasta and panini remain, with added dinner mains, desserts and a serious cellar and bar. Alternatively, visit the original *Terroni* at its Queen W location, where the perfectly structured pizzas, adventurous salads, antipasti, pastas and regional desserts pack in the fans. Mains start at $9.95.

Thirty-Five Elm 35 Elm St, at Bay St, Downtown ☎416/598-1766, ⓦwww.thirtyfiveelm.com. **Subway: Dundas.** Steps from the carnival-like stretch of Yonge near Dundas, Elm St feels like another world. In this renovated Victorian house, wood-burning ovens produce pizzas with a wide variety of toppings on delicate, thin crusts, and if that's not enough there are also pastas, fish (seafood and lake), and meaty mains, many of them sourced from local producers. Pizzas start at $15.

Trattoria Nervosa 75 Yorkville Ave, at Bellair St, Uptown ☎416/961-4642, ⓦwww.eatnervosa.com. **Subway: Bay.** Pretty *Nervosa* is a great spot for people- (and celebrity) watching. The open kitchen produces meal-sized salads, filling pastas (the capellini with goat's cheese and sundried tomatoes is a favourite) and delicious thin crust pizzas. The patio off the second-floor lounge has a terrific view of Yorkville, and service is unfailingly pleasant. Antipasti start around $9.95.

International

Delux 92 Ossington Ave, at Queen St W, West End ☎416/537-0134. **Streetcar: Queen (#501).** In a town famous for melding cuisines, *Delux*'s gastronomic hybrid is French-Cuban, which translates into fare such as chubby pressed Cuban sandwiches and flaky French pastries, both sweet and savoury. Look for the white arrow and the boho patrons clustered around the little café tables; this place is too hip for a sign. Meals start around $13.

Kalendar Koffee House 546 College St, at Euclid Ave, West End ☎416/923-4138. **Streetcar: Carlton/College (#506).** *Kalendar* is the loveliest café in town, with dark wood panelling and intimate booths providing an old-world atmosphere. Innovative light meals are served by excellent staff, and a well-stocked bar complements a full range of espresso drinks. Their signature sandwiches are naan wraps, which give a hint of the East. Mains start around $11.95.

▼ Kalendar Koffee House

Utopia Café & Grill 585 College St, at Euclid Ave, West End ☎416/534-7751, ⓦwww.utopiacafe.ca. **Streetcar: Carlton/College (#506).** The lion

lies down with the lamb at this semi-vegetarian, semi-carnivore bistro where most of the meaty menu options are replicated in a vegetarian version (or vice versa depending on your dietary inclinations). The menu selections are globally influenced, and if you can't stay there are plenty of take-out options. Sunday brunch starts at noon. Burgers start at $7.95.

North American

Black Camel 4 Cresent Rd, at Yonge St, Uptown ☎416/929-7518, ⓦwww.blackcamel.ca. **Subway: Rosedale.** Living up to the "good things come in small packages" maxim, this tiny Rosedale outfit serves delicious sandwiches of pulled pork shoulder, slow-cooked brisket and seared steak, plus serious chilli, to a discerning clientele.

Craft Burger 573 King St W, at Portland St, Downtown ☎416/596-6660. **Streetcar: King (#504).** True to its name, *Craft Burger* serves up flame-broiled burgers of all varieties (organic beef, chicken and vegetarian) on quality rolls with a variety of non-traditional, fresh toppings like avocado, blue cheese and roasted garlic. Crisp fries or onion rings complement the main event and milkshakes are available.

Edward Levesque's Kitchen 1290 Queen St E, at Leslie St, East End ☎416/465-3600, ⓦwww.edwardlevesque.ca. **Streetcar: Queen (#501).** In a town of celebrity chefs and tycoon restaurateurs, Edward "Ted" Levesque is one of Toronto's genuine characters. His diner-style restaurant offers a menu (mains from $9) that changes with the seasons, typically jumping up comfort fare like salmon fillets with tandoori spice, or serving pork rack with plums, sage and polenta studded with sharp pecorino cheese. Open Tues–Sat for dinner, Thurs & Fri for lunch, and Sat & Sun for the hugely popular brunch.

Four 187 Bay St (concourse level, Commerce Court), at Wellington St W, Downtown ☎416/386-1444, ⓦwww.fourtoronto.com. **Subway: King; streetcar: King (#504).** Tucked under the flashier *Far Niente* (see p.148) but sharing an executive chef and a vision, *Four* has two guiding principles: everything must be as fresh and local as possible; and no single item on the menu can top 650 calories. Could a travelling calorie-counter ask for more? The full menu borrows international styles for local produce, notably the lake fish mains and salads, along with plenty of vegetarian options and a guilt-free dessert sampler. Open for lunch and dinner Mon–Fri; items start around $5.

Fran's 20 College St, at Yonge St, Downtown ☎416/923-9867. **Streetcar: Carlton/College (#506). Also at 200 Victoria St, at Dundas St, Downtown. Subway: Dundas.** ⊛**www .fransrestaurant.com.** You can now have *Fran's* old-school-style or a fancy new *Fran's* alongside Dundas Square. Both stay true to a fifty-plus-year tradition of serving up fine diner-style dishes 24/7, just the way former regulars like Glenn Gould (see pp.54–55) and the King of Norway used to like them. House specialities include Fran's all-day breakfast and the classic grilled cheese sandwich. Meals start at $7.99.

Gilead Café 4 Gilead Place, near King St E, Downtown ☎647/288-0680, ⊛**www.gileadcafe .ca. Streetcar: King (#504).** Super-chef Jamie Kennedy (see p.145) is Toronto's leading locivor. His latest lunch stop and deli on tucked-away Gilead Place is all about serving food that is fresh, seasonal and sustainable. The best one-stop café to sample the regional producers everyone raves about for sit-down or take-away.

Golden Griddle 45 Carlton St, at Yonge St, Uptown ☎416/977-5044. **Subway: Carlton. Also 11 Jarvis St, at Front St, Downtown** ☎416/865-1263. **Subway: Union.** ⊛**www.goldengriddlecorp .com.** Optimistically billed as a family restau-rant, the *Golden Griddle* sees a late-night, early-morning clientele in its downtown branches that are an attraction in their own right. This 24-hour chain serves mainly an array of pancakes, but a full menu is also available. Items start at $5.99.

Harbord Room 89 Harbord St, at Sussex Mews, Uptown ☎416/962-8989. **Streetcar: Spadina (#510).** This sophisticated Annex gem features a stylish international menu, much of it locally sourced, that runs the gamut from comfort favourites like leg of lamb and root-veg mash to fresh pasta and tapas-type dishes for sharing. There are only 31 tables and a patio in the summer so reser-vations for dinner are recommended. Mains start around $18.

Insomnia Internet Bar Café Inc 563 Bloor St W, at Bathurst St, Uptown ☎416/588-3907, ⊛**www .insomniacafe.com. Subway: Bathurst.** Most cafés are set up to get their customers going first thing in the morning. *Insomnia* is there for you when you get your day started in the middle of the night. This fully licensed Internet

café has six computer terminals, DJs, and a kitchen that stays open until 2am, plus a large-screen TV and couches on which to snuggle. Booths are available, too.

Jamie Kennedy Wine Bar 9 Church St, south of Front St, Downtown ☎416/362-1957, ⊛**www.jamiekennedy.ca. Subway: Union.** Perhaps the best venue to see what all the chat about Jamie K is about – and the other Jamie, for that matter, as sommelier Jamie Drummond is also making a name for himself. An open kitchen, helmed by *chef de cuisine* Toby Nemeth, features ultra-fresh, regional food served tapas-style with suggested wine pairings. The seasonal fare is deceptively simple and deserves a slow sampling. Pulled pork poutine with JK's signature Yukon Gold fries and the smoked pickerel are classics. Items start at $5.

Mars Restaurant 432 College St, at Bathurst St, Uptown ☎416/921-6332. **Streetcar: Carlton/ College (#506).** The original *Mars* on College has been around so long (since 1951) it's in danger of becoming respectable. The all-day breakfast – eggs, rashers, toast and/or home fries – remains a Toronto cheap eats classic at $7.95, and the omelettes are still under $5.

Mel's Montreal Delicatessen 440 Bloor St W, at Howland Ave, Uptown ☎416/966-8881. **Subway: Bathurst.** This family-run deli is a smoked brisket slice of old-school Montréal, starting with the 24/7 hours. Poutine, matzo ball soup, omelettes and an all-day breakfast – it's all here in heaping portions. Mains start around $7.99.

Phil's Original BBQ 838 College St, at Ossington Ave, West End ☎416/532-8161. **Streetcar: Carlton/College (#506).** Serious BBQ is down to basics: meat, salt-n-spices, a special sauce and slow smoke. Phil has these elements under control. Aficionados are dedicated to the pork shoulder, although chicken and beef brisket also get the BBQ treatment.

Pic Nic 747 Queen St E, at Grant St, East End ☎647/435-5298. **Streetcar: Queen (#501).** A little bit of wine, a little bit of cheese (with a great Québec selection), and a small fixed menu featuring Gallic-influenced daily specials make this cosy, exposed-brick space with communal and private tables a popular low-key hang-out in the ever-evolving East End. You can design your own platters or build your own sandwiches in addition to ordering à la carte.

Rebel House 1068 Yonge St, at Roxborough St, Uptown ☎416/927-0704, ⊛www.rebelhouse.ca. Subway: Rosedale. An update on traditional Ontario farmhouse cuisine (barley risotto and meatloaf sandwiches being two favourites) plus a fine selection of Ontario wines, ciders and craft beers make this Rosedale hangout a popular eatery all week, but be prepared for the Sunday brunch line-ups. Specials start at $7.95.

Thai

Green Mango 730 Yonge St, at Charles St E, Uptown ☎416/928-0021, ⊛www.greenmango.ca. Subway: Bloor-Yonge. Also three other locations. One of Toronto's early Thai restaurants, this popular establishment offers sit-down dining and cafeteria-style take-away. Both are perfect for inexpensive, quick lunches. Spicy noodles are dressed up with tofu, chicken or vegetables, and fresh (not fried) spring rolls and sticky rice desserts are on the menu as well. Mains start at $7.95.

Pi-Tom's Thai Cuisine 6 Alexander St, at Yonge St, Uptown ☎416/966-1813, ⊛www.pi-tom .com. Subway: Carlton. A terrific find for lunch, though the five-course dinner specials are worthy of investigation as well. Offers a good selection of Royal Thai-style cuisine including tamarind fish, ginger duck, a variety of noodles and a choice of vegetarian mains. Lunch specials start at $8.75.

Salad King 335 Yonge St (entrance on Gould St), Downtown ☎416/971-7041, ⊛www.saladking .com. Subway: Dundas. *Salad King's* spiffed-up decor hasn't pushed the cost of a meal over $10, making it hugely popular with the nearby university's students. Thai food aficionados come for the home-made Panang curry. Items can be ordered according to a heat scale from one to twenty (don't go there unless you know what you're doing), and the vegetarian options are plentiful. Mains start at $6.45.

Thai To Go 452 Gerrard St E, near Sumach St, Downtown ☎416/515-8424, ⊛www.thai2go.com. Streetcar: Carlton/College (#506). A step in authenticity away from what most Torontonians think of as Thai food, this diminutive Cabbagetown take-away emphasizes the different sauces that dress the protein, sticks to either glass or thick rice noodles, and throws in a few house specialities like the delectable crêpes. Super-fresh ingredients and attractive presentation.

Vegetarian

Fresh, by Juice for Life 147 Spadina Ave, at Queen St W, Downtown ☎416/599-4442. Streetcar: Queen (#501). Also at 894 Queen St W, at Crawford St, West End (streetcar: Queen #501) and 326 Bloor St W, at Spadina Ave, Uptown (subway: Spadina) ⊛www.juiceforlife .com. Ya-hoo! Great-tasting vegetarian food served in vibrant, attractive surroundings. Rice bowls with names such as "Tantric" and "Warrior" are the speciality and feature delicious combinations of tempeh, tofu, greens and gravies over brown basmati rice. Burgers, sandwiches and wraps have optional sides of fries, and as well as the signature shakes, smoothies and juices, there are also espresso drinks, wines and micro beers. Mains start at $9.

King's Café 192 August Ave, at College St, Downtown ☎416/591-1340, ⊛www.kingscafe .com. Streetcar: Carlton/College (#506). This attractive café, in the heart of bustling Kensington Market, features mostly Chinese "mock meat" dishes, namely tofu-styled and presented to vaguely to resemble meat. It's an aquired taste for the most part, but even committed carnivores will find the rich desserts and espresso coffees more than enough reason to stop by. Mains start at $2.50.

Mela's Italian Vegetarian Café 7A Yorkville Ave, at Yonge St, Uptown ☎416/916-0619. Subway: Bloor-Yonge. Toronto's first and so-far only Italian vegetarian café is starting small with only twelve seats, but has been garnering rave reviews (the chef was formerly at the *Four Seasons Hotel*'s *Truffles* and *La Fenice*, after all), and the daily specials like breaded eggplant in tomato sauce, wholewheat cannelloni, crepes or panini sell out. The traditional Italian pastries are a huge draw as well. Lunch items start at $2.75.

Simon's Wok Vegetarian Kitchen 797 Gerrard St E, at Logan Ave, East End ☎416/778-9836. Streetcar: Carlton/College (#506). An excellent Chinese, vegan-vegetarian restaurant on the eastern outposts of Riverdale's Chinatown. Most of the dishes come from the ancient tradition of Buddhist monastic cooking and are thus suitable for vegans. Hot pots, mock meat dishes, stir-fries and house specialities like fragrant ginger rice have earned loyal support from a diverse crowd of patrons. Mains start around $7.95.

CAFÉS AND LIGHT MEALS | Light meals

8

Restaurants

Dining out is one of Toronto's most pleasurable experiences, and the passion with which residents embrace gastronomy is readily evident. Two of the city's most popular festivals, **Summerlicious** and **Winterlicious** (see p.209 & p.207) revolve exclusively around gaining access to high-end restaurants that may otherwise be prohibitively expensive to the average diner. Gastro-festivals aside, with more than five thousand **restaurants** in the city, everyone is sure to find a place where they can afford to educate their palates, discover new cuisines, or just enjoy a good meal. Competition between restaurants is fierce, so the **service** and the quality of the food are usually good to excellent.

A handy way to sample the fare and enjoy the ambience of pricier establishments is to take advantage of **lunch menus**, which tend to be much better value than dinner menus. As well, we've listed plenty of places where you can eat light or full meals in a more casual, affordable setting, see Chapter 7.

Restaurant **opening hours** and times of peak flow vary, so it's a good idea to call ahead. **Maps**, with all the restaurants in this chapter keyed to them, can be found in the back of the book.

For an up-to-the-minute scoop on who the best chefs are and where to dine, consult Ⓦwww.martiniboys.com or the glossy *Toronto Life* magazine, which publishes a much-coveted annual restaurant review guide, also available online at Ⓦwww.torontolife.com. You could also try Ⓦwww.dine.to, which offers deals and free coupons as well as listings for three thousand establishments.

Downtown

African

Sultan's Tent 49 Front St E, at Church St ☎416/961-0601. Subway: Union. This beautiful location in the St Lawrence Market neighbourhood gives two experiences: the front room is all natural woods and light; the back room is all silk tenting and belly dancers. The fixed-price four-course menu – featuring Moroccan delicacies such as pan-fried monkfish or couscous royale served up in conical tajines – starts at $39.95. Belly dancers shimmy away seven nights a week.

Chinese

Asian Legend 418 Dundas St W, at Huron St ☎416/977-3909, Ⓦwww.asianlegend.ca. Streetcar: Dundas (#505). The speciality here is peppery northern Chinese cuisines with a particular emphasis on regional dim sum goodies like rolled onion pancakes with sliced beef. The camphor-smoke duck, Kung Pao chicken, Moo Shu pork and Peking Duck are all highly esteemed. Prices range from $5.50 to $30.

🐀 **Lai Wah Heen** *Metropolitan Hotel*, 108 Chestnut St, at Dundas St ☎416/977-9899,

Celebrity chefs

Chefs really are Toronto's celebrities. Often, these culinary superstars are followed by their fans, who read avidly about them in gossip columns devoted to foodie chit-chat and save up for special occasions at their restaurants. Five-star Toronto chefs, and their respective restaurants, include:

Susur Lee	*Madeline's* (see p.145); *Lee* (see p.137)
Jamie Kennedy	*Jamie Kennedy at the Gardiner* (see p.152); *Jamie Kennedy Wine Bar* (see p.142) and *Gilead Café* (see p.142)
Mark McEwan	*Bymark* (see p.147)
Claudio Aprile	*Colborne Lane* (see p.146)
Greg Couillard	*Spice Room and Chutney Bar* (see p.151)

@ www.metropolitan.com. Streetcar: Dundas (#505). The name means "elegant meeting place", which it most certainly is. This high-end, split-level dining room is as elegant as its exceptional menus, which draw upon all the great regional Chinese cuisines and give them a fresh update taking in Guangdong-style fresh seafood, spicy northern beef dishes, Wuxi spare ribs and tea-smoked chicken ($24–36). The famous dim sum ($3.50–8) features new takes on classic regional Chinese ingredients such as the deep-fried jumbo prawns coated with taro root paste. Fixed-price menus, banquets, an extensive tea list and a very interesting wine list round out the wealth of offerings.

Pearl Harbourfront Queens Quay Terminal, 207 Queens Quay W, at York St @ 416/203-1233, @ www.pearlharbourfront.ca. LRT from Union. Perched on the edge of Lake Ontario, this upscale eatery patriotically features all the familiar Cantonese fare (from $8.75), attractively presented in a fine dining atmosphere.

Spadina Garden 116 Dundas St W, at Bay St @ 416/977-3413. Streetcar: Dundas (#505); subway: Dundas. A comfort food family favourite for almost three decades, *Spadina Gardens* features Hakka cuisine, a distinct branch of the Chinese diaspora living in India. China is the dominant influence on the extensive menu (look for perennial favourites like Crispy Ginger Chicken), but India holds sway in spicy noodle dishes and stews ($11).

French

Jules 147 Spadina Ave, at Richmond St @ 416/348-8886. Streetcar: Queen (#501). Tucked between coffee shops and the Fashion District wholesalers, *Jules* is a real

find. Huge bowls of steamed mussels in a garlicky white-wine sauce complement rosemary-rubbed chicken, while a daily selection of savoury crêpes or toothsome quiches are a bargain ($17–20; $25 set menu). The wine list is thoughtful if somewhat limited, and the desserts are delectable.

Fusion

Blowfish Restaurant & Sake Bar 668 King St W, at Bathurst St @ 416/860-0606, @ www.blowfishrestaurant.com. Streetcar: King (#504). This dressed-to-kill former bank stylishly presents grazing favourites and full meals with Korean and Japanese influences. Dishes range from sushi (from $4.50), through salmon salad ($14) to kobe beef seared on a hot stone ($38), while the tea list rivals the wine list in selection and scope.

Madeline's 601 King St W, at Bathurst St @ 416/603-2205, @ www.susur.com. Streetcar: King (#504). Susur Lee's latest venture, *Madeline's* gives the fusion treatment to mostly European cuisine. Set in a flamboyant Belle Epoque decor, *Madeline's* is fun and relatively affordable, with mains topping out around $24. The dishes pack the punch that Lee's admirers demand: Cornish hen in a gorganzola sauce ($17) combines Chinese cooking techniques with the most Occidental of ingredients; and the signature slow-cooked pork belly ($17) is a triumph.

Marben 488 Wellington St W, at Portland St @ 416/979-1990, @ www.marbenrestaurant.com. Streetcar: King (#504). This latest addition to a strip filling up fast with clubs and restaurants has a swanky interior and a menu that offers Japanese-style beef, Chinese-style noodles and duck with Cuban- and Portuguese-style sides (dinner mains $24–33). The cocktail list trumps the wine list for fun.

Monsoon 100 Simcoe St ☏ 416/979-7172, ⓦ www.monsoonrestaurant.ca. **Subway: St Andrew.** The Canad-Asian wood interior won awards, so pause for a martini at the bar before going into the dining room. Meals like Asian salmon tartar with wasabi cream arrive on delicate raku dishes, and the light, assured preparation boasts imaginative combinations. The menu pricing is clear: Small ($8–24), Large ($24–36) with sides at $4–8.

Rain 19 Mercer St ☏ 416/599-7246, ⓦ www .rain.ca. **Streetcar: King (#504).** *Rain* raised the bar for the retso-lounge scene with this sleek beauty, housed in a former women's prison. Mains such as the lobster-Muscovy duck ($37) and the Peking-style squab ($36) show off chef Michael Rubino's elegant, market-fresh Asian interpretations. Good but pricey wine list.

Indian

Babur 273 Queen St W, at John St ☏ 416/599-7720. **Streetcar: Queen (#501).** Buttery sauces, delicately spiced stews and fluffy naan breads are delivered to your table by helpful waiters. The luncheon buffet ($10.95) is a Queen W bargain.

Bombay Palace 71 Jarvis St, at King St E ☏ 416/368-8048. **Streetcar: King (#504).** Northern-style cooking with a nod towards Delhi is served up in a serene, smart dining room. Crispy pakoras and samosas are good bets for starters. Main courses à la carte start at $11.95 and include fish, meat and vegetable dishes.

Dhaba 309 King St W, at John St (upstairs) ☏ 416/740-6622. **Streetcar: King (#504).** *Dhaba* has been winning a dedicated following for chef P.K. Ahluwalia's subtle tweaks on standard northern dishes like roasted rack of lamb ($13.95) and Goan Xiacuttin, a spicy chicken dish with plenty of heat ($14.95). The sumptuous butter chicken and vegetarian mains are pretty rich for a pre-theatre meal, but combined with the swish decor are show-stoppers themselves.

International

Brassaii 461 King St W, at Spadina Ave ☏ 416/598-4730. **Streetcar: King (#504).**

Brassaii is great. Set back at the end of a courtyard, it boasts a sleek, sophisticated bar at the front, has a nice patio, and is even open for breakfast treats like croissants and Nutella with bananas, or blueberry buttermilk pancakes ($7). Lunches are comfort food, albeit sophisticated, such as the homemade burgers with truffles and cheese ($14) and the dinner menu features updates on stalwarts like pickerel on white bean and corn succotash ($24), fresh hand-rolled pasta ($19) and a first-rate steak tartare, all arriving in huge portions.

Colborne Lane 45 Colborne St, at Church St ☏ 416/368-9009, ⓦ www.colbornelane.com. **Streetcar: King (#504).** Chef Claudio's talent lies in mixing seemingly unmixable tastes and textures: think Peking duck with licorice and burnt honey sauce. The space is an old building with exposed brick and rubbed wood reflected in huge antique mirrors. Seating is a mix of cosy corners, smaller tables and a long communal table. Considering the setting and the hype, dinner mains are surprisingly affordable at about $33 on the dinner menu. Tasting and lunch menus are also available.

Ultra Supper Club 314 Queen St W, at Spadina Ave ☏ 416/263-0330. **Streetcar: Queen (#501).** Huge candelabra lit with twinkling pillar candles provide flattering light for the beautiful women and their hipster companions, while opaque silver curtains delicately divide tables for group reservations from the main room. The menu is an update of traditional French classics, like roast veal tenderloin with chanterelles and fennel-dusted sweetbreads ($33). A wonderful place to splash out and celebrate something.

Sen5es *SoHo Metropolitan Hotel*, **328 Wellington St W, at Blue Jays Way** ☏ 416/935-0400 ⓦ www .senses.ca. **Subway: Union; streetcar: King (#504).** Chef Patrick Lin is known for taking Asian ingredients and preparing them in the classical French/international method (pan-seared crispy duck breast with seared foie gras, shitake and oyster mushrooms and a port and fig purée at $37, for example). His fans praise the seamless taste transitions in his signature dishes and his restraint in doing simple things very well.

Rosewater Supper Club 19 Toronto St, at King St E ☏ 416/214-5888, ⓦ www.libertygroup.com. **Streetcar: King (#504).** This stylish charmer is all nineteenth-century elegance with an international-style menu that includes regional produce (such as Ontario rack of lamb, $39), and Canadian exotica (such as Nunavut wild caribou marinated in blackcurrent and juniper berry jus, $38). Lunch menus are seasonal, lighter and less expensive ($10–22) than dinner mains. The kitchen is visible behind a glass wall and a seat in the main dining space by the high fanlight windows creates the perfect balance between old and new.

Italian

Tutti Matti 364 Adelaide St W, at Spadina Ave ☎416/597-8839, ⓦwww.tuttimatti.com. **Streetcar: King (#504).** Pared-down Tuscan cuisine in all its seasonal variations. A Fall salad features roasted beets pricked up with horseradish vinaigrette ($9), or wild boar stew ($17); summer bounty offers spinach and ricotta stuffed into fresh, hand-cut ravioli pouches ($16). Dinner mains cover traditional favourites like roasted rabbit with olive and rosemary ($25), and the lunch menu includes a popular three-course *prix fixe* for $15.

Six Steps 53–55 Colborne St, at Church St ☎416/5404-4800. **Streetcar: King (#504).** *Six Steps*' lunch menu is Tuscan-inspired, featuring salads, pizzas and pastas ($8–16), while the dinner menu is largely regional and Canada-sourced meat and fish dishes – ribeye steak from Welllington County ($42), Nova Scotia lobster parpadelle ($32) – served with an Italianate flourish. The walls have been taken back to the original brick and beams, giving a warm, masculine quality to the beautiful rooms.

Japanese

Hiro Sushi 171 King St E, at Jarvis St ☎416/304-0550. **Streetcar: King (#504).** Hiro Yoshida raised the bar for Toronto's sushi establishments when he opened this sliver of a restaurant. It offers unparalleled subtlety in all respects: decor, presentation and the food itself, and many hold it to be the best sushi spot in town. Sushi selections start at $6.

Ki Bay Wellington Tower, BCE Place, 181 Bay St ☎416/304-5888, ⓦwww.kijapanese.com. **Subway: King.** The word *ki* means "pure" or "raw" in Japanese – not to be confused with "simple". *Ki* serves up sushi in all its expensive variations, as well as dainty salads, and *kushiyaki* – little snack-sized

skewers of grilled fish, meats or vegetables ($12–32).

Nami 55 Adelaide St E, at Victoria St ☎416/362-4745, ⓦwww.namirestaurant.ca. **Streetcar: King (#504).** *Nami* figured out what works, and sticks to a winning formula. This is an old-school Japanese restaurant with a dark, suave interior lined with private booths. The sushi bar serves the classics (from $10.45) and the menu includes some sushi using fresh local lake fish. There is also a robata counter, where grilled seafood is prepared in front of you. Fixed-price four-course menus start at $25 for dinner.

North American

360 CN Tower CN Tower, 301 Front St W, at John St ☎416/362-5411 ⓦwww.cntower.ca. **Subway: Union.** Why not schedule lunch or dinner around the inevitable visit? The restaurant, which is in the "donut" three-quarters up the CN Tower, slowly rotates a full 360 degrees in 72 minutes, thus affording an unrivalled view of the city and around. The uncomplicated, vegetarian-friendly menu, with dinner mains from $29 to $39 – pastas, seafood, sirloin steak with fries – is enhanced by the addition of regional dishes (smoked rainbow trout instead of tuna, for example), achieving an admirable balance between locals' tastes and visitors' demands.

Boiler House 55 Mill St, at Parliament St ☎416/203-2121, ⓦwww.boilerhouse.ca. **Bus: Front St (#72A).** Seafood stalwarts share space with mains fresh from the farm: citrus-marinated rack of lamb served with herbed mushroom strudel, or organic pork chops grilled with rosemary are regional alternatives to the surf'n'turf and ahi tuna, which remain on the menu ($22–36). The spacious two-storey interior of this former distillery boiler house features massive industrial beams and bricks stripped bare; the outdoor patio usually features live music to serenade diners. Weekend Brunch ($30 per person, until 3pm) is a huge spread, with fruits, salads, pastries, waffles, omelettes, cheeses, cured meats and more.

Bymark in the Toronto Dominion Tower, 66 Wellington St W, at Bay St ☎416/3777-1144, ⓦwww.bymarkca. **Subway: King or St Andrew.** Chef and restaurateur Mark McEwan immediately put *Bymark* on the map, not for the stylish, masculine decor by the Yabu-Pushelberg design team, or for the verve and nuance of his kitchen, but for the $37 hamburger with a side of fries served in a cone. A high-end power lunch could include the aforesaid burger, or the sumptuous grilled cheese sandwich made with aged brie, lobster, pancetta and a daub of citrus aioli ($27); dinner mains range from a reasonable $25 for *coq au vin* to $90 for striploin steak of Australian Wagyu beef.

Canoe in the Toronto Dominion Tower, 66 Wellington St W, at Bay St ☎416/364-0054. Subway: King or St Andrew. The minimalist splendour of Mies van der Rohe's Toronto Dominion Tower provides a dramatic venue for an excellent restaurant. Way up on the 54th floor, executive chef Anthony Walsh has stayed on top of the restaurant game by continually reinventing Canadian cuisine (East Coast seafood, Quebec cheeses, Yukon caribou, feral greens, wild berries) alongside one of the best wine lists in Toronto – indeed, some of Ontario's best vintages are produced exclusively for this sky-high venue. Six-course tasting menus start at $85.

Chez Victor 30 Mercer St, at John St ☎416/883-3431, ⓦwww.germaintoronto.com. Streetcar: King (#504). Sharing space with the *Hotel Le Germain* (see p.128), *Chez Victor's* Québec cheeses, Niagara charcuterie, Maritime scallops and much organic local produce get the maestro treatment by chef David Chrystian. Appetizers start around $9 and the upper-range beef mains are $36. The wine list is a source of pride, and pairings are suggested on the menu – keep an eye out for otherwise unavailable Ontario treats (Organized Crime's '06 Pinot Gris stands out).

Far Niente 187 Bay St, at Wellington St E ☎416/214-9922 ⓦwww.farnienterestaurant .com. Streetcar: King (#504). An excellent Financial District restaurant featuring seasonal, regional, vegetarian-friendly cuisine that crosses luxurious quality with comfort food cosiness. Try the lobster and grilled cheese sandwich or the fontina cheese fondue, glammed up with truffle honey and toasted hazelnuts (both $21). Serious carnivores will want to investigate the Angus striploin ($26). *Far Niente* has its own bakery on the premises, so don't spurn the carbs. It also has a first-rate wine list featuring rare Ontario vintages and, of course, a good representation of Californians.

Le Papillon on Front 69 Front St E, at Church St ☎416/367-0303, ⓦwww.lepapillonfront.com.

Subway: Union. A recent move around the corner has been a happy metamorphosis for this Toronto favourite, which continues to delight diners with its dinner-sized crêpes, plump with sweet or savoury fillings tweaked with Québecois flair (from $13). The menu also includes *tortier* (a Québec meat pie), as well as bistro standards like onion soup and steak-frites; there's also a comprehensive wine and beer list. The new address is an old building with high ceilings, exposed brick and beams, and dramatic chandeliers. Open for lunch, dinner and weekend brunch.

Lucien 36 Wellington St E, at Church St ☎416/504-9990, ⓦwww.lucienrestaurant.com. Subway: Union. *Lucien* is a handsome, whimsical slice of a mythical Europe in Toronto's St Lawrence Market district. The uncomplicated menu works around regional, seasonal produce so the challenge is to do simple things well. Individual courses are available as stand-alones, or you can order three-course ($75) or four-course ($85) *prix fixe* and let the chef and the wonderful staff take care of you.

Portuguese

Adega Restaurante 33 Elm St, at Yonge St ☎416/977-4338, ⓦwww.adegarestaurante.ca. Subway: Dundas or Carlton. This Portuguese charmer's signature platter, the *Petisco* (meaning a bit of everything), is a great bargain: grilled *chouriço*, gravlax, grilled sardines, grilled squid, fresh Portuguese goat's cheese and prosciutto for $29. Low lighting, dark wood accents, discrete booths and excellent service make this a great choice for an intimate evening.

Seafood

Starfish Oyster Bed & Grill 100 Adelaide St E, at Jarvis St ☎416/366-7827, ⓦwww .starfishoysterbed.com. Streetcar: King (#504). Seafood and lake fish get great billing as mains ($18–35) but the star treatment goes to the international array of oysters, from Malpeque, Prince Edward Island, all the way to Coromandel, New Zealand, priced according to availability and seasonality. Serious bivalve-lovers can shuck around with owner, oyster author and World Oyster Opening Champion Patrick McMurray every Thurs night after 10pm at the restaurant's Shucker's Club (bring your own knife).

Rodney's Oyster House 469 King Street W
☎416/363-8105. **Streetcar: King (#504).**
Toronto's favourite oyster bar serves more
than twenty varieties of the featured mollusk
and servings of scallops, crab, lobster and
shrimp complete the crustaceous collection.
Specials of the day feature market-fresh
grilled fish ($12–27). The wine and dessert
menus are short, but the selections of beer
and Scotch are impressive.

Steakhouses

Barberian's Steakhouse 7 Elm St, at Yonge St
☎416/597-0335, ⓦhttp://barberians.com.
Subway: Dundas. *Barberian's* hasn't changed
much since it opened in 1959, serving
Toronto's first shrimp cocktail (now $22.50)
and catering to Richard Burton and
Elizabeth Taylor when Burton opened the
first performances of *Camelot*. It continues
to offer the best no-nonsense steak in town,
with some seafood dishes thrown in for
good measure ($25–55). The wine cellar is
exceptional.

**Ruth's Chris Steak House 145 Richmond
St W, at University Ave** ☎416/955-1455,
ⓦwww.ruthschris-toronto.com. **Subway:
Osgoode.** This outlet of the Ruth's Chris
group is classic: dark wood booths,
tuxedoed waiters and dark red accents set
the stage for hand-cut steaks (from $40)
that arrive at your table in varying shades of
pink, sizzling away at the precise broiling
temperature of 180°F.

Thai

**Bangkok Paradise 506 Queen St W, at Ryerson
Ave** ☎416/504-3210, ⓦwww.bangkokparadise
.ca. **Streetcar: Queen (#501).** Funky Thai for the
Queen West crowd including a few
Malaysian additions such as Malay noodles
($8–12) and tofu *goering* ($8.75), plus a wide
range of vegetarian options, starting at $8.
The soups are wonderful and can be a meal
in themselves (small $4.50, large $8.25).

Vegetarian

**Bo De Duyen 254 Spadina Ave (upstairs), at
Queen St W** ☎416/703-1247, ⓦwww
.bodeduyen.com. **Streetcar: Spadina (#510).**
This popular walk-up greets guests with
puffs of incense and an ancestral shrine
halfway up the stairs. The absence of any
animal by-products means that even the

▼ Bangkok Paradise

strictest vegan can eat here with a clear
conscience. Pages and pages of selections
($5–12.95) include "mock" meat and
seafood items made of tofu or gluten, but if
you'd rather not remember meat, the rice,
noodle and hot-pot sections offer plentiful
alternatives. The wine list is thoughtful but
the teas and juices are better.

Le Commensal 655 Bay St (entrance off Elm St)
☎416/596-9364, ⓦwww.commensal.ca.
Subway: Dundas. The cafeteria-style, pay-by-
the-gram setup of this airy restaurant is its
only drawback. Notwithstanding this, the
place attracts a large number of non-
vegetarians with its excellent variety of
offerings, including soups, salads, potpies,
stews, casseroles and baked goods. All
items are clearly marked for vegans or
lacto-ovo vegetarians. A large dessert
counter tempts with delectables like maple
sugar pie, fruit cobblers and sweet pastries.

**Fressen Herbacious Cuisine 478 Queen St W,
at Spadina Ave** ☎416/504-5127, ⓦwww
.fressenrestaurant.com. **Streetcar: Queen (#501).**
An upscale vegan dining room, with a solid
cocktail bar: what a notion! Vegetarians,
vegans and their fellow-travellers finally have
an elegant place to go to. The service can
be uneven, but when the kitchen is firing on
all gas rings it produces innovative, seasonal
fare. Options include gluten-free and wheat-
free mains (from $9). A full meal can also be
made of the delicious appetizers, and the
juice and smoothie list is extensive.

Vegetarian Haven 17 Baldwin St, at McCaul St ☎416/504-5127. **Streetcar: Carlton/College (#506).** An attractive, pan-Asian vegetarian restaurant, *Haven* pulls out the stops on the use of meat substitutes, offering an abundance of tofu, tempeh (cultured soy beans), seitan (wheat gluten) and TVP (textured vegetable protein). A house speciality is the mock seafood "Souper-bowl". Suitable for vegans, with mains ranging from $9.99 to $11.99.

Uptown

African

Ethiopian House 4 Irwin Ave ☎416/923-5438. **Subway: Wellesley.** This two-storey restaurant offers meals graced with complex, aromatic spicing. Huge discs of sourdough bread called *injera* replace cutlery, and large platters (starting at $8.95) covered with yurt-like raffia caps replace plain old dishes. For a nominal fee, a full-blown coffee ceremony replaces a plain cup o' joe at the end of the delicious meal.

Manyata Hazelton Lanes, 55 Avenue Rd ☎416/935-0000, ⊛www.spiceroommanyata .com. **Subway: Bay (Cumberland exit).** The name is Kiswahili for "meeting place", coincidentally the original meaning for Toronto. Manyata draws upon the best of the African diaspora for inspiration: think jerk roasted turkey breast burgers ($12), *tilapia Wakupaka* ($15) – the tilapia is a fish origi-nally from the Congo and Wakupaka is a spicy Kenyan sauce – or Kikuya chicken pot pie with a puff pastry 'hat' and a silk'n'fire sauce of lemongrass, limeleaf, coconut milk and scotch bonnet chillis ($14). Pizzas and pastas are also on hand for less adven-turous diners.

Asian fusion

Indochine 4 Collier St ☎416/922-5840, ⊛www .indochinethaicuisine.com. **Subway: Bloor-Yonge.** This demure Thai/Vietnamese restaurant has hovered on the edge of Yorkville for so long it's easy to forget it was once the trailblazer for Southeast Asian cuisine in Toronto. The French accent in the Vietnamese dishes has been toned down over the years to bump up the Royal Thai dishes, fragrant with lemongrass, coriander and curry. Pho soups and noodle dishes are followed on the menu by a good seasonal selection of crab – their spicy tamarind crab dish is a house speciality – and lots of vegetarian options. The setting is attractive and the service smooth and efficient. Mains are $9–17.

Supermarket 268 Augusta Ave, at College St ☎416/840-0501, ⊛www .supermarkettoronto.com. **Streetcar: Carlton/College (#506).** In the ever-edgy heart of Kensington Market, *Supermarket* feeds the live bands, DJs, scenesters, hipsters and rockers with a Pan-Asian menu covering grilled calamari in Korean chimichuri, beef satay, tofu salad rolls with hosin sauce, pad thai in all its derivations, and globe-on-a-plate specials like the crispy fish fillets wok-fried in a sweet and sour, jalapeno sauce with a side of frites and tempura somen noodles. *Izakaya* (small side dishes) are $5–9 and mains $9–12.

French and Belgian

Bistro 990 990 Bay St, at Joseph St ☎416/921-9990, ⊛www.bistro990.ca. **Subway: Wellesley.** *The* Ground Zero eatery during the Toronto International Film Festival (see p.175). Beloved bistro standards like *magret de canard* ($27) and steak tartare ($30), buoyed by an excellent wine list, are served at this cosy, insider favourite. The superb staff, especially the adored Miss Susan, make everyone feel like a valued regular.

Gamelle 468 College St, at Markham St ☎416/923-6254, ⊛www.gamelle.com. **Streetcar: Carlton/College (#506).** Every neigh-bourhood should have a little bistro like *Gamelle* tucked in its midst. Touches of Québec and Morocco find their way onto the Gallic menu in the form of lentil salads or hearty roast pork. The wild mushroom risotto with dried apples and basil ($22) is inspired. Brunch is popular and space is limited, so be sure to make reservations.

Matignon 51 St Nicholas St, at Charles St ☎416/921-9226, ⊛www.matignon.ca. **Subway: Wellesley.** Traditional French mains are prepared with a light touch, such as the cloud-like omelettes, with sides of crisp frites ($11). Lunchtime salads and cheese plates ($9.50) make a civilized alternative to the nearby fast food.

Provence Délices 12 Amelia St, at Parliament St ☎416/924-9901. Streetcar: Carlton/College (#506). This renovated Cabbagetown cottage offers a compact, satisfying menu, with nouvelle cuisine leanings: there's plenty of attention to vegetables and meats served *au jus*, which saves room for the excellent crème brûlée. The three-course *prix fixe* meal ($29.95) is an excellent bargain; vegetarian options are available.

Indian, Nepalese and Sri Lankan

The Host 14 Prince Arthur Ave, at Avenue Rd ☎416/962-4678, ⊕ www.welcometohost.com. Subway: Bay (Cumberland exit). Brothers Jay and (chef) Sanjeev Sethi have been serving excellent tandoori favourites, seafood and meat curries, vegetarian dishes and Hakka (Chinese-Indian) cuisine here for over a decade. The polished woods and starched linens of the formal main dining room are lovely, but ask if a table in the glassed sunroom is available. Dinner mains range from $14 to $26.

Indian Rice Factory 414 Dupont St, at Howland Ave ☎416/961-3472. Subway: Dupont. Possibly the longest-established Indian restaurant in Toronto, the *Indian Rice Factory* has introduced generations to mostly North Indian cuisine. Satisfying mains ($15–20) include adventurous twists on tradition such as black cod in curry sauce with black mustard seeds. The time-honoured desserts, such as *gulab jamun* (fried balls of dough soaked in a rosewater, syrup and honey mixture), are very sweet.

Nataraj 394 Bloor St W, at Brunswick Ave ☎416/928-2925, ⊕ www.nataraj.ca. Subway: Spadina. This Annex address nudges the competition along by serving memorable meals with alchemic spicing. Try peppery stews, near-addictive shrimp pakoras and sugar-rush desserts. Vegetable mains start at $7.95 and fish or meat at $9.95.

Rashnaa 307 Wellesley St E, at Parliament St ☎416/929-2099, ⊕ www.rashnaa.com. Streetcar: Carlton/College (#506). Southern Indian and Sri Lankan dishes are on the menu at this tiny restaurant, crammed into a small Cabbagetown cottage. The red lentil linguine served with coconut chutney ($6.95–8.95) is a revolution, and *dosas*,

Sri Lankan crêpes (from $6.95) that come with a variety of fillings, are habit-forming.

International

C5 at the ROM 100 Queens Park Circle (Bloor St W entrance, Level 5) ☎416/586-7928, ⊕ www .rom.on.ca.dining. Subway: Museum. Tucked up in the Royal Ontario Museum's new Daniel Liebskind "crystal" addition (see p.72), *C5* offers spectacular views and opulent, seasonally inspired meals in a light-filled, architecturally adventurous setting. Both lunch and dinner menus (dinner Thurs–Sat only) contain touches of India, Asia, Europe and of course local Ontario flourishes. In other words, *C5* is the prow in the ship of multi-culti dining in Toronto. Lunch mains start around $17.

Greg Couillard's Spice Room and Chutney Bar 55 Avenue Rd, at Lowther Ave ☎416/935-0000. Subway: Bay (Cumberland exit). A glamorous mélange of spice-forward dishes from North Africa to the Caribbean, including jerk chicken, saffron scallops, and Berbere lamb rubbed with tomato jaggery, tamarind and a fig glaze, served on a vegetable biryani. Appetizers start at $10, mains hover around the $30 mark.

Italian

🏃 **Bar Mercurio** 270 Bloor St W, at St George St ☎416/960-3877, ⊕ www.barmercurio .com. Subway: St George. This charming bistro focuses on northern Italian approaches to pastas, salads, meat and fish; unexpected flourishes with spicing and presentation keep regulars coming back. A luscious array of desserts, such as tortes, fruit tarts and chocolate confections ($7–10), are paraded like beauty queens at the end of the meal.

Latin American and Spanish

Boulevard Café 161 Harbord St, at Borden St ☎416/961-7676, ⊕ www.boulevardcafe.sites .toronto.com. Streetcar: Spadina (#510); bus: Wellesley (#94). The menu at this popular Peruvian eatery highlights seafood and grill preparation – the *ceviche* (seafood marinated in lime juice; $13.95) and *quesadilla del mar* (tortilla with seafood, chillis, smoked cheese and tomatoes; $10.95) are perennial favourites. Located in a former house in the Annex neighbourhood, the cosy setting has upstairs and downstairs dining rooms and tables along a sidewalk terrace.

Segovia 5 St Nicholas St, at Wellesley St ☏416/960-1010. Subway: Wellesley. This long-time favourite does an excellent job with Spanish classics such as tapas, paella, and grilled seafood, chicken and roast meats ($9–20). A preferred venue for uptown power lunches with the civil service brass from nearby Queens Park, *Segovia* warms up in the evening as diners in search of a slice of sunny Spain generate buzz.

Middle Eastern

Pomegranate 420 College St, at Bathurst St ☏416/921-7557, ⓦwww.pomegranaterestaurant .com. Streetcar: Carlton/College (#506). The perfume of spices envelopes you as soon as you open the door to this pretty Persian eatery. The cuisine is poised between Middle Eastern and Indian, more complex than the former and less assertive than the latter. This balance is evident in the *baqali palo*, a saffron basmati rice dish studded with fava beans, braised lamb shank, Persian pickles and yoghurt ($14.95). There are plenty of vegetarian options and a list of daily specials.

North American

Gallery Grill 7 Hart House Circle, Hart House (University of Toronto campus) ☏416/978-2445. Streetcar: Carlton/College (#506); subway: Museum. On the Victorian-Gothic University of Toronto campus you'll find this imposing dining room, graced by soaring vaulted ceilings and hand-painted stained glass windows. Considered a hot find by foodies in the know, it offers very well prepared, presented, served and priced brunches and lunches (average prices $14–18), with seasonal menus that change regularly. It's open Mon–Sat 11.30am–1.30pm, and is closed in July & Aug.

Jamie Kennedy at the Gardiner 111 Queens Park Circle, at Bloor St and Avenue Rd ☏416/362-1957, ⓦwww.gardinermuseum.on.ca. Subway: Museum. Superstar chef Jamie Kennedy knows that what happens on his menu will influence the rest of the city's fine dining establishments. JK is all about sustainability and supporting regional farmers and producers: expect the most seasonal of offerings on the international-style menu (the pear and parsnip soup is the very taste of autumn as are heirloom tomatoes of summer), with some inspired suggested wine pairings. Mains range from $15 to $22.

Stone Grill on Winchester 51b Winchester St, at Parliament St ☏416/967-6565 ⓦwww .stonegrill.to. Streetcar: Carlton/College (#506). This upscale Cabbagetown favourite charms diners with its dark, polished wood and stone decor, and its Sunday brunch jazz band, but the whole thing about using incredibly hot squares of stone so patrons can individually sear their meals is the unique draw. Everything from portabello mushrooms and halloumi cheese to blue marlin and striploin can get the stone grill treatment. If that seems too complicated there are more conventionally prepared items as well. Mains range from $13 to $34.

Southern Accent 595 Markham St, at Lennox St ☏416/536-3211, ⓦwww.southernaccent.com. Subway: Bathurst. This taste of Louisiana doesn't stint on the full Creole and Cajun experiences, offering psychic readings and a squeeze-box house band called Swamperella. Specialities include hushpuppies (deep-fried corn bread), chicken fried steak, candied yams and vegetarian stews, with mains ranging from $16 to $34. Newcomers can take the stress out of decision-making and order the fixed-price meal (from $25).

Seafood

Joso's 202 Davenport Ave ☏416/925-1930, ⓦwww.josos.com. Subway: Bay, Cumberland exit; bus: Avenue Rd (#5). Described at length by Margaret Atwood in

▼ Joso's

her novel *The Robber Bride*, *Joso's* is famous for three things: its squid-ink risotto; the plethora of breasts and buttocks in owner Joso Spralja's paintings and statues that decorate the place (along with the odd Dalí and Picasso); and the celebrities who can't get enough of the signature Adriatic treatment of seafood. Pastas start at $15; mains from around $22.

Steakhouses

Mansion Keg 515 Jarvis St, at Wellesley St ☎416/964-6609, ⓦwww.kegsteakhouse.com. There are other *Kegs* and other steakhouses but this is the one to head to for a convivial evening with a group of friends or relatives. Apart from the competitive prices, this location has a Bring Your Own Bottle policy with a corkage fee of a mere $14.95 (per bottle). The setting – in a Victorian-Gothic mansion that once belonged to the wealthy Massey family (see p.71) – provides an atmospheric backdrop to the menu of sirloins, ribeyes and fillets in all their shapes and forms.

Morton's 4 Avenue Rd, at Bloor St W ☎416/925-0648, ⓦwww.mortons.com. Subway: Museum. This outpost of the Chicago-based chain is all about Big Meat for Big Men. Serves both prime Alberta and USDA cuts that start at $42. Californian reds are over-represented on the wine list, but that's a minor beef.

Vegetarian

Live Organic Food Bar 264 Dupont St, at Spadina Ave ☎416/515-2002, ⓦwww.livefoodbaar.com. Subway: Dupont. A name can't get any clearer – although there are a few cooked options as well. The guiding principle behind raw food cuisine – which involves a lot of labour-intensive chopping – is that the human digestive tract and not the kitchen is where food processing should take place. Thus a lasagne replaces noodles with zucchini and ricotta with cashew paste; a pad Thai switches rice noodles with shaved daikon radish, and the Thai "burger" has lettuce leaves rather than a bun. Dishes are suitable for vegans and gluten-free. Mains range from $12–$16.50.

East End

Greek

Avli 401 Danforth Ave, at Chester Ave ☎416/461-9577, ⓦwww.avlirestaurant.com. Subway: Chester. Owned and operated by chef Lambros Vassilou, *Avli* is the only Greek restaurant on the Danforth that combines authenticity, friendly service and culinary verve in equal parts. There's a variety of *meze* – the Greek version of tapas or dim sum – to get things started ($5.95 each or $14.95 for three). Classic seafood dishes like shrimp with ouzo ($12.95), a variety of potpies and sublime baklava round out the meal. The most theatrical dish in the house is *saganaki*, a slab of mozzarella-like cheese doused in brandy and set aflame.

Ouzeri 500a Danforth Ave ☎416/466-8158, ⓦwww.ouzeri.com. Subway: Chester. The later the hour, the more festive the atmosphere in this perennial favourite. A long list of classic *meze* starters like *skardalia* (garlic-infused mashed potatoes served cold), taramasalata, stuffed vine leaves, hummus and home-made pita ($5.95–13.95) vie with

mains such as moussaka, pasta and rack of lamb ($13.95–15.95). Large combination platters ($44) take the work out of choosing. A solid wine list, loud music and animated conversation make each visit a party.

Pan on the Danforth 516 Danforth Ave ☎416/466-8158, ⓦwww.panonthedanforth.com. Subway: Chester. Cyrillic script on the sign outside is the most traditional aspect of this restaurant, offering upmarket interpretations of Greek classics best described as nouvelle Hellenic. Their jumbo quail stuffed with sausage, mushroom and shallots ($21) is particularly good.

Thai, Cambodian and Japanese

Angkor 614 Gerrard St E, at Broadview Ave ☎416/778-6383, ⓦwww.angkorrestaurant.org. Streetcar: Carlton/College (#506). Thai standards (shrimp and coconut soup; spicy beef salad) coexist alongside less familiar Cambodian fare, a beguiling blend of Indian, Thai and French cuisines. Menu items include soups, salads, noodle dishes and simple chicken and seafood options

($7.95–10.95). Vegetarian meals are also available, and various requests are readily accommodated.

Diner's Thai 395 Danforth Ave, at Chester Ave ☎416/466-9222, ✆www.dinersthai.com. **Subway: Chester.** Improbably situated in the midst of the Danforth's Greek restaurants, this unassuming yet styled space serves up uncomplicated Thai food that is crisp, fresh and inexpensive. The vegetarian appetizer plate ($12.95) easily makes lunch for two. The satay dinners, including chicken, beef,

shrimp, squid, lamb and tofu ($8.95–14.95), are a house speciality.

Lily 86 786 Broadview Ave, at Danforth Ave ☎416/465-9991. **Subway: Broadview.** If you're after uncomplicated Japanese fare with the accent on sushi, this little neighbourhood place on the outskirts of Greektown is perfect. The "omakasi", Japanese for "I'm in your hands", is $86 for two and features broth sashimi, sushi and freshly prepared vegetables. À la carte mains range from $12 to $15.

West End

Eastern European

Czehkoski's 678 Queen St, at Euclid Ave ☎416/366-6787. **Streetcar: Queen (#501).** *Czehkoski's* was a Polish deli for fifty years and it keeps the old neighbourhood alive with a choice of deli-inspired items like smoked trout and pickled sardines, and beef cheeks. Otherwise, the options are decidedly upmarket – witness the Bourgeois Burger with striploin beef, a touch of foie gras, black truffles and smoked bacon ($37). Mains start around $19.

International

Beaconsfield 1154 Queen St W, at Beaconsfield Ave ☎416/516-2550. **Streetcar: Queen (#501).** Parkdale's hip strip between the *Drake* and *Gladstone* hotels is home to the ever-expanding *Beaconsfield*, which recently added a second-storey patio. The downstairs interior is all dark woods, moody lighting and huge *belle epoque*-style mirrors. Classic bistro menu offerings are based around market-fresh availability. Mains start at $9.95.

The Drake Dining 1150 Queen St W, at Beaconsfield Ave ☎416/531-5042. **Streetcar: Queen (#501).** The *Drake Hotel*'s dining room does many things well but particular mention must be made of their dry aged Angus ribeye ($36) and skirt steak ($25), locally sourced from Cumbrae Farm, butchers who are practically on first-name terms with their stock, should that kind of detail be important for your dining pleasure.

Italian

Coco Lezzone Grill & Porto Bar 602 College St, at Manning Ave ☎416/535-1489, ✆www.cocolezzone.com. **Streetcar: Carlton/College (#506).** Truth be told, there are better places in town for Italian fare, but stargazing over a plate of baked Chilean sea bass ($31) doesn't get any better than here, with the likes of Russell Crowe, Bono, Woody Harrelson and Steven Seagal stopping by when they're in town.

Noce 875 Queen St W ☎416/504-3463. **Streetcar: Queen (#501).** This exceptional Italian restaurant is located in a cottage-sized house. The pasta is hand-rolled, the *carpaccio* ($15) melts on the tongue and the meat from the roasted capon breast ($24) falls right off the bone. Service is personable and although the wine list is short, it is well considered.

Latin American

Caju 922 Queen St W, at Crawford St ☎416/532-2550. **Streetcar: Queen (#501).** A zingy taste of Brazil on the Queen West strip. *Caju*'s svelte interior is warmly minimal and the compact menu features just eight appetizers and eight main courses (dinner mains $16–24). Multiple uses of cassava (as flour, rosti, in stews, as chips) and cashews impart girth-enhancing richness to many dishes. Rounding out the menu are hearty soups of the day, stolid beef dishes, Brazilian classics like *feijoada* (a rich stew of black beans, salted pork and beef), and Portuguese-influenced favourites like salt cod fritters.

El Bodegón 537 College St, at Euclid Ave ☎416/944-8297. **Streetcar: Carlton/College (#506).** This College-strip standard doesn't tamper with a winning formula: zesty Peruvian seafood and hearty beefsteaks ($15–20) are the mainstays at this colourful family eatery.

Julie's Cuban Restaurant 202 Dovercourt Rd, at Foxley St ☎416/532-7397, ⊛www.juliescuban .com. **Streetcar: Queen (#501).** *Julie's* is love at first sight: the storefront entrance proclaims "Julie's Cuban Snack Bar: Take Out Service". Don't be deterred. Head inside to the Caribbean-coloured rooms filled with music, laughter and happy diners sharing the twenty-odd varieties of tapas, quaffing tropical cocktails, and tucking into platters of Cuban tamales, spicy pork, rice and beans and fried plantains. Hand-holding lovers get special solicitous treatment from Sylvia, the real Julie's daughter. Dinner mains range $13–19; tapas and sides start around $4.

Seafood

Oyster Boy 872 Queen St W, at Crawford St ☎416/534-3432. **Streetcar: Queen (#501).**

Maritimers homesick for a taste of Down East visit *Oyster Boy* for tasty bivalves with names that read like a map of the East Coast: Malpeque, Caraquet Vert and Tatamagouches. A half dozen of two each starts at $14.50. Other options include clam fritters, fish and chips in beer batter and lobster. The house-party atmosphere, superior brew list, and rare Ontario vintages also warrant a visit.

Tibetan/pan-Asian

Little Tibet 712 Queen St W ☎416/306-1896. **Streetcar: Queen (#501).** A few pan-Asian concessions to Western tastes may affront purists (rice rather than millet, no yak), but plenty of Tibetan specialities found their way to this Toronto outpost. Dishes from Buddhist monasteries keep vegetarians happy, while peppery pork and beef offerings satisfy the carnivores. The spicing is closer to the Indian subcontinent, but the staples, especially the popular steamed dumplings called *momos* ($8.50–11.95), have a more Eastern character.

Suburbs

French

Didier 1496 Yonge St, at St Clair Ave ☎416/925-8588. **Subway: St Clair.** Chef Didier Leroy's latest establishment is seriously French in the classical way. Nevertheless, the lunch and brunch menus are accessible as well as affordable, featuring bistro favourites like *croque monsieur* ($16) and *steak tartare* ($18). Dinner mains include veal shank with olives, or the *assiette Canadienne*, a platter of fresh fish. The three-course dinner *prix fixe* is $58 and the four-course Chef's Table is $75.

Indian

Gujarat Durbar 1386 Gerrard St E, at Coxwell Ave ☎416/406-1085. **Streetcar: Carlton/College (#506).** This vegetarian restaurant serves up aromatic dishes from India's northwest Gujarati region. Your best bet is the generously proportioned *thali*, a tray featuring a variety of daily curries, dhal, pickles and rice ($6.95).

Jaipur Grille 2066 Yonge St, at Eglinton Ave ☎416/322-5678, ⊛www.jaipurgrille.com. **Subway: Eglinton.** An unexpected find in the confluence of offices, high-tech cinemas and singles bars, this quiet hideaway offers a menu that transcends stereotypes, thanks to owner-chef Pawan Mahendro's lightness of touch with oil and heat, and careful orchestration of spices and textures. Channas, dhals, vegetable and meat stews and other northern Indian specialities ($13–19) are skilfully executed and attractively presented.

Siddhartha 1450 Gerrard St E, at Hiawatha Rd ☎416/465-4095, ⊛www.thesidhartha.com. **Streetcar: Carlton/College (#506).** This is a top-notch addition to Little India's restaurants. The chicken tikka masala is in a class of its own. Trout gives an unexpected Ontario twist to the delectable tandoori options, and vegetarians are wooed with outstanding *mali kofta* (vegetable dumplings) for $8.99.

Italian

Grano 2035 Yonge St ☏416/440-1986, 🕸www
.grano.ca. **Subway: Davisville.** This is where
Salman Rushdie chose to first read his
novel *The Enchantress of Florence* to
Toronto audiences. The family feel here is
no illusion: the Martellas own *Grano*, live
upstairs and work downstairs, and when
you step into the restaurant you know
you're a true guest. Family recipes make
the pastas, seafood and meat dishes a
personal slice of Tuscany; the brilliant
antipasti – fried zucchini blossoms, golden
rice balls with a mozzarella centre, perfectly
grilled eggplant – are positively addictive.
The charming back patio is closed only
during the depths of winter. Pastas start at
$12.50, mains at $22.

Il Fornello 1560 Yonge St, at Delisle Ave
☏416/920-7347, 🕸www.ilfornello.com.
Subway: St Clair. There are six other *Il
Fornello* locations but the St Clair version is
the best. More than one happy customer
has proclaimed its delicate, individually
sized, ultra-thin-crust, wood-fired oven
pizzas the best they have ever enjoyed.
Toppings range from the virginal "Semplice"
(tomato sauce, herbs and mozzarella, at
$8), to the decadent lushness of a mascar-
pone, fig, prosciutto, pardano and
honey-drizzled creation ($14.89). The pasta
dishes and trattoria mains ($14–22) are not
in the same league but nothing is perfect.
Ontario-fresh produce, wines and cheeses
are proudly featured. Gluten-free crusts are
also available.

Japanese

Rikishi Japanese Restaurant 833 Bloor St
W, at Shaw St ☏416/538-0760. **Subway:
Christie.** Stuck out among Portuguese,
Cuban and Somalian sports bars, this little
gem not only serves well-prepared traditional Japanese dishes – either individually
or in fixed-price bento boxes – but also
offers over thirty makki options. Dishes,
decor and service are all very authentic and
the staff are extremely helpful and attentive.
All mains below $20.

Middle Eastern

Jerusalem 955 Eglinton Ave W, three blocks
west of Bathurst St ☏416/783-6494. **Bus #32
(Eglington West).** This venerable establishment is still going strong after three
decades. Everything is ultra fresh, with an
emphasis on the many small dishes from
the Levant (falafel, hummus, baba ghanouj,
etc) that can be shared as a memorable
meal. Combination platters start at $30.

Bars and pubs

For a city that didn't serve mixed drinks until 1948 and is still subject to Ontario's often puzzling liquor regulations, Toronto is home to a remarkably vital **bar scene**. You'll find everything from grizzled taverns to sleek cocktail bars, and from decades-old neighbourhood pubs to the recent crop of frayed-but-styled club-like establishments that are currently in vogue.

Most bars and lounges featuring entertainment have a weekend **cover charge** after 9pm ranging between $10 and $20. Cover charges may also apply during the week if there's a special act, performance or top guest DJ. The legal drinking age throughout Ontario is 19, and **last call** at all establishments is usually 2am, although this can be pushed back to 4am in Downtown bars during some festivals, notably the Toronto International Film Festival. Last call doesn't, however, necessarily herald an end to the night's festivities: after-hours bars riddle the city, and the people who will generally be able to guide you to them are the very bartenders serving your last orders. Be aware, though, that speakeasies (known locally as **booze cans** and roughly defined as unlicensed, after-hours clubs serving alcohol) are flat-out illegal and can be raided.

All Toronto bars are required to serve **food**, presumably to soak up some booze – though the quality and service of this is often sorely lacking. As a general hint, if you don't see anyone eating, the food probably isn't worth ordering. **Smoking** is no longer permitted in Toronto bars, but it *is* permitted on outside patios. Laws pertaining to **drinking and driving** are strict, so if you end up drinking too much, leave your car in a car park, or, better yet, don't take it along in the first place. **Taxicabs** are far easier to find than parking spots, and **public transport** roams the city's main arteries 24 hours a day.

Downtown

Black Bull 298 Queen St W, at Soho St ☎416/593-2766. Streetcar: Queen (#501). The line of gleaming motorcycles parked outside gives an idea of who the regular patrons are at this popular spot, one of the oldest taverns in Toronto. The *Black Bull* also has an excellent summer patio, plus a grill menu heavy on the burgers.

Bovine Sex Club 542 Queen St W, at Ryerson Ave ☎416/504-4239. Streetcar: Queen (#501). The *BSC* has held its own for about fifteen years now, and in all that time has never invested in a sign. The exterior is encrusted with layers of industrial scrap and bicycle parts, offering no glimpse of the playground within, which is filled with kinetic sculptures built from old portable record players, as well as a couple of bars and pool tables.

C'est What? 67 Front St E, at Church St ☎416/867-9499. Subway: Union. Over twenty microbrews are on tap in this St Lawrence Market spot – including the popular house brand, hemp beer – plus there's an impressive selection of single malt

Scotches and hearty pub food. The performance space here has seen the likes of Bare Naked Ladies and Jeff Buckley, to name just a few.

Dominion on Queen 500 Queen St E, at River St ☎416/368-6893. Streetcar: Queen (#501). The recently restored Romanesque building shrugs its massive plum granite shoulders at trends and celebrates its return to being a neighbourhood taproom. Flea market club chairs, beer tasting "flights" and a solid menu draw a steady crowd. Lots of live bands throughout the week and live jazz Sun afternoons.

Esplanade Bier Market 58 The Esplanade, at Lower Church St ☎416/862-7575. Subway: Union. Even though mussels and frites are served here, this place's primary purpose is to pour big glasses of Belgian (and other) beer to a mostly young, mostly male clientele, usually fresh from viewing a hockey game over at the nearby Air Canada Centre.

Foundation Room 19 Church St, at Front St E ☎416/364-8368. Subway: Union. The only way most people stumble across this hidden gem with a Moroccan flair is by running into the doormen, who try to remain discreet. Virtually carved into the early nineteenth-century foundation of the building above, this is a perfect spot for an intimate nightcap.

The Keg Steakhouse Bar 165 York St, at Queen St W ☎416/703-1773. Streetcar: Queen (#501). Yes, there is a chain steakhouse attached to this dark-wood, expensive-subdued-lighting, buzzing bar, but it is of tertiary considera-tion. This is pick-up central for the Financial District. Very popular with young, mostly single straight guys if that's who you're looking for.

The Last Temptation 12 Kensington Ave, at Dundas St W ☎416/599-2551. Streetcar: Dundas (#505). A change of ownership and a much-needed renovation saved this Kensington Market spot from sheer nastiness. Now, in place of the former gritti-ness, it has a smooth club ambience inside and a generous patio out front. There's a Middle Eastern/Mediterranean menu, but the main reason to pop in is to have a drink and watch the lively street life.

Library Bar in the *Fairmont Royal York Hotel*, 100 Front St W, at York St ☎416/368-2511. Subway: Union. One of the few places left in town where the staff knows how to make a good martini and, better still, brings a little

flask holding the other ounce of your drink. The bar also sports huge leather wingback chairs and racks of newspapers, plus it never plays loud music.

Mill Street Brew Pub 55 Mill St, at Parliament St ☎416/681-0338. Streetcar: King (#504). This is where the good stuff is: *Mill Street Brewery* produces some fine handcrafted beers and its Organic is one of the best brews in town. The historic building is stripped back to the brick, and the sweet scent of hops fills the air when brewmaster Michael Duggan is at work.

The Paddock 176 Bathurst St, at Queen St W ☎416/504-9997. Streetcar: Queen (#501). Rising phoenix-like from a grotty past, *The Paddock* reclaimed its original, authentic Deco glory when it reopened in 1998. It boasts the world's longest Bakelite-topped bar, and the crowd is mainly smart young filmmakers and TV types. The kitchen produces straightforward, meat-and-potatoes-type fare.

Pravda Vodka Bar 36 Wellington St E, at Victoria St ☎416/306-2433. Streetcar: King (#504). The recent trend in vodka bars finds its expression here in a beautiful old space near the St Lawrence Market. The decor looks like a Romanov or two sold off the last of the palace drapes and chandeliers. Best after 11pm.

Reservoir Lounge 52 Wellington St E, at Church St ☎416/955-0887. Subway: Union. An intimate subterranean club with a good selection of wines by the glass and micro-brews on tap. Live jazz on the weekends.

The Rivoli 332 Queen St W, at Spadina Ave ☎416/504-1320. Streetcar: Queen (#501). Thankfully, some things don't change, such as the high-backed booths lining either side of Queen West's original hipster haven. There's a long bar beside the dining room (which serves Wookie balls, Asian noodle soups and a global selection of appetizers), a cabaret space in the back, and a pool-and-billiards room upstairs.

Savage Garden 550 Queen St W, at Ryerson Ave ☎416/504-2178. Streetcar: Queen (#501). If cyberpunk is the old/new Goth, *Savage Garden* is Toronto's premier cyberpunk bar. More G.G. Gieger these days than Dark Angel, the metal sculptures, cages and post-apocalyptic distressed paint finishes perfectly complement the DJ-ed industrial thrash.

Tattoo Rock Parlour 567 Queen St W, at Dennison Ave ☎416/703-5488. Streetcar: Queen (#501). Just what your mum always wanted for you: a bar featuring a full-time tattoo artist on staff, just in case you wanted to immortalize the night out somewhere on your skin. The *TRP* has got definite grit and features loud rock bands or memorable turntable artistes like DJ Steve Aoki.

Toad in the Hole 525 King St W, at Brant St ☎416/593-8623. **Streetcar: King (#504).** Once an outpost of sorts for cheap beer and pub grub, today the *Toad* offers much the same

but amid the fancy lounges and restaurants that now line King West.

The Wheat Sheaf 667 King St W, at Bathurst St ☎416/504-9912. **Streetcar: King (#504).** Toronto's oldest public house, *The Wheat Sheaf* served its first pint in 1849. In the century and a half since then, not much has changed – except for indoor plumbing, refrigeration and a television permanently tuned to sporting events.

Uptown

Amber 119 Yorkville Ave, at Bellair St ☎416/926-9037. **Subway: Bay (Bellair exit).** Many beautiful and famous people have been spotted sipping martinis at this very of-the-moment spot. The interior is dark and cosy with a vaguely Moroccan vibe, but it's the patio overlooking little Cumberland Walk that is the main attraction.

Andy Poolhall 489 College St, at Palmerston Ave ☎416/923-5300. **Streetcar: Carlton/ College (#506).** If you want the opportunity to sit down – the seats were salvaged from the Concord's VIP lounge at New York's JFK airport – then come early. If you want to see what the buzz is all about, then come late. Named for Andy Warhol, this place gets top marks for its Factory-like retro-kitsch atmosphere, great bar service, and excellent DJs. One of the College strip's best hangouts.

Annex Wreckroom 794 Bathurst Ave (second-floor entrance, beside *George's BBQ*), at Bloor St W ☎416/536-0346. **Subway: Bathurst.** Any place located over a *Pizza Pizza* is going to attract a certain student element, but the *Wreckroom* – a North Americanism for a finished basement that kids can't really damage – is a fun place to get goofy on beer and cycle through a long playlist of Eighties wondertunes.

Artful Dodger 10 Isabella St, at Yonge St ☎416/964-9511. **Subway: Wellesley.** This English-style pub looks and feels authentic. A second home for many locals, the *Dodger* also sees any number of social clubs and darts teams hanging out amid its red velvet banquettes and flock wallpaper.

🏃 **Avenue in the *Four Seasons* Hotel, 21 Avenue Rd, at Yorkville Ave** ☎416/324-1568. **Subway: Bay (Cumberland exit).** The *ne plus ultra* watering hole in town, and the

place where visiting movie stars hang out during the Toronto International Film Festival. The luxurious interior, with its long bar and dark woods, makes a stylish setting to sit back and enjoy the excellent wine list and great selections of stylish martinis and aperitifs.

The Brunswick House 481 Bloor St W, at Brunswick Ave ☎416/964-2242. **Subway: Spadina.** This old neighbourhood fixture has been pulling pints and serving pitchers of cheap draught to poets, students and working stiffs since the 1880s. Despite a recent paint job and a few new pieces of furniture, the *Brunswick* remains true to its proletarian roots and eschews anything faddish or trendy. There is always some community event or other going on in one of the taprooms, and weekends usually see live rock. Thursday's cheap-pitcher night is an excellent time to stop by.

🏃 **College Street Bar 574 College St, at Clinton Ave** ☎416/533-2417. **Streetcar: Carlton/College (#506).** One of the last true neighbourhood bars on a strip that was once was home to many. A great long bar with huge old, gilt mirrors, twinkling chandeliers and votive candles warm up the sparse interior that, truth be told, doesn't have a lot of design involved in the basic table-and-chairs set up. Who cares? It fills up early and has a clientele devoted to their Soul Sundays as well as the regular line-up of live music and lounge-loving DJs.

Eat My Martini 649 College St, at Grace St ☎416/516-2549. **Streetcar: Carlton/College (#506).** While it is possible to eat here, the main attraction, not surprisingly, is the extensive martini list, which boasts over eighty concoctions to put you over the top at the end of a long day.

Flow 133 Yorkville Ave, at Avenue Rd ☎416/925-2143. **Subway: Bay (Cumberland exit).** *Flow's* vibe is one of chocolate-coloured wood, lots of glass, brushed metal and an electronic beat sound system as over-processed as some of the customers' hair.

Hemmingways 142 Cumberland St, at Avenue Rd ☎416/968-2828. **Subway: Bay (Cumberland exit).** This is almost an anti-Yorkville Yorkville bar. It's also an outpost for Toronto-based Kiwis looking for a little slice of New Zealand. The downstairs bars and patio are fine but head up onto the covered, all-weather rooftop patio for the best seats.

The Madison 14 Madison Ave, at Bloor St W ☎416/927-1722. **Subway: St. George.** This massive multi-floor pub has two pool rooms, a piano bar and a dancefloor. Popular with students, especially fraternity types, from the University of Toronto.

Mini Market By Tempo 596 College St, at Clinton St ☎416/531-2822. **Streetcar: Carlton/College (#506).** First this location was the neighbourhood mini market, then it was the resto-lounge *Tempo* and now it is both if only in name. The long thin space maintains *Tempo's* serenity which melts in the face of a busy night. Stylish College Street haunt, perfect for a sake cocktail.

Pauper's 539 Bloor St W, at Lippincott St ☎416/530-1331. **Subway: Bathurst.** This former bank has been performing a far more useful function as a two-storey beer hall for about a decade now. *Pauper's* is rightly esteemed for its rooftop patio, which can tend toward loud boisterousness on the weekend evenings.

The Pilot 22 Cumberland St, at Bay St ☎416/923-5716. **Subway: Bay (Bay exit).** A thorough and much-needed renovation has put this long-time favourite (established in 1944) back on the map. Their Flight Deck is an ace Yorkville patio in summer.

▼ Pauper's

Roof Lounge in the *Park Hyatt Hotel*, 4 Avenue Rd, at Bloor St W ☎416/924-5471. **Subway: Bay or Museum.** Long a retreat for establishment literati, the *Roof Lounge* offers a spectacular view of the city and hands down the very best martinis in Toronto (the bartender has been perfecting his method for almost four decades). Sofas, a fireplace and silken smooth service make this spot a treasured oasis.

Souz Dal 636 College St, at Grace St ☎416/537-1883. **Streetcar: Carlton/College (#506).** The extensive cocktail list and dark ambience are the main draws at this spot on College strip. The backroom is really a walled patio, open to the stars and lit exclusively by banks of votive candles. Waiters drop by with little dishes of pistachios and keep the drinks coming. A great place to end an evening out.

East End

Myth 417 Danforth Ave, at Chester Ave ☎416/461-8383. **Subway: Chester.** A cavernous space with a huge suspended TV screen that silently plays Hollywood films with Greek mythological themes, like *Jason and the Argonauts*. Although you'll find better Hellenic fare elsewhere on the Danforth, *Myth's* lively late-night crowd is a major draw – as are the massive chandeliers hanging from twenty-foot ceilings, exposed beams and pillars burned with runic symbols and beautiful blonde-wood bar.

West End

LeVac Block 88 Ossington Ave, at Queen St W ☎416/916-0571. **Streetcar: Queen (#501).** A perfect spot to hang out with your pals and check out the best efforts of local brewers. The large front windows of this restored Victorian beauty are perfect vantage points for street action.

Odd Fellows 936 Queen St W, at Shaw St ☎416/627-4128. **Streetcar: Queen (#501).** This nifty neighbourhood hangout has extra verve thanks to the design job by Castor, (which, incidentally, is Latin for beaver, Canada's national rodent) and an interesting approach to recreational shopping. If you like the decor, such as the bundle of twenty-feet-long light rods, ask about its availability: Castor retails furniture right out of the bar.

The Ossington 61 Ossington Ave, at Queen St W ☎416/850-0161. **Streetcar: Queen (#501).** An outstanding watering hole on a great party strip, this former art gallery space is the unofficial clubhouse for the current crop of hipsters. The vibe stays as cool as the beer and their martini bar will amuse and delight you.

Resperado 136 Ossington Ave, south of Dundas St W ☎416/532-6474. **Streetcar: Dundas (#505).** This is a quality tequila bar, and no, that is not an oxymoron. A somewhat church-like interior allows patrons to get serious with premium brands of Mexico's national tipple. For those who dare to dilute, the margaritas are excellent.

Sweaty Betty's 13 Ossington Ave, at Queen St W ☎416/535-6861. **Streetcar: Queen (#501).** Reputed to be *the* heaving, hopping, happening bar that started the groove rush to the Ossington strip. It's nothing fancy but that's part of the charm.

10

Clubs and live music

Toronto's **nightlife** has blossomed in recent decades, and the city's reputation for rolling up its sidewalks after 10pm is history. Today, there are **clubs**, **lounges** and **discos** for every taste, with most of the action taking place between Thursday and Sunday.

The latest "Now Squad" district is along **Ossington Avenue**, between Dundas Street West and Queen Street West, which specializes in retro chic interiors and speakeasy ambience. Beyond this nexus are the clubs and performance venues around the **Roncesvalles neighbourhood**, where Dundas Street bends up to Bloor Street West. Also in the West End is the exuberant **West Queen West** strip of bars, clubs and art galleries that stream out from the *Drake* and *Gladstone* hotels (see p.131) into the formerly sketchy neighbourhood of Parkdale. The highest density of lounges and dance clubs in Canada is along the **Richmond Street** strip, just south of Queen Street West, which is itself home to a number of **live-band venues**. This four-block chunk of Downtown is a weekend magnet for young suburbanites. The **College Street** strip, west of Palmerston Avenue, once the sharp edge of edgy, is now more attuned to lounges and DJs. Also in the mix are trend-defying venues that staunchly support **jazz**, **blues** or **R&B**, and whose clientele bemoan the fact that they can no longer smoke indoors.

Most clubs and lounges serve **alcohol** and the last call is at 2am. That means that all drinks have to be consumed and bottles taken away by 3am. On the weekends, however, most clubs will stay open until 4am, though live-music spots tend to wind things down earlier. For venue **listings**, consult *NOW* or *eye*, two free weekly newspapers that are available in stores, restaurants and in news boxes on the street. A great online source of hot club information is the Martini Boys website at Ⓦwww.martiniboys.com – you can also sign onto club guest lists at either Ⓦwww.torontonightclub.com or Ⓦwww.clubcrawlers.com.

Toronto's **comedy clubs** are another good nightlife option. The city has a proven track record when it comes to showcasing emerging comedic talent, and several venues around town are specifically dedicated to stand-up or improv, with comedy cabarets finding a regular slot in some of the more varied venues.

Live music

Toronto is a stand-out city for its **live music scene.** Artists like Ron Sexsmith, Fiest, Broken Social Scene, Nelly Furtado, Jane Bunnett, and Jully Black found launch pads in Toronto's clubs, and they continue to drop in on their old haunts.

The contemporary music scene goes well beyond guitar-based rock. **Jazz** features prominently, as does **Latin dance**, whether it's salsa, mambo, tango or merengue. On the other end of the dance spectrum is a lively **hip-hop** scene, and the city's large Afro-Caribbean population ensures a fairly consistent offering of **break**, **reggae** and **soca** music. Clubs used to specialize in World Beat; now they simply reflect the global tastes of their patrons: Portuguese *fado*, South Asian trance dub, Hong Kong lounge acts, Celtic fiddling ravers and sublime African songsters are all represented.

Downtown

Big Bop 651 Queen St W, at Bathurst St ☎416/504-6699. Streetcar: Queen (#501). This vast space is actually three clubs in one – *Kathedral*, *Reverb* and *Holy Joe's* – catering to the live alternative rock scene.
Cameron House 408 Queen St W, at Cameron St ☎416/703-0811, Ⓦwww.thecameron.com. Streetcar: Queen (#501). A line of huge metal ants march up the side of this legendary place and the front is subject to ever-changing murals of women's faces. You can't miss it. The interior is a clash of Beaux Arts boudoir and honky tonk bar, and the stage at the back of the room has provided a showcase for emerging talent of every genre.
FUNHAUS Club & Concert Hall 562 Queen St W, at Ryerson Ave ☎416/703-4999. Streetcar: Queen (#501). An upstairs thrash-punk Goth nest for the next generation of Dark Ones. They know who they are.
Grace O'Malley's 14 Duncan St, at Pearl St W ☎416/596-1444. Streetcar: King (#504). In addition to all the auld country standards, bands playing the *Grace* usually have a wonderful repertoire of Canadian traditional songs from Cape Breton reels to Métis laments, and also take requests.
Horseshoe Tavern 370 Queen St W, at Spadina Ave ☎416/598-4753. Streetcar: Queen (#501). Lots of Toronto bands like the Cowboy Junkies and Blue Rodeo their start here, and now-famous names still swing by to play a set or one-off concert. The interior is relentlessly unglamorous, but the low (or no) cover charge and music industry promo specials are a major compensation.
🏃 **Phoenix Concert Theatre** 410 Sherbourne St, at Carlton St E ☎416/323-1251. Streetcar: Dundas (#505). This five-bar, three-venue concert emporium specializes in booking big-name acts longing for intimate gigs (the Stones debuted their 2005 Bigger Bang tour here). Everyone from Matisyahu to Richard Thompson, Cesaria Evora to the Misfits has performed here.
The Rex Hotel Jazz Bar and Grill 194 Queen St W, at McCaul St ☎416/598-2475. Subway: Osgoode; streetcar: Queen (#501). In fierce arguments about which is the best jazz club

in town, this one is consistently near the top of the list. A natty crowd lounge about admiring the spiffed-up interior, but any reservations about pretensions evaporate once the music – which is always top-notch – begins.

The waterfront

Guverment and Kool Haus 132 Queens Quay E, at Lower Jarvis St ☎416/869-0045, Ⓦwww.theguverment.com. Subway: Union. This huge barn of a dance club houses seven distinct venues on the shores of Lake Ontario. Features DJs, live music and special events. One ticket gets you into everything.

Uptown

Grossman's Tavern 379 Spadina Ave, at Cecil St ☎416/977-7000. Streetcar: Carlton/College (#506). When *El Mocambo* across the street closed its sticky doors, *Grossman's* took over the role of being Chinatown's chief purveyor of quality jazz and R&B. Broken Joe's Old Timey Tuesdays are a particular treat.
Lee's Palace 529 Bloor St W, at Bathurst St ☎416/532-1598. Subway: Bathurst. The continued popularity of *Lee's* has nothing to do with the decor, the food or even the draught beer; its reputation is based entirely on the often outrageous bands it usually books. The equally popular *Dance Cave* is upstairs.
Silver Dollar 486 Spadina Ave, at College St ☎416/975-0909. Streetcar: Carlton/College (#506). Self-billed as "Toronto's Premier Blues Club", this sketchy-looking venue books top blues artists. Arrive early if you want a seat with a good view.
Sneaky Dees 431 College St, at Bathurst St ☎416/603-3090. Streetcar: Carlton/College (#506). A no-attitude slacker palace with live rock bands, pinball, pool and Tex-Mex grub until 5am seven days a week.

East End

Black Swan 154 Danforth Ave, at Broadview Ave ☎416/469-0537. Subway: Broadview. A neighbourhood beer joint that brings in Blues performers and open jams.

Opera House 735 Queen St E, at Broadview Ave ☎416/366-0313. Streetcar: Queen (#501). This former theatre is the outpost for hardcore rock acts who like to thrash the night away. Despite the bad sound system, seatless interior and utter absence of decor, the venue books cult rock and electronica bands from England and the US.

West End

Cadillac Lounge 1296 Queen St W, at Dufferin Ave ☎416/ 536-7717, ⓦwww.cadillaclounge .com. Streetcar: Queen (#501). Half a Cadillac hangs above the entrance of this Parkdale establishment, renowned for its excellent summer patio, country-rock, inexpensive drinks, and the sit-in bands for the Cadillac Ranch Matinee every Sat at 4pm.

Dakota Tavern 249 Ossington Ave, at Dundas St W ☎416/856-4579. Streetcar: Dundas (#505). Don't be dismayed by the exterior's hint of shabby urban cowboy blues. The *Dakota* has the buzz. It's a place where bands such as the ever-popular Fembots can walk the line between raucous and rowdy or soft as a whisper. A great crowd, no hassles, no dress codes.

Gladstone Hotel 1214 Queen St W, at Gladstone Ave ☎416/531-4635, ⓦwww.gladstonehotel .com. Streetcar: Queen (#501). Each of this hotel's three venues – *The Ballroom, The Melody Bar* and *The Art Bar* – is likely to be booked out with something worth attending.

In homage to its seedy, recent past, it showcases bands like Cajun favourite Swamperella, alongside burlesque dancers as the adjunct acts.

Mod Club 722 College St, at Dovercourt Rd ☎416/588-4663. Streetcar: Carlton/College (#506). Possibly the hippest spot for live shows in Toronto right now. This place draws the bands with the biggest buzz, and the crowds to match. All that atmosphere means that beer can be expensive and shows sell out very quickly.

The Orbit Room 580A College St (upstairs), at Euclid Ave ☎416/535-0613. Streetcar: Carlton/College (#506). Long a favourite of the terminally hip, the *Orbit* specializes in sit-ins when internationally celebrated musicians just happen to drop by and play with the local bands.

Suburbs

Hugh's Room 2261 Dundas St W, at Roncesvalles Ave ☎416/531-6604. Subway: Dundas West. An excellent reason to visit the west, West End, and a place to hear leading-edge music in every genre from Canada, the US and around the world, performed by the best up-and-comers as well as long-time legends: Dr. Draw, Jane Bunnett and the Cuban All Stars, the Satellites, Richie Havens … the list is long. *Hugh's* doubles as a supper club, so be prepared to order (an inexpensive) dinner if you want the best seats in the house.

Clubs and lounges

New strains of **clubs** are springing up in Toronto, assuring a quality night out whatever your tastes. Weekends tend to be busy, and the more popular spots can have long lines year round. **Cover charges** are usually between $15 and $20, but can be higher if the headliner act is a really big name. Some clubs book live bands on occasion, but most stick to the DJ formula. **Lounges** rarely have live music – space being at more of a premium – but they don't always have cover charges, either. One of the recent trends in patron quality and crowd control is the online guest list. Consult ⓦwww.clubcrawlers.com to sign up or get listed for parties. As well, you can check the listings in the free *NOW* or *eye* papers, (see p.162) to see which DJs are playing where.

Downtown

C Lounge 465 Wellington St W, at Spadina Ave ☎416/260-9393. Streetcar: Spadina (#510). A spa-inspired lounge featuring a South Beach-style deck, lots of leather, wood, and

relaxing down-tempo beats make this a nice alternative to the regular club scene. In winter the pool/patio area becomes a really cool ice bar – literally.

Cabana 289 Richmond St W, at Peter St ☎604/555-5555. Streetcar: Queen (#501). This newcomer to the packed clubzone offers mainstream house, mash-ups, hip-hop and sundry on the dancefloor and a hint of the tropics in the decor.

Circa 126 John St, at Richmond St W ☎416/530-0011, ⊛www.circatoronto.com. **Streetcar: Queen (#501).** This four-storey bling palace sports a circus theme and a cavernous main stage with all the lights, bells and whistles. Odd touches include the upstairs KidRobot Room, filled with curvy glass cases of Paul Budnitz's little dolls, and the faintly perverse Washroom Bar. Whatever. Weekdays are for private events so visit weekends.

Fluid 217 Richmond St W, at Duncan St ☎416/593-6116, ⊛www.fluidlounge.net. **Subway: Osgoode.** If you're looking for a glamorous backdrop, *Fluid* is the perfect spot. The doormen, line-ups and shower of glass tears suspended from the ceiling are enough to make anyone feel special.

Lot 332 332 Richmond St W, at Peter St ☎416/599-5332. **Streetcar: Queen (#501).** The big deal here is the retractable glass roof over the dancefloor which, during a warm summer's weekend night, is magic. Seating is arranged so that every space seems like a pricey private one. DJs spin club anthem, hip-hop, Latin and reggae Wed, Fri & Sat.

Republik 261 Richmond St W, at John St ☎416/598-1632, ⊛www.republiknightclub.com. **Streetcar: Queen (#501).** This place aims to impress: two-storey ceilings accommodate lasers, strobes, fireworks, and numerous rotating plasma screens. A monster sound system says that *Republik* wants you up on your feet in the midst of a heavy, sweaty mass, at the mercy of DJs like Johan Gielen, D:Fuse and DJ Scwarma.

Rockwood 31 Mercer St, between John St and Peter St, Downtown ☎416/351-1100. **Streetcar: King (#504).** This lounge/disco has bars and a dancefloor plus a upstairs patio, open to the sky. This is an expensive venue for a discerning, bottle-service kind of crowd. House music exclusively.

This Is London 364 Richmond St, at Spadina Ave ☎416/351-1100. **Streetcar: Queen (#501).** Although the entrance is in an alley, it's easy to spot *TIL* by the maddeningly long lines outside. Popular for its DJ's selection of disco, soul and Top 40 beats, perhaps the real draw is the Ladies' Spa, where hairdressers and make-up artists are on hand for touch-ups. Not a good choice of clubs if your date already spends too much time powdering her nose. Dress codes apply.

The waterfront

The Docks 11 Polson St ☎416/461-2625. This 41,000-square-feet complex is like a theme park for clubbers. The music veers from old-school disco and R&B to Top 40 and dance, so no one should feel left out. Public transport is spotty so take a cab.

Guverment 132 Queens Quay E, at Lower Jarvis St ☎416/869-0045, ⊛www.theguverment.com. **Subway: Union.** This barn of a dance club houses seven distinct venues on the shores of Lake Ontario. Features DJs, live music and special events. One ticket gets you into everything.

Uptown

Neutral 349A College St, at Augusta St ☎416/926-1212. **Streetcar: Carlton/College (#506).** Worlds collide at this hipster walk-down on the cusp of Kensington Market and the College Street strip. Its forte is Eighties Brit Rock, which has a large, loyal and multi-generational Toronto fan base. *Neutral* also has a karaoke thing going, as well as DJ dance parties and live bands.

West End

Camera Bar 1026 Queen St W, at Ossington Ave ☎416/530-0011, ⊛www.camerabar.ca. **Streetcar: Queen (#501).** Director Atom Egoyan and film distributor Hussain Amarshi (of Mongrel Media) concocted this sleek little martini bar with a screening gallery in the back to show an eclectic selection of their favourite films.

The Chelsea Room 923 Dundas St W, at Bellwoods Ave ☎416/364-0553. **Streetcar: Dundas (#505).** The *Chelsea*'s no beauty queen but she has plenty of admirers. A smallish dance venue, this is where to come to find up-and-coming DJs seven days a week.

🏃 **Communist's Daughter 1149 Dundas St W, at Dovercourt Rd** ☎416/647-435-0103. **Streetcar: Dundas (#505).** There is no better antidote to the chrome-and-glass theatre of the lounge scene than this frayed little bar. The sign above the door reads "Nazzarre", referring to a prior tenant, while "Communist's Daughter" comes from a Neutral Milk Hotel song lyric. Flea market furnishings and a willful dishevelment imported from Ontario's north make it the trendiest dive in town.

Drake Lounge **1150 Queen St W, at Beaconsfield Ave** ☎416/531-5042. **Streetcar: Queen (#501).** This space has been a hit since the doors reopened in 2004. A wet bar serving house tipples like the Dorothy Parker cocktail (vodka, cranberry juice and Chambord) and a sushi bar keep the crowd satisfied as they sprawl on fat sofas, club chairs or loungers. Over the fireplace, a huge flat-screen TV projects live or taped shows held in the basement performance space.

El Convento Rico **750 College St, at Dovercourt Rd** ☎416/588-7800, ⊛www.elconventorico.com. **Streetcar: Carlton/College (#506).** Walking into this lively joint, replete with red velvet flock wallpaper and baroque spot welding, makes you feel like you've stumbled onto the best party in town. The crowd ranges from earnest suburbanites to dishy Latino drag queens, and the DJs spin Latin and disco classics until 4am six nights a week (until 10pm on Sun).

Lula Lounge **1585 Dundas St W, at Duffrin St** ☎416/588-0307, ⊛www.lula.ca. **Streetcar: Dundas (#505).** Bastion of all things Latin, this thriving dance palace regularly features top salsa, *son* and other performances. If you don't know how to dance they'll teach you.

Not My Dog **1510 Queen St W, at Jameson Ave** ☎416/532-2397, ⊛www.notmydog.com. **Streetcar: Queen (#501).** Patrons who eschew bottle service and theme lounges – or virtually any decor at all – love *Not My Dog*, which is about as rough and ready as the name suggests. The house band, the Kensington Hillbillies, and the Everybody Has a Song Wednesday night open mics are pretty darned real.

Comedy clubs

Absolute Comedy **2335 Yonge St, at Roehampton Ave, Uptown** ☎416/486-7700, ⊛wwwabsolutecomedy.ca. **Subway: Eglinton.** Pros do stand-up Thurs–Sun, Wed night is Pro/Am, when the pros and the amateurs mix – or not.

ALT.COMedy Lounge at the Rivoli **332 Queen St W, at Spadina Ave, Downtown** ☎416/596-1908. **Streetcar: Queen (#501).** The cabaret space in the back of the *Rivoli* hosts an alternative comedy night on Mon at 9pm and the Sketch Comedy Lounge on Tues. Acts vary from wobbly stand-up routines to truly inspired silliness, such as Minimalist Puppet Theatre (no puppet, just the hand).

Bad Dog Theatre **138 Danforth Ave, at Broadview Ave, Uptown** ☎416/491-3115, ⊛www.baddogtheatre.com. **Subway: Broadview.** This former newspaper office regularly hosts "Theatresports" on Wed evenings, in which teams of comics compete in improv showdowns, and at midnight on Fri, "Late Late Horror shows" mix Grand Guignol with horror movie spoofs. (Free popcorn is generously thrown in.) Performances are Wed, Fri & Sat, and comedy classes and workshops take up the rest of the week.

The Bagel **285 College St, at Spadina Ave, Uptown** ☎966-7555. **Streetcar: Carlton/College (#506).** University of Toronto students have been catching inexpensive breakfasts at *The Bagel* for over sixty years. Now they can come back at night and catch the stand-up comedy routines. Not to be confused with the *Thai Angel* at the same street address.

Second City **51 Mercer St, at Blue Jays Way, Downtown** ☎416/343-0011, ⊛www.secondcity.com. **Streetcar: King (#504).** This Toronto scion of the Chicago company spawned John Candy, Martin Short, Catherine O'Hara and the SCTV crowd. Time has not dulled the troupe's taste for political satire. A good place to learn all you need to know about local as well as global affairs.

The Tim Sims Playhouse **56 Blue Jay Way, at King St W, Downtown** ☎416/343-0011. **Streetcar: King (#504).** *TTSP* specializes in staging an amorphous, improvisational comedy matrix. It could be about a mob wedding, it could be based on a 1950s game show or it could morph into who knows what.

Yuk-Yuks Downtown **224 Richmond St W, at John St, Downtown** ☎416/967-6425. **Streetcar: Queen (#501).** This is the place where stand-ups have to make it in order to move up the food chain. Everyone has played *Yuk-Yuks* at some point or another, including homeboys/girls Russell Peters, Kenny Robinson and Elvira Kurt.

Performing arts and film

Toronto is internationally recognized as a vibrant centre for the **performing arts** and **film**. As Toronto strides confidently through the twenty–first century, the arts are what the city has chosen to stake its claim on, and in the last few years a flurry of construction has seen some of the world's most famous architects take on one cultural institution after another.

Perhaps Toronto's main strength is the diversity of its population, which lends itself to dynamic and exciting artistic expressions. Visitors can enjoy varied **dance**, **opera** and **musical performances**, as well as a year-round **theatre scene** that's the third-largest in the English-speaking world (after London and New York, respectively). Additionally, Toronto is justifiably proud of the many arts **festivals** it hosts throughout the year – the most renowned being the **Toronto International Film Festival**, which is the world's largest public film festival and second only to Cannes in terms of its importance in the film industry.

The high season for most of the performing arts is late September to May, bringing cheer to Toronto's long winter months. The summertime is livened by a slew of outdoor festivals and events; for more information, see Chapter 16.

Theatre

Home to more than six hundred opening nights a year, Toronto offers an exceptionally varied array of **theatre** productions, from opulent international hits to idiosyncratic fringe affairs. Classical drama rubs shoulders with edgy improvisational comedy, and big, Broadway-bound musicals coexist with Baroque period pieces.

As if the wealth of choice during peak season were not enough, Toronto also hosts a number of arts-related events at other times of the year. The biannual **World Stage** theatre festival, held at the Harbourfront Centre in April (☎416/973-4000, ⓦwww.harbourfrontcentre.com/worldstage), is a major international affair, featuring alternative theatre companies from more than twenty countries, while the annual **Fringe Festival of Toronto** showcases approximately eighty workshops and alternative performances in ten days in early July. Additionally, Toronto's newest repertory company, Soulpepper, bucks the trend of a fall-to-spring season and treats audiences to bracing interpretations of works by contemporary masters, as well as underperformed classical

Newmindspace

Kevin Bracken and Lori Kufner met as a pair of University of Toronto students looking for a cheap way of spreading instant joy and amusement. This they achieve with their website ⓦ**www.newmindspace.com**, dedicated to "interactive public art", "cultural interventions" and "urban bliss dissemination". Thanks to the magic of the internet (especially Facebook and Flickr), the site rallies like-minded funsters for Toronto public space happenings: pyjama parties on TTC subway cars, pillow fights in Nathan Phillips Square, bubble blowing, tricycle racing, and flag capturing (a sort of treasure hunt race) are all conjured up as examples of interactive public art – or fun. A New York branch has recently started up and their site has an online starter kit to coordinate similar happenings in one's own city. If you would like to propose something in time for your Toronto visit contact love@newmindspace.com or keep an eye on the site to see what's up next.

pieces, during the summer months. Lastly, although they aren't within the confines of Toronto proper, the Stratford Festival and the Shaw Festival (see p.115 & p.109), both held two hours from Toronto in the towns of Stratford and Niagara-on-the-Lake, respectively, are two of the largest and most respected theatre festivals in North America.

Toronto's main **theatre district** is **Downtown**, encompassing the area around Yonge Street, Front Street, King Street West and John Street. This is where the oldest and most established theatres are located, such as the beautiful Elgin and Winter Garden theatres, and the graceful Royal Alexandra – though there are also plenty of contemporary offerings to spice things up. **Uptown** is home to another vibrant theatre scene where you'll find some of the best alternative companies, especially in and around the **Annex** neighbourhood, east of Bathurst, between Dupont and Bloor. Further venues, primarily small fringe establishments, dot the city's East End, West End and suburbs.

For all theatrical events, **prices** – which range from $17 for shows by smaller companies to $90 for major ones – can be cut in half for same-day perform-ances at **T.O. TIX office** (Tues–Sat noon–7.30pm; ☎416/536-6468 ext 40, ⓦwww.totix.edionysus.com), located on the southeast corner of Dundas Square, right across from the Eaton Centre. Tickets go on sale at noon, so it's a good idea to get in line a half hour before; cash, credit cards (Visa, MasterCard) and Interac are accepted, and no reservations are made by phone. When deciding on seats in an unfamiliar venue, check the front section of Toronto's *Yellow Pages*, which thoughtfully includes the seating charts for the Humming-bird Centre, Roy Thompson Hall and Massey Hall.

Should half-price tickets still exceed your means, look for PWYC ("Pay What You Can") performances listed in publications such as *NOW*. These have a suggested ticket price of about $15, but the boldest or poorest can get away with offering a few bucks (or maybe even nothing at all).

Downtown

Alumnae Theatre 70 Berkeley St, at King St E ☎416/962-1948, ⓦwww.alumnaetheatre.com. Streetcar: King (#504). Original productions with low-budget charm has long been the Alumnae Theatre's mandate. Low on frills, high on fringe.

Artworld Theatre 75 Portland St, at King St W ☎416/366-7723, ⓦwww.artword.net. Streetcar: King (#504). This intimate,150-seat stage and gallery space features consistently innova-tive programming that reflects Toronto's many diverse communities.

Berkeley St Theatre 26 Berkeley St, at King St E ☎416/368-3110, ⓦwww.canstage.com.

Streetcar: King (#504). In addition to being the second stage of the Canadian Stage Company, which presents its more experimental pieces here, this location often houses avant-garde or workshop performances, and is an excellent place to see young talent.

Cameron House Backroom 408 Queen St W, at Cameron St ☎416/703-0811. **Streetcar: Queen (#501).** Situated behind the much-loved and ever-popular Cameron House (which also hosts live bands and DJs; see p.163), this fifty-seat space is best known for its twice-yearly Video Cabaret performances of Michael Hollingsworth's *The History of the Village of the Small Huts*, which satirizes Canada's colonial history.

Canon Theatre 265 Yonge St, at Dundas St E ☎416/872-1212; box office 244 Victoria St, ☎416/593-1962, ⓦ www.mirvish.com. **Subway: Dundas.** Just up the street from the Elgin Theatre and Winter Garden, the Canon, formerly the Pantages, was saved from demolition and restored to its former vaudeville glory in 1989 by impresario Garth Drabinsky, who used it for his Toronto production of *The Phantom of the Opera*. These days, the Canon is used for visiting theatre companies and short-run Broadway productions (*The Producers*, *Wicked*), and special guest acts (Dame Edna Everage).

Elgin Theatre and Winter Garden 189 Yonge St, at Queen St E ☎416/314-2901, ⓦ www.heritagefdn.on.ca. **Subway: Queen.** The Elgin and Winter Garden are the last functioning double-decker theatres in the world, with the latter built on top of the former. From 1987 to 1989, the Ontario Heritage Foundation, under the watchful eye of architect Philip Ziedler, fully restored them to their exact original specifications. While the downstairs Elgin is a treat, with its plush, red upholstery and gilt-plaster ornaments, it's the upstairs Winter Garden that really takes your breath away. This tiny gem was constructed to look like a garden, its ceiling replete with real leaves and its pillars clad to look like tree trunks. Tours are given on Thurs at 5pm, and on Sat & Sun at 11am. Today, the Elgin specializes in dramatic and musical productions, as well as Gala screenings of the Toronto International Film Festival; the Winter Garden uses its more intimate setting to host special events.

Factory Theatre 125 Bathurst St, at King St W ☎416/504-9971, ⓦ www.factorytheatre.ca. **Streetcar: King (#504).** This spot, with its

▼ Factory Theatre

pressed-tin decorative ornaments and seemingly fragile balcony, has a special charm. Since opening in 1970, the Factory was the first theatre in Canada to devote itself to producing Canadian plays exclusively, thereby launching many careers, notably those of playwrights George F. Walker and Adam Pettle; additionally, actors such as R.H. Thompson and Eric Peterson take time from their film and television careers to perform here. Its downstairs sister, the cabaret-like Factory Studio Café, has nurtured a reputation for innovative contemporary theatre.

Lorraine Kisma Theatre for Young People 165 Front St E, at Sherbourne St ☎416/862-2222, ⓦ www.lktyp.ca. **Streetcar: King (#504).** This muscular, Romanesque-style building, which used to be a stable, was saved from the wrecking ball in 1977. The innovative productions shown here are geared towards a young audience, but they're often as intriguing as many of the city's more mainstream offerings (see also Kids' Toronto, pp.203–206).

Princess of Wales Theatre 300 King St W, at John St ☎416/872-1212, ⓦ www.Mirvish.com. **Subway: St Andrew.** Built in 1993 to accommodate the helicopter in *Miss Saigon*, this beautiful theatre has an intimate feel despite its two thousand seats. The murals and loge reliefs by artist Frank Stella are an added visual treat.

Royal Alexandra Theatre 260 King St W, at Simcoe St ☎416/872-1212, ⓦ www.Mirvish .com. **Streetcar: King (#504).** The dowager of Toronto theatres, the graceful, Beaux Arts "Royal Alex", as it's known to locals, was designed in 1906 by architect John Lyle. Today it puts on everything from classical repertory theatre to exuberant Broadway or

West End musicals, such as *Mamma Mia*. The dramatically cantilevered balcony ensures clear sightlines from every seat.

St Lawrence Centre for the Arts 27 Front St E, at Scott St ☎416/386-3100, ◍www.stlc.com. **Subway: Union.** The St Lawrence Centre, home to the Canadian Stage Company, contains two stages: the Bluma Appel Theatre, the facility's main stage, where primarily new works by contemporary artists are shown, and the upstairs, studio-sized Jane Mallett Theatre, which presents experimental and workshop productions and is home to the Toronto Operetta.

Soulpepper Theatre 55 Mill St, Distillery District ☎416/203-6264, ◍www.soulpepper.ca. **Streetcar: King (#504).** Albert Schultz's electrifying leadership of the young Soulpepper Theatre Company, which performs a classical repertory, has lured leading talents from the likes of the Stratford and the Shaw festivals (see p.115 & p.109). The Young Centre for the Performing Arts, which opened in fall 2005 in the Distillery District, is the troupe's new home.

Theatre Passe Muraille 16 Ryerson Ave, at Queen St E ☎416/504-7529, ◍www.passemuraille.on.ca. **Streetcar: Queen (#501).** The unusual configuration of this former bakery and attendant stables allows set designers a lot of dramatic possibilities. A beloved venue for challenging, contemporary drama.

Waterfront

Harbourfront Enwave Theatre 231 Queens Quay W ☎416/973-4000, ◍www.harbourfrontcentre.com. **LRT: Queens Quay.** Hosts a wonderful variety of international dancers, musicians and theatrical productions.

Uptown

12 Alexander Street Theatre 12 Alexander St, at Yonge St ☎416/975-8555, ◍www.artsexy.ca. **Subway: Wellesley.** Tucked away on a tree-shaded side street, 12 Alexander is home to the gay-specialist "Buddies in Bad Times/Art Sexy" company (see p.180). When not showcasing the best in original queer-culture theatre, the space hosts visiting alternative companies and concert performances, and serves as home base for the annual Rhubarb! Theatre Festival (see p.208).

Annex Theatre 730 Bathurst St, at Bloor St W ☎416/538-1772, ◍www.randolphacademy.com. **Subway: Bathurst.** Like the next-door Bathurst Theatre, this former parish hall is home to the Randolph Academy for the Performing Arts and is used for both training and as a venue for festivals and special event performances.

Bathurst Street Theatre 736 Bathurst St, at Bloor St W ☎416/531-6100, ◍www.randolphacademy.com. **Subway: Bathurst.** The acoustics in this more than five-hundred-seat venue (formerly a nineteenth-century church) are excellent, and the performances tend towards the fringe side. Home to the Randolph Academy for the Performing Arts.

New Annex Theatre 296 Brunswick Ave, at Bloor St W ☎416/888-6133, ◍www.gilweb.net/annextheatre/home.htlm. **Subway: Bathurst.** Multimedia performances, screenings and music acts inhabit the former Poor Alex space.

Panasonic Theatre 651 Yonge St, at Isabella St ☎416/8721111, ◍www.Mirvish.com. **Subway: Bloor-Yonge.** The old New York Theatre was stripped to the studs and rebuilt in 2004 to accommodate the indefinite Toronto run of the ever-popular Blue Man Group.

Tarragon Theatre 30 Bridgman Ave, at Howland Ave ☎416/531-1827, ◍www.tarragontheatre.com. **Subway: Dupont.** By consistently presenting challenging, innovative performances, the Tarragon, a renovated factory space, has contributed much to Toronto's thriving theatrical community.

Transac Club 292 Brunswick Ave, at Bloor St W, ☎416/923-8137. **Subway: Spadina.** Not to be confused with the Tranzac Club, a clubhouse for expat Kiwis and Aussies – and confusion is easy because they share the same address – the Transac is a professional theatre venue especially popular with fringe-type productions.

East End

Obsidian Theatre Company 943 Queen St E, at Carlaw Ave ☎416/463-8444, ◍www.obsidian-theatre.com. **Various venues.** Obsidian focuses mainly on producing plays written by Afro-Canadian playwrights. The international company is not only pan-Canadian but also has members from the US, the UK and the West Indies.

West End

Poor Alex Theatre 772A Dundas St W, at Markham St ☎416/324-9863, ⊛www.pooralex .com. Subway: Spadina. The Poor Alex Theatre has made the move over to a new address but the cabaret venue remains a launching pad for many a career, mostly of the alternative/bohemian variety.

Suburbs

DanCap Productions 5000 Yonge St (Suite 1705) ☎416/644-3665, ⊛www.dancaptickets.com.

Various venues. Dancap is the new kid in town specializing in Brodway-type, big box musical productions such as *Jersey Boys*, *My Fair Lady* or the triumphant Toronto return of the *Drowsy Chaperone*. **Papermill Theatre** 67 Pottery Rd, west of Broadview Ave ☎416/396-2819. A beautiful new theatre in the historic Todmorden Mills, once a Victorian industrial space and now an art gallery, theatre and wildflower preserve. The playbills of visiting companies vary widely, from the musical *The Wiz* to Molière's *Tartuffe*.

(11)

Classical music, opera and dance

Thanks to strong moral and fiscal support from a dedicated fan base, Toronto maintains a diverse programme of **opera**, **dance** and **classical music**. In the summer of 2006 the city's ongoing attempt to build a permanent opera house finally paid off: the acoustically pristine, two-thousand-seat ⫚ **Four Seasons Centre for the Performing Arts** (⊛www.fourseasonscentre.ca) is now the home of the Canadian Opera Company and the National Ballet.

Single adult **ticket prices** for opera, dance and classical music performances range from \$35 to \$195. As with theatre tickets you can take your chances at **T.O. TIX** (see p.168), in a kiosk at the northeast corner of Dundas Square, which sells day-of-show seats at half price. Consult either the free copies or online edition of Wholenote at ⊛www.thewholenote.com for a full array of concert **listings**. Additionally, *NOW* magazine has listings for smaller music venues, which feature wonderful performers such as the Orpheus Choir (☎416/530-4428), the Music Umbrella concerts series (☎416/461-6681) – a loose coalition of classical and, increasingly, world musicians who put together small, professional, inexpensive concerts – and free lunchtime recitals, often organ but sometimes choral, given in different churches throughout the city.

Classical music

Glenn Gould Studio 250 Front St W, at John St, Downtown ☎416/205-5555, ⊛www .glenngouldstudio.cbc.ca. Streetcar: King (#504). Named for the great pianist and composer, this small, boxy hall in the Canadian Broadcasting Centre is so sprung for sound that enthusiastic performances leave audiences vibrating. The programming is first-rate and generally showcases Canadian talent. A particularly life-like bronze statue of Gould by Ruth Abernathy lounges on a bench outside the door.
Massey Hall 178 Victoria St, at Young St, Downtown ☎416/872-4255, ⊛www .masseyhall.com. Subway: Dundas. This turn-of-the-century recital hall with great acoustics has hosted a wide variety of

performers – everyone from Enrico Caruso and Maria Callas to Jarvis Cocker. The austere architecture is offset by Moorish details, like the fanciful moulding along the balconies.
⫚ **The Music Gallery Centre for New and Unusual Music** 197 John St, at Queen St W, Downtown ☎416/204-1080, ⊛www .musicgallery.org. Streetcar: Queen (#501). Housed in the new, ecclesiastical space in tiny St George the Martyr, the Music Gallery offers one of the most intense, tantalizing performance schedules in the city and is always up for experimentation. A great place to see Toronto originals such as diva Fides Kruker, thrilling pianist Eve Egoyan or the unusual Glass Orchestra, whose musical instruments, as the name suggests, are made entirely of glass. Guest artists come

from around the world, and performances are linked with lectures and workshops.

Roy Thompson Hall 60 Simcoe St, at King St W, Downtown ☎416/593-4828, ⓦwww .roythompson.com. Subway: St Andrew. Roy Thompson Hall is home primarily to the **Toronto Symphony Orchestra** (☎416/593-4828), though it also hosts the Toronto Mendelssohn Choir (☎416/872-4255) and visiting superstars such as Cecila Bartoli and Midori. The building, finished in 1982 to a design by Arthur Erickson, looks like an upturned café au lait bowl by day, but at night the place is transformed, as the glass-panelled walls glow, casting light over the reflecting ponds and a public square outside. Inside, the circular hall has excellent sightlines, and its acoustics have been recently improved.

Toronto Centre for the Arts 5040 Yonge St, at Elmwood Ave, Suburbs ☎416/872-2222, ⓦwww.tocentre.com. Subway: North York Centre. The classical wing of the Toronto Centre for the Arts, the George Weston Recital Hall is an acoustically precise performance venue that competes with the Roy Thompson Hall for top-name classical acts. Although some distance from Downtown, it's easy to reach, being right next to North York subway.

Trinity-St Paul's Centre 427 Bloor St W, at Spadina Ave, Uptown ☎416/964-9562 or 416/964-6337, ⓦwww.tafelmusik.org. Subway: Spadina. Toronto's riveting Tafelmusik Baroque Orchestra, renowned worldwide for historical performances using period instruments, is gliding gracefully towards its third decade. Under concert master and musical director Jeanne Lamon's leadership, Tafelmusik (German for table music) performs over fifty concerts a year in Toronto.

Opera

Canadian Opera Company Four Seasons Centre for Performing Arts, 145 Queen St W, at University Ave, Downtown ☎416/363-6671, ⓦwww .coc.ca. Subway: Osgoode. Canada's national opera troupe, the COC has dazzled international audiences for years, particularly with its daring approach to the modern opera repertoire. It now has a new artistic director, Alexander Neef, to go with its superb new opera house, designed by Toronto architect Jack Diamond. Seats sell out quickly, particularly for the eagerly anticipated season premières, so reserve as far in

advance as possible – ticket prices vary widely, from $35 to $175.

Opera Atelier various venues, Downtown ☎416/25-3767, ⓦwww.operaatelier .com. Offers sumptuous productions of seventeenth- and eighteenth-century operas, dramas and ballets, though only a handul of times a year. Ticket prices range from $45 to $90.

Opera Lirica Italia 43 Allengrove Crescent, Uptown ☎ 416/882-0246, ⓦwww .operaliricaitalia.com. Various venues. Noting Opera Atelier's success with historical productions and the Canadian Opera Company's tendency to be anything but traditional, this brave, relatively new opera company dares to stage mainly Italian chestnuts for very affordable prices.

Tapestry New Opera 55 Mill St, The Cannery, Studio 316, The Distillery District, Downtown ☎416/537-6066, ⓦwww.tapestrynewopera .com. Streetcar: King (#504). This company is dedicated to supporting and producing new operas by Canadian composers, such as *Iron Road* by Chan Ka Nin, about the Chinese migrant labourers who built the Canadian Pacific Railway, and Nic Gotham and Anne-Marie MacDonald's *Nigredo Hotel*, which tells the story of a man forced to spend the night in a creepy roadside motel. New one-act works are annual stages under the programme heading *Opera To Go*. Performances are staged in a variety of venues.

Dance

Harbourfront Centre Theatre 231 Queens Quay W, the waterfront ☎416/973-4000, ⓦwww .harbourfrontcentre.com. LRT: Queens Quay (from Union Station). Part of the Harbourfront Centre, this modern theatre hosts dance recitals, as well as the occasional theatrical or musical performance.

National Ballet of Canada Four Seasons Centre for Performing Arts, 145 Queen St W, at University Ave, Downtown ☎416/363-6671, ⓦwww .national.ballet.ca. Subway: Osgoode. This company has proven that it is one of the most accomplished corps anywhere, performing classical ballet and contemporary dance with equal artistry. The artistic director (and former prima ballerina) Karen Kain is revered as a national treasure. The seventy-plus dancers in the company are replenished by the Company's own ballet school.

Fleck Dance Theatre (formerly Premier Dance Theatre) 207 Queens Quay W, the waterfront ☎416/973-4921, ⦿ www.harbourfrontcentre .com. LRT: Queens Quay (from Union Station). A beautiful facility built specifically for dance performances, this space also hosts a number of visiting dance companies associated with the many cultural festivals that take place throughout the year (see pp.207–211).
Toronto Dance Theatre 80 Winchester St, at Parliament St, Downtown ☎416/967-1365, ⦿ www.tdt.org. Streetcar: Carlton/College (#506). In a city once infamous for its repressive "Sunday Blue Laws" – which, among other things, forbade theatrical performances on Sun – it is fitting irony that this, like many of Toronto's contemporary theatres, is housed in a former church. Tucked deep in the heart of the historic Cabbagetown neighbourhood, the Toronto Dance Theatre and its affiliated school offer daring, original productions.

Film

First-run cinemas in Toronto range from multiplex shoeboxes (invented by infamous Torontonian Garth Drabinsky) to old-fashioned picture palaces – although, as elsewhere, the latter are dwindling in number as cinemas, and are steadily being converted into event spaces. Home entertainment, from X boxes to DVDs, have had an impact on independent **second-run** or **repertory cinemas**, whose programmes are no longer as eclectic as they once were. On the plus side, some of the multiplex chains have become much more innovative in their programming, and contemporary world cinema finds its way to Toronto screens for first-run films. The gap between the old-school rep houses and the first-run screens is filled in Toronto by the never-ending stream of **film festivals**. Every Toronto community worthy of the name seems to have one of its own and the programming is usually very good to excellent. Now, in addition to learning about one another through the happy medium of food and restaurants, Torontonians can explore one another's cultures and states of mind (there's a mental health film festival) through the art of cinema.

First-run cinemas

Beach Cinemas 1651 Queen St E, at Coxwell Ave, Suburbs ☎416/646-0444. Streetcar: Queen (#501). A plump suburban multiplex serving the growing number of young families in this East End neighbourhood.

Canada Square 2200 Yonge St, at Eglinton Ave W, Suburbs ☎416/646-0444. Subway: Eglington. A sprawling thirteen-screen cineplex offering a mix of foreign, independent and mainstream films.
Carlton 20 Carlton St, at Yonge St, Uptown ☎416/598-2309. Subway: College. When

Moviemaking in Toronto

Over the last three decades, **filmmaking**, animation and television production in Toronto has developed into a billion-dollar industry. Occasionally the Canadian dollar gives an advantage to producers working in US currency, but few large cities capable of handling a major film shoot have such a diversity of landscape and architecture to use as a backdrop. In a relatively short period of time a cinecity of studios and production facilities has sprung up along the lakeshore in the east end. Of equal significance is Toronto's status as a theatre town: it has a large pool of talented artists to draw on for costumes, wigs, sets and lighting, plus there is an abundance of classically trained actors to fill various roles. Add to these resources a Canadian genius for film animation and it's no wonder that Toronto is a filmmaking centre of international stature. Examples of high-profile Toronto-based **filmmakers** include Deepa Mehta, Atom Egoyan, Don McKellar, and the great David Cronenberg.

Garth Drabinsky's Cineplex chain muscled in on the Toronto scene, a number of arthouse cinemas closed. To compensate for this, Drabinsky set aside the Carlton to show first-run art films, and its eleven screens are still doing just that. The café and espresso bar offer nice alternatives to standard concessions fare, although that too is available.

Cumberland 4 159 Cumberland St, at Avenue Rd, Uptown ☎416/646-0444. Subway: Bay. Contrary to its name, this multiplex actually has five screens. Located in the heart of Yorkville, this Uptown version of the Carlton caters to arthouse film fans. Larger screens and more leg room make for more comfortable viewing than at the Carlton, however.

Docks Lakeview Drive-in 11 Polson St, the waterfront ☎416/461-3625. If you have a car and crave that quintessential North American experience of the drive-in movie, the Docks has double bills nightly at dusk, as long as there's not snow.

Scotiabank Movie Theatre (formerly the Paramount) 259 Richmond St W, Downtown ☎416/368-5600. Streetcar: Queen (#501). Perfect venue for filmgoers who want to feel like extras in *Blade Runner*. Half the spectacle is in the theatre itself, with a mammoth pixel-board cube showing film clips to the club-hoppers outside, an almost vertical ride up the escalator to the cinemas and, of course, a sound system that will blast you out of your seat. The complex also houses an IMAX theatre.

Rainbow Market Square 80 Front St E, at Church St, Downtown ☎416/494-9371. Subway: Union. Another Downtown multiplex; this one is close to lots of restaurants and a few bars for after-film meals and discussions.

Regent 551 Mount Pleasant St, at Davisville Ave, Uptown ☎416/480-9884. Subway: Davisville. Wonderful single-screen Art Deco cinema with a great chrome box office and illuminated marquee. Features mainstream fare.

Silvercity Yonge 2300 Yonge St, at Eglinton Ave, Suburbs ☎416/544-1236. Subway: Eglinton. Aimed squarely at the youth market – with dazzling banks of video games and a cornucopia of junkfood – this premium-priced movie venue attempts to be an entertainment complex unto itself.

Varsity 55 Bloor St W, at Belmuto St, Uptown ☎416/961-6303. Subway: Bloor-Yonge. A recent expansion has turned this two-screener into an eleven-cinema behemoth,

replete with displays of Hollywood costumes, costly full-service amenities (drinks and snacks delivered to your seat) VIP screening rooms and regular cinemas with good sightlines, fancy sound systems and deep, comfortable seats.

Independent and repertory cinemas

Al Green Theatre 750 Spadina Ave, at Bloor St W, Uptown ☎416/924-6211. Subway: Spadina. Housed in the Miles Nadal Jewish Community Centre, this little theatre has an incredibly ambitious agenda. The Jewish Film Festival, Toronto Lesbian and Gay Film and Video Festival, Latin Media Festival, Worldwide Short Film Festival, and many more all have screenings here. Between festivals the menu is strictly foreign and art films, sometimes with director nights or discussion forums.

Bloor Cinema 506 Bloor St W, at Bathurst St, Uptown ☎416/516-2330. Subway: Bathurst. Though this cinema won't win any beauty contests, it's a great place to view films. Frequently plays host to the numerous film festivals in Toronto.

Cineforum 463 Bathurst St, at College St, Uptown ☎416/603-6643. Streetcar: Bathurst (#511) or Carlton/College (#506). An independent among independents, Cineforum is indispensable to film students and buffs who want to catch up on the history of film without resorting to cropped video and DVDs.

Cinémathèque Jackman Hall, Art Gallery of Ontario, 317 Dundas St W, at McCaul St, Downtown ☎416/968-3456. Streetcar: Dundas (#505). Cinémathèque is a year-round extension of the Toronto International Film Festival. The senior programmer, James Quandt, is so respected that the French awarded him a Chevalier des Arts et des Lettres and recently the Japan Foundation awarded him a Special Prize for Arts and Culture. The quality of prints he finds are beyond compare, and the retrospectives on the world's great directors are particularly notable.

The Fox 2236 Queen St E, at Beech Ave, Suburbs ☎416/691-7330. Streetcar: Carlton (#506). This former vaudeville theatre, mentioned several times in Michael Ondaatje's *In the Skin of the Lion*, is an alternative to its multiplex cousin, Beach Cinemas, up the road. There's no glitzy marquee and the popcorn

Film festivals

At any given point in the year, someone is sure to be holding a **film festival** in Toronto, whether it's the Latin Media Festival, the Worldwide Short Film Festival, the Jewish Film Festival, or the Toronto Lesbian and Gay Film and Video Festival. The most famous of the group is the **Toronto International Film Festival** (TIFF); ☎416/968-3456, ⓦwww.tiffg.ca. Many regular TIFF attendees are people who plan their holidays around the event, buying passes or books of tickets in advance, which is a somewhat more economical method. There are a variety of plans to choose from, but, because of the festival's popularity and prestige, bargains are hard to find. For more information, see p.210.

is best avoided – just comfortable seats and a good selection of films.

Kingsway Theatre 3030 Bloor St W, at Royal York Rd, Suburbs ☎416/236-1411. Subway: Royal York. This place epitomizes the small theatre experience from the movie-house heyday, before the chains and multiplex theatres moved in.

Ontario Place Cinesphere 955 Lakeshore Rd W, at Remembrance Drive, Harbourfront ☎416/314-9900. Streetcar: Harbourfront (#509) or free shuttle (May–Sept) from Union Station. Located inside Ontario Place and open year-round, the world's first IMAX theatre, Cinesphere, plays both 35mm and IMAX

films on a massive screen. Admission is separate from admission to Ontario Place.

Revue Cinema 400 Roncesvalles Ave, at Marmaduke Rd, Suburbs ☎416/531-9959. Subway: Dundas West. Well worth the trip, this cinema has long had a reputation for some of the finest programming outside of the festival circuit.

The Royal 608 College St, at Clinton St, Uptown ☎416/516-4845. Streetcar: Carlton/College (#506). Situated in the humming midst of Little Italy, The Royal is one of the most attractive cinemas in Toronto, with its lovingly restored original Art Deco interior and forty-feet silver screen.

12

Gay Toronto

oronto's relationship with gays and lesbians has evolved from blunt intolerance to enthusiastic celebration over the past three decades. In addition to hosting one of the largest **Pride** celebrations in the world, the lesbian and gay community now has significant economic, political and social clout. Toronto boasts the largest out population of any city in Canada, thanks in no small part to the city's liberal response to diversity in all its forms.

The neighbourhood at the centre of the activity – commonly known as the **Gay Village** – is at the intersection of Church and Wellesley streets, about one block east of Yonge Street and running south to Carlton Street. Gay establishments are not exclusive to this neighbourhood – the influx of galleries on West Queen West has generated a nascent scene in the Parkdale area – but the lion's share of lesbian/gay/bisexual/transgendered (**LGBT**) community services, bars, clubs and restaurants are at Church and Wellesley. As is the case in many cities, the gay scene is far more conspicuous than its lesbian counterpart – though this neighbourhood is nothing if not inclusive. Even if the bars seem to be specifically for gay men, lesbian and bi women should call for information on dyke nights, women–only events and mixed–theme nights.

One of the more interesting developments over the past decade has been the addition of a family element to the neighbourhood. For those who remember the monogenerational lesbian and gay communities of decades past, it's a joy to watch supportive parents with their LGB offspring, or

Same-sex marriage

On June 10, 2003 the Ontario Supreme Court ruled the exclusion of **same-sex couples** from the Marriage Act unconstitutional under Canada's Charter of Rights and Freedoms. Two hours after that ruling Michael Stark and Michael Leshner, a crown attorney, were married in a civil ceremony in Toronto by an Ontario Supreme Court judge. On June 11 Toronto became wedding-central for same-sex couples across North America. By July 21, 2005 Supreme Court Chief Justice Beverly McLachlin signed Bill C-38 into law, thus legalizing same-sex marriages across Canada. Under Canadian law there is no distinction between hetero- and same-sex couples. Both unions are equally legal and solemn, carrying the same entitlements, commitments and responsibilities. Couples wishing to marry in Toronto can obtain their marriage license from any municipal office for $110 CND and must fulfill the stated requirements. Couples do not require residency or Canadian citizenship.

ⓦ www.city.toronto.on.ca

ⓦ www.samesexmarriage.ca

Alexander Wood

Along with other Toronto communities, the Gay Village celebrates its place in the city's life with a **statue**, in this case a large bronze of **Alexander Wood**, at the corner of Church and Alexander (named for Wood) streets. A magistrate, Wood found himself the subject of an 1810 sex scandal while inspecting the penises of male suspects in a rape case (the victim claimed she had scratched the penis of her attacker during the assault). Whether or not there was any misconduct on Wood's part during his inspections is unknown. What's certain, however, is that the magistrate became the object of ridicule and persecution – owing to allegations of his homosexuality – and was forced to flee to Scotland.

openly gay parents and their children, sorting through the minutiae of day-to-day life in a tolerant, open environment. Interestingly, Bert Archer, author of *The End of Gay*, makes his home in Toronto – a city that bears out his polemic on the increasing normalcy of same-sex relationships in many ways, not least when the Canadian Armed Forces set up a recruitment booth at the big Pride parade here.

The passage of Bill C-38, the so-called same-sex legislation (see box opposite), has undoubtedly contributed to this evolution. There is also strong community recognition of transsexual and transgendered people, whose place in the LGB community is becoming more prominent.

Contacts and information

Anyone interested in finding out about issues, programmes and resources relating to the city's LGB and transsexual communities should contact the **519 Community Centre** at 519 Church St, Uptown (☎416/392-6874, ⓦwww.the519.org; subway: Wellesley). Once a private club, this solid building in the heart of the gay quarter is now the hub for the city's LGB and transsexual outreach and awareness programmes, as well as the neighbourhood's community centre. Over three hundred groups, mostly part of the LGBT communities, utilize this expanding space.

Additionally, look for the **free gay weeklies**, notably *Xtra!*, distributed in newsboxes throughout the city and in many Downtown bars and restaurants. Several **websites** cater to the LGB community: ⓦwww.gaycanada.com has extensive **listings** of what's going on in Toronto; ⓦwww.outintoronto.com has a basic overview of the gay community; and ⓦwww.gaytoronto.com, ⓦwww.gayguidetoronto.com and ⓦwww.fabmagazine.com are excellent online resources.

Accommodation

The following listings are shown on the colour "Uptown" map at the back of this book.

🏃 **Banting House** 73 Homewood Ave, at Wellesley St E, Uptown ☎416/924-1458, ⓦwww.bantinghouse.com. Streetcar: Carlton/College (#506); subway: Wellesley. A luxuriously appointed Edwardian house with nine themed guest rooms (with both en-suite or shared baths), and a suite with its own entrance. Fresh-baked treats are included in the buffet-style continental breakfast. Doubles start at $110.

Bent Inn 107 Gloucester St, at Church St, Uptown ☎416-925-4499, @www.bentinn.com. **Subway: Wellesley.** Billed as "Toronto's only leather guesthouse with a fully equipped dungeon", the *Bent Inn* rounds out the amenities of any self-respecting B&B with rubber floors, sling-ready beds, and a variety of disciplinary furniture and implements. Double occupancy starts at $175 and Dungeon privileges are included in the daily rate in place of the standard continental breakfast.

Cawthra Square Bed & Breakfast Inns 10 Cawthra Square, at Wellesley St E, Uptown ☎416/966-3074, @www.cawthrasquare.com. **Subway: Wellesley.** A beautifully restored, handsomely furnished Victorian mansion-turned-B&B in the heart of the Gay Village. Upscale amenities include PC access, fax, voicemail, afternoon tea, and spa facilities. Doubles start at $269, deluxe Queen at $299, and a Superior from $339. It's hugely popular for weddings and honeymoons and a wedding consultation service is available, so advance bookings are suggested.

Dundonald House 35 Dundonald St, at Yonge St, Uptown ☎416/961-9888 or 800/260-7227, @www.dundonaldhouse.com. **Subway: Wellesley.** For some, a visit to Toronto wouldn't be right without a stay at this well-established Downtown B&B. Hosts Warren, Dave and Rio the dog offer attractive rooms with internet access, a/c, cable TV, an on-site gym, touring bikes, parking and sumptuous breakfasts. Doubles start at $135 with lots of special package offers.

Victoria's Mansion Inn & Guesthouse 68 Gloucester St, at Church St, Uptown ☎416/921-4625, @www.victoriasmansion .com. **Subway: Wellesley.** The rainbow flag flies proudly over this Victorian mansion, whose rooms are all equipped with fridges, microwaves and coffeemakers. Guests are frequently repeat visitors, giving this establishment a genuine warmth and hominess. Doubles start at $105. All rooms are en suite with a/c, maid service, high-speed internet access, coffeemakers and fridges, and can be rented daily, weekly or monthly.

Bars, clubs and restaurants

The Barn 418 Church St, at Carlton St, Uptown ☎416/593-9696, @www.thebarnnightclub.com. **Subway: College.** Three floors and a patio continue founder Janko Najilic's goal of providing a safe cruising environment. Once a focal point of gay life in Toronto, if not Canada, and still a great place to buy a fella a beer. Closed Mon & Tues.

Black Eagle 457 Church St, at Alexander St, Uptown ☎416/413-1219, @www .blackeagletoronto.com. **Subway: Wellesley.** A popular leather and denim cruise spot, with two full bars (dungeon equipment by Master R's Dungeon; murals by Jay Dampf) and a rooftop patio that boasts "best smoking patio" in town. Strict fetish dress code in effect on Frid & Sat, with an emphasis on leather. Popular events include a wet jocks contest on the first Thurs of every month.

Byzantium 499 Church St, at Wellesley St E, Uptown ☎416/922-3859. **Subway: Wellesley.** If the Church-Wellesley neighbourhood owned a Little Black Dress it would be *Byzantium*: stylish and literally tasteful, the long, slim space divides itself into a cocktail bar and a dining room. Reservations recommended on weekends.

Gay Pride

When Toronto's first **Gay Pride** celebration was held at Hanlan's Point on the Toronto Islands in 1971 only one hundred brave people showed up. Today, the celebration stretches over an entire week at the end of June, and the concluding parade attracts an annual attendance of over 800,000. Festivities promoting gay awareness fill the week and culminate with the Gay Pride Parade, beginning at Church and Wellesley and unrolling down Yonge Street. To show solidarity with Toronto's LGBT population, the Mayor and Premier of Ontario ride at the front of the parade. For more information, see @www.torontopride.com.

▲ Gay Pride

Club Toronto Mansion 213 Mutual St, at Carlton St, Uptown ☎416/977-4629, ⓦwww .clubtoronto.com. Subway: College. Another spin on the men's club theme, this gay men's playhouse rents rooms and lockers and stands back to let guests amuse themselves. There are two floors with private rooms, two with party rooms, and the cell block. Further facilities include two lounges, a common room, a sling room, swimming pools and a sauna. Foodwise it's Summer BBQs and the ever-popular Sunday brunch.

Church Street Bar 501 Church St, at Wellesley St E, Uptown ☎416/323-0399. Subway: Wellesley. Sporting three floors (including a decorous lounge with a fireplace and a retrofit dancefloor), this is also home to ManCandyRadio (ⓦwww.mancancy.com). Inclusivity is the theme and all shades, types and orientations are as welcome as they want to be.

Fly Nightclub 8 Gloucester St, at Yonge St, Uptown ☎416/410-5426, ⓦwww .flynightclub.com. Subway: Wellesley. One of the top dance clubs featuring their own DiverCity programming, from signature Besharam (South Asian dance trax) to Golden Age classics. Special events are held on Fri, while the party on Sat lasts until 7.00am Sun morning.

Hair of the Dog 425 Church St, at Carlton St, Uptown ☎416/964-2708, ⓦwww .hairofthedog.org. Subway: Wellesley or Carlton. A popular upscale bistro, pub and cocktail bar featuring heady 3oz cocktails, *Hair of the Dog* has one of the Gay Village's better kitchens. Lunch focusses on comfort foods, including an upscale mac'n'cheese, while dinner mains are lighter versions of traditional seafood and steak combos. By day, a good place for a business lunch, and at night for a serious date.

Pegasus on Church 489B Church St (second floor), at Wellesley St E, Uptown ☎416/927-8832, ⓦwww.pegasusonchurch.com. Subway: Wellesley. Billiard and pool tables, darts and satellite TV give the distinct impression of your average gay/lesbian sports bar. A tad cruisey, but that's the point.

Slacks 562 Church St, at Wellesley St E, Uptown ☎416/928-2151, ⓦwww.slacks.ca. Subway: Wellesley. One of the city's few decisively lesbian bars, a recent rennovation has refreshed and warmed a neighbourhood favourite. The menu is serious and mains weigh in a hefty $20 average, but the bar action is solid. Check regularly for themed events.

Straight 553 Church St, at Gloucester St, Uptown ☎416/926-2501, ⓦwww .straightonchurch.com. Subway: Wellesley.

Brenda Abdo's latest property is a stylish dance club/lounge currently open Thurs–Sun with special themed nights and Straight Girl events. Brenda welcomes all comers to this new jewel in Toronto's LGBT crown.

Tallulah's Cabaret 12 Alexander St, at Yonge St, Uptown ☎416/975-8555. **Subway: College or Wellesley.** A popular bar/cabaret space attached to the Buddies in Bad Times theatre. Hosts a youngish LGB and transsexual crowd, in addition to the thespians.

Woody's/Sailor 465-467 Church St, at Alexander St, Uptown ☎416/972-0887, Ⓦwww .woodystoronto.com. **Subway: Wellesley.** Five bars equipped with 21 video monitors, an excellent selection of microbrews and draught ales, daily specials and a popular weekend brunch – not that anyone comes here for the food. There are competitions for various parts of the male anatomy Thurs–Sun, themed nights, special events and many men.

Zelda's Bar and Restaurant 542 Church St, at Wellesley St E, Uptown ☎416/922-2526, Ⓦwww.zeldas.ca. **Subway: Wellesley.** Canada has its queen and Toronto has Zelda: Zelda's patio is the place for a ringside seat during the Gay Pride celebrations, and the flotilla of pink flamingos is Divine. A varied, culturally diverse menu reflects patrons' tastes, and the Sunday brunch in particular is fabulous. That goes doubles for the bar. The party room is highly esteemed as a wedding venue, and if that isn't enough excitement, Zelda herself occasionally whooshes in to hold court.

Zipperz/Cellblock 72 Carlton St, at Church St, Uptown ☎416/921-0066, Ⓦwww .zipperz-cellblock.ca. **Streetcar: Carlton/College (#506).** *Zipperz* is a rather good piano bar with the action starting around 10pm, and *Cellblock* is a dance club with themed nights Wed–Sun featuring drag, line-dancing, college nights, and retro music Sun.

Theatre

Gay theatre in Toronto makes its home at the excellent 12 Alexander Street Theatre, at 12 Alexander St, near Yonge Street (☎416/975-8555, Ⓦwww .artsexy.ca; subway: Wellesley. See p.170). Here, the Buddies in Bad Times company puts on a repertoire of queer-culture performances of original works, as well as the annual Rhubarb! Festival (see p.208 for more), prized by all Toronto theatre-goers.

Shops

Come as You Are 701 Queen St W, at Markham St, West End ☎416/504-7934, Ⓦwww.comeasyouare.com. **Streetcar: Queen (#501).** A worker-owned cooperative sex-toy shop and bookstore that caters primarily, though not exclusively, to lesbians and bisexual women.

Glad Day Bookstore 598A Yonge St (upstairs), at Wellesley St, Uptown ☎416/961-4161, Ⓦwww .gladdaybookstore.com. **Subway: Wellesley.** Information central for the LGBT community since 1970, this bookstore was once the only overt sign that a gay community existed in Toronto. Sells books, music, videos and periodicals.

He & She Clothing Gallery 263 Queen St E, at Sherborne St, Downtown ☎416/594-0171. **Streetcar: Queen (#501).** For work or play, these exuberantly sleazy outfits are deliberately provocative and loads of fun. There's a full range of stiletto pumps in sizes big enough to accommodate both sexes.

Priape 465 and 501 Church St, at Wellesley St E, Uptown ☎416/586-9914, Ⓦwww.priape.com. **Subway: Wellesley.** Wittily described as Toronto's "gay insight centre", this is more than a boy-toy-boy emporium: books, magazines, costumes, a huge selection of men's knickers and a knowledgeable staff guide customers towards the realization of their secret and not-so-secret desires.

Gay baths and spas

Cellar 78 Wellesley St E, at Church St ☎416/944-3779. Subway: Wellesley. Open 24/7 but famous for its "Wild Wednesdays". Use the back entrance. Really.

Club Toronto Mansion 213 Mutual St, off Carlton St (one block east of Chuch St) ☎416/977-4629, ⓦ www.clubtoronto.com. Streetcar: Carlton/College (#506); subway: College. There are two floors with private rooms, two with party rooms, and the cell block. Facilities include two lounges, a common room, a sling room, glory holes, swimming pools and a sauna. Foodwise it's summer BBQs and the ever-popular Sunday brunch. Open 24/7.

Spa Excess 105 Carlton St, at Jarvis St, Uptown ☎416/260-2363, ⓦ www.spaexcess.com. Streetcar: Carlton/College (#506). Except for the brass lettering "Excess", the discrete wooden doors of the office-like building give no hint of the four floors of safe environment for casual encounters inside.

Steamworks 540 Church St (second floor), at Wellesley St, Uptown ☎416/925-1571, ⓦ www .steamworks.ca. Subway: Wellesley. The proud boast here is that Steamworks is "Toronto's largest legal cruise and play space". Anonymity assured with a key deposit system; memberships optional.

13

Shops and galleries

Toronto offers the widest range of **shops** in Canada. Stores run the gamut from chain store ubiquity to boutique exclusivity and there is something for every price range, age, style and taste. **Business hours** are fairly consistent: most shops are open seven days a week, Monday to Thursday from 10am to 7pm, with somewhat longer hours on Friday and somewhat earlier closing times on Saturday. Sunday hours are usually between noon and 6pm. Smaller, independent boutiques have variable hours so if in doubt, call ahead.

Toronto is composed of numerous **shopping districts**. The intersection at Yonge and Dundas streets, with its huge pixel billboards, neon lights, noise and ongoing roster of events in **Dundas Square**, teems with teenagers flocking here from suburbs across North America and beyond. This area has the highest concentration of retail outlets in Toronto, including the **Eaton Centre**, a huge mall stretching from Sears at Yonge Street on its northern edge, south to The Bay at Queen and Yonge. It houses every youth-oriented brand store, entertainment device, fashion trend and frippery a youthful shopper could want, and is within easy reach of everywhere in Downtown Toronto.

Continuing north up Yonge Street to Bloor Street West takes you to **Yorkville**, a nest of streets that run between Yonge and Avenue Road, including Cumberland Street, Yorkville Avenue, Hazelton Avenue and Scollard Street. Yorkville was Toronto's Flower Power epicentre in the 1960s, but the neighbourhood went upscale in the 1980s and is now filled with costly boutiques, private **galleries** and multi-million-dollar condos. While not the place to look for bargains, Yorkville is home to some shops and services that are on the affordable side of luxury, and the area offers prime quality people-watching.

Queen Street West, and now **West Queen West**, are the shopping districts most closely associated with independent fashion and all things decidedly trend-forward. The further west you go from University Avenue the more avant garde Queen West becomes. Currently the area around Queen West and **Ossington Avenue** has the greatest combination of edge and style.

Areas primarily known as residential neighbourhoods such as the **Bloor West Village**, **Forest Hill Village**, **Leslieville**, **Bayview**, **Rosedale** and **Roncesvalles** all have retail pockets of antiques, home design, gourmet food shops and art galleries, and are easily accessible by public transport.

Antiques and home furnishings (contemporary and vintage)

Absolutely Inc 1132 Yonge St, at MacPherson Ave, Uptown ☎416/324-8351. Subway: Rosedale. Also at 1236 Yonge St, at Walker Ave, Uptown ☎415/922-6784. Subway: Summerhill. Stacks of wonderful finds piled high in every possible nook and cranny. Huge sea sponges perch atop delicate pedestals, antique hat forms adorn Georgian desks, and Venetian mirrors reflect everything, doubling the sense of wondrous clutter.

▼ Absolutely Inc antiques

L'Atelier 1224 Yonge St, at Alcorn Ave, Uptown ☎416/966-0200. Subway: Summerhill. A series of rooms give out to one another, each filled with treasures: L'Atelier specializes in quality French Deco furniture and decorative objects with a somewhat masculine flair.

Ethel – 20th Century Living 1091 Queen St E, at Brooklyn Ave, East End ☎416/778-6608, ⓦwww.ethel20thcenturyliving.com. Streetcar: Queen (#501). Lighting, furniture and accessories from International Modern luminaries such as Ray and Charles Eames, Frank Gehry, and Eero Aarnio, as well as fun Pop plastics, chunky ceramics, and slender teak accessories.

MachineAgeModern 1000 Queen St E, near Carlaw Ave, East End ☎416/461-3588, ⓦwww.machineagemodern.com. Streetcar: Queen (#501). A mix of Modernism (1920s through to 1980s) with some contemporary Modernism-inspired pieces. Excellent range of chairs and mirrors.

Ministry of the Interior 80 Ossington Ave, north of Queen St W, West End ☎416/533-6684, ⓦwww.ministryoftheinterior.net. Streetcar: Queen (#501). If someone opened a high concept home design store instead of forming a grunge band you'd have Ministry of the Interior. In addition to the often amusing furniture it offers outstanding wallpapers like the Timorous Beasties pattern, and highly imaginative accessories.

The Paisley Shoppe 77 Yorkville Ave, at Bellaire St, Uptown ☎416/923-5830. Subway: Bay. Housed in the last Yorkville Regency cottage, this Toronto institution specializes in fine antiques – mostly French, English and Irish, with some Chinese.

Phil'z 20th Century Design 792 Queen St E, near Broadview Ave, East End ☎416/461-9913. Streetcar: Queen (#501). A great source for twentieth-century design, including surrealist pieces remade by the original manufacturers such as an exquisite Merit Oppenheim gilt consul with chicken legs. Modernist masters like Gehry, Mies van der Rohe and Jensen can also be spotted.

Queen West Antique Centre 1605 Queen St W, near Roncesvalles Ave, West End ☎416/588-2212. Streetcar: Queen (#501). Uptown retailers have been spotted sourcing this cache of twentieth-century home and industrial furniture, including Arts and Crafts, Modern, Danish Modern and superb clear acrylics.

Toronto Antique Centre 276 King St W, at Duncan St, Downtown ☎416/345-9941, ⓦwww.torontoantiquectr.com. Streetcar: King (#504); subway: St Andrew. Over 25 different antique dealers migrated north from the former Harbourfront Antique Market and settled under one ample roof, each specializing in a different niche. Perfect for browsing before or after a play or concert.

Books

Toronto loves **books**, literature, poets and authors. It hosts the world's largest literary festival (see p.210), has a year-round authors' reading series at the waterfront, and is home to a large population of authors. Reflecting this bibliophilic disposition are a number of excellent bookstores, both specialist and general.

New

Bookcity 348 Danforth Ave, at Chester Ave, East End ☎416/469-9997. Subway: Chester. Also three other locations. A solid neighbourhood bookstore with a good range of new-release literature, magazines and children's selections. If you can't find what you're looking for, first-rate staff will make special orders.
David Mirvish Books 596 Markham St, at Bathurst St, West End ☎416/531-9975, ⓦwww.dmbooks.com. Subway: Bathurst. The recent addition of fiction, non-fiction, poetry, travel and culinary ranges supplements the fine art and design collection. Mirvish's connection with American artist Frank Stella is apparent: his remarkable mural "Damascus Gate Stretch Variation" adorns the back wall.
Indigo Books, Music & Café 55 Bloor St W, at Bay St, Uptown ☎416/925-3536, ⓦwww.indigo.ca, and other locations. Subway: Bay. This Canadian chain decks out its locations in blond wood and provides seating to encourage browsing. CD, software and gift sections supplement the books. High marks for its children's book selection and championship of Canadian authors.
Nicholas Hoare 45 Front St E, at Church St, Downtown ☎416/777-2665. Subway: Union. A beautifully appointed store replete with Gothic folly flourishes, this bibliophile refuge provides comfy chairs and sofas and a working fireplace. The large selection runs the gamut but excels with its design and architecture section.
Pages 265 Queen St W, at John St, Downtown ☎416/598-1447. Streetcar: Queen (#501). Toronto's number-one bookstore for sophisticated readers with alternative tastes. The stock is the edgiest, most comprehensive collection of contemporary literature and social criticism in town, and includes an extensive range of magazines and small-press publications.
This Ain't the Rosedale Library 86 Nassau St, at Bellevue Ave, Downtown ☎416/ 929-9912, ⓦwww.thisaint.ca. Streetcar: Carlton/College (#506). After nearly thirty years on Church St, owner Charlie Huisken moved to Kensington Market. A lifeline to emerging authors, TATRL continues to offer a kaleidoscope of magazines, recent fiction, gay and lesbian culture, and literary, film and art criticism.
Type Books 883 Queen St W, at Walnut Ave, West End ☎416/366-8973, ⓦwww.typebooks.ca. Streetcar: Queen (#501). Also at two other locations. Stocks a small but select collection of fiction and non-fiction making the lists and winning the awards, and carefully chosen magazines.
World's Biggest Bookstore 20 Edward St, at Yonge St, Downtown ☎416/977-7009. Subway: Dundas. A sprawling space where slow sellers go for really deep discounts. There are always treasures to be found if you have time and patience.

Used and antiquarian

Acadia Art & Rare Books 232 Queen St E, at Jarvis St, Downtown ☎416/364-7638, ⓦwww.acadiabooks.com. Streetcar: Queen (#501). The neighbourhood remains a stranger to gentrification but this is where the uptown dealers come for high-quality antiquarian books and prints. Authenticity guaranteed.
Babel Books & Music 123 Ossington Ave, north of Queen St W, West End ☎416/533-9138. Streetcar: Queen (#501). Great resource for hard-to-find, out-of-print titles that will nevertheless cost no more than $8. Select vinyl in LPs and 45s.

D & E Lake 237 King St E, at Jarvis St, Downtown ☎416/863-9930, ⓦwww.delake.com. Streetcar: King (#504). A Dickensian brick building with paned windows, creaky floors, and teetering canyons of old and arcane books. A collector's first stop: the wide selection includes military, art, architecture and medical books, in museum quality condition.

Eliot's Bookstore 584 Yonge St, at Wellesley St, Uptown ☎416/925-0268. Subway: Wellesley. A favourite for browsing, with a good general and scholastic collection and a growing culinary section. Also has a used magazine selection that is particularly strong on arts and music.

Specialist

Bakka Phoenix Science Fiction Books 697 Queen St W, at Markham St, Downtown ☎416/963-9993, ⓦwww.baakkaphoenixbooks.com. Streetcar: Queen (#501). This is where speculative fiction authors like Tanya Huff and Robert J. Sawyer got their start – as sales clerks while writing their early novels. A quality selection of SF and fantasy with a solid representation of horror.

The Cookbook Store 850 Yonge St, at Yorkville Ave, Uptown ☎416/920-2665, ⓦwww.cook-book.com. Subway: Bloor-Yonge. This compact Yorkville shop has long been a temple for bibliophilic foodies, celebrity chefs and culinary novices. It offers special events, book-signings, cooking demonstrations and, of course, cookbooks ranging from the latest cooking trend to the classics.

Swipe Books on Advertising and Design 401 Richmond St W, at Spadina Ave, Downtown ☎416/363-1332, ⓦwww.swipe.com. Streetcar: Queen (#501). Totally dedicated to design, this remarkable resource covers areas such as architecture, typography, green design, urbanism, and – of course – advertising.

Theatre Books 11 St Thomas St, at Bloor St W, Uptown ☎416/922-7175, ⓦwww.theatrebooks.com. Subway: Bay. An exceptional bookstore specializing in all aspects of film and the performing arts, including theatre, opera, dance and even arts administration. An excellent resource centre and a beautiful shop, housed on a chic little street off Bloor West's Golden Mile in a Victorian brick house.

Toronto Women's Bookstore 73 Harbord St, at Spadina Ave, Uptown ☎416/922-8744, ⓦwww.womensbookstore.com. Streetcar: Spadina (#510). A hub of feminist literature for 35 years and now the largest feminist and humanist bookstore in Canada, the TWR has a strong background in activism and community outreach and maintains a busy events schedule.

Home and garden accessories

At Design 5 McPherson Ave, at Yonge St, Uptown ☎416/323-0315, ⓦwww.atdesignhome.com. Subway: Rosedale. This teensy little cottage is a mannerist/surrealist design emporium squashed full of treats: Fornasetti textiles, Jonathan Adler's Muse series, and Michael Aram's Skeleton, Earth, and Water collections predominate.

Belle Epoque 1066 Yonge St, at Roxburgh St, Uptown ☎416/925-0066, ⓦwww.belleepoque.ca. Subway: Rosedale. Little vestiges of its French flea market days linger but what you'll mostly find are fresh takes on classics, an interesting line in glass furniture, and tempting accessories for the home or Madame.

French Country 6 Roxborough St, Uptown ☎416/944-2204, ⓦwww.frenchcountry.ca. Subway: Rosedale. This fine French furnishings and home accessories cottage is well worth a visit. Their prices for quilts and bedding beat any market in Provence, and their glass and tableware items are first rate.

Putti Fine Furnishings 1104 Yonge St, at Roxborough St, Uptown ☎416/972-7652. Subway: Rosedale. A jewel box of beautiful objects, some old and some new, from antique boudoir tables and Venetian glass mirrors, to Limoge pill boxes and fine writing paper. In season, the Christmas tree ornaments are so desirable that people who don't celebrate the holiday end up buying them.

Shopgirls 1342 Queen St W, at Brock Ave, West End ☎416/534-7467, ⓦwww.shopgirls.ca. Streetcar: Queen (#501). This Parkdale retail/studio design collective is specifically for Canadian (and mostly Torontonian) designers, including knitwear by Priscilla Gomes, jewellery by Jodi Foreman, birch

"Bubble Chairs" by Graham McNally, and other soon-to-be-household names.

Studio Brillantine 1518 Queen St W, at Macdonell Ave, West End ☎416/536-6521, ⓦwww.studiobrillantine.com. **Streetcar: Queen (#501).** A highly select, international collection of award-winning, everyday objects by architects, designers, and artisans including Alessi, Fornasetti, Georg Jensen, Masato Yamamoto, et al.

Teatro Verde Hazelton Lanes, 87 Avenue Rd, at Yorkville Ave, Uptown ☎416/966-2227, ⓦwww.teatroverde.com. **Subway: Bay (Cumberland exit).** The ultimate one-stop shopping for the Downtown gardener: you can get a floral arrangement, find the perfect addition to your container garden, interior accessories for your next dinner party, and even a really good facial mudpack. An upcoming move around the corner to Yorkville Ave is anticipated.

Umbra Concept Store 165 John St, at Queen St W, Downtown ☎416/599-0088, ⓦwww.umbra.com. **Streetcar: Queen (#501).** A splashy new building in Karim Rashid's signature Pink & White, there are two floors of affordable design items, furniture and accessories for every room in the house including over twenty of Rashid's best-known designs for Umbra (Oh Chair, garbino cans, magino tables.)

Clothing

Independent designers

Champagne & Cupcakes Dress Boutique 1114 Queen St W, at Dovercourt Rd, West End ☎416/533-2253. **Streetcar: Queen (#501).** Pretty party girl dresses by owner/designer Caroline Lim plus the frilly lingerie to put under them *and* cupcake-shaped bath products.

Damzels in this Dress/Doll Factory Studios 1122 Queen St E, near Jones Ave, East End ☎416/598-0509, ⓦwww.damzelsinthisdress.com. **Streetcar:** Queen (#501). Fans of the Damzels – Kelly Freeman and Rory Lindo – include Kirsten Dunst and Neve Campbell. The femme-with-edge dresses and the Doll Factory "Albums" – bikinis, capris, chemises and slips packaged in twelve-inch-by-twelve-inch record sleeves with guitar pick earrings – are supplemented with Sailor Jerry accessories.

Delphic Clothing Limited 706 Queen St W, at Manning Ave, West End ☎416/603-3334. **Streetcar: Queen (#501).** Some women's but mostly men's street and club wear. The speciality is the house-brand jeans but there are also solid of-the-moment lines like Acne and Filippa K.

Pam Chorley Fashion Crimes 322 ½ Queen St W, at Yonge St, Downtown, ☎416/592-9001, ⓦwww.fashioncrimes.ca. **Subway: Queen.** A dramatic exterior and wow windows barely hint at the show-stopper outfits inside: designer Pam Chorley's creations have been described as the most beautiful dresses in Toronto. Their exclusive fabrics and exceptional attention to detail make them equally popular with Prom Princesses and visiting VIPs looking for something special.

Propaganda 686 Yonge St, north of Wellesley St, Uptown ☎416/961-0555. **Subway: Wellesley.** Owner Regina Sheung has provided a launching pad for lots of local and Canadian clothing, accessory and jewellery designers (Oligarchy, House of Spy, Momo, Bloodline) with an accent on fresh and fun. Help spread the word.

▼ Shopping in Toronto

Toronto fashion design

Toronto's fashion design scene has developed and matured to the point that it is positively booming, spurred by the emergence of the Toronto-based Fashion Design Council of Canada and its sponsorship of the biannual **Toronto Fashion Week** (Ⓦwww.torontofashionweek.ca). Brave new local labels and their outlets include:

Damzels in this Dress,1122 Queen St E, near Jones Ave, East End ☎416/598-0509, Ⓦwww.damzelsinthisdress.com. Streetcar: Queen (#501).

House of Spy at Spy Lab, 247 Queen St W, at Peter St, Downtown ☎416/599-4779, Ⓦwww.houseofspy.com. Streetcar: Queen (#501).

Pink Tartan, Holt Renfrew, 50 Bloor St W, at Bay St, Uptown ☎416/922-2333, Ⓦwww.pinktartan.com. Subway: Bay (Bay exit).

Y5 5 Yorkville Ave, at Yonge St, Uptown ☎416/920-9173. Subway: Bloor-Yonge. Visionary designer Ula Zukowska has carved a place for herself on Toronto's fashion design scene, and fans of her inspirational approach to knits, textiles, form and cut are loyal and growing in number. Be prepared to buy it something fits and you want it: items move fast and space is at a premium.

Designer labels and haute couture

Chanel Boutique 131 Bloor St W, at Bay St, Uptown ☎416/925-2577. Subway: Bay. Purveyors of the ultimate power suit for Ladies Who Lunch, Chanel offers dependable excellence at couture prices.

Corbo Boutique 119 Yorkville Ave, at Hazelton Ave, Uptown ☎416/928-9898. Subway: Bay (Cumberland exit). Men's and women's top-of-the-line suits, dresses, outerwear, shoes and accessories in labels for those who take their forward haute couture seriously and have the budgets to match: YSL, of course, some Junya Watanabe, Olivier Theyskens, Jimmy Choo, et al.

Hazel 99 Yorkville Ave, at Bellair St, Uptown ☎416/925-3380. Subway: Bay. One of the most exclusive stores in Canada, with staggering sticker-shock prices to match. This is where the one-offs from the European mega-labels like Chanel, Gucci and Escada can be found, and the store rightly treats these exquisite garments as wearable textile art by giving them the gallery treatment. Mostly women's but some men's plus a few luxe accessories.

Holt Renfrew 50 Bloor St W, at Bay St, Uptown ☎416/922-2333. Subway: Bay. Toronto's premier couture destination for both men

and women. Specializes in signature collections from the likes of Jean-Paul Gaultier, Gucci, Sonia Rykiel and Armani, as well as upper-echelon Canadian designers such as Pink Tartan and Lida Baday. Holt aims to wrap its customers in full-service, and so provides a concierge desk by the main entrance, two cafés, a full day spa and a great staff to help you out.

Indiva 144 Yorkville Ave, at Avenue Rd, Uptown ☎416/962-3482, Ⓦwww.indivaretail.com. Subway: Bay (Cumberland exit). A recent move to Yorkville serves to concentrate attention on some of India's best contemporary designers, including Wendell Rodricks' very latest collections. The sumptuous textiles are also shown off in a homeware accessory line.

Over the Rainbow 101 Yorkville Ave, at Hazelton Ave, Uptown ☎416/967-7448, 877/967-7448, Ⓦwww.rainbowjeans.com. Subway: Bay. Like finding perfect shoes, a great hat or underwear that fits, body sculpting, comfortable, of-the-moment jeans are worth the price. This is *the* place to buy jeans. OTR has an excellent staff and full lines of tops and belts that will be worthy of your jean purchase. Labels include Denim Design Lab, Chinese Laundry, Toronto's Line Sweaters and more.

Prada 131 Bloor St W, at Bay St, Uptown ☎416/513-0400. Subway: Bay (Bay exit). Prada's Toronto boutique offers a representative range of the latest Men's and Women's apparel, accessories, shoes and handbags for both the Prada and Miu-Miu lines.

TNT Woman, TNT Man, TNT Blu Hazelton Lanes mall (see p.190), 55 Avenue Rd, Uptown ☎416/975-1810. Subway: Bay (Cumberland exit). Flirty little items and techno-power suits or even T-shirts don't come cheap here, and a teensy bit of label obsession is probably a customer requisite. Lines include Teenflo, Diesel, Robert Rodriguez and Iceburg.

Hats, shoes and accessories

Accessity 136 Cumberland St, at Avenue Rd, Uptown ℡416/972-1855. Subway: Bay (Cumberland exit). A visit to Accessity begets more visits because you can't see everything at once. Jewellery, scarves, belts, separates, lingerie, hose, hair accessories, bags and hats represent Toronto and Canadian designers (Zokai, Jane Abbot) and international lines, especially from India, the US and Italy.

Heel Boy 682 Queen St W, at Euclid Ave, West End ℡416/362-4335, ⓦwww.heelboy.com. Streetcar: Queen (#501). A trove of feminine footwear selectively clustered under one roof. Big brand favourites such as Steve Madden and Kenneth Cole are supplemented by some lesser-known must-haves.

Lilliput Hats 462 College St, at Markham St, Uptown ℡416/536-5933. Streetcar: Carlton/College (#506). Millinery is almost a lost art, so Toronto is particularly blessed to have Karen Gingras and her Lilliput Hats in its midst. In addition to the breathtaking variety of finished headwear, the open studio is in the shop, steaming, stitching and forming fabrics into each unique creation. Men's and women's special orders are welcome.

Vintage

Brava 553 Queen St W, at Spadina Ave, Downtown ℡416/504-8742. Streetcar: Queen (#501). An excellent collection of vintage jewellery and spiffy duds for men and women from the Thirties to the Nineties. Shoes, handbags, kimonos and Fifties bowling shirts can all be found in pristine condition.

Courage My Love 14 Kensington Ave, at Dundas St, Downtown ℡416/979-1992. Streetcar: Dundas (#505). Vintage clothing for men and women augmented with an eclectic selection of beads, amulets and buttons. The clientele here ranges from high school girls looking for funky prom dresses to fashion-magazine editors looking for cheap chic.

Divine Decadence Originals 2nd floor, 136 Cumberland St, at Avenue Rd, Uptown ℡416/324-9759. Subway: Bay (Cumberland exit). An unmatched collection of vintage

haute couture, including Chanel from the 1930s, Dior from the 1950s, Pucci from the 1960s, and museum-quality accessories, jewellery, beaded bags, fragile cocktail hats plus vintage bridal. An absolute must for connoisseurs.

Gadabout Vintage 1300 Queen St E, at Leslie St, East End ℡416/463-1254, ⓦwww.gadabout.ca. Streetcar: Queen (#501). Top-quality vintage, linens, shoes, hats and jewellery with an emphasis on the 1920s to the 1970s, plus rare Edwardian pieces. Features top examples of twentieth-century couture including Bespoke, de Givenchy, Lavin and Suzy Perette. Some men's items are available.

I Miss You Vintage 63 Ossington Ave, near Queen St W, West End ℡416/916-7021, ⓦwww.imissyou.ca. Streetcar: Queen (#501). Excellent finds from the 1930s to the 1980s with an emphasis on Sixties and Seventies designer dresses, accessories, hats, shoes and bags. Fendi, Pucci, Gucci, Hermès and even Schaiparelli have been sighted.

Stella Luna 1627 Queen St W, at Roncesvalles Ave, Suburbs ℡416/536-7300. Streetcar: Queen (#501). Stella Luna is a secret Torontonians tend to keep to themselves. Bargain-hunters slip in here for the killer jet and sparkly jewellery, vintage designers (Halston, Valentino) and the marvellous shoes. If you make the trek, be sure to bring cash. Credit and debit cards belong to a different era.

Thrift

Grrreat Stuff 870 Queen St W, at Crawford St, West End ℡416/533-7680. Streetcar: Queen (#501). An end-of-line/sample store filled with label clothing at deep discount prices for men. Two floors of solid labels – Hugo Boss, Clinique, Kenneth Cole – plus some local designers.

Honest Ed's 581 Bloor St W, at Bathurst St, Uptown ℡416/537-1574, ⓦwww.honesteds .sites.toronto.com. Subway: Bathurst. Although Ed himself is gone, his name lives on in the two-and-a-half-storey neon sign with dancing light bulbs stretching around a city block. Toronto's ultimate discount store stocks homeware, hardware, groceries, clothing, toys, electronics – whatever you need for bargain basement prices. Its colourful clientele adds further interest.

Marilyn's 200 Spadina Ave, at Sullivan St, Downtown ℡416/504-6777, ⓦwww.marilyns .com. Streetcar: Spadina (#510). It's a store, it's an event space, it's a post-grad school in efficient closet arrangement; Marilyn's wants women from sizes 2 to 24 to dress for less, whatever the occasion. Check out the collection of fanciful umbrellas; try to resist the $20 Temptation rack.

Tom's Place Men's Clothing 190 Baldwin Ave, at Kensington Ave, Uptown ☎416/596-0297, Ⓦwww.toms-place.com. Streetcar: Spadina

(#510). This Kensington Market institution offers a wide selection of men's and women's designer clothes at discount prices. The actual price tags are more or less suggestions for bartering with the deeply courteous, real-life Tom Mihalik. The more he likes you, the better the deal. The staff is top-notch and alterations are speedily performed on-site.

Crafts and design

Art Gallery of Ontario Gallery Shop 317 Dundas St W, at McCaul St, Downtown ☎416/979-6610. Subway: St Patrick. The Gehry-designed space is retail intoxication. In addition to items themed around current exhibits, the AGO's shop stocks items by local jewellers, artisans and designers, and has a large poster section. There's also an excellent selection of children's toys, books and multimedia teaching aids.

Bounty 235 York Quay Centre, Waterfront ☎416/973-4993. Streetcar: Spadina/ Harbourfront; (#509/#510). This consignment shop and exhibition space features the work of visiting and resident artisans, who produce beautiful stained and blown glass, jewellery, baskets, fired clay, ironware, turned wood and more in glass-walled studios on site.

Corktown Designs Bldg no.59–102, 55 Mill St, Distillery District, Downtown ☎416/861-3020, Ⓦwww.corktowndesigns.com. Streetcar: King (#504); bus: Parliament St. Robyn Berman's studio-like store features innovative designers including Burnt Sienna, George Dragonov of Dragonfly and Rarebloom.

Distill Canadian Art Craft Design Bldg no.47, 55 Mill St, Distillery District, Downtown ☎416/304-0033, Ⓦwww.distillgallery.com. Streetcar: King (#504); bus: Parliament St. One of the most popular stores in the Distillery District, Distill features textiles (could include dresses, scarves, hats, and baby duds) by Funk Shui and Akra, ceramics by Janet MacPherson, Jennifer Graham and Julie Moon, glass by

Julia Hilyer and a new line in hockey stick furniture by Urban Products.

Gardiner Museum Shop 111 Queen's Park Circle, Uptown ☎416/586-5699. Subway: Museum. Perhaps the best place in town to find innovative, one-off ceramics, the Gardiner's gift shop carries design-forward jewellery, glass and some textiles.

🏃 **The Guild Shop 118 Cumberland St, at Bellair St, Uptown ☎416/921-1721. Subway: Bay.** The Guild Shop has represented Canadian artists and artisans for seven decades. They mix newcomers with collectible veterans and carry glass, ceramics, textiles, jewellery and turned wood. It is also Toronto's oldest Inuit and First Nations art dealer (also see p.191), and sells Inuit statuary and prints. An excellent place to begin a collection.

The ROM Shops 100 Queen's Park Circle, Uptown ☎416/586-5775. Subway: Museum. The gift shops at the Royal Ontario Museum carry scarves, jewellery and intriguing widgets themed to major exhibits and reproductions of items in the permanent collection. The dramatic new space has a section of items made from recycled materials, and the book section has a range of titles emphasizing Canadian and First Nations history and culture. The children's section is chock-full of educational books and toys themed to the museum's collections with a predictable emphasis on dinosaurs.

Department stores and malls

Department stores

The Bay 176 Queen St, at Yonge St, Downtown ☎416/861-9111. Subway: Queen. Also at intersection of Bloor and Yonge, Uptown ☎416/972-3333. Subway: Bloor-Yonge. Ⓦwww.thebay.com. The name is taken from the Hudson's Bay Company, the

The largest mall in Toronto is invisible from the surface, buried beneath the streets in 27 kilometres of tunnels known as the **Underground City**, with 1,200 retail outlets and services sprawling over 371,600 square meters/four million square feet. The entrances and connections to the Underground City are brightly marked with the **PATH** logo. This subterranean network of plazas co-evolved with the banking towers that dominate the street level, when their developers had the idea of creating shopping environments for the hundreds of thousands of workers who pour into the city's core daily (they've been administered by the City of Toronto since 1987). The system hooks into TTC stations, malls, municipal buildings, hotels and department stores, so, no matter how bad the weather, you can always go shopping, visit a gallery or find something to eat in the retail labyrinths beneath Toronto.

world's oldest corporate entity and former owner of most of the Canadian North. You can still purchase the Hudson's Bay Blanket here (a must-have item during the fur trade), but the rest of the basic department-store stock is decidedly contemporary.
Sears 290 Yonge St, at Dundas St, Downtown ☎416/343-2111, ⓦwww.sears.ca. **Subway: Dundas.** Once the flagship of Canada's oldest department store chain (Eaton's), it now flies the Sears flag, carrying fashion, perfume, cosmetics and houseware unavailable in the average outlet of the utilitarian American department store chain.

Malls

Brookfield Place 161–181 Bay St, at Front St, Downtown. Subway: Union. Known to most Torontonians by its old name of BCE Place, this Financial District office and retail complex incorporates the walls of Toronto's oldest surviving stone building and a block of Victorian shops into the soaring development. Its centrepiece is a five-storey galleria with a vaulted ceiling, designed by Spanish "starchitect" Santiago Calatrava. The glass

roof allows sunlight to pour in, providing a welcome antidote to the subterranean fluorescent lighting of the Underground City (see above).
Eaton Centre 290 Yonge St, at Queen St W, Downtown. Subway: Queen or Dundas. Anchored at its northern boundary by the Sears department store (see above), this mall spans two subway stops, contains hundreds of stores on five levels and takes the better part of an afternoon just to walk from one end to the other. It is perhaps the best place to shop if you have limited time, simply because every chain store of any significance is here. The layout follows one general rule: high-end shops are on the third level, mid-price shops on the second, and the cheap stuff is on the bottom.
Hazelton Lanes 55 Avenue Rd, at Yorkville Ave, Uptown. Subway: Bay. This mall is almost too classy to be so labelled. It has high-end clothing, home decor and is home to Toronto's only Whole Foods, mixed in with a few restaurants and cafés. Wonderful for browsing if the weather outside is too cold, too hot, or too wet.

Food and drink

See also "Markets", too, p.192.

Gourmet

Caviar Direct St Lawrence Market, Downtown ☎416/361-3422, ⓦwww.caviarforsale.com. **Subway: Union.** For a friendly counter in the St Lawrence Market, this little outlet handles all the luxury biggies: sturgeon, tobiko and

golden caviars, white and black truffles, foie gras, and Canadian Atlantic and Pacific varieties of wild smoked salmon.
Pusateri's 57 Yorkville Ave, at Bay St, Uptown ☎416/785-9100, ⓦwww.pusateris.com. **Subway: Bay.** The downtown Pusateri "deli", and café (see p.136) aims to provide the

very best foodstuffs and comestibles, be they cheeses, fruits, meats, pastries or olive oils. The valet parking is a nice touch too. Catering, personal shopping and cooking classes are also available.

Soma Chocolatemaker Bldg no.48, 55 Mill St, Distillery District, Downtown ☎416/815-7662. Streetcar: King (#504); bus: Parliament St. People who are really serious about their cocoa beans come here, and if you never understood the passion people have for this food of the gods, you will after a visit.

Summerhill Station LCBO 10 Scrivner Square, at Yonge St, Uptown ☎416/922-0403, ⊛www .lcbo.com. Subway: Summerhill. One of the coolest, best stocked liquor stores anywhere, this thirty-thousand-square-feet outlet was once a railway station, complete with marble walls and clock tower. Today it carries more than five thousand wines, spirits and beers from around the world, with a vintages section, tasting sections and a demonstration kitchen.

Bakeries and patisseries

Brick Street Bakery Bldg no.45A, 55 Mill St, Distillery District, Downtown ☎416/214-4949. Streetcar: King (#504); bus: Parliament St. Offers a variety of breads, puff pastries, desserts and take-away sandwiches, all totally organic.

Carousel Bakery St Lawrence Market, Jarvis St, at Front St, Downtown ☎416/363-4247. Subway: Union. Toronto's famous peameal back bacon on a fresh kaiser roll is available here. Accept no imitations. The Carousel also gets high marks for its speciality breads, including brioche, focaccia and all kinds of rolls.

Daniel et Daniel 248 Carlton St, at Parliament St, Uptown ☎416/968-9275, ⊛www.danieletdaniel .ca. Streetcar: Carlton/College (#506).

Classically French, Daniel et Daniel creates superb cakes, jewel-like fruit tarts and dainty pastries. Look-out for traditional, seasonal French favourites such as the Gallette des Roi.

Queen of Tarts 283 Roncesvalles Ave, at Dundas St W, Suburbs ☎416/651-3009, ⊛www .thequeenoftarts.ca. Subway: Dundas West. Streetcar: Carlton/College (#506). The Queen not only produces luscious clafoutis, toothsome macaroons and pies and tarts of every description, but also turns out an excellent line in politically informed ginger-bread people.

Health food

Big Carrot Natural Food Market and Wholistic Dispensary 348 Danforth Ave, at Jackman Ave, East End ☎416/466-2129, ⊛www.thebigcarrot .ca. Subway: Chester. This whole food super-market collective provides one-stop shopping for organic food and earth friendly household items. Although vegetarian-friendly, the Big Carrot also stocks organic meat, poultry and fish. It has a popular vegetarian deli counter/café, personal care section and herbalist shop.

The House of Spice 190 Augusta Ave, at Baldwin St, Downtown ☎416/593-9724. Streetcar: Carlton/College (#506). No matter how intricate the dish, House of Spice will have all the hard-to-find spices under its new addition roof. In addition to the fragrant range of exotic condiments, it also has a fine range of teas and coffees.

Whole Foods 87 Avenue Rd, at Yorkville Ave, Uptown ☎416/944-0500, ⊛www.wholefoods .com. Subway: Bay. The Toronto outlet of the US health food supermarket chain, Whole Foods, carries a full selection of organic produce, fish and meat, bulk and frozen foods, deli counter and bakery.

Inuit and First Nations galleries

For more on Inuit and First Nations art, see *Canadian Art* colour section.

Fehley Fine Arts 14 Hazelton Ave, at Yorkville Ave, Uptown ☎416/323-1373, ⊛www.feheleyfinearts .com. Subway: Bay (Cumberland exit). Fehley's is an international leader in the complex and diverse area of Inuit art, representing artists and sculptors from across the enormous expanse of the Canadian Arctic, and patron-ized by serious collectors. The superior print

collections make an excellent start to under-standing the genre.

Isaacs Inuit Gallery 9 Prince Arthur Ave, at Avenue Rd, Uptown ☎416/921-9985. Subway: St George or Museum. Collectors have long patronized Isaacs, which carries Inuit sculpture, prints, drawings and wall hangings.

Kinsman Robinson Galleries 108 Cumberland St, at Bellair St, Uptown ☎416/964-2374, ⓦ www.kinsmanrobinson.com. Subway: Bay (Bellair exit). The principle dealer for Norval Morriseau's estate, this Yorkville gallery also carries Haida artist Robert Davidson and Canadian figurative sculptor William McElcheran.

Maslak-McLeod Gallery 118 Scollard Ave, Uptown ☎416/944-2577, ⓦ www.maslakmcleod.com. Subway: Bay (Cumberland exit). This gallery carries some of the most important names in First Nations and Inuit painting, including Woodland School masters like Norval Morrisseau and Goyce Kagegamic, and Inuit sculptor Floyd Kuptna.

Markets

Dufferin Grove Farmers' Market 875 Dufferin St, at Dufferin Grove Park rinkhouse, West End ☎416/392-0913, ⓦ www.dufferinpark.ca. Subway: Dufferin. This community market brings together "locivor" producers all year and also features its own bread, baked in the park's outdoor ovens. Thurs 3–7pm year-round.

The Farmers Market (North Market) 92 Front St E, at Jarvis St, Downtown ☎416/392-7219. Subway: Union. These vendors are usually the producers offering fresh honey, pots of herbs, home-baked goods, fresh cheeses and fruits and vegetables straight off the farm. Open Sat only, from 5am to 5pm. On Sun the same space transforms into a good flea market.

Kensington Market Dundas St W, at Kensington Ave, Downtown, ⓦ www.kensington-market.ca. Streetcar: Dundas (#505). A United Nations of food: one street is stuffed with Ethiopian, Vietnamese, Trinidadian, Bahamian, Chinese, Portuguese and Jewish food shops, while around the corner merchants from throughout Latin America congregate with vendors from the Middle East, the Mediterranean and Central Europe. If you can't find it here, the odds are you won't find it anywhere. In addition to the edibles there are vintage clothing stores, over-the-edge designers,

pubs, cafés and patios. Open daily; Sun are car-free and very quiet.

Riverdale Farm Organic Market Riverdale Farm, 201 Winchester St, at Parliament St, Uptown ⓦ www.friendsofriverdalefarm.com. Streetcar: Carlton/College (#506). The best overall organic neighbourhood market in town. In addition to seasonal fruits and veg, regional vendors sell honey, baked goods, jams and preserves, and organic meats and cheeses. Open Tues 3–7pm from May–Oct.

St Lawrence Market 92 Front St, at Jarvis St, Downtown, ☎416/392-7219, ⓦ www.stlawrencemarket.com. Subway: Union. On the site of Toronto's first city hall, this market boasts two levels of stalls, shops and bins filled with tantalizing international goods. The busiest and most festive day to visit is Sat, when buskers of every description play to the crowds. Apart from the array of international items, you can sample treats specific to Canada, like peameal bacon sandwiches (back bacon coated in a cornmeal crust), fiddlehead ferns, salmon cured in maple syrup and an astonishing variety of mustards, rice, cheeses and meats. The lower level also has prepared foods and a crafts market with hats, scarves, jewellery and wooden toys. Tues–Sat.

Music

Entertainment corporations use Toronto's diverse, cosmopolitan population as a test market for CDs, DVDs and games, and consequently you'll find a wide selection of new-release titles for some of the best prices in North America. The standard CD price is $15, going up to $21–23 for expensive imports and speciality labels. However, the popularity of MP3 players and downloading has put the squeeze on both independent and big box music stores.

New

L'Atelier Grigorian 70 Yorkville Ave, at Bay St, Uptown ☏416/922-6477. **Subway: Bay.** The comprehensive selection of classical and ancient music here includes many imported labels and hard-to-find titles. Nothing comes cheap, but if you really need that four-disc set of Byzantine liturgical music, this is the place to shop.

HMV 333 Yonge St, at Dundas St, Downtown ☏416/586-9668. **Subway: Dundas.** The four comprehensively stocked floors here are packed with the Top 40 of most musical genres. An equally large selection of DVDs and games fill the racks.

Rotate This 620 Queen St W, at Bathurst St, Uptown ☏416/504-8447. **Streetcar: Queen (#501).** A bit further down the Queen West strip and therefore less likely to be filled with young things from the suburbs on a Sat afternoon. Stocks a diverse selection of many genres.

Soundscapes 572 College St, at Manning Ave, Uptown ☏416/537-1620. **Streetcar:**

Carlton/College (#506). Alternative indie labels like Merge and Thrill Jockey, and imports at commiserate prices.

Used

Second Vinyl 2 McCaul St, at Queen St W, Downtown ☏416/977-3737. **Subway: Osgoode.** Despite the name, this store carries only a limited selection of records. One side of the store is devoted to used jazz and classical CDs, and the other is filled with rock and alternative titles.

She Said Boom 372 College St, at Bathurst St, Uptown ☏416/944-3224. **Streetcar: Carlton/ College (#506).** An emporium devoted to popular culture and sounds, filled with new and used CDs and books.

🏃 **Wild East 360 Danforth Ave (upstairs), at Chester Ave, East End** ☏416/469-8371, ⊛www.johnnyrockomet.com. **Subway: Chester.** A mix of new and used CDs and DVDs, this small walk-up is the elite of the off-beat.

Speciality stores

Kidding Awound 91 Cumberland St, at Bay St, Uptown ☏416/926-8996, ⊛www.kiddingawound .com. **Subway: Bay.** A large turning key over the door warms you up for this delightfully goofy store, where you can buy quality rubber chickens, punching nuns, metal lunch boxes decorated with Hindu gods, huge dragon puppets or a variety of keychains.

Northbound Leather 7 St Nicholas St, at Wellesley St, Uptown ☏416/972-1037. **Subway: Wellesley.** Spiffy duds in latex, leather and PVC, with a full complement of masks, whips and other props for erotic home theatre. Beautiful workmanship, high-quality materials and a broad-minded, attentive staff willing to answer questions or take special orders.

Sporting goods

Hogtown Extreme Sports 401 King St W, at Spadina Ave, Downtown ☏416/598-4192. **Streetcar: King (#504).** Hogtown specializes in skateboarding equipment, baggy clothes and snowboards, though they also do a nice line in bike gear.

Mountain Equipment Co-op 400 King St W, at Peter St, Downtown ☏416/340-2667. **Streetcar: King (#504).** An annual membership (for a nominal fee) gets you access to the city's most extensive range of top-flight sports

equipment. If you're planning to dog-sled in the Arctic, bike across China, climb mountains or go deep-sea diving, you can buy everything you need here at better-than-average prices. Mountain Co-op also does daily rentals of bicycles, cross-country skis, canoes and kayaks for the urban outdoors person. The building itself is even interesting: it's made from recycled materials and has a wildflower garden on the roof.

14

Sports and outdoor activities

J ust as Toronto's arts and culinary scenes have exploded and expanded to match the city's diversity, so too has **sports** – testified by the growing popularity of professional basketball and soccer, for example, reflecting Toronto's changing demographics (and adding to the year-round excitement provided by the traditional **spectator sports** of ice hockey, baseball and Canadian football). But you don't have to stick to watching: Toronto offers ample opportunities for participating in sports and **outdoor activities**, thanks in no small part to the remarkable amount of **parkland** and **green space** maintained within the city limits (more than twelve percent of the entire city land mass is a park of one type or another). Within those parameters are some three million trees and 1500 named parks, in addition to numerous playgrounds, community centres, swimming pools, tennis courts, golf courses and even a labyrinth in Trinity Square Park, behind the Eaton Centre. There are also all-night baseball diamonds, basketball courts, soccer pitches, hiking and cross-country skiing trails, greenhouses and gardens and wildlife sanctuaries. To find a facility or to check on opening hours and fees, contact **Toronto Parks and Recreation** (☎416/392-1111, ⓦwww.toronto .ca/parks) or check the Municipal Blue Pages in the phone book.

Major sporting venues

There are three main venues for spectator sports in Toronto, all located downtown:
Air Canada Centre 40 Bay St, off the Gardiner Expressway, Downtown ☎416/815-5500, ⓦwww.theaircanadacentre.com. Subway: Union. Home of the Toronto Maple Leafs hockey team and the Toronto Raptors basketball squad.
BMO Field 170 Princes Blvd, at the Exhibiton grounds off Lakeshore Blvd W ☎416/360-4625, ⓦwww.bmosoccerfield.com. Brand-new home for the brand-new Toronto FC of the relatively new Major League Soccer (MLS).
Rogers Centre (formerly the SkyDome) 1 Blue Jays Way, at Front St W, Downtown ☎416/341-3663, ⓦwww.rogerscentre.com. Subway: Union. Hosts the Toronto Blue Jays baseball team and the Toronto Argonauts football team, as well as numerous special events and concerts. See p.42 for more on the building and tours.
Single **tickets**, when available, to all major sporting events may be purchased through Ticketmaster, ☎416/872-5000 or ⓦwww.ticketmaster.ca.

▲ The Toronto Maple Leafs

Ice hockey

Ice hockey is Canada's national pastime, and with players hurtling around at nearly 50kph and the puck clocking speeds of over 160kph, this would be a high-adrenaline sport even without all the combat that takes place on the ice. Truth be told, the **Toronto Maple Leafs** haven't won the Stanley Cup since 1967 but this dismal record has not dimmed Toronto's blind affection for the team in the least. On the contrary, it can be difficult to get tickets for even exhibition games.

Although the Maple Leaf Gardens still hulks on the corner of Church and Carlton, the Leafs decamped in 1999 to the then new **Air Canada Centre** (☎416/815-5500). This state-of-the-art complex is replete with pixelboard gadgetry, bone rattling sound systems and costly corporate suites. The Centre also hosts Toronto's professional basketball franchise, the **Toronto Raptors**. The ACC is connected to Union Station by an underground walkway and is very easy to reach by public transport.

The regular **hockey season**, which lasts from October to May (and sometimes June), is composed of approximately ninety games. Single **ticket prices** range from $65 to a whopping $495, depending on availability, the other team, and of course proximity to the ice. In the rare years when the Leafs do make the playoffs, tickets are virtually impossible to obtain.

Canadian football

Professional **Canadian football**, played under the aegis of the Canadian Football League (CFL), is a somewhat different affair from the American version, played by the National Football League. In Canada the playing field is longer, wider and has a deeper end zone, and there are twelve rather than eleven players on each team. There is also one fewer "down" in each series of the game, meaning that after kick-off the offensive team has three, rather than four, chances to advance the ball ten yards and regain a first down. The limited time allowed between plays results in a more fast-paced and high-scoring sport, in which ties are often decided in overtime or in a dramatic final-minute surge.

Toronto's team, **the Argonauts** (or "Argos"), has become a force to be reckoned with under the tutelage of their wildly popular head coach, **Michael "Pinball" Clemons**, once Argo running back and now the team's CEO – a unique transition in either the CFL or NFL. With a height of five feet and six inches (167cm), Pinball earned his nickname because his size allowed him to dart between the bulkier players and take full advantage of the CFL's faster game. The Argos (☎416/341-2746; ⊛www.argonaughts.ca) share the Rogers Centre stadium with the Toronto Blue Jays baseball team. The **season** takes place between August and November, and culminates in playoffs for the Grey Cup, Canadian Football's championship trophy. The Grey Cup weekend is a Canadian tradition, involving lots of house parties and, if the Argos win, general revelry throughout the city. Single **tickets** range from $20 to $75 for a regular game and over $100 for a Grey Cup match.

Baseball

When the **Toronto Blue Jays** (☎416/341-1234; ⊛www.toronto.bluejays .mlb.com) won their first World Series in 1992, more than a million people jammed Downtown to celebrate the victory. When the Jays repeated the feat in 1993, Toronto's newfound love for baseball was sealed. Fans anticipate a return to glory now that **Clarence "Cito" Gaston**, who brought the Jays to their back-to-back World Series wins, has returned as head coach. The Blue Jays (affiliated with Major League Baseball's American League) play about eighty home games a season, which lasts from April to October. Games are played in the afternoon or at night and can last anywhere from two to four hours. Without a doubt, the Jays Twoonie Tuesdays are the best sports deal in town: seats in the 500 Level go for a mere $2 and regular home game **ticket prices** can start at $10, going up to $65 for an infield seat; but for pennant games prices can get up over the $200 mark.

Basketball

Canadians are fond of annoying Americans with the fact that **basketball** was invented by a Canadian, James Naismith, who took his game south of the border in 1891 where it actually took off.

Toronto had a professional basketball team in the Thirties and Forties, but when the American divisions reorganized themselves into the National Basket-ball Association (NBA) in the Fifties, the Toronto franchise was dropped. Toronto didn't rejoin the professional ranks until 1995, when the **Toronto Raptors** became part of the NBA.

The Raptors play home games from November to May at the ultramodern **Air Canada Centre**. Ticket prices range from $27 to $175, although the upper range prices are even higher for an all-star game. Currently the Raptors are far from being a top NBA team; however, it's well worth attending a game to marvel at the sheer athleticism of professional basketball players.

Soccer

When in April 2007 Toronto finally got its own soccer-specific stadium, the **BMO Field**, to go with its very own pro team, **Toronto FC** (☎416/263-5700, Ⓦ www.torontofc.com), the pent-up demand from fans hit like a wave: in its first two seasons every home game sold out, with over three-quarters of the seats filled by season ticket holders. Fans keenly anticipate manager Mo Johnston and coach John Carver's next moves to build up the young team. Prices for single tickets for the 20,522-seat, open-air stadium range from $15 to $200 and there is a standing-only Supporters' Section. The BMO field is also home turf to Canada's **National Soccer Team** (Ⓦ www.CanadaSoccer.com) and it hosted the FIFA U-20 World Cup in 2007. An interesting aside reflecting the local fan base is the wide diversity of snack food available at the BMO Field during a game. You can get a chip butty, scotch egg, panini and pizzas, samosas, souvlaki, Jamaican patties, vegetarian wraps, BBQ pork, peameal bacon sandwiches, and curry fries (ie chips), an interesting new hybrid everyone seems to enjoy, and all of these can be washed down with beer and non-alcoholic beverages.

Lacrosse

Although ice hockey is Canada's national sport, the first and perhaps most truly Canadian game is **lacrosse**, which is enjoying a vigorous resurgence in popularity. This fast, rugged sport was invented by the Iroquois people of the Six Nations Confederacy, whose games would include hundreds of players on both sides and were mistaken by the first European sports spectators for battles. The rules of play, simplified and codified in the mid-nineteenth century, state that the objective is simply to send the ball through the opponent's goal as many times as possible while preventing the opposing team from scoring. There are ten players to a team and the long-handled, racket-like implement, called the crosse, used to toss and catch the ball, is the most distinctive feature of the game. As in hockey, players face off in midfield with their crosses touching the ground, and the referee drops the ball between them. Other similarities include body checks and penalties for slashing, tripping and fist-fighting. The **Toronto Rock** is the city's **National Lacrosse League** team and the NLL's premier team. When managed by the late Les Bartley, the Rock won the championship five times in seven years and went on to win two more division championships. From January to April the Rock plays eight intense home games at the **Air Canada Centre**. Single **tickets** range from $27 to $73.

Cycling and inline skating

Bicycles have proliferated in Toronto, both as a means of transportation and for recreation. Indeed, the municipal government even has a **Cycling Committee**, which devotes itself to protecting the interests of Toronto cyclists. The city also sponsors a variety of group rides and bike-friendly activities, and maintains an extensive **website** for cyclists featuring bike route maps, cyclist events, newsletters, blogs and so on (Ⓦ www.toronto.ca/cycling). In addition, the **Toronto Bicycling Network** (Ⓦ www.tbn.ca) arranges group rides, weekend trips and mixers for both cyclists and inline skaters.

    Bike lanes have made an appearance on the main traffic arteries throughout Toronto; there are currently ninety kilometres of bike lanes, but the proposed goal of the Toronto Bicycle Plan is 495km of designed roadway space for the exclusive use of bicycles and a thousand kilometres of off-road cycling routes, mostly through the city's parklands. For the novice or visitor, two popular routes are the **Leslie Street Spit** (officially known as Tommy Thompson Park), a car-free zone that stretches out like a skinny finger into Lake Ontario from the foot of Leslie Street beyond Ashbridges Bay; and the **Belt Line trail**, a route that follows the old Belt Line surburban rail link that ran down through Rosedale, around the Don Valley, and through Mount Pleasant. Branches expand through Riverdale and the Don River, up Pottery Road along the old Brickworks and Bayview, and through the Avoca Ravine. For more details on these routes, see Ⓦ www.ontariobikepaths.com.

Note that cyclists under the age of 18 must wear a protective helmet. Bicycles are allowed on streetcars, subways and buses, except during the weekday rush hours of 6.30–9.30am and 3.30–6.30pm. **Rental fees** are around $45 a day and an additional security deposit is required; hourly rates vary.

Though no longer the craze it once was, **inline skating** (rollerblading) still makes another fun way to get about on wheels. As with cycling, it's important to rent adequate safety gear, especially helmets, along with the equipment. A good outfit to rent skates from is Wheel Excitement (see below).

Bike and inline skate rentals

Cogs Cycle 1 Howland Rd, at Gerrard St E, East End ☎416/465-7677, Ⓦ www.cogscycle.com. Both new and used bikes are for sale in this long-established Riverdale bicycle repair shop. Also does rentals.

Curbside Cycle 412 Bloor St W, at Brunswick Ave, Uptown ☎416/972-6948, Ⓦ www.curbside.on.ca. Fancy bikes like the folding Brompton and the Dutch Batavus and stylish cyclist accessories can be found in this Annex shop.

The Cyclepath 2106 Yonge St, at Manor Rd E, Suburbs ☎416/487-1717, Ⓦ www.cyclepath toronto.com. Road bikes and mountain/hybrid bikes.

Europe Bound 47 Front St E, at Yonge St, Downtown ☎416/601-1990, Ⓦ www.europe bound.com. Standard and mountain bikes.

🏃 **Mountain Equipment Coop 400 King St W, at Spadina Ave, Downtown** ☎416/340-2667, Ⓦ www.mec.ca. Wide range of standard and mountain bikes. Small coop member-ship fee necessary.

Toronto Island Bicycle Rental on Centre Island ☎416/203-0009. Quad, tandem and standard bikes. See p.86.

Wheel Excitement 249 Queens Quay W, the waterfront ☎416/260-9000, Ⓦ www .wheelexcitement.ca. Mountain bikes and inline skates. Cycle and skate rentals start at $15 an hour or $30 for 24 hours.

Skateboarding, snowboarding and skiing

Although the modernist plazas surrounding Downtown's skyscrapers are a serious temptation for skateboard enthusiasts, boarding those areas is rarely tolerated by authorities. There are, however, plenty of **skateboarding** parks ringing the city. The most popular – and the only indoor – Downtown Toronto skatepark is Shred Central, 19 St Nicolas St, near Yonge and Wellesley (☎416/923-9842 or 416/924-2589; Ⓦ www.shredcentral.com). The best bowl is reputed to be Vanderhoof Skatepark at Laird Drive and Vanderhoof Avenue, near Eglinton Avenue E (Ⓦ www.skatersinc.com), which has the added bonus of being free, as is the Cummer Skateboard Park, at 6000 Leslie St, at Cummer Avenue (Ⓦ www.toronto.ca/parks).

Skateboarding's winter twin, **snowboarding**, as well as **cross-country skiing**, can be experienced without leaving the city limits. In the hilly northern suburbs of Toronto, lessons are available for beginners at the Snowhawks Raven

Ski and Snowboard School, 166 Lytton Blvd, Willowdale (☎416/487-6271, ⓦwww.snowhawks.com). Two municipal centres that rent equipment and provide lessons are the North York Ski Centre (☎416/395-7931), located in Earl Bales Park at Sheppard and Bathurst streets, and the Centennial Park Ski Hill at Renforth and Rathburn streets (☎416/394-8754). Rentals, equipment and local skatepark tips can be found at Hogtown Skateboard & Snowboard Shop, 401 King St W, at Spadina Ave (☎416/598-4192; ⓦwww.hogtownextreme.com).

Ice skating

From mid-November to early spring, 47 municipally operated indoor and outdoor iced surfaces operate seven days a week from 10am to 10pm. One of the most popular **rinks** is at City Hall's **Nathan Phillips Square**. It has the added advantage of being beautifully lit at night, especially during Toronto's Cavalcade of Lights (see p.211), and skate rentals are available. Another public rink where you can rent skates is at Harbourfront Park (☎416/973-4000). Adult **skate rentals** are a flat $7 and should you wish to rent the skates for another rink they start at $14 an hour. For information on the various locations, hours of operation and ice conditions, call the parks service Mon–Fri 8.30am–4.30pm at ☎416/338-7465.

Hiking and walking

Toronto's parklands, ravines and neighbourhoods offer plenty of opportunities for **hiking** and **walking**, in particular along nine self-guided **Discovery Walks**

Guided hikes and city walks

If you're keen to get hiking in Toronto's nearby wilderness areas but don't feel like going it alone, the perfect solution could be to join a **guided hike** with the **Toronto Bruce Trail Club** (☎416/690-4453, ⓦwww.torontobrucetrailclub.org). This voluntary organization maintains a fifty-kilometre section of the remarkable **Bruce Trail**, which extends from the Niagara Escarpment all the way up to the Bruce Peninsula in Georgian Bay. The club runs a regular year-round hiking program, including plenty of "bus hikes", which transport hikers to the starting point of the hike, and then bring them back at the end.

Alternatively, for something a little less taxing, you could try the following city **walking tours**:

A Taste of the World ☎416/923-6813, ⓦwww.torontowalksbikes.com. Shirley Lum's culinary tours of Chinatown, especially on the advent of Chinese New Year, are charming, informative and a brisk workout. She also has a great line in Literary Toronto walking tours and has introduced bicycle tours into her touring repertoire.

Bruce Bell Tours ☎647/393-8687, ⓦwww.brucebelltours.ca. Accept no substitutes. Bruce is a local historian, former actor, and bon vivant extraordinaire whose walking tours, including the St Lawrence Market and the Distillery District, are the best in the city hands down.

ROMwalks ☎416/586-8097, ⓦwww.rom.on.ca/programs. Volunteers from the Royal Ontario Museum lead guided walking tours through architecturally and historically significant Toronto neighbourhoods.

(☎ 416/338-0338, ⓦ www.toronto.ca/parks/discoverywalks). These meandering routes are peppered with maps and interpretive signs explaining the local flora and fauna and the historical significance of the trails. Perhaps surprisingly, the **Downtown Toronto Discovery Walk** is the most intriguing, as much of the natural landscape features, such as the buried creeks, continue to exist beneath the concrete surface. The best coastal paths are the Western and Eastern Ravines and **Beaches Discovery Walks**, which lead to a shoreline boardwalk through natural ponds, marshes and lakeshore parks. From here, it's hard to believe you're still within Toronto's city limits. One of the more physically challenging (and rewarding) Discovery Walks is the **Humber River route** that leads from the Old Mill, dating back to 1793, through the ancient Carrying Place Trail,

▲ Discovery Walk sign

Green Roof Project

In addition to the parkland on the ground or in Lake Ontario, Toronto has a number of sky-high gardens. The city's Green Roof Project has over 307,000 square feet of rooftop gardens on municipal property alone. The new Royal Ontario Museum's Crystal addition is the latest green roof; the Mountain Equipment Coop's meadowland rooftop is perhaps the oldest; the *Fairmont Royal York* hotel maintains a herb garden and apiary on its rooftop; and there are numerous private gardens atop many new condo and coop developments. Rooftop gardens help cool the city in the summer, offset carbon emissions, insulate their buildings in the winter, and provide an oasis-like habitat for sky-dwelling urban wildlife. **Tours** of the Toronto City Hall's Green Roof Project can be arranged by calling ☎ 416/338-0338 .

currently known as Riverside Drive. This trail was used by First Nations peoples for millennia and was once the connecting route between Lake Ontario and the upper Great Lakes to the north. This path will also take you along the Humber River Marsh, one of the last river marshes in the Toronto area and a breeding ground for waterfowl, turtles and varieties of fish.

Another self-guided walking tour is the **Murmur Project** (Ⓦ www .murmurtoronto.ca). You go along a route mapped with distinctive street signs shaped like ears. Call the number on the sign on your mobile and a recording tells you about the exact spot you are standing in, usually from the perspective of personal histories and experiences. The Murmur Project first started in Toronto in 2003 and has since spread around the world. There are six oral histories: Fort York, Spadina, Kensington, The Junction, Little India and the Annex.

Golf

More than two hundred public and semi-private eighteen-hole **golf courses** exist within an hour's drive of Toronto, some of which, like Glen Abbey (☎ 905/844-1800), are PGA circuit courses where a full round can cost hundreds of dollars. More cost-effective options are located within the city, namely five city-owned public courses that offer beginners and experienced duffers alike the opportunity to whack a few balls around.

All of Toronto's golf courses have club houses and pro shops with rental equipment. Greens fees typically range from $14 to $19 for nine holes, and from $22 to $46 for eighteen holes; renting equipment is of course extra. To get up-to-the-minute course information, visit Ⓦ www.toronto.ca/parks/golf, Ⓦ www .torontogolf.com or Ⓦ www.toronto.com.

Golf courses and driving ranges

City Core Golf and Driving Range
2 Spadina Ave, at Bremner Blvd,
Downtown ☎ 416/640-9888. A privately owned facility that is beside the Metro Convention Centre and only a hop, skip and a jump away from the Rogers Centre.
Dentonia Park Golf Course on Victoria Park Ave, just off Danforth Ave, East End ☎ 416/392-2558. An eighteen-hole, par-three course that hosts a nine-hole Family Golf Night, helps

various community groups plan tournaments and even has a well-established Ladies League. Offers enough variety for experienced golfers and novices alike.
Don Valley Golf Course at the intersection of Yonge St and William Carson Crescent, Suburbs ☎ 416/392-2465. Eighteen-hole, par-71 course. Five-minute walk from the York Mills subway stop.
Humber Valley Golf Course on Beattie Ave, east of Albion Rd, Suburbs ☎ 416/392-2488. A challenging par-70 course.

Inner Golf Course **99 Sudbury St (Unit #103), at Lisgar St, Downtown** ☎ 416/538-4653, 🌐 www.innergolf.ca. A Downtown driving range with all sorts of electronic monitoring gizmos to tell you everything about your swing, stance and anything else you need to know.

Scarlett Woods Golf Course **Scarlett Rd and Jane St, south of Eglinton Ave E, Suburbs** ☎ 416/392-2484. A par-62 course suitable for beginners.

Tam O'Shanter Golf Course **on Birchmount Rd, north of Sheppard Ave E, Suburbs** ☎ 416/392-2547. The city's premier golfing facility, with eighteen holes ranked at par-70. Can be reached via public transport, on either the Birchmount (#17) or Sheppard East (#85 or #85A) buses.

Watersports

Toronto is a port city with an active **waterfront**. Sailing, windsurfing, water skiing and cruise boating are popular summertime pursuits. **Swimming** in the lake is possible again due to a concerted clean-up effort, but some beaches can still be temporarily closed for swimming due to pollution. Swimming or no, the public **beaches** are still favourite places for sunning, picnics, beach volleyball and general carousing. Hanlan's Point Beach on the Toronto Islands (see p.88) is a clothing optional beach, meaning that nudity is an option, not a requirement.

Canoeing and **kayaking** are popular activities, as Toronto not only has the Toronto Island lagoons and a protected harbour to paddle around in, but also two navigable rivers to traverse. Lessons, rentals and guided tours (twice a week in early fall) are available at The Harbourfront Canoe and Kayak School, 283A Queens Quay W (☎ 416/203-2277 or 1-800/960-8886, 🌐 www.paddletoronto .com). Another urban outfitter worth checking out is Toronto Kayak and Canoe Adventures (☎ 416/536-2057, 🌐 www.torontoadventures.ca), which specializes in trips along the Humber River. Voyageur Quest (☎ 416/486-3605 or 1-800/794-9660, 🌐 www.voyageurquest.com) offers four-hour, naturalist-guided canoe tours of the Toronto Islands with a picnic thrown in for groups of ten, and you can rent anything from canoes and kayaks to cross-country skis at Mountain Equipment Co-op, 400 King St W (☎ 416/340-2667).

Public marinas

If you happen to be visiting Toronto with your own boat in tow, slip into one of these marinas:

Bluffer's Park Marina **at the end of Brimley Rd, Suburbs** ☎ 416/266-4556, 🌐 www.blufspark marina.com. A four-hundred-slip marina that also offers trophy fishing charters for salmon and trout and a sailing school.

 Harbourfront Marina **235 Queens Quay West, the waterfront** ☎ 416/973-8030, 🌐 www.harbourfrontcentre.com/thewaterfront /marine. Talk about convenient! Downtowners with boats maintain their slips here for easy access.

Toronto Island Marina **between Muggs Island and Centre Island** ☎ 416/203-1055. Charges a nominal fee for overnight stays.

15

Kids' Toronto

T
oronto has a deserved reputation for being a safe, clean North American city and for all those words imply it is a welcoming place for visiting **children**. As well as the mainstream attractions that are appealing to children of various ages (see box below), there are plenty of further options – both indoor and outdoor – for entertaining your children in Toronto, including parks, playgrounds, swimming pools and petting zoos.

Toronto also has many family-friendly shops, restaurants and services reflecting a continued trend of urban as compared to suburban family life, and children are generally welcome in adult settings. It must be said, however, that infant children attending the latest trendy restaurant, midnight concert or theatrical extravaganza will attract disapproving looks. Childcare services are available at the larger Downtown hotels and some B&Bs. Finally, nursing mothers have the right to **breastfeed** their children in public, and restaurants or attractions that suggest otherwise should be reported. Breastfeeding-friendly restaurants have stickers ("Anywhere, Anytime") and nursing mothers may wish to consult ⓦ www.toronto.ca/health/breastfeeding/feedingfriendly.htm for up-to-the-moment information.

Gardens, parks and zoos

For an account of **Toronto Zoo**, see p.91. See also the account of **Canada's Wonderland** on p.98.

Allen Gardens Conservatory 19 Horticultural Ave, at Jarvis St (between Carlton and Gerrard sts), Uptown. Streetcar: Carlton/College (#506). The Victorian greenhouses that collectively form the centrepiece of this off-leash park and gardens are among the city's architectural treasures, and the wide variety of plants filling the 16,000-square-feet interior

---

Child-friendly attractions

Many adult-sized attractions also feature special children's programming, play spaces and installations:

Art Gallery of Ontario	pp.60–65	Fort York National Historic Site	pp.47–48
Bata Shoe Museum	p.75	Harbourfront Centre	p.81
Black Creek Pioneer Village	p.97	Royal Ontario Museum	pp.72–74
Casa Loma	pp.78–80	Toronto Islands	pp.85–86
CN Tower	p.40	Toronto Zoo	p.91

are the vegetative equivalent of a zoo. Allen Gardens is especially magical during its Victorian Christmas Flower Show, when the Palm House is lit with candles and its fountains and tropical plants seem a world away from the snow outside. Admission is free and it's open daily 10am–5pm, with special extended hours in Dec.

Centreville Amusement Park and Petting Zoo Centre Island ☎416/203-0405, ⓦ www .centreisland.ca. Centreville is an amusement park that is not garish, raunchy, flashy or loud. It offers swan boats, an antique carousel, twirling teacups and pony rides. There are bumper boats, a ghost ride and machines that will lift, rotate and accelerate their occupants, but none of the thirty rides, such as the small Ferris Wheel, will make tummies roil in the pursuit of fun. For opening times and ticket prices for the rides, see p.87. Right beside the amusement park, Far Enough Farm is a petting zoo where children are encouraged to caress and interact with the goats, ponies, and domesticated critters.

Riverdale Farm Winchster St, at Sumach St, Uptown ☎416/392-6794, ⓦ www.friendsof riverdalefarm.com. Streetcar: Carlton/College (#506). Smack in the middle of Cabbage-town (see p.77), and formerly the site of the Toronto Zoo, Riverdale Farm is a version of a working farm circa 1905. Some of the original zoo buildings are still standing but a transported farmhouse and barn now take the place of the zoo cages. Animals include cattle, sheep, horses, donkeys, chickens, geese, swans, pigs and rabbits, and the organic garden produce is sold in a little shop along with hot chocolate and cookies. At the foot of the property, a wetlands preserve is home to turtles, herons, owls, and mallard ducks. The arrival of the spring lambs and kids are an especially popular time to visit, and scheduled activities help children better understand their environment and agricul-ture. Daily 9am–5pm; free.

Indoor pursuits

Laser Quest 1980 Eglinton Ave E, at Warden Ave, Suburbs ☎416/285-1333. Bus: Eglinton Ave E or Warden Ave. This electronic team sport allows participants to inhabit a video game, arms them with laser (ish) weapons and turns them loose in a multi-tiered environment to pursue one another through labyrinths, along catwalks and up and down ramps. Heavy mood mist, special audio-visual effects and atmospheric lighting accentuate the experience. Games vary in effects and complexity depending on players' age, experience and objectives. Open Mon–Thurs 5am–9pm, Sat 10am–11pm, Sun 10am–8pm; from $8 per person.

Lillian H. Smith Library 293 College St, at Spadina Ave, Uptown ☎416/393-5630. Streetcar: Carlton/College (#506). Statues of a lion and griffin guard the main door to two special collections, the Merril Collec-tion of Science Fiction, Speculation and Fantasy and the Osborne Collection of Early Children's Books. The latter has rare and first-edition children's books dating back to the fourteenth century, and includes a first edition of *Alice in Wonder-land*. Special children's events here (and throughout the Toronto public library system) are detailed on ⓦ www .torontopubliclibrary.com.

Water and wave play

City Splash & Wades There are 64 splash pads and 110 wading pools open in parks throughout the city during the summer to keep younger children cool and their parents cool-headed. Splash pads are unsupervised water play areas so parents are reminded to keep a watchful eye on their children. For more information, call ☎416/388-7665.

Soak City Ontario Place, 955 Lakeshore Blvd W, by Exhibition Place, the waterfront ☎416/14-9900. Streetcar: Bathurst (#511). Soak City is one of Toronto's great family attractions. The Pink Twister, with its eerie Purple Pipeline, gushes six thousand gallons at gleeful waterbabies. The Twister is a three-storey water slide and the Pipeline approximates the experience your unwanted

goldfish had when you flushed it down the loo. As well, the Hydrofuge shoots riders along a tube on thin sheets of water at speeds of up to 50km per hour before whooshing them out into an enormous green funnel. Smaller children have Waterplay to splash around in – an area which includes a goofy sprinkler system and water-dumping buckets. Conservationists take note: all this whooshing water is treated and re-circulated. Soak City is included in Ontario Place's "Play All Day" pass (see p.84).

Toronto Hippo Tours 151 Front St W, at Simcoe St (beside East Side Mario's), Downtown ☎416/703-4476, ⍟www.torontohippotours .com. These bulbous-looking amphibian tour buses deliver a 90min "urban safari" by land and water that includes the Hockey Hall of Fame and the CN Tower. It then heads to

the lakeshore and literally dips into Lake Ontario to tour the waterfront over to Ontario Place. Tours depart hourly 11am–5pm from May 1 to Oct 31. Child fares $25; students and seniors $33; adults $38.

The Wave Pool 5 Hopkins Ave, Richmond Hill (off Major Mackenzie Dr W and Yonge St), Suburbs ☎905/508-6673. Car needed. This pool generates three-feet-high waves that alternate with the 160° twisting waterslide at 15min intervals. When the pool isn't generating waves it offers "Leisure Swims". A 95° F Swirl Pool and sauna offers parents and grandparents a break. Leisure swims start at $2 and Wave Swims at $5. During the summer, wave swims operate daily 1.30–4pm and Fri–Sun 4.30–7pm; at other times of year, Fri–Sun only. For leisure swim timetables, call ahead.

Shopping

Jacadi 87 Avenue Rd, at Bloor St W, Uptown ☎416/923-1717. A branch of the Parisian chain that introduces kids to well-tailored taste at a very young age. The clothes are beautifully made from top-quality fabrics and look like teensy versions of adult togs *à la bon chic bon genre*.

Kidding Awound 91 Cumberland St, at Bay St, Uptown ☎416/926-8996. Subway: Bay. The

revolving key above the door hints at the playfulness within. This is where you can find truly cool gag toys and all sorts of wind-up, battery-operated, shake'n'swirl, bubble-blowing stuff.

Mabel's Fables Childrens' Bookstore 662 Mount Pleasant Rd, at Hillsdale Ave E, Suburbs ☎416/322-0438, ⍟www .mabelsfables.com. Bus: Eglinton E;

Mt Pleasant. This independent bookstore stocks an excellent range of children's books, based on the premise that children deserve a bookstore as varied, topical and interesting as their parents do.

Magic Pony 694 Queen St W, at Euclid Ave, West End ⓦwww.magic-pony.com. Streetcar: Queen (#501). Head here for the very latest in those whacked little collectable figures, Yoshitomo Nara T-shirts, Crazy Jim jewellery and books, games and decor necessities.

Mastermind 3350 Yonge St, at St Germain Ave, Suburbs ⓣ416/487-7177. Subway: Lawrence. An excellent toy store specializing in puzzles, games and other problem-solving intellectual amusements for kids.

Polka Dot Kids 917 Queen St W, across from Trinity Bellwoods Park, West End ⓣ416/306-2279. Streetcar: Queen (#501). Traditional (mostly European) toys, books and clothing for children aged 0–4 made from wood, organic fabrics and other natural materials.

Roots Kids at the Eaton Centre, 220 Yonge St, at Dundas St W, Downtown ⓣ416/593-9640. Subway: Dundas. Miniaturized versions of Roots' classic fleeces, hats, leathers and accessories.

Science City 50 Bloor St W (downstairs in underground mall), at Bay St, Uptown ⓣ416/968-2627. Subway: Bay. Science-based games, books, puzzles and toys for all skill and age levels crowd this popular store, tucked underground in the glitzy plaza beneath Holt Renfrew. Junior entomologists, geologists, astronomers and paleontologists' enthusiasms are expertly catered to.

The Toy Shop 62 Cumberland St, at Bay St, Uptown ⓣ416/961-4870. Subway: Bay. The creative, well-crafted toys sold here come from around the world and are geared toward infants through teens. You'll find high-end lines of classics, including puppets, tin soldiers, porcelain dolls and a full range of soft toys.

Treasure Island Toys 581 Danforth Ave, near Pape Ave, East End ⓣ416/778-4913. Subway: Pape. This independent toy store maintains a first-class, affordable cache of interesting children's books, toys and crafts.

Eating

Old Spaghetti Factory 54 The Esplanade, at Scott St, Downtown ⓣ416/864-9761. Subway: Union. This cavernous restaurant hasn't really changed since it opened in 1971, neither in terms of decor or menu. The fare is what the name suggests: spaghetti and pastas, with kid-size portions and plenty of treats.

Pickle Barrel 40 Dundas St W, at Yonge St, Downtown ⓣ416/977-6677, ⓦwww.picklebarrel .ca. Subway: Dundas. This is not a traditional deli but it will appeal to most children from all cultural backgrounds because a) they fry most things; b) they concoct huge, ultra-sweet desserts; and c) they've appropriated every big food fad from the past three decades.

Shopsey's 33 Yonge St, at Front St, Downtown ⓣ416/365-3333. Subway: Union. An integral part of Toronto for three generations, *Shopsey's* remains a great family restaurant with a comfort food forte, featuring deli classics (such as knish and atkas), grills, soups, breakfasts, pancakes and more.

Richtree Market 42 Yonge St, at Wellington St, Downtown ⓣ416/863-0108. Subway: King. Also at the Eaton Centre, 220 Yonge St, at Dundas St W, Downtown ⓣ416/351-8783. Subway: Dundas. Patrons visit a variety of food stations where their orders – anything from crêpes, omelets or waffles to kid-sized portions of pizza, pasta and grill favourites – are prepared before their eyes. Esteemed as a particularly good place to take young diners to Sunday brunch. Take-out available.

Festivals and events

Toronto hosts a large number of **festivals** and annual **events**, particularly in the summer months. From June to September there is something big going on every weekend; even better, most of these happenings are free, or have free components. Although things slow down during winter, free events continue to take place, and Toronto's historical homes such as Spadina House, Mackenzie House and Colborne Lodge in High Park observe holiday dates and special occasions with music, food and open-house activities. Check Ⓦwww.toronto.ca under special events or parks for details. Meanwhile, places like the Harbourfront Centre (Ⓦwww.harbourfrontcentre .com) host various music festivals throughout the summer, as well as rosters of touring bands.

For further **information** about various other goings-on, contact Tourism Toronto at Ⓣ416/203-2600, or visit their website at Ⓦwww.tourismtoronto .com. You can also call Ontario Tourism at Ⓣ1-800/668-2746, (Ⓦwww .ontariotravel.net) for a seasonal guide. Two excellent – and often overlooked – sources of events information are the front sections of the Toronto Yellow Pages and the fliers that hang over the exit doors on the TTC's streetcars (see also Ⓦwww.ttc.ca). Note that while actual **dates** for events may vary from year to year, the months generally stay the same.

January

Niagara Ice Wine Festival second and third weekends of the month. The little towns of Jordan and Niagara-on-the-Lake set up ice bars in the middle of the street, bring in bands and host ice carving competitions, and the wineries of the Niagara region lay on ice wine flights and all sorts of ice-wine-infused treats in the world's only wine harvest festival held in the middle of winter. Ⓦwww.niagarawine festival.com.

Robbie Burns Day Jan 25 Traditional Scottish *ceilidh* (house party) on the Caledonian Bard's birthday, held at Mackenzie House and featuring poetry readings, Scottish music and dancing. A haggis is ushered in to the sound of bagpipes. Years when Robbie Burns Day and Chinese New Year overlap have spawned the Gung Haggis Fat Choy hybrid. Ⓣ416/392-6915, Ⓦwww .gunghaggisfatchoy.com.

Winter City Festival late Jan to early Feb For two weeks, right when everyone needs a lift, Toronto becomes the self-designated "world's coolest city" and has a party featuring free outdoor concerts and performances by troupes from around the world, plus online coupons for attractions such as the CN Tower and the Bata Shoe Museum. As part of the festival, the hugely popular **Winterlicious** event (Ⓣ416/395-0490) offers over a hundred affordable *prix-fixe* menus in some of the glitziest restaurants in town. Ⓦwww.city.toronto.on.ca.

February

Asian Lunar New Year last week of Jan or first week of Feb Cultural institutions like the Harbourfront Centre hold special events centring on Chinese and Southeast Asian arts and feasts. The daily newspapers will keep you up to date on the most auspicious things to say, do, wear and eat on any given day of the festival.

Kuumba and African Heritage Month all month African cultures and histories are celebrated throughout Feb. Festivities include Kuumba Festival, at the Harbourfront Centre during the first two weekends of the month. Open to all ages, the events include special guest performers, storytelling, arts and crafts exhibits, film screenings and culinary events. ☎416/973-3000, Ⓦwww .harbourfrontcentre.com.

Rhubarb! Theatre Festival three weeks of the month The largest new-works festival curated by a Canadian company, the Rhubarb! serves as both a theatre lab and a launching pad for the best and brightest in Toronto stage. Held at the 12 Alexander Street Theatre (see p.170). ☎416/975-8555, Ⓦwww.artsexy.ca.

March

Canada Blooms Flower Show usually the second weekend of the month This massively popular event features plants, plants and more plants. Landscape artists, architects and horticulturalists of every description descend on the Metro Convention Centre and transform it into an oasis of herbaceous wonders. ☎1-800/730-1020, Ⓦwww .canadablooms.com.

St Patrick's Day Parade the Sun closest to March 17 On this day, all Torontonians claim to be Irish. Indulge in Irish step dancing, music, food, poetry and, of course, Guinness. ☎416/487-1566, Ⓦwww .topatrick.com.

April

Sprockets International Children's Film Festival usually second and third weekends Children's films from around the world, plus behind-the-scenes events for kids aged 4 and up, are featured at this event, run by the people responsible for the Toronto International Film Festival. ☎416/967-7371, Ⓦwww.bell.ca/sprockets.

Hot Docs Film Festival late April/early May From very humble origins, Hot Docs is now North America's largest documentary film festival with over a hundred selections from everywhere. ☎416/637-2155, Ⓦwww .hotdocs.ca.

May

Santé – The Bloor Yorkville Wine Festival early May A five-day, Yorkville-based wine festival in early May involving fifty Canadian and international wineries. Tastings, seminars, food and wine pairings and oenophilic discussions on the subject of viticulture – it's all here. ☎416/928-3553 ext 27, Ⓦwww.santewinefestival.net.

Toronto International Circus Festival mid-May Indoor and outdoor circus acts, featuring celebrated acrobats, unicyclists, fire-eaters, stilt-walkers, musicians, face painters and, yes, clowns make it easy to run away to Harbourfront and see if you would like to join the circus. Ⓦwww .tocircusfestival.com.

Doors Open Toronto third weekend This is the ultimate insider event that everyone can get into: Toronto's historical buildings of note, many of which are normally closed to the public, open their doors for guided tours the third weekend of May. A great opportunity to get deep into Toronto history. ☎416/338-0496, Ⓦwww .doorsopen.org.

June

Luminato early June The latest Toronto festival of the arts brings in the big multidisciplinary acts in early June for a week's worth of dance, music, theatre and celebrity sighting opportunities in venues throughout Downtown. Ⓦwww.luminato.com.

North by Northeast Music and Film Festival mid-June For five days in June five hundred bands in over fifty clubs and bars flaunt their talents and vie for cash awards in this showcase festival for indie bands – and now film directors – mainly from Canada and the US but also from further afield. ☎416/863-69-63, Ⓦwww.nxne.com.

TD Canada Trust Toronto Downtown Jazz Festival last week of the month Jazz headliners representing all the genre's disciplines play venues throughout the city for free. ☎416/928-2033, Ⓦwww .tojazz.com.

Pride Week and Parade last week of the month Toronto celebrates gay pride for a full week with various events, culminating in a massive parade. Rapidly becoming the largest pride celebration anywhere. ☎416/927-7433, Ⓦwww.pridetoronto.com.

Canadian art

Often neglected, frequently overlooked, Canadian art has a depth and range that surprises many visitors. The Europeans who set the painterly scene in the eighteenth and nineteenth centuries produced stirring evocations of their new homeland and later, with the pre-eminent Group of Seven, came a distinctive Canadian style that paid lavish tribute to the stark, chill beauty of Ontario's vast northern wilderness. The Group cast a long shadow, but modern Canadian artists are an adventurous crew with their heady installations and idiosyncratic juxtapositions filling many a Toronto gallery.

Beginnings

No one captured the imagination of colonial Canada quite like **Joseph Brant**, a Mohawk chieftain, Freemason and Anglican who was loyal to the British interest through thick and thin. A whole raft of painters queued up to do his portrait, some emphasizing his Mohawk credentials, others – like **George Romney** – presenting him as an ersatz European, albeit in unusual gear. The same problem – quite how to present this alien country in a suitably genteel, European manner – affected **Paul Kane**, whose Canadian landscapes can look remarkably like Switzerland, but not his contemporary **Cornelius Krieghoff**, whose anecdotal scenes of Québec life possess a genuine sense of time and place.

Portrait of Joseph Brant by George Romney ▲

Indian Encampment on Lake Huron, Paul Kane ▼

Following the Moose by Cornelius Krieghoff ▼

The Group of Seven

In the spring of 1912, a commercial artist by the name of **Tom Thomson** ventured north from Toronto bound for Algonquin Park, where he spent the summer travelling by canoe, painting the wilderness. Upon his return to the city, Thomson's friends, many of them fellow employees of the Toronto art firm Grip Ltd, saw Thomson's naturalistic approach to indigenous subject matter as a pointer away from the influence of Europe, declaring the "northland" as the true Canadian "painter's country". World War I and the death of Thomson – who drowned in 1917 – delayed these artists' ambitions, but in 1920 they formed the **Group of Seven**. Initially, the group comprised Franklin H. Carmichael, Lawren Harris, A.Y. Jackson, Arthur Lismer, J.E.H. MacDonald, F.H. Varley and Frank Johnston; later, they were joined by A.J. Casson, L.L. Fitzgerald and Edwin Holgate, and they also had strong connections with Emily Carr. Working under the unofficial leadership of **Lawren Harris**, they explored the wilds of Algoma in northern Ontario in the late 1910s, travelling around in a converted freight car, and later foraged even further afield, from Newfoundland and Baffin Island to British Columbia.

They were immediately successful, staging forty shows in eleven years, a triumph due in large part to Harris's many influential contacts. However, there was also a genuine popular response to the intrepid **frontiersman element** of their aesthetic. Art was a matter of "taking to the road" and "risking all for the glory of a great adventure", as they wrote in 1922, whilst "nature was the measure of a man's stature", according to Lismer, with the lone pine set against the sky becoming the Group's favourite symbol.

▲ Red Barn, A.Y. Jackson

▼ Western Forest, Emily Carr

▼ Canoe Lake, Tom Thomson

Where to see what

Colonial Canadian art the Art Gallery of Ontario (AGO) and the Royal Ontario Museum (ROM). See p.60 and p.72 respectively.

Contemporary art Power Plant Contemporary Art Gallery (see p.84) and the AGO (see p.60).

Group of Seven the AGO (see p.60) and the McMichael Canadian Art Collection (see p.98).

Inuit and First Nations art the AGO (see p.60) and the Toronto Dominion Gallery of Inuit Art (see p.45).

Buying A good place to start is the Distillery District (see p.53), where several galleries are clustered close together. There are also some excellent galleries in Yorkville, Uptown, specializing in Inuit and First Nations art – see p.191 for details.

Edward Burtynsky ▲

Inuit sculpture of a boy and seal ▼

Inuit artist Kenojuak Ashevak ▼

The **legacy** of the Group of Seven was double-edged. On the one hand, the Group rediscovered the Canadian wilderness and established the autonomy of Canadian art, but well into the 1950s it was difficult for Canadian painters to escape their influence.

Modern times

Amongst **contemporary** artists, Toronto's own **Michael Snow** has proved to be one of the most enduring, his assorted drawings, paintings, sculptures and photographs a regular feature of the exhibition circuit. Snow has also completed several public commissions, with the geese in the Eaton Centre perhaps being the best known. Look out also for **William McElcheran**, whose trademark is bronzes of chubby businessmen, and **Edward Burtynsky**, whose photographs possess a crystalline realism that has proved so popular that the AGO hired him to record the gallery's recent multimillion-dollar renovation.

Inuit art has been very collectible since the 1960s. Some Inuit artists choose to work in bone and/or ivory, but most opt for soapstone, creating elemental carvings of **animals, deities and fellow Inuit** supplemented by a variety of **metamorphic figures** – in which an Inuit adopts the form of an animal, either in full or in part. Several of the best-known Inuit sculptors come from Cape Dorset, in the far north of Canada, including **Kumakuluk Saggiak** and **Kenojuak Ashevak**. The success of Inuit art has encouraged many First Nations painters and sculptors, perhaps most memorably the Ojibwa **Norval Morrisseau**, whose brightly coloured paintings employ traditional iconography to fine advantage.

Canada Day Celebrations July 1 On this national holiday celebrating Canada's birthday, festivities are held throughout the city, and a full roster of concerts and fun events are held in Queen's Park or at City Hall. ⓦwww.toronto.ca/events.

Canada Dry Festival of Fire early July A two-week pyrotechnical extravaganza explodes over Lake Ontario from the vantage point of Ontario Place. ⓦwww.ontarioplace.com.

Beaches International Jazz Festival usually second weekend of the month Toronto's favourite neighbourhood jazz festival heats up the Beach neighbourhood with big bands, world beat and calypso along with the classical jazz standards. ⓦwww.beachesjazz.com.

Summerlicious second weekend How could a food festival featuring $15–20 *prix-fixe* lunch menus and $25–35 dinner menus at Toronto's best restaurants not be a huge success? Check online for participating restaurants and availability. ⓦwww.toronto.ca/events.

Toronto Outdoor Art Exhibition second weekend Nathan Philips Square, outside of Toronto's swooping City Hall, fills with over five hundred established and emerging artists exhibiting their works for juried awards. An excellent opportunity to acquire a new piece. ☎416/408-2754, ⓦwww.wx.toronto.ca.

Masala! MehndiMasti! mid-July Billing itself as the "largest Desi festival of its kind", this very hip South Asian festival of music, dance, theatre, film and food is gaining international accolades for its sensational programming and introduction of South Asian artists to North American audiences. At Exhibition Place ☎416/666-9494, ⓦwww.masalamehndimasti.com.

Toronto Fringe Theatre Festival mid-July For twelve days, an international assortment of theatre troupes, established and aspiring actors, playwrights and some people who just have a story to tell take over the smaller theatres and a few parks. Big-time hits (*The Drowsy Chaperone*; *Two Pianos, Four Hands*; *Da Kink in My Hair*) got their start here. ⓦwww.fringetoronto.com.

Caribana third week of month through to long weekend at end Begun in 1967 as a community heritage project, this two-week festival of Caribbean culture culminates in

▼ Caribana

one of North America's biggest street parties, with an eye-popping parade featuring hundreds of floats, dazzling costumes, steel bands and jaw-dropping dancing. The 1.5km parade route goes along Lakeshore Blvd and continues on to the Toronto Islands for a huge picnic. Check the daily schedule of events. ☎416/391-5608, ⓦwww.caribana.com.

Just For Laughs Comedy Festival late July A recent Montréal import, this Toronto branch features sketch comedy, stand-up and improv. This being Toronto, its most popular shows are the Ethnic Comedy Super shows. ☎416/979-3824, ⓦwww.hahaha.com.

August

Annual Vegetarian Food Fair late Aug North America's largest vegetarian celebration, this two-decade-plus food festival is held at the Harbourfront Centre. Features over a hundred exhibitors, cooking demos, activist booths, music, and lots of free food to sample. ⓦwww.veg.ca/foodfair.

Buskerfest late Aug Just so you know, the mime artists, clowns and human statues assembled along Front St in late Aug came from across North America and beyond to be part of an actual festival. If they hit you up for spare change it will go to the Epilepsy Foundation. ☎416/964-9095, ⓦwww.torontobuskerfest.com.

Canadian National Exhibition (CNE) second week until Labour Day An annual ritual signalling the beginning of the end of summer for generations of Toronto youth, the CNE is pure carny, love it or leave it. Kids will always enjoy the rides, shell games and junk food, and the Midway at night can still be a thrill. There are many special events such as the air show and the concert series, and permanent on-site pavilions are filled with agricultural and industrial exhibits. ☎416/393-6300, ⓦwww.theex.com.

Krinos Taste of the Danforth second weekend By far the largest food festival in Canada, the stretch of Danforth Avenue between Broadview and Donlands attracts over a million people with its bands, family activities and "tastes" from over one hundred local restaurants. ☎416/469-5634, ⓦwww.toronto.com/tasteofthedanforth.

September

Toronto International Film Festival ten days following the first weekend The Toronto International Film Festival is the only major film festival open to the public, which is why it's so phenomenally successful. Movie stars, living-legend directors, big-time producers and thousands of film nuts take over the city's Downtown cinemas for ten days, making this one of the biggest parties of the year. Passes go on sale towards the end of July and are snapped up quickly, although rush tickets are available fifteen minutes before scheduled screenings. ☎416/967-7371, ⓦwww.tiffg.ca.

Cabbagetown Cultural Festival second weekend The oldest and largest of Toronto's many neighbourhood festivals, this one includes its own film festival, pub crawl, arts-and-crafts fair, tour of homes, folk dancing, musical performances and a slew of children's events. The epicentre of activities is Riverdale Park and its little farm. ☎416/921-0857, ⓦwww.oldcabbagetown.com.

Niagara Grape and Wine Festival last twenty days of month Other wine festivals have come and gone, but for three decades the oenophilic St Catherines and Niagara Falls region has honoured the grape. ☎905/688-0212, ⓦwww.niagarawinefestival.com.

Nuit Blanche late Sept/early Oct From 7pm–7am designated zones of Downtown Toronto turn into an all-night art fair. This event draws hundreds of thousands out into the night to experience art and features museums, galleries, happenings, art parks, clothed buildings, dancing in the street, light sculptures, and one-night-only installations by some of the world's leading artists. ⓦwww.scotiabanknuitblanche.ca.

October

Toronto Marathon and Half Marathon second weekend The largest athletic event in town hits the road in the cool of autumn during the second weekend of the month. ⓦwww.TorontoMarathon.com.

Thanksgiving weekend of second Sun Americans celebrate it at the end of Nov, but Canadian Thanksgiving, which entails the same family gatherings and food, is held over a long weekend beginning the second Sun of Oct. Thanksgiving Weekend is generally the closing weekend for summer attractions.

International Festival of Authors third week One of the world's largest and most prestigious literary events, held at the Harbourfront Centre, features on-stage interviews, special events, a lecture series and readings of fiction, poetry, drama and biography. ☎416/973-4760, ⓦwww.reading.org.

Halloween Oct 31 This is a holiday everyone likes to indulge in. Private residences outdo one another in constructing chilling lawn tableaux; children are escorted from house to house to trick-or-treat; and the closest Sat to Oct 31 is an occasion for costumed adult revelry and impromptu parades. Special events such as ghost walks and haunted house storytelling are featured in the city's historic properties. ⓦwww.toronto.ca.

November

Royal Agricultural Winter Fair from the first weekend, for two weeks The Royal has promoted agricultural and equestrian excellence for more than seven decades. City folk flock to see languorous bovines, exotic poultry, giant vegetables and butter sculptures, while horse lovers thrill to events like the Royal Horse Show and the National Showcase of Champions. ☎416/263-3400, ⓦwww.royalfair.org.

Santa Claus Parade first weekend Superlatives abound: the first ever department store parade, the oldest parade for children in the world and the unofficial beginning of the Christmas shopping season. This tradition features clowns, brass bands, animated floats, hundreds of costumed paraders and, of course, the jolly old man himself. Check for route specifics and dates. ☎416/249-7833, ⓦwww.thesantaclauseparade.org.

Canadian Aboriginal Festival last weekend Held at the Rogers Centre (formerly the SkyDome), North America's largest, multi-disciplined aboriginal arts event features theatre, music, arts-and-crafts, dancing competitions, fashion shows, educational programmes and a marketplace where First Nations peoples from across North America can sell their wares. ☎519/751-0040, ⓦwww.canab.com.

Cavalcade of Lights end of the month Into its fourth decade, Toronto fights off winter gloom from late Nov to the end of Dec with lighting displays in neighbourhoods throughout the city, fireworks and free concerts at City Hall, Programming includes Sat night walking tours and ice skating day and night. ⓦwww.toronto.ca/events.

One of a Kind Craft Show and Sale end of the month What started as a neat idea for crafts-people and artisans has blossomed into a remarkable celebration of creativity, innovation and idiosyncrasy. A great place to look for a Christmas gift for that hard-to-shop-for friend. Held at the Direct Energy Centre in the Exhibition Palace. ☎416/960-3680, ⓦwww.oneofakindshow.com.

December

Victorian Christmas all month The sights, sounds and tastes of nineteenth-century Toronto Christmases past are recreated in the city's heritage properties of Colborne Lodge, Spadina House and Mackenzie House. Yuletide concerts, activities and baked goods are all part of the historically accurate festivities. ⓦwww.toronto .ca/events.

The Christmas Story every weekend until Christmas A tradition since 1937, this nativity pageant is held in the charming Church of the Holy Trinity in Trinity Square, behind the Eaton Centre. The Biblical Christmas story is told through mime, narration, organ music and carols sung by an unseen choir. ☎416/598-8979, ⓦwww .holytrinitytoronto.org.

🏃 **Kensington Festival of Lights on the winter solstice** Founded as a neigh-bourhood event to celebrate the diversity of Kensington's residents, this lantern-lit neigh-bourhood pageant begins at dusk on the solstice and incorporates images and tradi-tions from Hanukkah, Christmas and other celebrations from around the world. ⓦwww .kensington-market.ca.

Hogmanay! Happy New Year! Dec 31 A New Year's Eve party at historic Mackenzie House at 82 Bond St, with traditional Scottish music, holiday food and gas-lit tours of the house. ☎416/392-6915, ⓦwww.city .toronto.on.ca/culture/museums/events.

Toronto Zoo New Year's Eve Dec 31 A New Year's Eve party that's literally a zoo. This family fest features bands, buskers, treats and, of course, the critters themselves. ☎416/392-5929, ⓦwww.torontozoo.com.

⑯

FESTIVALS AND EVENTS

Contexts

Contexts

History

Colonial in conception, Toronto only emerged as a major international metropolis in the 1950s. Since then, Toronto has made up for lost time, dimming the lights of its Canadian rivals – primarily Montréal – to become one of North America's most invigorating cities.

Beginnings

In prehistoric times, the densely forested northern shore of **Lake Ontario** was occupied by nomadic hunter-gatherers, who roamed in search of elk, bears, caribou and perhaps mammoths, supplementing their meaty diet with berries and roots. Around 1000 BC, these nomads were displaced by **Iroquois-speaking peoples**, who gained a controlling foothold in what is now modern-day southern Ontario, upper New York and Québec. The settlers of this period (usually called the **Initial Woodland** period – 1000 BC to 900 AD) differed from their predecessors only in so far as they constructed burial mounds and used pottery. In the **Terminal Woodland** period (900–1600 AD), however, these same Iroquois-speakers developed a comparatively sophisticated culture, based on the cultivation of corn (maize), beans and squash. This agricultural system enabled them to lead a fairly settled life, and the first Europeans to sail up the St Lawrence River stumbled across large communities, often several hundred strong. Iroquois villages were invariably located on well-drained ground with a reliable water supply. They comprised a series of longhouses, up to 50m long, built of saplings covered in bark and heated by several open hearths situated in a line down the middle. Pits were dug around the longhouses for food storage, and a timber palisade encircled each village. Archeologists have discovered the remains of over 190 Iroquois villages in the Toronto area alone and the restored settlement of **Sainte-Marie among the Hurons** (see p.121) illustrates all these features.

Iroquois society was divided into matriarchal clans, each of which was governed by a female elder. The clan shared a longhouse, and when a man married (always outside his own clan), he moved to the longhouse of his wife. Tribal chiefs (*sachems*) were male, but they were selected by the female elders of the tribe and they also had to belong to a lineage through which the rank of *sachem* descended. Once selected, a *sachem* had to have his rank confirmed by the federal council of the inter-tribal league – or confederacy – to which his clan belonged. These **tribal confederacies**, of which there were just a handful, also served as military alliances, and warfare between them was endemic. In particular, the **Five Nations** confederacy, which lived to the south of Lake Ontario, was almost always at war with the **Hurons** to the north.

The coming of the Europeans

In the sixteenth century, **British and French fur traders** began to inch their way inland from the Atlantic seaboard. The French focused on the St Lawrence River, establishing Québec City in 1608. From their new headquarters, it was a fairly easy canoe trip southwest to **Toronto** (the Huron word for "place of meeting"), which was on an early portage route between Lake Ontario and Georgian Bay. The French allied themselves with the Hurons, and in 1615 **Samuel de Champlain** led a full-scale expedition to southern Ontario to cement the alliance and boost French control of the fur trade. When he arrived, Champlain handed out muskets to his allies, encouraging them to attack their ancient enemies, the Five Nations. He also sent **Étienne Brulé**, one of his interpreters, down to Toronto with a Huron war party in the first recorded visit of a European to Toronto.

In the short term, Champlain's actions bolstered France's position, but the Five Nations never forgave the French for their Huron alliance, and thirty years later they took their revenge. In 1648, **Dutch traders** began selling muskets to the Five Nations to enhance their own position. The Five Nations were duly grateful and the following year they launched a full-scale invasion of Huron territory, massacring their enemies and razing the settlement of Sainte-Marie among the Hurons to the ground.

The rise of the British

The destruction of Sainte-Marie was a grisly setback for the **French**, but it didn't affect their desire to control southern Ontario. In the second half of the seventeenth century, they rushed to encircle Lake Ontario with a ring of forts-cum-trading posts. The **British** did the same. Initially, the French out-colonized the British, and they also crushed the Five Nations confederacy in the 1690s, forcing them deep into New York State. Furthermore, in 1720, the French established a tiny fur-trading post at Toronto, the first European settlement on the site, and although it was soon abandoned, the French returned thirty years later to build a settlement and a stockade, **Fort Rouillé**, on the lakeshore. This was to be the high-water mark of French success. During the Seven Years' War (1756–63), the British conquered New France (present-day Québec) and overran the French outposts dotted around the Great Lakes. The Fort Rouillé garrison didn't actually wait for the British, but prudently burnt their own fort down and hightailed into the woods before the Redcoats arrived. The site lay abandoned for almost forty years until hundreds of United Empire Loyalist settlers arrived following the American Revolution.

Early Toronto (1793–1812)

In the aftermath of the American Revolution (1775–83), thousands of Americans fled north to Canada determined to remain under British jurisdiction. These migrants were known as the **United Empire Loyalists**, and several hundred of them settled along the northern shore of Lake Ontario. The British parliament responded to this sudden influx by passing the **Canada Act** of 1791, which divided the remaining British-American territories in two: Upper and Lower Canada, each with its own legislative councils. Lower Canada was broadly equivalent to today's Québec, and Upper Canada to modern-day Ontario. The first capital of Upper Canada was Niagara-on-the-Lake, but this was much too near the American border for comfort, and the province's new lieutenant-governor, the energetic **John Graves Simcoe**, moved his administration to the relative safety of Toronto in 1793. Simcoe named the new settlement **York** in honour of Frederick, the Duke of York and a son of George III, and began his residence with an elaborate imperial ceremony, complete with a 21-gun salute from the warship on which he had arrived. Eton- and Oxford-educated, Simcoe was a man of vim and gusto, who brought his home with him in the form of a large "tent" (which included wooden walls, insulating boards and proper doors and windows). Curiously, the "tent" had originally been made for Captain Cook's Pacific trips and Simcoe's soldiers were much impressed. Simcoe's wife, Elizabeth, made a marked impression of her own: her witty diaries remain a valuable source of information on colonial life, and her watercolours are among the first visual records of Native American life along the Lake Ontario shoreline.

Lieutenant-Governor Simcoe promptly arranged for the surrounding area to be surveyed, but he was already very grumpy. He had wanted the new capital to be established further inland in a much more benign location, but his superior, Governor Dorchester, vetoed his choice with the dismissive comment that the only way of getting to the spot preferred by Simcoe was by hot-air balloon. Despite this reverse, Simcoe decided to make a go of things, and he certainly thought York's harbour was first-rate, but he became increasingly exasperated by the marshy conditions, writing, "the city's site was better calculated for a frog pond ... than for the residence of human beings". Three years later, Simcoe had had enough and sailed off back to England, leaving control in the hands of **Peter Russell**, a one-time British soldier, slave owner and compulsive gambler. Despite his checkered history and his relatively advanced age – Russell was 63 when Simcoe left – Russell proved a good administrator, improving Toronto's roads and setting land aside for a church, a courthouse and a market. Nevertheless, the capital, now nicknamed "**Muddy York**", failed to attract many settlers, and twenty years later it had just seven hundred inhabitants.

The War of 1812

In the early nineteenth century, the main deterrent to settlement was the festering relationship between Britain and the US, which culminated in the **War of 1812**, whereby the Americans hoped to eject the British from Canada once and for all. The Americans thought this would be a fairly straightforward proposition and expected to be greeted as liberators. In both respects, they were quite wrong, but they did capture York without too much difficulty in 1813. Most of the American casualties came when the garrison of Fort York (see p.47) blew up their own munitions and incidentally pulverized the approaching US army. The Americans stayed for just twelve days, and returned for an even shorter period three months later. Neither occupation was especially rigorous, with the Americans content to do a bit of minor burning and looting. Even this, however, was too much for the redoubtable **Reverend John Strachan**, who bombarded the Americans with demands about the treatment of prisoners and the need for the occupiers to respect private property. The **Treaty of Ghent** ended the war in 1814, and under its terms the US recognized the legitimacy of British North America.

The Family Compact

The Canada Act had established an Upper Canada government based on a **Legislative Assembly**, whose power was shared with an appointed assembly, an executive council and an appointed governor. This convoluted arrangement ultimately condemned the assembly to impotence. At the same time, a colonial elite built up chains of influence around several high-level officials, and by the 1830s economic and political power had fallen into the hands of an anglophile oligarchy christened the **Family Compact**. This group's most vociferous opponent was a radical Scot, **William Lyon Mackenzie** (see p.57), who promulgated his views both in his newspaper, the *Colonial Advocate*, and as a member of the Legislative Assembly. Mackenzie became the first mayor of Toronto, as the town was renamed in 1834, but the radicals were defeated in the elections two years later, and a frustrated Mackenzie drifted towards the idea of armed revolt. In 1837, he staged the **Upper Canadian Rebellion**, a badly organized uprising of a few hundred farmers, who marched down Yonge Street, fought a couple of half-hearted skirmishes and then melted away. Mackenzie escaped across the border and two of the other ringleaders were executed, but the British parliament, mindful of their earlier experiences in New England, took the hint, quickly liberalizing Upper Canada's administration instead of taking reprisals. In 1841, they granted Canada **responsible government**, reuniting the two provinces (Upper and Lower Canada) in a loose confederation that prefigured the final union of 1867 when Upper Canada was re-designated Ontario as part of the British **Dominion of Canada**. Even Mackenzie was pardoned and allowed to return. His pardon seemed to fly in the face of his portrayal of the oligarchs as hard-faced reactionaries - indeed, this same privileged group pushed through a range of comparatively progressive social measures.

Victorian Toronto

Toronto boomed in the second half of the **nineteenth century**, consuming and exporting the products of its agricultural hinterland and benefiting from its good harbour and excellent maritime connections. Soon, Toronto had become a major manufacturing centre and, as a result, a railway terminus as well. Like every industrial city of the period, Toronto was characterized by a discordant mixture of slums and leafy residential areas, its centre dotted with proud Victorian churches, offices and colleges.

Politically, the city was dominated by a conservative mercantile elite, which was exceedingly loyal to the British interest and maintained a strong Protestant tradition. This elite was sustained by the working-class **Orange Lodge**, a sectarian fraternal order that originated in Ireland and sought to advance Protestant interests in government. The Lodge's reactionary influence was a key feature of municipal politics – spurring Charles Dickens, for one, to write disparagingly of the city's "rabid Toryism" when he visited in the 1840s. That said, the Protestant working class was enthusiastic about public education, as were the Methodist-leaning middle classes, who spearheaded social reform movements like Suffrage and Temperance.

The Victorian period came to an appropriate close with a grand visit by the future **King George V**, who toured Toronto in 1901 with his extravagantly dressed entourage – all bustles and parasols, bearskins and pith helmets.

The early twentieth century

In the **early twentieth century**, Toronto's economic successes attracted immigrants by the thousands: in 1850, the city had 30,000 inhabitants, 81,000 in 1882, and 230,000 in 1910. Most of these immigrants came from Britain, and when **World War I** broke out in 1914 the citizens of loyalist Toronto poured into the streets to sing "Rule Britannia". Thousands of volunteers subsequently thronged the recruiting stations – an enthusiasm which would cost many of them their lives: no fewer than seventy thousand Torontonians fought in the war, and casualties amounted to around fifteen percent.

Immediately after the war, Canada hit the economic buffers and, just when it appeared that matters were on the mend, the economy was hit by the stock market crash of 1929. During the **Great Depression** unemployment reached astronomical levels – between thirty and thirty-five percent – and economic problems were compounded by the lack of a decent welfare system. The hastily established Department of Welfare was only able to issue food and clothing vouchers, meaning that thousands slept in the streets. Fate was cruel too: Toronto experienced some of the severest weather it had ever had, with perishing winters followed by boiling hot summers.

At the start of **World War II**, thousands of Torontonians rushed to join the armed forces once again. The British were extremely grateful and Churchill visited Canada on several occasions, making a series of famous speeches here. The war also resuscitated the Canadian economy – as well as that of the United States – and Toronto's factories speedily switched to war production. Boatloads of British kids were also shipped to Toronto to escape the attentions of Hitler's Luftwaffe. After the war, Toronto set about the process of reconstruction in earnest. There was a lot to do. The city's infrastructure had not kept pace with the increase in population, and the water, transportation and sewage systems were desperately in need of improvement. Political change was also needed. A jumble of politically independent municipalities now surrounded a burgeoning core, with industries strung along the lakeshore and residential districts spreading beyond. The need for an overall system of authority was self-evident. Vigorous horse-trading resulted in the creation of **Metropolitan Toronto** in 1953, its governing body an elected council comprising 24 representatives, 12 apiece from the city and suburbs. The dominant figure of Metro politics for the first ten years was the dynamic **Frederick G. Gardiner**, aka "Big Daddy", who authorized the construction of the Gardiner Expressway.

The late twentieth century

Nevertheless, for all its status as the capital of Ontario, Toronto remained strikingly provincial in comparison with Montréal until well into the 1950s. It was then that things began to change, the most conspicuous sign being the 1955 defeat of the incumbent mayor, Leslie Saunders, by **Nathan Phillips**, who became the city's first Jewish mayor. Something of a *bon viveur*, Phillips was often criticized for neglecting city business in favour of banquets and festivals, but he was very popular, being elected no less than four times between 1955 and 1962. Other pointers were the opening of the city's first cocktail bars in 1947 (there'd been taverns before, but none that sold liquor), and, three years later, a closely fought referendum whose result meant that public sporting events could be held on Sundays. Up until then, Sundays had been preserved as a "day of rest", and even Eaton's department store drew its curtains to prevent Sabbath-day window-shopping. The opening of the **St Lawrence Seaway** in 1959 also stimulated the city's economy, though not quite as much as had been anticipated – only after its completion did it become obvious that road transport would render much waterborne traffic obsolete.

In the **1960s** the economy rocketed, and the city's appearance was transformed by the construction of a series of mighty, modernist **skyscrapers**. This helter-skelter development was further boosted by the troubles in Québec, where the clamour for fair treatment by discontented francophones prompted many of Montréal's anglophone financial institutions and big businesses to up sticks and transfer to Toronto. Much to the glee of many Torontonians, the census of 1976 showed that Toronto had become **Canada's biggest city**, edging Montréal by just one thousand inhabitants, and since then the gap has grown much wider. Meanwhile, Toronto's **ethnic complexion** was changing, and by the early 1970s Canadians of British extraction were in the minority for the first time. There was a burgeoning cultural scene too, with the hippy delights of Yorkville, aided and abetted by US draft dodgers from the Vietnam war, morphing into all sorts of artistic groups as well as community alliances, who kept the developers (temporarily) at bay.

In the 1980s and 1990s, Toronto's economy followed the cycles of boom and retrenchment common to the rest of the country, but the city lost its sense of commonweal and commonwealth in a haze of greed – real estate specula-tion, for example, verged on the frantic for most of the 1980s. Things got even more reactionary in the mid-1990s, when the **Progressive Conservatives** took control of Ontario under their hard-nosed leader, **Mike Harris**. A hated figure amongst the province's liberals and socialists, Harris's conservative social policies were often blamed for the dramatic increase in the number of homeless people on the city's streets and Harris certainly attacked public services with a large financial hatchet. Nonetheless, he and his fellow PCs still managed to get themselves re-elected in 2000 with the large-scale support of small-town and suburban Ontario. It was Harris who, in 1998, pushed through a major govern-mental reorganization, combining the city of Toronto with its surrounding suburbs. This **GTA** (**Greater Toronto Area**) – or "**Mega City**", as it has come to be known – has a population of around 5.5 million and covers no less than ten thousand square kilometres. The first mayor of the GTA was **Mel Lastman**, who had made a fortune with his Bad Boy furniture chain. Initially very popular, the exuberant Lastman horrified many of his fellow Torontonians during the **SARS crisis** (Severe Acute Respiratory Syndrome) of 2003, by appearing gauche and ignorant in equal measure. An outbreak of SARS had prompted the World Health Organization to issue an advisory concerning the advisability of delaying all non-essential travel to Toronto. The city was desperate for good leadership, but up popped Lastman on CNN to say he had never heard of the World Health Organization – and hands went up in front of faces all over Toronto.

Toronto today

In 2002, Mike Harris passed the premiership over to another Progressive Conservative, **Ernie Eves**, the province's 23rd premier – a less divisive figure perhaps, but one who maintained his predecessor's conservative policies, albeit in a rather less confrontational manner. The Eves regime was, however, short-lived. The following year, the Liberals under **Dalton McGuinty** finally ousted the provincial Conservative government and, in an allied development, Mayor Lastman hung up his spurs to be replaced by an energetic and progressive city councillor, **David Miller**, who had been a member of the left-of-centre New Democratic Party, but was elected without any formal political affiliation. Miller was re-elected in 2006, McGuinty in 2007. Miller and McGuinty agree on many things, and Miller certainly supported McGuinty's ambitious programme of investment in public services after years of neglect by the Harris-Eves regime. It will take time for the effects of this investment to show, but show it will – as will the efforts both of them are making in the provision of affordable housing and, as part of a wider, green agenda, the improvement of public transport. At last, Toronto seems to have politicians up to the standard of a high-ranking international metropolis.

Literary Toronto

Although there has been a literary scene in Toronto since the middle of the nineteenth century, Toronto as a theme in Canadian literature has emerged only in recent decades. From the diaries of Elizabeth Simcoe to the fiery editorials of William Lyon Mackenzie and the fond sketches of Henry Scadding, late eighteenth- to early twentieth-century writings about Toronto were almost entirely non-fiction. When writers did delve into fiction, their subjects were often lofty discussions on matters of church and state, not the pastoral aspects of Toronto life. As early Canadian novelist Sara Jeanette Duncan (1861–1922) wrote of the fictional Ontario town of Elgin in *The Imperialist*, "Nothing compared with religion but politics, and nothing compared with politics but religion." These were the topics worthy of serious discussion.

Social realism

Social realism became a popular literary theme in the aftermath of World War I, but this gritty real-world writing style was slow to take off in Canada, where people preferred historical romances and small-town settings. Two important exceptions were **Morley Callaghan** (1903–90) and **Hugh Garner** (1913–79), who wrote about their native Toronto from a class perspective, focusing on aspects of life that had none of the high moral tones or Gothic romance associated with nineteenth-century novelists. Garner and Callaghan also tended to hover on the left of the political spectrum, far from the peculiarly Canadian Red-Tory brand of social satire best captured by humorist **Stephen Leacock** (1869–1944). The overwhelming emphasis was on small-town Ontario, which obscured the fact that the urban population of Toronto was awash in a sea of change. In Callaghan's *Such is My Beloved* (1934), a description of the demographic shift in a Toronto parish between world wars has a contemporary ring, even though it describes a social construct that no longer exists:

The Cathedral was an old, soot-covered, imitation Gothic church that never aroused the enthusiasm of a visitor to the city. It had been in that neighbourhood for so long it now seemed just a part of an old city block. The parish was no longer a rich one. Wealthy old families moved away to new and more pretentious sections of the city, and poor foreigners kept coming in and turning the homes into rooming houses. These Europeans were usually Catholics, so the congregation at the Cathedral kept getting larger and poorer. Father Anglin really belonged to the finer, more prosperous days, and it made him sad to see how many of his own people had gone away, how small the collections were on Sunday and how few social organisations there were for the women. He was often bitter about the matter, although he should have seen that it was really a Protestant city, that all around his own Cathedral were handsome Protestant Churches, which were crowded on Sunday with well-dressed people, and that the majority of the citizens could hardly have told a stranger where the Catholic Cathedral was.

The Hugh Garner Co-operative Housing Development on Ontario Street is named in testament to Garner's novel *Cabbagetown*. The book is set in the

Depression and takes its name from the Toronto neighbourhood that Garner famously described as the largest Anglo-Saxon slum in North America. An unexpurgated version of the novel did not appear until 1968, by which time the streets he described had either been turned into tracts of sanitized public housing or refurbished as upscale Victorian residences for moneyed professionals. The improbable transformation of the Cabbagetown neighbourhood (see p.77) is documented in Garner's 1976 novel *The Intruders*.

The 1950s and 1960s

In the late 1950s and early 1960s, Toronto was the home base for a remarkable flowering of prose, poetry, painting and theatre. Many of Canada's leading poets, essayists and novelists, most notably **Margaret Atwood**, emerged from the milieu that crowded into the all-night poetry readings at the Bohemian Embassy on St Nicholas Street. Other major talents from that era were **Milton Acorn**, known across Canada as "The People's Poet", **Gwendolyn MacEwen**, and **b.p. nichol** and **Paul Dutton**, both of whom belonged to the Four Horsemen, a poetry performance group. These artists and their contemporaries set up awards to encourage new writers and sustain established ones; they mentored one another at every opportunity, and took many newcomers under their wings. They encouraged a school of writing that considered place, in this case Toronto, to be fundamental to storytelling. For them, Toronto was not, as Robert Fulford said, "a place to graduate from", it was a place to stay. In this passage from *In the Skin of a Lion* (1987), by **Michael Ondaatje** (who came later, though the passage still applies), Commissioner Harris, who built Toronto engineering feats like the Bloor Street Viaduct and the Water Filtration Plant, describes a vision:

One night, I had a dream. I got off the bus at College – it was when we were moving College Street so it would hook up to Carlton – and I came to this area I had never been to. I saw fountains where there used to be an intersection. What was strange was that I knew my way around. I knew that soon I should turn and see a garden and more fountains. When I awoke from the dream the sense of familiarity kept tugging me all day. In my dream the next night I was walking in a mysterious park off Spadina Avenue. The following day I was lunching with the architect John Lyle. I told him of these landscapes and he began to laugh. "These are real," he said. "Where?" I asked. "In Toronto?" It turned out I was dreaming about projects for the city that had been rejected over the years. Wonderful things that were said to be too vulgar or too expensive, too this, too that. And I was walking through these places, beside the traffic circle at Yonge and Bloor, down the proposed Federal Avenue to Union Station. Lyle was right. These were real places. They could have existed. I mean, the Bloor Street viaduct and this building here are just a hint of what could have been done here.

In 1965 Stan Bevington and Wayne Clifford took over a back-lane carriage house space where Marshall McLuhan had lectured and founded **Coach House Press**, which became the incubator for all that was new and adventurous in Canadian literature. In addition to publishing the early works of Atwood and Ondaatje, whose *In the Skin of a Lion* is perhaps the definitive Toronto novel – Coach House began a tradition of giving talented new writers their first break: Paul Quarrington, Susan Swan and anthologist Alberto Manguel are just three examples. The company continued to expand its interests, putting out textbooks and a Québec translation series featuring emerging Québecois authors like Jacques Ferron, Nichole Brossard and Victor-Levy Beaulieu. A turbulent period of conflict on the editorial board and financial difficulties caused the press to be dissolved in 1996, but in 1997 Bevington announced the birth of Coach House Press Books, an establishment devoted to beautiful, handmade limited editions and, way at the other end of the publishing spectrum, online novels for the internet.

▲ Michael Ondaatje

The 1970s and 1980s

More prominent Toronto-based authors followed in the wake of this particularly fertile period, including **Timothy Findley** and **Robertson Davies**. Findley's third novel, *The Wars* (1977), established him as a major literary talent, and more recent novels such as *Headhunter* (1993) and *The Piano Man's Daughter* (1995), both set in Toronto, make great use of local history, lore and settings.

Robertson Davies, one of the most significant novelists of the postwar era, uses quirky, thinly veiled descriptions of Toronto institutions such as the University of Toronto in novels like *The Rebel Angels* (1981), which is imbued with a strong sense of place. Both Davies and Findley have a knack for recognizing the rich stories that have yet to be told about the people and the city of Toronto. Rather than portraying Toronto as a stuffy, provincial town, the characters of a Findley or Davies novel are flamboyant, mystical, and are often based on obscure events in Canadian history.

In the Seventies and Eighties, new voices continued to find their way into Canadian literature. The **immigrant experience** in Toronto has been covered since the early nineteenth century, but early writers usually saw themselves as importing values and mores, and they shared similar cultural backgrounds and religions. Writers like **Austin Clarke**, who was born in Barbados, **Michael Ondaatje**, who was born in in Ceylon, and **M.G. Vassanji**, who is originally from Kenya, contributed a different perspective of immigrant life in Toronto. In Vassanji's *No New Land*, customary activities become strange, and the landmarks native Torontonians see as everyday landmarks become exotic:

What would immigrants in Toronto do without Honest Ed's, the block-wide carnival that's also a store, the brilliant kaaba to which people flock even from the suburbs? A centre of attraction whose energy never ebbs, simply transmutes, at night its thousands of dazzling lights splash the sidewalk in flashes of yellow and green and red, and the air sizzles with catchy fluorescent messages circled by running lights. The dazzle and sparkle that's seen as far away as Asia and Africa in the bosoms of bourgeois homes where they dream of foreign goods and emigration. The Lalanis and other Dar immigrants would go there on Sundays, entire families getting off at the Bathurst station to join the droves crossing Bloor Street West on their way to that shopping paradise.

The 1990s and the 2000s

By the edge of the millennium, a full generation of Torontonians had grown up surrounded by different cultures and was fully equipped with the language of diversity that an earlier generation had struggled to create. For example, novelist **Dionne Brand**'s recent work, *What We All Long For*, explores the weave of personal relationships and social histories among Toronto's visible minorities – a phrase increasingly outdated – who are Canadian born or raised. Brand uses the metaphor of locales and buildings that are always changing from one reality (a bank, a pizza parlour, a house) into another (a pub, a boutique, a parking lot) to illustrate her city's fluid demography. And while there has always been an ambiguity about Toronto that has made capturing the city's essence difficult, poet-turned-novelist **Anne Michaels** beautifully explored the city's many faces in *Fugitive Pieces* (1996):

Like Athens, Toronto is an active port. It's a city of derelict warehouses and docks, of waterfront silos and freight yards, coal yards and a sugar refinery; of distilleries, the cloying smell of malt rising from the lake on humid summer nights.

It's a city where almost everyone has come from elsewhere – a market, a caravansary – bringing with them their different ways of dying and marrying, their kitchens and songs. A city of forsaken worlds; a language a kind of farewell.

It's a city of ravines. Remnants of wilderness have been left behind. Through these great sunken gardens you can traverse the city beneath the streets, look up to the floating neighbourhoods, houses built in the treetops.

It's a city of valleys spanned by bridges. A railway runs through back yards. A city of hidden lanes, of clapboard garages with corrugated tin roofs, of wooden fences sagging where children have made shortcuts. In April, the thickly treed streets are flooded with samara, a green tide. Forgotten rivers, abandoned quarries, the remains of an Iroquois fortress. Public parks hazy with subtropical memory, a city built in the bowl of a prehistoric lake.

The above description would have confounded earlier generations of the city's writers, who lived in Toronto but uniformly placed their poems and novels elsewhere. Likewise, the perspective of outsiders who came to Toronto in the nineteenth and early twentieth centuries almost always stressed the city's perceived rigidities. From Charles Dickens to Ernest Hemingway and Wyndham Lewis, literary visitors often took Toronto's social and political milieu to be narrow and provincial. While it is true that the city's growing maturity and self-confidence bolstered a literary reflection of these sentiments, the creation of prestigious literary awards with large purses unquestionably did a lot to focus serious attention on the city's literary scene. Most notable of these is the **Giller Prize**, founded in 1995 in the memory of journalist and *Toronto Star* columnist Doris Giller. Since 2005 it has formally become the Scotiabank Giller Prize, with a top purse of $40,000. While national in scope, The Giller is emphatically Toronto-based. More specifically, the **Toronto Book Award** is awarded by the City of Toronto and brings welcome attention as well as a total of $15,000 in prizes to the many excellent works of fiction and prose set in Toronto or about Torontonians.

Books

Most of the following books should be readily available in bookshops or online (®www.amazon.com), though you may have a little more difficulty tracking down those few titles we mention which are currently out of print, signified o/p. Titles marked with the 🏃 symbol are especially recommended.

Travel and general

Katherine Ashenburg *Going to Town: Architectural Walking Tours in Southern Ontario.* This book is a terrific, day-trip guide to a variety of lesser-known towns that are within comfortable driving distance of Toronto. No fewer than three hundred photos – and eleven maps. Three of the towns Ashenburg selects – Niagara-on-the-Lake, Goderich and Stratford – feature in our Day-trips chapter (see pp.102–124).

Bruce Bell *Toronto: A Pictorial Celebration.* Thoroughgoing cruise round the city, visiting everything of interest and then some.

Anna Jameson *Winter Studies and Summer Rambles in Canada.* Originally published in 1839, these tart observations of early Toronto's colonial society are marked by a sense of wonderment at the vastness of Canada's untamed land.

Elliott Katz *Great Toronto Bicycling Guide.* A useful guide to Toronto-area bike paths as well as background information about the region itself. Also Katz's *Great Country Walks Around Toronto.*

William Kilbourn *Toronto Remembered: A Celebration of the City* (o/p). A collection of over a century of imaginative descriptions of Toronto.

🏃 **A.B. McKillop** *The Spinster and the Prophet: H.G. Wells, Florence Deeks, and the Case of the Plagiarized Text.* In 1925 Toronto teacher and armchair historian Florence Deeks sued the great H.G. Wells for the then-fabulous sum of $500,000 for his supposed literary piracy of her manuscript about the history of the world. Did he do it? Was she simply an overwrought spinster? Read on.

George Rust D'Eye *Cabbagetown Remembered* (o/p). An intimate portrait and historical account of this popular Toronto neighbourhood, its people and its landmarks. Wonderful photographs, but could do with an update – it was last published in 1987.

Henry Scadding *Toronto of Old* (o/p). Originally published in 1873, and written by a member of one of Toronto's founding families, these sketches and pen-and-ink illustrations have an immediacy and charm that give insight to Toronto's early years.

🏃 **Elizabeth Simcoe** (ed: Mary Innis) *Mrs. Simcoe's Diary.* The wife of Upper Canada's first lieutenant-governor and an early resident of York (Toronto), Elizabeth Simcoe was an energetic woman who kept a detailed and very well-written diary. This provides intriguing observations on the landscape and the city's way of life, plus astute political comments on the major historical figures of the time - like Chief Joseph Brant.

William H. White (ed) *Dateline: Toronto: The Complete Toronto Star Dispatches, 1920–1924* (o/p). Ernest Hemingway's first professional writing job was with the *Toronto Star* as both a local reporter and a European correspondent. This is a collection of his dispatches for the paper.

History

Carl Benn *The Iroquois in the War of 1812*. In 1812, the United States, which was at war with Canada, invaded and briefly occupied York (later Toronto). The role played by the Five Nations and Iroquois peoples in the war was pivotal to Canada's survival, and the ramifications of the war affected the aboriginal people of Ontario for years to come. Thoroughly researched and well-written.

Pierre Berton *Flames across the Border*. Berton (1920–2004) was one of Canada's finest and most approachable historical writers. This particular book describes the American raids across the border into Ontario in 1813–14. Other Berton titles include *The Last Spike: the Great Railway 1881–1885*, an account of the history and building of Canada's transcontinental railway; and *Vimy*, which details the World War I battle fought mainly by Canadians that Berton saw as a turning point in the nation's history.

Robert Bothwell *The Penguin History of Canada*. Accessible and well-written history from prehistoric times onwards. Covers all the key moments and all the key themes – economic, social and political – in just 432 pages.

Craig Brown (ed) *The Illustrated History of Canada*. Lavishly produced title that combines the work of several leading historians in a well-considered whole. Lots of fascinating historical titbits too, though some readers have accused it of excessive political correctness.

William Dendy *Lost Toronto* (o/p). This book documents the unfortunate loss of countless historically important Toronto buildings to the wrecking ball, fire and neglect. An eye-opener for those who only think of Toronto as a modern urban landscape.

Derek Hayes *Historical Atlas of Toronto*. Vintage Toronto maps with a well-written historical account as accompaniment. Published in 2008.

Harold Innis *The Fur Trade in Canada: An Introduction to Canadian Economic History*. Words like dramatic, sweeping and engaging are not usually associated with books on economic history, but in this case they fit the bill. Innis's study is invaluable for the insight it gives to pre-European Canada and its trading relations with Ontario's native peoples.

Randall White *Toronto The Good: Toronto in the 1920s* (o/p). A detailed portrait of the evolution of a modern city and its people. Stuffed with intriguing facts, observations and photographs.

George Woodcock *A Social History of Canada* (o/p). A man of leftish persuasion, George Woodcock (1912–95) was the outstanding Canadian historian of his generation – indeed many would say he was the finest historian Canada has ever produced. His books are erudite, perceptive and beautifully written, and – although none of his books about Canada are currently in print – they are all worth seeking out, including this particular title, which was first published in 1988.

Architecture and the arts

Jeremy Adamson *Canadian Paintings (The Thomson Collection at the AGO)*. Authoritative text whose series of essays gets to grips with the highlights of the Thomson collection in the Art Gallery of Ontario (see p.60).

Robert Fulford *Accidental City* (o/p). This entertaining book on the vagaries of the city's development pokes in some unlikely nooks and crannies. The central thesis is somewhat bogus (almost all cities develop haphazardly), but it's a good read all the same.

Glenn Gould *The Glenn Gould Reader* (ed. Tim Page). Sometimes chatty, sometimes pompous, Gould's voice and erudition shine through this collection of essays, articles and letters written from early adulthood to the end of his short life. If this whets your appetite, move onto *Glenn Gould: Selected Letters* (ed. John Roberts & Ghyslaine Guertin).

Anne Newlands *Canadian Paintings, Prints and Drawings*. Lavishly illustrated exploration/investigation paying due honours to 164 Canadian artists from the seventeenth century onwards.

Mark Osbaldeston *Unbuilt Toronto: A History of a City that Might Have Been*. Entertaining study on what the city would have/could have/ should have looked like if all the cool buildings and civic projects ever planned had gone ahead. Speculative nostalgia on a grand scale.

Dennis Reid *A Concise History of Canadian Painting*. Not especially concise, this book is a thorough trawl through Canada's leading artists, with bags of biographical detail and lots of black-and-white (and a few colour) illustrations of major works. Published in 1989.

David P. Silcox *The Group of Seven and Tom Thomson*. Authoritative and carefully researched book in which no painterly stone is left unturned. Especially good on Thomson; lavishly illustrated.

Fiction

Margaret Atwood *The Robber Bride*. Torontonian readers had a field day with the thinly veiled descriptions of famous and infamous locals. A snapshot of time and place, this book lives up to Atwood's high storytelling standards. First published in 1993.

David Bezmozgis *Natasha: And Other Stories*. Seven razor-sharp short stories about Toronto's Russian-Jewish community.

Dionne Brand *What We All Long For*. Covers the entwined lives of four friends, Jackie, Carla, Oku and Tuyen, and Tuyen's older brother, Quy, who was separated from the family in 1970s Vietnam. Set in the summer of 2002 with the World Cup series as the backdrop.

Robertson Davies *The Cunning Man*. Jonathan Hullah is a Toronto doctor befuddled by the death of one Father Hobbes, some twenty years earlier. As he recalls

the circumstances surrounding the priest's death, Hullah also finds time to ruminate on theatre, art, God and the strange secrets of a doctor's consulting room. A fine novel by one of Canada's most distinguished and prolific authors, who died in 1995.

Timothy Findley *Headhunter* (o/p). A sombre, futuristic novel that brings aspects of Conrad's *Heart of Darkness* to contemporary Rosedale, an haute bourgeois Toronto neighbourhood.

Barbara Gowdy *Helpless*. A truly courageous writer, Gowdy has mastered the art of finding beauty and tenderness in the things that everyone else looks away from. Set in her Cabbagetown (see p.77) neighbourhood, Gowdy's latest novel tackles the issue of a child's abduction.

Vincent Lam *Bloodletting and Miraculous Cures*. A dozen interweaving short stories about a group of young doctors from the University of Toronto whose diverse backgrounds and shared medical profession provide an unusual slant on the city. Lam's own background, in the emergency ward of a large Toronto hospital, inform much of the narrative.

Gwendolyn MacEwen *Norman's Land* (o/p). MacEwen once called Canada the most exotic place in the world, and she defends her thesis admirably in this enormously creative novel about a character she first introduced in her short-story collection *Norman*.

Alice Munro *Lives of Girls and Women*; *The Progress of Love*; *The Beggar Maid*; *Friend of My Youth*; *Dance of the Happy Shades*; *Who Do You Think You Are?*; *Something I've Been Meaning to Tell You*; *Runaway*; *The Moons of Jupiter*; and *Hateship, Friendship, Courtship, Loveship and Marriage*. Amongst the world's finest living short-story writers, Munro deals primarily with the lives of women in the semi-rural and Protestant backcountry of southwest Ontario. Unsettling emotions are never far beneath the surface. Among her more recent works, *Open Secrets* focuses on stories set in two small Ontario towns from the days of the early settlers to the present. Otherwise, start with *Who Do You Think You Are?*

Michael Ondaatje *In the Skin of a Lion*. This is the novel that introduces readers to the characters in the more famous *The English Patient*. It spans a period between the end of World War I and the Great Depression in East End Toronto.

Michael Redhill *Consolation*. A transplanted family, evolving histories and the search for vindication in an evolving city are the background to this Toronto-based novel. Winner of the 2007 Toronto Book Awards.

Nino Ricci *Where Has She Gone?* (o/p). The third in a trilogy that began with *Lives of the Saints*, this book is about an Italian-Canadian family's sometimes tragic, sometimes comic attempts to find its identity.

Robert J. Sawyer *Calculating God*. Hollus, an alien scientist, comes to earth, specifically Toronto, believing that the fossil collection at the Royal Ontario Museum will prove the existence of God. Hollus enlists the assistance of the ROM's human palaeontologist, a life-long atheist dying of cancer.

Russell Smith *Muriella Pent*. An Oxford-educated Caribbean poet is billeted in the nouveau riche mansion of a Toronto socialite. Smith addresses Toronto's heterogeneity through the protagonist's frequently brittle relationships.

Susan Swan *The Wives of Bath*. At a Toronto girls' school in the Sixties, the protagonist, Mouse, struggles with notions of feminine beauty as her best friend struggles with gender identity. A wry novel written in a genre the author describes as "sexual Gothic".

Small print and

Index

A Rough Guide to Rough Guides

Published in 1982, the first Rough Guide – to Greece – was a student scheme that became a publishing phenomenon. Mark Ellingham, a recent graduate in English from Bristol University, had been travelling in Greece the previous summer and couldn't find the right guidebook. With a small group of friends he wrote his own guide, combining a highly contemporary, journalistic style with a thoroughly practical approach to travellers' needs.

The immediate success of the book spawned a series that rapidly covered dozens of destinations. And, in addition to impecunious backpackers, Rough Guides soon acquired a much broader and older readership that relished the guides' wit and inquisitiveness as much as their enthusiastic, critical approach and value-for-money ethos.

These days, Rough Guides include recommendations from shoestring to luxury and cover more than 200 destinations around the globe, including almost every country in the Americas and Europe, more than half of Africa and most of Asia and Australasia. Our ever-growing team of authors and photographers is spread all over the world, particularly in Europe, the USA and Australia.

In the early 1990s, Rough Guides branched out of travel, with the publication of Rough Guides to World Music, Classical Music and the Internet. All three have become benchmark titles in their fields, spearheading the publication of a wide range of books under the Rough Guide name.

Including the travel series, Rough Guides now number more than 350 titles, covering: phrasebooks, waterproof maps, music guides from Opera to Heavy Metal, reference works as diverse as Conspiracy Theories and Shakespeare, and popular culture books from iPods to Poker. Rough Guides also produce a series of more than 120 World Music CDs in partnership with World Music Network.

Visit www.roughguides.com to see our latest publications.

Rough Guide travel images are available for commercial licensing at www.roughguidespictures.com

SMALL PRINT

Rough Guide credits

Text editor: Melissa Graham
Layout: Pradeep Thapliyal
Cartography: Deshpal Dabas
Picture editor: Scott Stickland
Production: Rebecca Short
Proofreader: Margaret Doyle
Cover design: Chloë Roberts
Photographer: Enrique Uranga
Editorial: Ruth Blackmore, Andy Turner, Keith Drew, Edward Aves, Alice Park, Lucy White, Jo Kirby, James Smart, Natasha Foges, Róisín Cameron, Emma Traynor, Emma Gibbs, Kathryn Lane, Christina Valhouli, Monica Woods, Mani Ramaswamy, Harry Wilson, Lucy Cowie, Amanda Howard, Helen Ochyra, Alison Roberts, Joe Staines, Peter Buckley, Matthew Milton, Tracy Hopkins, Ruth Tidball; **Delhi** Madhavi Singh, Karen D'Souza, Lubna Shaheen
Design & Pictures: **London** Scott Stickland, Dan May, Diana Jarvis, Mark Thomas, Chloë Roberts, Nicole Newman, Sarah Cummins, Emily Taylor; **Delhi** Umesh Aggarwal, Ajay Verma, Jessica Subramanian, Ankur Guha, Sachin Tanwar, Anita Singh, Nikhil Agarwal

Production: Vicky Baldwin
Cartography: **London** Maxine Repath, Ed Wright, Katie Lloyd-Jones; **Delhi** Rajesh Chhibber, Ashutosh Bharti, Rajesh Mishra, Animesh Pathak, Jasbir Sandhu, Karobi Gogoi, Alakananda Bhattacharya, Swati Handoo
Online: **London** Georgina Atwell, Faye Hellon, Jeanette Angell, Fergus Day, Justine Bright, Clare Bryson, Aine Fearon, Adrian Low, Ezgi Celebi, Amber Bloomfield; **Delhi** Amit Verma, Rahul Kumar, Narender Kumar, Ravi Yadav, Debojit Borah, Rakesh Kumar, Ganesh Sharma, Shisir Basumatari
Marketing & Publicity: **London** Liz Statham, Niki Hanmer, Louise Maher, Jess Carter, Vanessa Godden, Vivienne Watton, Anna Paynton, Rachel Sprackett, Libby Jellie, Laura Vipond, Vanessa McDonald; **New York** Katy Ball, Judi Powers, Nancy Lambert; **Delhi** Ragini Govind
Manager India: Punita Singh
Reference Director: Andrew Lockett
Operations Manager: Helen Phillips
PA to Publishing Director: Nicola Henderson
Publishing Director: Martin Dunford
Commercial Manager: Gino Magnotta
Managing Director: John Duhigg

Publishing information

This fifth edition published July 2009 by
Rough Guides Ltd,
80 Strand, London WC2R 0RL
14 Local Shopping Centre, Panchsheel Park, New Delhi 110017, India
Distributed by the Penguin Group
Penguin Books Ltd,
80 Strand, London WC2R 0RL
Penguin Group (USA)
375 Hudson Street, NY 10014, USA
Penguin Group (Australia)
250 Camberwell Road, Camberwell, Victoria 3124, Australia
Penguin Group (Canada)
195 Harry Walker Parkway N, Newmarket, ON, L3Y 7B3 Canada
Penguin Group (NZ)
67 Apollo Drive, Mairangi Bay, Auckland 1310, New Zealand
Cover concept by Peter Dyer.

Typeset in Bembo and Helvetica to an original design by Henry Iles.
Printed and bound in Singapore by SNP Security Printing Pte Ltd
© Phil Lee and Helen Lovekin 2009

240pp includes index
A catalogue record for this book is available from the British Library
ISBN: 13: 978-1-84836-074-7

The publishers and authors have done their best to ensure the accuracy and currency of all the information in **The Rough Guide to Toronto**, however, they can accept no responsibility for any loss, injury, or inconvenience sustained by any traveller as a result of information or advice contained in the guide.

1 3 5 7 9 8 6 4 2

Help us update

We've gone to a lot of effort to ensure that the fifth edition of **The Rough Guide to Toronto** is accurate and up-to-date. However, things change – places get "discovered", opening hours are notoriously fickle, restaurants and rooms raise prices or lower standards. If you feel we've got it wrong or left something out, we'd like to know, and if you can remember the address, the price, the hours, the phone number, so much the better.

Please send your comments with the subject line "**Rough Guide Toronto Update**" to ©mail @roughguides.com. We'll credit all contributions and send a copy of the next edition (or any other Rough Guide if you prefer) for the very best emails.

Have your questions answered and tell others about your trip at
®community.roughguides.com

SMALL PRINT

Acknowledgements

Helen would like to thank all the Torontonians whose energy, creativity and passion make the city a wonderful place to be. Special thanks to John, Phil, Melissa and Kattrin.

Phil would like to extend a special thanks to Diane Helinski of Ontario Tourism for all her help

and kindness. Thanks also to my delightful editor, Melissa Graham, who has brought organization and order to the updating of this book. Last but certainly not least, a big round of applause for my co-author, Helen, who, as ever, was great to work with.

Readers' letters

Thanks to all the readers who have taken the time to write in with comments and suggestions (and apologies if we've inadvertently omitted or misspelt anyone's name):

Friederike Albrecht; Xavier Balducci; Tim Burford; Chris Clayton; Gordon Craig; Haruna Dankaro; Paulo Dorabela; Beni Downing; Dwight Elliot; Carole Embrey; Ian Embrey; Andrea Fahrmeyer; Ute Frank; Sandra Ganahl; Marie-Helene Gauthier; Suzette Gibson; Viele Grube; Jennifer Haak; Brian Hislop; Simon Hollows; June Hornby; Bernadette Hyland; Ian and Claire Inglis; Claude Jouhannet; Arnelle Kendall; Jocelyn Labbé; Stefan Loose; Gloria Marsh; Michael Mossley; Philip Nyman; Roger Pebody; Stéphanie Pelletier; Piergiorgio Pescali; Tom Petch; Serge Poulin; Dee Powell; Keith Rohman; Carol & John Rowley; Grube von Anke Rowold; Julie Sanderson; Ernie Savage; David Saville; Frank Sierowski; Mike Smallenberg; Julia Speht; Chantal Tardif; Geoff Thomason; Alexis Thornely; Lynn Ulrey; Belinda Walker; Serena Webber; Andrew Young.

SMALL PRINT

Index

Map entries are in colour.

H

I

J

K

L

M

N

Map symbols

maps are listed in the full index using coloured text

-----	International boundary	⌣	Bridge
	Canadian highway	ⓘ	Information office
	US interstate highway	Ⓢ	Streetcar station
	US highway	♦	Place of interest
	Provincial highway	⊠	Post office
	Major road	◉	Accommodation
	Minor road	▣	Restaurant
-----	Path	✈	Airport
	Railway	⚲	Lighthouse
	Funicular railway		Church (town maps)
	Metro line		Building
	Coastline/river	⬭	Stadium
– –	Ferry		Cemetery
	Wall		Park

SOUTHWEST ONTARIO

Algonquin Park

Georgian Bay

Georgian Bay Islands

Severn Sound

Honey Harbour

Ste Marie Among the Hurons

Penetanguishene

Midland

Nottawasaga Bay

Orillia

Owen Sound

Lake Simcoe

Barrie

Peterborough

Primrose

Bradford

Aurora

Oshawa

Richmond Hill

Markham

Kleinburg

Woodbridge

Brampton

Toronto

See Toronto maps

Lake Ontario

CANADA
USA

Kingston

Mississauga

Waterloo

Kitchener

Oakville

Burlington

Stratford

Cambridge

Dundas

Niagara-on-the-Lake

Ancaster

Hamilton

St Catherines

Woodstock

Brantford

Grimsby

Niagara Falls

Buffalo

Welland

Tillsonburg

Port Colborne

Fort Erie

Hamburg

Lake Erie

CANADA
USA

Dunkirk

Fredonia

Goderich & Bayfield

N

0   25 km

TORONTO'S SUBURBS

0   5 km

Canada's Wonderland

RUTHERFORD ROAD

CENTRE STREET

NEW WESTMINSTER DR.

407

400

STEELES AVE. W

■ Black Creek Pioneer Village

DUFFERIN STREET

DREWRY AVE.

BAPS Shri Swaminarayan Mandir

FENMAR DR.

FINCH AVE. W

ALBION ROAD

ROAD

FINCH AVENUE WEST

NORFINCH DRIVE

JANE STREET

KEELE STREET

NORTH YORK

YONGE STREET

27

REXDALE BOULEVARD

MARTIN GROVE

KIPLING AVENUE

ISLINGTON AVENUE

WESTON ROAD

SHEPPARD AVE WEST

BATHURST STREET

Ford Centre

427

401

CARLINGVIEW DRIVE

BELFIELD ROAD

409

401

WILSON AVENUE

MACDONALD CARTIER FREEWAY

11

✈ Pearson International Airport

DIXON ROAD

LAWRENCE AVE. WEST

AVENUE RD.

LAWRENCE AVE WEST

GLENCAIRN AVE.

11A

EGLINTON AVENUE WEST

ETOBICOKE

EGLINTON AVENUE WEST

YORK

①

BATHURST ST.

SPADINA RD.

② **③**

PLEASANT ROAD

YONGE STREET

KIPLING AVENUE

ISLINGTON AVENUE

ROYAL YORK ROAD

JANE STREET

KEELE STREET

DUFFERIN STREET

ALLEN RD.

④
⑤

ST CLAIR AVE. WEST

DAVENPORT ROAD

DUNDAS ST.

PRINCE EDWARD DR.

E

See 'Uptown Toronto'

5

BLOOR ST. WEST

⑥

BLOOR ST WEST

AVENUE RD.

BLOOR ST. WEST

NORSEMAN ST.

High Park

HARBORD ST.

See 'West End Toronto'

427

2

THE QUEENSWAY

GARDINER EXPRESSWAY

QUEEN ST. W

SPADINA AVE.

UNIV. AVE.

YONGE ST.

F

QEW

EVANS AVE.

QEW

KING ST. W

See 'Downtown Toronto'

HORNER AVE.

Humber Bay

Ontario Place

LAKE SHORE BLVD.

Toronto City Centre Airport

Inner Harbour

2

Toronto City Centre Airport

See 'The Toronto Islands'

Outer Harbour

See 'Uptown Toronto'
See 'West End Toronto'
See 'Downtown Toronto'
See 'The Toronto Islands'

Stratford & Goderich ◀ C & D

Niagara Falls ◀

G & D

WEST END TORONTO

⑨ COLLEGE STREET **⑩**

⑪

GLADSTONE AVENUE

DUNDAS STREET WEST

DOVERCOURT ROAD

OSSINGTON AVENUE

ROXTON ROAD

STREET

MONTROSE AVE.

BEATRICE ST.

GRACE ST.

AVENUE

STREET

MANNING AVENUE

EUCLID AVENUE

PALMERSTON AVENUE

MARKHAM STREET

DUNDAS STREET WEST

Trinity Bellwoods Park

SHAW STREET

CRAWFORD STREET

BELLWOODS AVENUE

CLAREMONT STREET

⑫

ARGYLE STREET

LISGAR STREET

DOVERCOURT RD.

BEACONSFIELD ST.

⑬

ROBINSON STREET

G **H**

QUEEN STREET WEST

⑭

⑰ **⑱**

⑮ **⑯**

RICHMOND STREET W.

RESTAURANTS

Angkor	24	Gujurat Durbar	8
Avli	23	Il Fornello	4
Beaconsfield	13	Jaipur Grille	2
Caju	14	Jerusalem	1
Coco Lezzone Grill		Julie's Cuban Restaurant	12
& Porto Bar	9	Lily 86	19
Czehoski's	16	Little Tibet	15
Didier	5	Noce	18
Diner's Thai	20	Ouzeri	21
Drake Dining	H	Oyster Boy	17
El Bodegón	11	Pan on the Danforth	22
Gamelle	15	Rikishi	6
Grano	3	Siddhartha	7

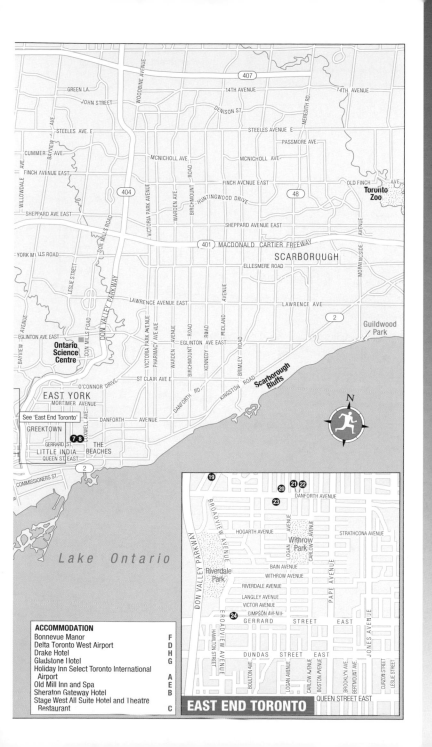

ACCOMMODATION

Bonnevue Manor	F
Delta Toronto West Airport	D
Drake Hotel	H
Gladstone Hotel	G
Holiday Inn Select Toronto International Airport	A
Old Mill Inn and Spa	E
Sheraton Gateway Hotel	B
Stage West All Suite Hotel and Theatre Restaurant	C

EAST END TORONTO

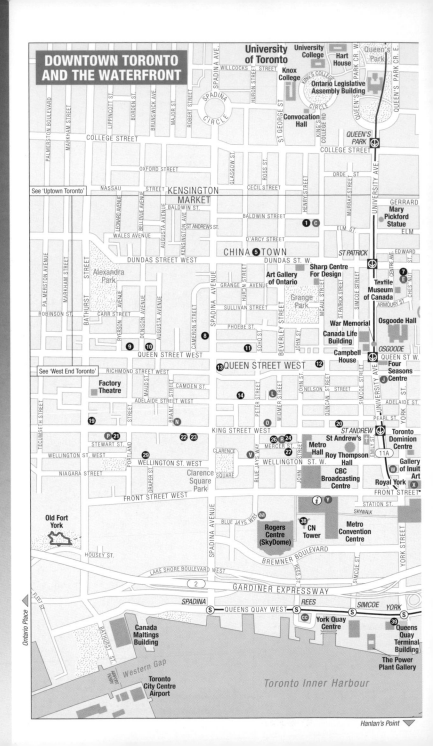

DOWNTOWN TORONTO AND THE WATERFRONT

University of Toronto

University College

Hart House

Queen's Park

Knox College

Ontario Legislative Assembly Building

Convocation Hall

QUEEN'S PARK

COLLEGE STREET

SPADINA CIRCLE

SPADINA AVE.

WILLCOCKS STREET

HURON STREET

ST GEORGE ST.

KING'S COLLEGE RD

QUEEN'S PARK CR. W.

QUEEN'S PARK CR. E.

COLLEGE STREET

PALMERSTON BOULEVARD

MARKHAM STREET

LIPPINCOTT ST.

BORDEN ST.

BRUNSWICK AVE.

MAJOR ST.

ROBERT STREET

OXFORD STREET

GLASGOW STREET

ROSS ST.

ORDE ST.

MURRAY STREET

UNIVERSITY AVE.

GERRARD

Mary Pickford Statue

See 'Uptown Toronto'

NASSAU STREET

KENSINGTON MARKET

CECIL STREET

HENRY STREET

ELM ST.

ELM

LEONARD AVENUE

BELLEVUE AVENUE

AUGUSTA AVENUE

KENSINGTON AVE

ST ANDREWS ST.

BALDWIN ST.

BALDWIN STREET

❶ Ⓒ

WALES AVENUE

D'ARCY STREET

CHINA ❺ TOWN

ST PATRICK

EDWARD

CENTRE AVE.

CHESTNUT

❼ Ⓔ

DUNDAS STREET WEST

DUNDAS ST. W.

Sharp Centre For Design

Textile Museum of Canada

P.A. MERSTON AVENUE

MARKHAM STREET

BATHURST STREET

Alexandra Park

RYERSON AVENUE

DENISON AVENUE

AUGUSTA AVENUE

CAMERON STREET

SPADINA AVENUE

GRANGE AVENUE

HURON STREET

McCAUL STREET

ST PATRICK STREET

SIMCOE STREET

Art Gallery of Ontario

Grange Park

ARMOURY ST.

Osgoode Hall

ROBINSON ST.

CARR STREET

SULLIVAN STREET

PHOEBE ST.

SOHO ST.

JOHN ST.

BEVERLEY STREET

War Memorial

Canada Life Building

❾ ❿ ⓫

❽

Campbell House

OSGOODE

QUEEN ST. W.

Four Seasons Centre

QUEEN STREET WEST

❾ ❿

QUEEN STREET WEST

⓭ **QUEEN STREET WEST** ⓬

See 'West End Toronto'

RICHMOND STREET WEST

Factory Theatre

CAMDEN ST.

MAUD ST.

BRANT STREET

PETER STREET

JOHN STREET

NELSON STREET

DUNCAN STREET

SIMCOE STREET

UNIVERSITY AVE.

YORK ST.

ADELAIDE STREET WEST

ADELAIDE STREET WEST

⓮ Ⓛ

WIDMER STREET

PEARL ST.

❿

TECUMSETH STREET

STREET

Ⓝ

KING STREET WEST

Ⓞ

❿

ST ANDREW

❷⓪

Toronto Dominion Centre

⓲

Ⓟ ㉑

STEWART ST.

㉒ ㉓

MERCER ST.

㉖ Ⓡ ㉔

BLUE JAYS WAY

St Andrew's

Metro Hall

Roy Thompson Hall

11A

WELLINGTON ST. WEST

WELLINGTON ST. WEST

CLARENCE

Ⓥ

㉗

Gallery of Inuit Art

NIAGARA STREET

DRAPER ST.

PORTLAND

㉙

Clarence Square Park

JOHN STREET

CBC Broadcasting Centre

Royal York

Ⓧ

FRONT STREET WEST

Clarence Square

FRONT STREET WEST

FRONT STREET

ⓘ Ⓨ

STATION ST.

SKYWALK

Old Fort York

SPADINA AVENUE

BLUE JAYS WAY

❽ₐ

Rogers Centre (SkyDome)

㊳ **CN Tower**

Metro Convention Centre

YORK STREET

SIMCOE ST.

REES ST.

HOUSEY ST.

BREMNER BOULEVARD

LAKE SHORE BOULEVARD WEST

FLEET ST.

BATHURST ST.

Ontario Place

GARDINER EXPRESSWAY

2

SPADINA

REES

SIMCOE

YORK

Ⓢ QUEENS QUAY WEST Ⓢ Ⓢ Ⓢ

Ⓒⓒ

York Quay Centre

㊴ **Queens Quay Terminal Building**

Canada Maltings Building

The Power Plant Gallery

Western Gap

Toronto City Centre Airport

Toronto Inner Harbour

Hanlan's Point ▽

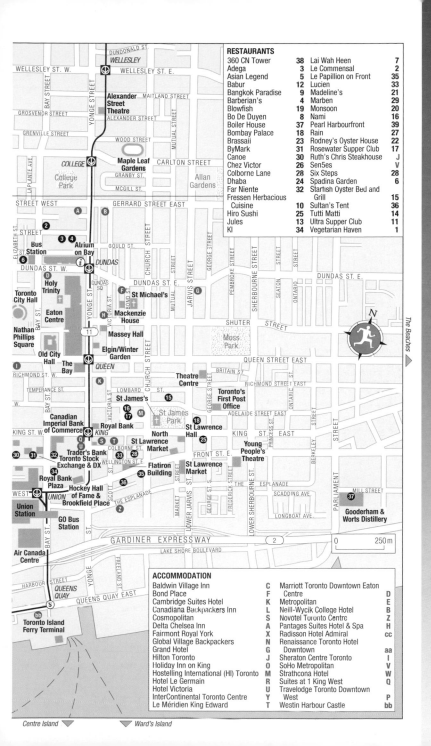

RESTAURANTS

360 CN Tower	38	Lai Wah Heen	7
Adega	3	Le Commensal	2
Asian Legend	5	Le Papillon on Front	35
Babur	12	Lucien	33
Bangkok Paradise	9	Madeline's	21
Barberian's	4	Marben	29
Blowfish	19	Monsoon	20
Bo De Duyen	8	Nami	16
Boiler House	37	Pearl Harbourfront	39
Bombay Palace	18	Rain	27
Brassaii	23	Rodney's Oyster House	22
ByMark	31	Rosewater Supper Club	17
Canoe	30	Ruth's Chris Steakhouse	J
Chez Victor	26	Sen5es	V
Colborne Lane	28	Six Steps	28
Dhaba	24	Spadina Garden	6
Far Niente	32	Starfish Oyster Bed and	
Fressen Herbacious		Grill	15
Cuisine	10	Sultan's Tent	36
Hiro Sushi	25	Tutti Matti	14
Jules	13	Ultra Supper Club	11
KI	34	Vegetarian Haven	1

The Beaches ▷

ACCOMMODATION

Baldwin Village Inn	C	Marriott Toronto Downtown Eaton	
Bond Place	F	Centre	D
Cambridge Suites Hotel	K	Metropolitan	E
Canadiana Backpackers Inn	L	Neill-Wycik College Hotel	B
Cosmopolitan	S	Novotel Toronto Centre	Z
Delta Chelsea Inn	A	Pantages Suites Hotel & Spa	H
Fairmont Royal York	X	Radisson Hotel Admiral	cc
Global Village Backpackers	N	Renaissance Toronto Hotel	
Grand Hotel	G	Downtown	aa
Hilton Toronto	J	Sheraton Centre Toronto	I
Holiday Inn on King	O	SoHo Metropolitan	V
Hostelling International (HI) Toronto	M	Strathcona Hotel	W
Hotel Le Germain	R	Suites at 1 King West	Q
Hotel Victoria	U	Travelodge Toronto Downtown	
InterContinental Toronto Centre	Y	West	P
Le Méridien King Edward	T	Westin Harbour Castle	bb

Centre Island ▽   ▽ Ward's Island

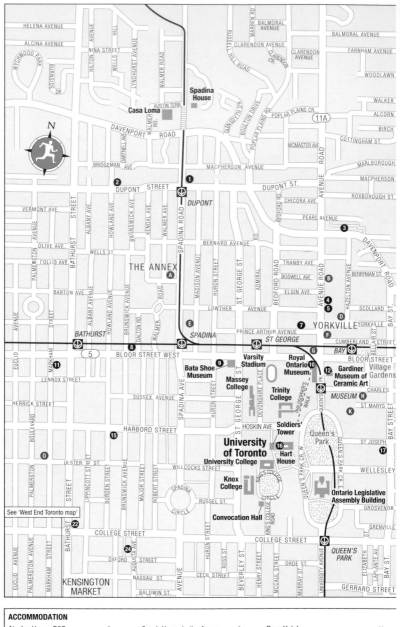

ACCOMMODATION			
Ainsley House B&B	C	Coach House in the Annex A	Days Hotel V
Banting House B&B	T	Comfort Hotel Downtown	Dundonald House B&B P
Bent Inn	N	Toronto I	Four Seasons F
Best Western Primrose	W	Courtyard by Marriott	Hazelton Hotel D
Cawthra Square B&B	Q	Downtown Toronto U	Howard Johnson Yorkville B

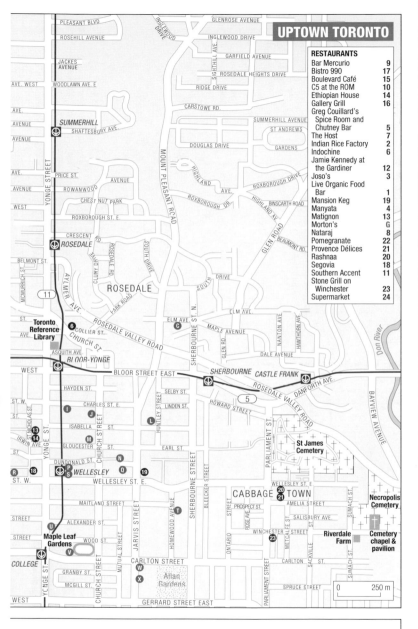

Madison Manor Boutique Hotel	E	Sutton Place	R	University of Toronto,
Mulberry Tree	L	Town Inn Suites	J	St Michael's College	K
Park Hyatt	G	University of Toronto,		Victoria's Mansion	M
Posh Digs	O	Victoria College	H	Wellesley Manor
Ramada Plaza Hotel	X			Boutique Hotel	S

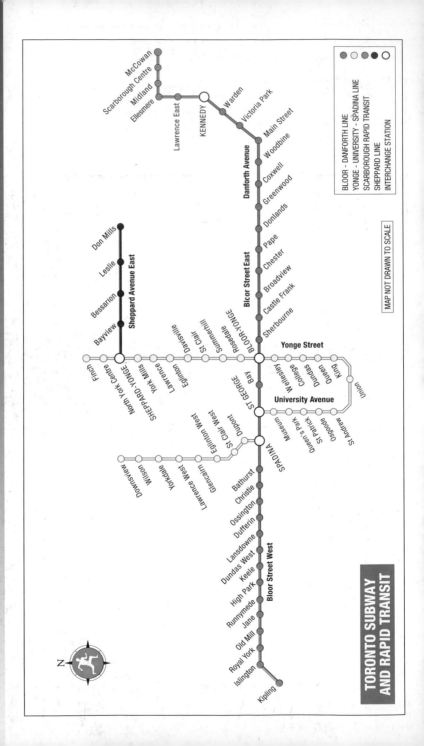